On Beckett, On!

On Beckett, On!

A collection of essays from the
Journal of Modern Literature

Edited by Jean-Michel Rabaté
and Laurel Garver

Indiana University Press

This book is a publication of

Indiana University Press
Herman B Wells Library 350
1320 East 10th Street
Bloomington, Indiana 47405 USA
https://iupress.org

© 2025 by Indiana University Press

All rights reserved

No part of this book may be reproduced or utilized in any form or by any means, electronic or mechanical, including photocopying and recording, or by any information storage and retrieval system, without permission in writing from the publisher.

First Printing 2025

Library of Congress Cataloging-in-Publication Data

Names: Rabaté, Jean-Michel, Laurel Garver, co-editors
Title: On Beckett, on! : a collection of essays from the Journal of modern literature / edited by Jean-Michel Rabaté and Laurel Garver.
Description: Bloomington : Indiana University Press, 2025. | Includes bibliographical references and index. | Summary: "This collection of essays was born from a wish to show to a wider audience how exciting and productive Samuel Beckett scholarship has become, at a time when there are more essays and books written about Beckett than about any key modernist authors like Joyce and Woolf. This volume contains numerous essays on Beckett that the Journal of Modern Literature has published in the last decade. Their enduring quality proves that Beckett's oeuvre has maintained its appeal today because it attracts original scholars who are also interested in issues like philosophy, psychoanalysis, ethics, contemporary history, and literary theory"—Provided by publisher.
Identifiers: LCCN 2025008860 (print) | LCCN 2025008861 (ebook) | ISBN 9780253074836 paperback | ISBN 9780253074843 ebook | ISBN 9780253074850 adobe pdf
Subjects: LCSH: Beckett, Samuel, 1906–1989—Criticism and interpretation | Modernism (Literature) | LCGFT: Literary criticism | Essays
Classification: LCC PR6003.E282 O63 2025 (print) | LCC PR6003.E282 (ebook) | DDC 848.91409—dc23/eng/20250317
LC record available at https://lccn.loc.gov/2025008860
LC ebook record available at https://lccn.loc.gov/2025008861

CONTENTS

    Introduction   1
    Jean-Michel Rabaté

I. From the Dialectics of Nothingness to the Neuter

    1. Nothing is Impossible: Bergson, Beckett, and the Pursuit of the Naught   13
       Jeremy Colangelo

    2. Beckettian Habit and Deictic Exhaustion   26
       Shuta Kiba

    3. Glitches in Logic in Beckett's *Watt*: Toward a Sensory Poetics   42
       Amanda M. Dennis

    4. Beckett's Vessels and the Animation of Containers   56
       Hunter Dukes

    5. Blanchot in Infinite Conversation(s) with Beckett   71
       Arleen Ionescu

II. Art and History in the Context of Posthumanism

    6. Beckett, Painting and the Question of "the human"   91
       Kevin Brazil

    7. Art of Impoverishment: Beckett and *arte povera*   109
       Erika Mihálycsa

    8. Beckett, War Memory, and the State of Exception   127
       Emilie Morin

    9. Putting the Impossible to Work: Beckettian Afterlife and the Posthuman Future of Humanity   144
       Ruben Borg

    10. Dogging the Subject: Samuel Beckett, Emmanuel Levinas, and Posthumanist Ethics   162
       Karalyn Kendall-Morwick

III. Writing the Body: Disabled Ethics and Residual Laughter

11. A Defense of Wretchedness: *Molloy* and Humiliation   185
    Rick de Villiers

12. Who Hobbles after the Subject: Parables of Writing   203
    in *The Third Policeman* and *Molloy*
    Yael Levin

13. " 'Tis my muse will have it so": Four Dimensions   220
    of Scatology in *Molloy*
    Andrew G. Christensen

14. "Strange laughter": Post-Gothic Questions of Laughter   235
    and the Human in Samuel Beckett's Work
    Hannah Simpson

15. The Illusionless: Adorno and the Afterlife of   254
    Laughter in *How It Is*
    Michelle Rada

    Editors   271

    Index   272

Introduction

Jean-Michel Rabaté

This collection was born from a wish to show to a wider audience how exciting and productive Samuel Beckett scholarship has become, at a time when there are more essays and books written about Beckett than about any key modernist authors like Joyce and Woolf. However it is not quantity that matters. We wanted to show how imaginative, perceptive, and creative the group of younger Beckettians can be. This collection is a selection made among numerous essays on Beckett that the *Journal of Modern Literature* has published in the last decade. Their enduring quality proves that Beckett's oeuvre has maintained its appeal today because it attracts original scholars who are also interested in issues like philosophy, psychoanalysis, ethics, contemporary history, and literary theory.

The collection's title alludes to what H. Porter Abbott had called the "trope of Onwardness" in Beckett (32–42), by which he refers to the recurrent injunction to keep on moving forward that was so often identified with a Victorian ideology of progress. The ending sentences of *The Unnamable* have been often quoted and are seen on T-shirts and coffee mugs: "I can't go on. I'll go on." The paradoxical form does not undo the impetus, the urge to keep on doing, moving, writing. There is an "imperative of narration" (see Wulf) in Beckett's texts and plays that keeps asserting its urgent necessity despite its proclaimed impossibility. The Beckettian narrator evinces an obsessive need to write, which is inextricably intertwined with his suspicion of language. As the narrator only lives if the narrative is perpetuated, there is life-and-death situation in which the urge to tell stories is explained as a Kantian imperative.

In more general terms, any artist will be simultaneously conscious and unconscious of a universal drive to create, which can then be formulated as a law: You will go on. One of the densest later prose texts, "Worstward Ho" flaunts this imperative in a minimalist syntax that remains startling. The text begins thus: "On. Say on. Be said on. Somehow on. Till nohow on. Said nohow on" (101). I have discussed Beckett's despair at not being able to translate this into French because he could not find a French expression capable of rendering the basic reversal of "On" and "No," and suggested possible solutions that were not as condensed but workable (see Rabaté 164–66). We encounter here one of the recurrent problems in Beckett's work, the systematic hesitation between a purely motivated form (his formalism, as it were) and his use of philosophical concepts (his way of engaging thought). The hiatus has forced commentators to be aware of Beckett's huge philosophical culture, now proved by the recent publication of his philosophy notes, while noticing that traditional philosophemes hinging around issues of Being, negativity, Time, existence, etc., are relentlessly parodied. On top of that, this hesitation had to be replayed in two languages, French and English, which generated important distortions. One can understand the endless appeal of Beckett's texts!

However, it is not only in the opaque texts of the later years that one finds a mixture of disarming simplicity in the expression and loaded philosophical meanings presented in an abbreviated manner. I'll give one example by choosing an apparently simple and descriptive French poem composed in the late thirties, entitled "Rue de Vaugirard." Here is the short poem:

> à mi-hauteur
> je débraye et béant de candeur
> expose la plaque aux lumières et aux ombres
> puis repars fortifié
> d'un négatif irrécusable (Beckett, *Poems* 100)

I had taken this to refer to bicycle ride up rue de Vaugirard, a thoroughfare linking the circular boulevards in the South-West of Paris with the lower reaches of the Latin quarter. Beckett's apartment 6 rue de Favorites was almost at the corner with rue de Vaugirard. He would immediately go up that street whenever he wanted to go toward the Luxembourg. Going down South would lead him to Montparnasse, where his favorite cafés and restaurants were. However, I learned from a note in the 2012 edition of the *Poems* that Beckett had told his friend Lawrence Harvey that basis of the poem was a moment when he was walking in that street (386). I had seen a faint allusion to the beginning of Dante's epic ("in the middle of our life") and a parallel with Dante's numerous moments of hesitation as he explores first hell, then purgatory and paradise. But why did Beckett use the technical verb "débrayer" (to declutch) to talk about himself? This suggests a conception of the body-machine in line with a Cartesian view. Is the soul then a photographic plaque? Would the "plaque" make the entire body function like a camera with a moment of over-exposure generating pure white as in "candor"? Keeping these questions in mind, I offer two translations of the five lines:

> Rue de Vaugirard
>
> half-way up
> I declutch agape with candor
> exposing the plate to lights and shadows
> then start again fortified
> by an unimpeachable negative

or:

> Rue de Vaugirard
>
> reaching the middle of the way
> I release the clutch and candidly beaming
> expose the film to sun and shade

> then go on strengthened
> by an irrefutable negativity

What seems clear enough is that the speaking subject experiences a moment of pause that allows him to feel "candid." This makes him register the scene within visual coordinates marked by stark opposites of blackness and whiteness, after which he senses that he has gained something like courage thanks to that moment of insight. He can then "go on," having encountered on the way a sort of Hegelian negativity that cannot be disputed or contested. Having touched the bottom, as it were, he can move on again, strengthened as the Cartesian subject was after the experience of radical doubt that led him to a sense of his indisputably thinking *cogito*. Both Alain Badiou and Theodor W. Adorno would applaud to the deployment of "negative dialectics" that usher in an ethics of courage. One may object that I have alluded to Dante, Descartes, Hegel, Adorno and Badiou just to make sense of just five lines . . . This referential or intertextual excess derives from the extraordinary compression of Beckett's writing, be it prose or poetry.

If we pay attention to the form, we see that this poem is quite complex in its composition, with a longer line in the middle that should be read as an alexandrine, which involves a number of decisions to make about the *e muets*, the ultimate phonological resource of French verse. The line: "expose la plaque aux lumières et aux ombres" should not be read (as would be the case in today's spoken French), with all *e muets* elided, which would give a halting rhythm, something like: "expos' la plaqu' aux lumièr' et aux ombr'. . . ." No, the line should be read with a strong e at the end of the verb "expose," which lengthens it, to give it more meaning; it should have an elided e at the end of "plaque" because of the following vowel; however, the -es of "ombres" should be similarly long, with two syllables for the word, and no dieresis expected on "lumière" (which means that it cannot be read "lumi-ère" as the word has to be read in a famous line from Jean Racine's *Phèdre*, "La lumière du jour, les ombres de la nuit.") In fact, the line should sound like this: expose*uh* la plaqu' *aux* (6 syllables) lumière*szet* aux ombre*uhs* (6 syllables).

The very presence of an alexandrine is sufficient to call up all the ghosts of French poetry, which accounts for the central position of the line in the quaintain; it brings about a dialectical intervention during which light and darkness exchange their properties. A negative remains imprinted, which means that the single instant will not be forgotten. What is more, the aesthetic apprehension also yields ethical comfort: noone can "refute" or disqualify the "negative" that has been apprehended then. The poet can go on resolutely—he still has a long way to go, rue de Vaugirard being the longest street in Paris.

It is noticeable that Beckett did not try to translate this poem into English. Had he tried, he would have had a hard time finding an equivalent for the rhyme that makes "mi-hauteur" and "candeur" chime with one another while subtly echoing "Vaugirard." What Beckett slyly suggests is that if he is still a Candide in his use of the French language, the naïve quester will soon become a true and full (not half) "author," if we see "auteur" hidden in "hauteur." Of course I have alluded to Dante, Descartes, Adorno, and Badiou above all because they are names that recur in Beckett scholarship. I could also adduce Karl Marx, whose first novel, *Scorpion and Felix,* looks very much like *Watt.* Marx was also armed with an "irrefutable negativity." Like Beckett later, Marx was inspired by an Irish writer, Laurence Sterne, as we can verify when we read this amusing meditation on the Nothing that is also a parody of Hegelian dialectics:

> If anyone desires to obtain a clear and not abstract conception of the Trinity, not the Greek Helen or the Roman Lucretia, but the Holy Trinity, I could not advise him better than to dream of **N o t h i n g**, as long as he does not fall asleep, but on the contrary to watch in the Lord and to examine this sentence, for in it lies a clear concept. If we ascend to its height, five flights of stairs above our present position, floating over it like a cloud, we are confronted by the gigantic "NOT," if we descend to its middle, we behold in fear the enormous "**N o t h i n g**," and if we sink down into its depth, both are again harmoniously reconciled in the "**NOT**" which in its upright, bold characters of flame, springs to meet them: "Not"—"**N o t h i n g**"—"**NOT**" (Marx, ch. 39)

The spectacular deployment of this Nothing, underlined, in bold and in capitals, whether dialectical or not, explains why Beckett has kept his appeal today. Perhaps also because his innate pessimism fits our current anxieties. Indeed, Beckett is felt to be relevant in a world marked by an increased gap between the rich and the poor, a world riven by radicalism, religious, racial, or ethnic intolerance, in a planet destroyed by an unprecedented ecological crisis, a world made one only because of the rapid spread of a universal pandemic. Despite being a work of the twentieth century, Beckett's texts and plays speak to us in a way that has no equivalent among key modernists authors like Joyce, Woolf, Kafka, or Proust. They initiated a revolution in literary language from which Beckett profited and to which he remained faithful, but they all died before the end of WWII. Beckett's career spans the twentieth century, from the beginnings of Irish rebellion against British colonialism during WWI to the fall of the Berlin wall. In between, there were the horrors of mass barbarism in the Holocaust and conflicts marked by the widespread use of torture, as during the Algerian war of Independence and the Argentinian "dirty war" against civilians.

Without being explicitly political, Beckett's work has responded to these challenges in a manner that is both historical and supra-historical, as the essays by Emilie Morin and Erika Mihálycsa remind us, and what's more, he has the ability to make us laugh. The essays we have selected revolve around three main domains: Beckett's contemporary philosophical appeal, his conversation with dominant theories and practice of art after 1945, and the issue of the human in a context of poshumanism, which paradoxically leads to an ethics of laughter and courage.

Many of the essays gathered here allude either to philosophical systems or to theories of esthetics. Since our first section focuses upon philosophical issues, it had to take its point of departure in the concept of Nothing. In "Nothing is Impossible: Bergson, Beckett, and the Pursuit of the Naught," Jeremy Colangelo discusses Beckett's obsession with negativity. The theme of Nothing in Beckett's works has been thoroughly documented—see Daniela Caselli's excellent collection *Beckett and Nothing*—and it is here tackled via Henri Bergson, one of the philosophers read by Beckett when he was working on Marcel Proust. For Bergson, nothingness is not a pure void but a form of ontological codependency, and manifests itself not as an absence but as a striving toward absence. Adding useful references to Jean-Luc Nancy's philosophy of "being-with," Jeremy Colangelo analyzes this striving for an aphasic nothing in Beckett's feminine characters, like Mouth in *Not-I*, and one poem, contending that such a dynamic Nothing is a necessary condition for a renewed creativity.

In the second essay, "Beckettian Habit and Deictic Exhaustion," Shuta Kiba goes back to a key issue for Bergson and Proust, that of "habit" understood as a "compromise" between spontaneity and social erosion, or as Beckett puts it melodramatically: "Habit is the ballast that chains the dog to his vomit. Breathing is habit" (*Proust* 19). Beyond the deadening function of habit imposed by life in society, Beckett's theory of habit is tested in formalistic experiments to generate the idea of exhaustion as developed by Gilles Deleuze. Because Beckett's exhaustion led to an accumulation of moments of deixis, the particular event resists the tendency of the habituating process. Here-and-now deixis inscribes readers in the text; with *Molloy*, this produces a sense of confusion and compulsion, which simultaneously propels and undoes our habits of reading aiming at reaching the end quickly. Participating more actively in the present of writing, we then discover an adventurous and innovative writing that mobilizes us fully.

A similar sense of physical mobilization of the reader is explored by Amanda Dennis in "Glitches in Logic in Beckett's *Watt*: Toward a Sensory Poetics." Dennis is also echoing Bergson, replacing him in a longer philosophical genealogy going from Aristotle to Wittgenstein via Kant and Mauthner so as to tackle the problematics of logical exhaustion. Here Dennis focuses on *Watt's* logical games and shows how they parody the binary oppositions underlying rationality. Beside the critique of language that they enact, the novel's "glitches" in logic initiate a sensual poetics, in which sound and sense tend to annul one another. Beckett dismantles all rational systems by exposing their tendency to elide the body. He shows that if rationality is unable to approach mathematical infinity or the realm of affects, when the zeroes and ones of binary codes are made to flounder into pure absurdity, other possibilities for meaning emerge. These are entwined with a phenomenology of lived experience and of desire. *Watt* demonstrates that the body is the indispensable site for the construction of new meaning in language.

Hunter Dukes also starts from the body, a paradoxical body in which the inside is also the outside, a body that can be pictured as a Moebius strip or a Klein bottle. In "Beckett's Vessels and the Animation of Containers," Dukes harnesses André Breton's metaphor of the "communicating vessels" that aimed at evoking the interaction between dreams and real life to show how it is enacted with a vengeance by Beckett in novels like *Murphy* and *The Unnamable*. Indeed, as

Dukes argues, all of Beckett's novels and plays are filled with double vessels, and stage a subjectivity at the cusp between the human and the nonhuman. *Malone Dies* is brought in contact with anthropological theories of the homunculus. By adopting material containers as surrogate bodies or by imagining life in hollow vessels, Beckett's characters encounter a self that exceeds the limits of the body—a form of projective identification that anticipates what the psychoanalyst Wilfred R. Bion had theorized as the paradox of the "container-contained."

If Beckett had learned a lot from Bion during his almost two years of psychoanalysis in London, he later found in Maurice Blanchot a subtle and well-read critic who fully understood him, to the point that their aesthetic programs sounded identical in the 1940s. Arleen Inonescu throws new light on the long and fruitful exchange between the two writers in "Blanchot in Infinite Conversation(s) with Beckett." She describes a polyphonic dialogue between Blanchot and Beckett that moved both ways, Beckett approaching Blanchot's work with some reverence, Blanchot continuing to engage both critically and creatively with Beckett's texts. In *Awaiting Oblivion* and *The Infinite Conversation*, we see Blanchot quoting and rewriting Beckett. *Awaiting Oblivion* parallels *Waiting for Godot* thematically while mirroring fragments from *How It Is* and *Texts for Nothing*. Beckett's voice, even if it is "ill-heard," "ill-murmured," and "ill-recorded" is crucial because it ushers in Blanchot's key concept of the Neuter, an experience of radical passivity and subjective dispossession that literature alone can produce.

The second section takes Beckett's ongoing confrontation with the visual arts as a way of tackling the momentous question of the human, or rather the "posthuman" in his general attitude. Kevin Brazil begins with the post-war critical debate about what constituted "the human," a debate that traversed the spheres of aesthetics, politics, and philosophy. In "Beckett, Painting and the Question of 'the human,'" Brazil brings Beckett's criticism into contact with that Jean-Paul Sartre, Francis Ponge, Maurice Merleau-Ponty, and Martin Heidegger. Brazil argues that we need both a more historicized reading of Beckett's art criticism and an awareness of the political stakes of his work. He takes as prime examples "The End," *Eleutheria*, and *Molloy* to show that Beckett's art criticism as well as his fiction should be understood as part of the history of critical theory.

Exploring the same postwar moment, Erika Mihálycsa compares Beckett's aesthetic theories stressing impoverishment with the theories and practices of the Italian *arte povera* movement. In "Art of Impoverishment: Beckett and *arte povera*," Mihálycsa compares Beckett's works with those of Alberto Burri. Beckett's postwar writings abandon a late modernist aesthetic to branch into momentous departures observed in *arte povera*. One of its major practitioners, Alberto Burri, appears very close to Beckett, both being at the crossroads of prewar Surrealism, *art informel*, and postwar abstraction. Their common post-humanist artistic practice of impoverishment rejects any notion of achievement, an attitude seen as the only possible response to the crisis of humanist European culture. Burri's 1940s and 1950s works converge with Beckett's visual aesthetics to embody an aesthetics of radical finitude and artistic poverty. Any mastery is rejected so as to reach a degree zero in art and writing, foregrounding a material imagination of indigence grounded in detritus. This response to the disaster of contemporary history abolishes the symbolic unity of the work of art. Dispossession, non-knowing, impotence, and waste matter become valorized.

Here is also the site inspected by Emilie Morin who has renewed the approaches to politics in Beckett. Complementing Morin's wonderful 2017 *Beckett's Political Imagination*, this new essay, "Beckett, War Memory, and the State of Exception," meditates on the political knowledge and experiences of the postwar work. The texts Beckett wrote in the fifties remain tied to forms of war memory that resonate with conflicts past and present. However, the type of political situation that Beckett pondered most consistently over the course of his career remains connected not to states of war, but to states of exception. The state of chronic suspension that has come to characterize his postwar texts has particularly powerful historical and transnational underpinnings and owes much to the cultural memory and political legacies of states of siege and emergency that have made so much of modern history.

From the horrors of contemporary history to a sense of futurity is but a step, a step that Beckett asks us to take, as Ruben Borg contends. In "Putting the Impossible to work: Beckettian Afterlife and the Posthuman Future of Humanity," Borg zooms in on the "posthuman future of humanity," a temporal contradiction at the heart of the discourse of the posthuman. Beckett's depiction of a posthumanity comes about in response to huge ethical and epistemological challenges. At the same time, it renders the use of words like "subjectivity," "history," and "experience" obsolete. An experience of the impossible derived from Georges Bataille and Jacques Derrida informs the moment of a posthuman self-reflection. Borg associates this posthuman turn with the experience of being in between life and death, or rather the concepts of death-in-life and seeing-oneself-dead, finding key examples in *Dream of Fair to Middling Women, More Pricks than Kicks, Malone Dies*, and *The Unnamable*.

Starting from another debate with Jacques Derrida, Karalyn Kendall-Morwick takes the trope of the dog as a companion and as a witness to tease out the implications of posthumanist theory. In "Dogging the Subject: Samuel Beckett, Emmanuel Levinas, and Posthumanist Ethics." Kendall-Morwick studies the role of dogs in Beckett's fiction along with Emmanuel Levinas's philosophy. Levinas's allegory of a stray "German" dog while he was a war prisoner in Germany was discussed by Derrida who took the example of this animal to point to gaps in Levinas's humanist conception of subjectivity. Similarly, Beckett's depictions of animal suffering collapse the distinction between the human as rational animal and the animal as living machine. For Beckett and Levinas, dogs do not merely represent the animal in a generic sense. The animal encounters of *Watt* and *Molloy* echo with Levinas's "The Name of a Dog." If dogs define through negation the humanist subject, their participation in violence against other animals complicates the ethical quandary of humanist discourse vis-à-vis the animal.

The image of the dog allows Beckett and Levinas to present a posthumanist ethics responding to radical alterity and heterogeneity.

The third section continues the interrogations about suffering and the posthuman but to bring these themes into contact with concepts of degradation, humiliation, scatology and laughter. In "A Defense of Wretchedness: *Molloy* and Humiliation," Rick de Villiers explores the recurrent motif of humiliation as experienced by most of Beckett's characters to wonder about its implications for the current scholarship. If humiliation and responses to it define Beckett's "creatures," what can we deduce about an ethics that takes suffering as a given? In *Molloy*, humiliation exhibits as an ontologically determining phenomenon while disallowing the morose enjoyment of private suffering. Alongside many instances of wretchedness and abuse, the novel posits humility as an ethical imperative which is needed to approach the suffering of others. Only tears and laughter can welcome them, pushing the main ethical maxim of humility taken as a key value by Arnold Geulincx, the Flemish philosopher revered by Beckett, towards an original "low modernism."

With so many maimed or disabled characters, it was inevitable to take into account the approaches via disability studies to assess Beckett's impact. This is what Yael Levin does in "Who Hobbles after the Subject: Parables of Writing in *The Third Policeman* and *Molloy*" by comparing the novels of Beckett and those of Flann O'Brian. Disability studies call attention to a lack of agency and autonomy, which means that the Cartesian subject has to be reconfigured. The disabled protagonists of *Molloy* and *The Third Policeman* dramatize a writing that abandons all creative agency and dramatize their contingency, their dependence, and their ontological uncertainties. A "dismodernist" subject is forcibly posited within a discourse of supplementarity and exhaustion. A similar treatment of disability should force us to rethink the links between Irish modernism and contemporary ethical interrogations about excluded and disenfranchised others.

Another exclusion bears about waste, excrement, and the scatological humor that pervades Beckett's texts. Andrew G. Christensen provides the systematic account of scatology in Beckett. His "'Tis my muse will have it so': Four Dimensions of Scatology in *Molloy*" details the various functions of scatology in satire, humor, and critique. In *Molloy*, scatology is deployed not only for satire but also as a metaphor exhibiting language as excess. In religious discourse, the scatological can be elevated alchemically through mythology or used to bring religion down. As Christensen demonstrates, *Molloy* traverses both paths in a parody of Catholicism. If excrement functions as a leveler among humans and of humans, it brings us back to an essential determination of our being beyond shame and disgust: it touches upon a universal existential anxiety.

Laughter is Beckett's weapon against anxiety, and he deploys a surprising variety of manifestations. In "'Strange laughter': Post-Gothic Questions of Laughter and the Human in Samuel Beckett's Work," Hannah Simpson shows how strange and unsettling his characters' laughter can be. Often readers do not feel prompted to join. If we laugh in response to the Beckettian text, we are often shocked by our own lack of propriety. Simpson surveys laughter theory with a focus on the Gothic genre to analyze exactly why Beckettian laughter is so disconcerting: it touches on the limits between he human and non-human, and reaches down to the foundation of identities.

Finally Michelle Rada completes the analysis of Beckettian laughter by looking closely at *How It Is*. In "The Illusionless: Adorno and the Afterlife of Laughter in *How It Is*," Rada argues that the comedy of *How It Is* differs from Beckett's previous texts because it is much more scarce, almost imperceptible, in a text characterized by torture scenarios, monotonous repetition, and the dismantling of syntactical coherence. However, Rada finds humor in abundance as she explores comedic events through Adorno's readings of Beckett in which humor figures as a critical element. While Adorno's work on Beckett is based on *The Unnamable*, *Godot*, and *Endgame*, the theorization of laughter and the comedic event in these texts should be read in *How It Is* as well, for this novel is a work that comes alive in the wake of laughter. Rada considers then Badiou's reading of *How It Is* in terms of alterity next to Adorno's texts in order to argue that the experience of a residual laughter is a performative gesture as well as a transformative event.

Works Cited

Abbott, H. Porter. *Beckett Writing Beckett: The Author in the Autograph*. Cornell UP, 1996.

Beckett, Samuel. *The Collected Poems*. Edited by Seán Lawlor and John Pilling. Faber. 2012.

———. *Proust and Three Dialogues*. Calder, 1965.

———. "Worstward ho." *Nohow On*. John Calder, 1989.

Caselli, Daniela, editor. *Beckett and Nothing: Trying to Understand Beckett*. Manchester UP, 2010.

Marx, Karl. *Scorpion and Felix*. Marxists.org, www.marxists.org/archive/marx/works/1837-pre/verse/verse41.htm.

Rabaté, Jean-Michel. *Think, Pig! Beckett at the Limit of the Human*. Fordham UP, 2016.

Wulf, Catharina. *The Imperative of Narration: Beckett, Bernhard, Schopenhauer, Lacan*, new ed. Sussex Academic P, 2014.

JEAN-MICHEL RABATÉ, professor of English and comparative literature at the University of Pennsylvania, co-editor of the *Journal of Modern Literature*, co-founder of Slought – Public Trust Foundation is a fellow of the American Academy of Arts and Sciences. He has authored or edited fifty books on modernism, psychoanalysis, philosophy, and literary theory. Recent monographs include *Beckett and Sade* (2020), *Rires Prodigues: Rire et jouissance chez Marx, Freud et Kafka* (2021), *James Joyce, Hérétique et Prodige* (2022), *Lacan l'irritant* (2023), and *Jacques Lacan Against Psychoanalytic Obsolescence* (2024).

I. From the Dialectics of Nothingness to the Neuter

1 Nothing is Impossible: Bergson, Beckett, and the Pursuit of the Naught

Jeremy Colangelo

*from impenetrable self to impenetrable unself by way of neither
as between two lit refuges whose doors once neared gently close, once turned
away from gently part again
beckoned back and forth and turned away*

—Samuel Beckett,
"Neither"

"NOTHING HAPPENS, TWICE"[1]

The concept of Nothing[2] is an old topic in Beckett studies, to the extent that the importance of the concept has become something of an in-joke, as indicated by a story in the satirical newspaper *The Onion* entitled, "Scholars Discover 23 Blank Pages That May As Well Be Lost Samuel Beckett Play." Despite the headline's obvious absurdity, it points to an important fact: Beckett, despite his reputation, was never able to produce Nothing, not merely in the sense of his never having been able to stop writing, but also in the sense of his work always being irreducibly significant. No matter how much he trimmed away, Something always remained. From where does this problem arise? The source becomes clearer when we look to Henri Bergson, with whom Beckett was familiar, and who in his interrogation of the concept shows himself to be Beckett's precursor.

Bergson reveals to us an ontological co-dependency between existence and non-existence that bears a strong resemblance to the system described in Jean-Luc Nancy's *Being Singular Plural*. This co-dependency echoes throughout Beckett's works, especially his play *Not I* (in French, *Pas Moi*) and his final published poem "What is the Word" (in French, "*Comment dire*"), the two focal texts considered here. These two late works, in addition to being exemplary instances of Bergsonian Nothingness, also indicate the manner in which Beckett's engagement with

Nothing takes the form of a pursuit, indeed an endless one. In these texts we see that the adage "seek and you will find" is not a cause for hope, since in finding something one always *finds Something* and so must extend the search for Nothing still further.

The dialogic ontologies expressed in these three works articulate an inability to delve down all the way to Nothingness that is in line with Henri Bergson's critique of the concept.[3] While for Nancy being is always "being-with," for Bergson it is Nothingness that arises from co-existence. In Bergson's system, negation is *additive*, in that one arrives at Nothing by *adding* a negation to the concept of Everything. Thus, attempts to reduce existence to Nothingness inevitably rebound against a limit.

The characters in Beckett's fiction find themselves caught between these two competing ontologies: they each exist, as Nancy would say, in relation to another, yet that other is precisely Nothing, and is thus unreachable. One can imagine the characters in these stories as two stars in a binary system, orbiting around a point of empty space defined by their competing gravitational fields. In *Not I*, Mouth oscillates between a similar external definition on the one hand, and a "being-with" of *internal division* on the other, an oscillation that manifests in the Auditor figure's increasing redundancy and eventual disappearance. Finally, in "What is the Word," we see the poem's speaker attempt to find a Nothing to relate to without the benefit of a second body to define its orbit. This absence leads to a pattern of aphasia, with words always on the tip of the tongue but never released. In each case, we encounter characters embedded in dialogic ontologies seeking a Nothing structured in Bergsonian terms.

"That Beckett knew of Bergson ...," as Anthony Uhlmann writes, "is incontestable" (29). Manfred Milz places Beckett's first exposure to Bergson's ideas as far back as 1923, during his time as a student of the philosopher Arthur Aston Luce (144). The evidence for Beckett's exposure is three-fold. The most obvious is Beckett's close reading of Marcel Proust, who was perhaps the modernist author most strongly influenced by Bergson's ideas.[4] Though this reading would not acquaint Beckett with the particulars of Bergson's philosophy, it does provide a vicarious connection. The second major point of contact is Beckett's 1949 translation of Georges Duthuit's *Les fauves: Braque, Derain, van Dongen, Dufy, Friesz, Manguin, Marquet, Matisse, Puy, Vlaminck*. Duthuit's *Les fauves* was his "most extended work on a Bergsonian conception of space" (Addyman 138), and so Beckett's translation of the text (and his relationship with Duthuit generally) would provide ample second-hand exposure to Bergson's ideas.

In addition to these two, less-compelling pieces of evidence, there is a third and more conclusive indication in the form of lecture notes taken by Rachel Burrows during Beckett's brief time teaching at Trinity College Dublin, which show him interacting with Bergson's ideas directly. As the notes describe, the lesson touched on several key Bergsonian concepts:

[C]onflict v. intelligence & intuition. Bergson—interested in this ... Suggests that intuition can achieve total vision that intelligence can't. ... Passionate justification of "La vision intuitive" ... Taken up by Symbolists and Dadaists—last interested in his [Bergson's] idea of inadequacy of the word to translated impressions registered by instinct. (Qtd. in Uhlmann 29; original emphasis)

S.E. Gontarski, commenting on these notes reads as their central "ontological and epistemological issue" the question of "why all art must inevitably and perpetually fail," and why "at best ... what art can offer is a snapshot of time ... which spatializes [its] flow" ("Introduction" 5). As we shall see, failure is an important component of Bergson's idea of Nothing, as certainly it is also vital to Beckett's writings generally. And as the evidence shows, Bergson was emphatically on Beckett's mind during the earliest days of his career—both directly, in his Trinity College Dublin lectures, and indirectly, in the aesthetics of Proust and philosophy Duthuit. It is thus with this historical background that I proceed into my examination of this one facet of the Beckett-Bergson relationship.

Bergson's primary dilation on Nothing occurs in the first section of *Creative Evolution*'s fourth chapter. It is an attack on the validity of the concept similar to his response to Zeno's Paradox in his earlier *Time and Free Will*. Rather than disproving or invalidating the paradox, he undermines it and characterizes it as a pseudo-problem.[5] According to Bergson, philosophers usually understand Nothing as an eternal substratum upon which existence rests (*Creative Evolution* 276). Nothing is, effectively, a universal and yet despite (or perhaps because) of this, it is impossible to positively define on its own. Instead, one understands Nothing by imagining Everything and then negating it (280). Which means, in essence, that Nothing, which supposedly undergirds Everything, is in fact derived from Everything. Or, as Bergson concludes, "if now we analyze this idea of Nothing we find that it is at bottom the idea of Everything" (296).[6]

But this is not where the problem ends. For, according to Bergson, Nothing is not a pseudo-concept simply because under examination it proves to be paradoxical, but also because it is itself impossible to attain. The process of taking Everything and paring it down into Nothing cannot run to its end: a kernel of existence always remains. "Reality," writes Bergson, "has appeared to us as a perpetual becoming. It makes itself or it unmakes itself, but it is never something made" (272). As such, whenever Bergson attempts to apprehend Nothing phenomenally, he runs into a roadblock: "I subsist ... and cannot help myself subsisting. ... At the very instant that my consciousness is extinguished, another consciousness lights up ... it had arisen the instant before, in order to witness the extinction of the first" (278). According to Bergson, in negating we are faced with a choice. Either we enter a state of total external negation, a state of Cartesian doubt, and like Descartes are left with only a mote of self-presence in the *cogito*, or we can understand ourselves as fully negated, but in so doing posit negation as itself an entity in a wider world, a kind of anti-*cogito*. The concept of Nothing arises from the space between these two poles, between "a naught of external perception" and "a naught of internal perception," where we can "perceive both, having reached the point where the two terms come together, and the image of Nothing, so defined, is an image full of things" (279).

Nothing is thus unreachable, and the concept of Nothing is itself only conceivable through an ontological co-dependence between inner and outer states of nonexistence. And it is for this reason that I analyze Beckett's engagement with the concept of Nothing through process of *co*-existence. As Jean-Luc Nancy writes in *Being Singular Plural*, "if Being is being-with, then it is ... the 'with' that constitutes Being" (30). Indeed, though the ontology presented in Nancy's text is largely Heideggerian and Derridian, it bears many striking similarities to Bergson's critique of Nothing, particularly in Nancy's observation that "pure unshared presence—presence to nothing, of nothing, for nothing—is neither present nor absent" (2). Nancy's usefulness here, beyond simply the affinities between his and Bergson's ideas, is that they allow for the extension of Bergson's ontology into the social. "Being-with," for Nancy, is an explicitly inter-personal state in a way that it is not for Bergson, and as we will see later on the social nature of the "with" is of the utmost importance. It is in this manner that I will characterize the fruits of Beckett's pursuits of Nothing in terms of a dialogic, or co-dependant, ontology, where the process of reduction leads to multiplication, the creation of inner naughts and outer naughts between which the concept of Nothing hangs as though caught between two magnetic fields.

"WHAT? ... WHO? ... NO! ... [WE]!"[7]

In a sense, *Not I* depicts what it is like to be a siren. Not a mindless one, like in Kafka's "The Silence of the Sirens" (a story that is similarly Bergsonian in its treatment of Nothing), but one containing multitudes; not one that maliciously draws in others with the pull of desire, but still one who stays withdrawn upon her rock, doubled yet alone. The image is a famous one: the rapid-moving mouth of Mouth (and, in the play's most famous performance, of Billie Whitelaw), speaking from the void at great speed. But the play has another figure—the Auditor, so easily forgotten, the character that Beckett once himself dismissed as "an error of the creative imagination," in part due to how tricky it was to stage (qtd. in Knowlson 617). I do not contest the difficulty of finding a place for the Auditor on stage, but I diverge with Beckett in seeing this fact as a creative error.

The staging of *Not I* presents a kind of ontological solipsism. The actor playing Mouth stands on a platform in the middle of the stage; the lights are dimmed, and a single thin spotlight falls on her mouth, circled in black face makeup so that only the lips, teeth, and tongue are visible to the audience. That Mouth, in this position, then delivers a monologue while the Auditor remains silent, cannot help but draw attention away from the second toward the first, so that it is quite likely that most members of the audience will miss the Auditor's four movements during Mouth's silence. They might well forget that there was anyone else on stage to begin with. Likewise, in the text of the play, the Auditor is nearly absent, the name appearing only once in the stage directions (*Not I* 376). Beckett instead indicates the Auditor's actions with the word "movement," and describes this movement in a note:

> Movement: this consists in simple sideways raising of arms from sides and their falling back, in a gesture of helpless compassion. It lessens with each recurrence till scarcely perceptible at third. There is just enough pause to contain it as MOUTH recovers from vehement refusal to relinquish third person. (375)

The pauses, and "refusal[s] to relinquish third person," here occur after each instance of Mouth uttering the phrase that I took for the title of this section: "what? ... who? ... no! ... she!" But the Auditor's reaction lessens at each instance, eventually disappearing—for when Mouth repeats the phrase for a fifth time, there is no longer a stage direction noting a movement (*Not I* 382).[8] Seemingly superfluous in staging, direction, and perhaps in Beckett's own mind, the Auditor becomes superfluous finally in the world of the text itself.

So at second glance—if not first—the apparent needlessness of the Auditor seems to be "part of the point." But what is this point? We can find an answer to this question, and see how it relates to Bergson, by re-examining the note that in its last sentence links the Auditor's actions and their receding intensity not merely to Mouth's pauses, but also the cause of those pauses: her "vehement refusal to relinquish third person." Mouth is an internally doubled character. Having suffered some kind of trauma (its nature unclear) she has tried to escape it by relinquishing the first person, describing her life story as though it belongs to a "she" of her own creation.

In this sense, she is in good company among Beckett's characters: *Malone Dies*, *The Unnameable*, and *Embers* (to name just a few examples) all have figures who produce similar auto-fictitious narratives. But the presence of the Auditor also aligns Mouth with a different set of characters—those like Vladimir and Estragon, Hamm and Clov, Mercier and Camier, Molloy and Moran, paired figures whose relationship is in some way the center of the story. What Beckett protagonists rarely are is alone, for even the loneliest of them usually invent some other character to talk about. But *Not I* occupies a middle ground, showing an internally split yet singular character established beside a semi-independent double, in a situation somewhat resembling the chess game with Mr. Endon in *Murphy*.

Not I's doubled doubling puts the play in a peculiar relationship with the concept of Nothing. While scholars like Stephen Thomson have noticed Beckett's Bergsonian recognition of the unreachability of Nothing,[9] what remains obscure is the type of ontology generated by this unreachability. The key for *Not I* lies in the dichotomy Bergson drew between voids of internal versus external perception, between complete solipsism and the eradication of the independent self.

Bergson explores this concept through a thought experiment: "I am going to close my eyes," he writes, "stop my ears, extinguish one by one the sensations that come to me from the outer world" (*Creative Evolution* 278). He proceeds from this point to greater extremes, from the eradication of sensory perception, to that of memory, the present, and the self. But at this final moment, a swerve occurs. A second self appears so to see the first snuffed out, "for the first could disappear only for another and in the presence of another" (278). Thus, for Bergson, these two ontological extremes are mutually exclusive. Internal emptiness calls out for another consciousness to perceive it, while the closure of the external world is predicated on a minimum level of internal complexity.

Mouth faces a choice between, essentially, the internalized duality of *The Unnameable* and the externalised duality of *Waiting for Godot*. It is for this reason that the Auditor is so important to the play's structure: the presence of this second figure makes Mouth's refusal to accept the first person pronoun a true dilemma. The Auditor beckons her with his silence, but she is too internally split to formulate a response. Yet, too, the outside world for Mouth has not been extinguished.

Throughout the play, there is always a question as to whether Mouth is capable of feeling anything. Early on she describes how she "found herself in the dark ... and not exactly ... insentient ... insentient ... for she could still hear the buzzing ... so-called ... in the ears" (*Not I* 377, original ellipses). Her description of hearing some kind of buzz persists throughout the monologue, with one notable instance occurring after a series of her screams, each of which is followed by silence. It is as though she were expecting an echo but, to her approval, did not hear one, was instead "spared that"—she says, instead, that she hears only silence "but for the buzzing" (378). The constant, silence-spoiling buzz is but the most notable example of her failed attempts at sensory deprivation. Later on the same page, for example, Mouth claims that there is "no part of her moving ... that she could feel ... just the eyelids." That she specifies that she can still feel her eyelids moving is interesting given that we do not see them, since only her mouth is visible to the audience. The floating mouth is, of course, the most obvious example of the incompleteness of her reduction, but the constant invocation of an external world, in part though her senses and in part through the lengthy but impermanent states of silence she claims to undergo, confirms for us that the extensive personal eradication that we see on stage is in large part wishful thinking.

These scenes are much like the moment in *Endgame* where Clov peeks out the window, providing the smallest hint of a world external to the hermetically-sealed and self-consistent chess game present on stage. Surprisingly, given Beckett's reputation as an arch-minimalist, his works always seem to present just slightly *too much* presence, too much embodiment, as though the great ambition of his reductionism makes its failures all the more egregious.

It is Beckett's excessiveness that returns us to the Auditor, and to the character's frequent (and author-approved) neglect in productions of *Not I*. As Nancy tells us, existence is always predicated on co-existence, and yet the play presents us with an excess of even that. In light of Bergson, we can see reduction as an asymptotic drive toward self-sufficiency, toward a Nothing ungrounded from the all, a naught without end. But because this reduction has so clearly failed, and because Mouth's rejection of the "I" is constantly in question, the character exists *enough*, which is to say, *too much*. As Hugh Kenner remarks in his analysis of *All That Fall*, in the radio plays that populate Beckett's late theatre, "a purely aural landscape capitaliz[es] ... on the fact that whatever falls silent disappears" (168).

Ironically, Mouth's extensive history of silence can only be expressed through speech, and so she is inexorably present physically, mentally, and audibly—far from being silent and invisible, she is the most conspicuous character on stage. Speech has for Mouth become "a pathological habit, beyond intentional control" (Maude 817). The presence of the Auditor, whose frequent overtures toward some connection with Mouth (which occur, tellingly, during her short, infrequent lapses into silence), present us with the possibility of Mouth replacing her external Nothing with an internal one, and adopting a "being-with" of a different kind. Thus, the Auditor at times seems superfluous because the character in a sense *is* superfluous—a Vladimir without an Estragon, a Moran without a Molloy.[10] The Auditor's disappearance at the end of the play—the "silence" noted with a lack, not of speech, but of movement—indicates not only the fragile self-sufficiency that Mouth has attained, but the loss of being suffered by an internal Nothing.

A HYPOTHETICAL POEM

The final act of Beckett's engagement with Nothing comes with the concluding work of his career, in which Mouth's incessant need to speak turns in on itself to become aphasia. Beckett, like Joyce, ended his literary career on an incomplete sentence. But unlike Joyce, its other half cannot simply be found by turning to the first page of the book. Beckett wrote "What is the Word" by hand in a notebook, and accompanied the draft with the note "Keep! for the end," which Dirk Van Hulle interprets as "a note by the author to himself, indicating that whatever he would write next" the poem should "round off his oeuvre with an open ending" (193).

Indeed, the poem is best described as a series of sentence fragments. It begins:

folly—
folly for to—
for to—
what is the word— (lines 1–4)

The refrain that ends each segment, and that gives the poem its title, is also the only non-fragment in the entire work. Yet each instance represents a small failure, an inability to find the conclusion to the increasingly long and Byzantine sentence that the speaker is actually trying to write. It is in this sense that the poem can be said to have left the end of Beckett's oeuvre open, for it turns this poem and its speaker essentially into half a being, a speaker who, because unlistened to, continually lapses into silence.

Let us examine the longest version of the sentence that the speaker is trying to assemble: "folly for to need to seem to glimpse afaint afar away over there what—" (50). The sentence, whose elements we can see scattered throughout the rest of the poem, constantly gestures outward. We see hedging and qualification indicative of indecisiveness (not a "glimpse" but a "*need* to *seem* to glimpse"), a lack of confidence that the poem had earlier been building up to:

> folly for to see what—
> glimpse—
> seem to glimpse—
> need to seem to glimpse— (45–48)[11]

What the speaker "seems" to "glimpse" we do not know, but we do know that it is faint, "far," and "over there." It is deftly external, a sentence—itself the (characteristically absent) center of the poem—completely oriented around some unseen, unknown entity that (not despite, but because it is far away) props up this lean-to of a phrase just long enough for us to read it. This externalization is completely necessary. The movement from "see" to the less-sure "glimpse," and then eventually from an actual glimpse to the *need* for one, tallies along with the enlargement of the sentence. The degree to which the sentence becomes unstable, and to which it approaches its collapse back into "what is the word," appears to rise in proportion to its nearness to self-sufficiency.

"What is the word" thus seems to act as a reset button to reduce the speech to a basic question, itself an outward gesture, that the poem must then provide an answer for. For if silence in a radio play may indicate absence, then the same can be said of the white space at the end of a page.[12] So, just like in *Not I*, the monologue before us becomes a battle over ontology, in this case over one of the characteristic problems that Bergson poses in *Creative Evolution*.

As previously noted, one of the issues at stake in Bergson's critique of Nothing was his understanding that Being, and the perception of Being, is a process of becoming that forces the subject to apprehend existence continually in relation to another temporal location. "It is necessary," he writes, "in order to see it ... to turn our back on reality, which flows from the past to the present, advancing from behind ... [so a person cannot] determine his actual position except by relation to that which he had just quitted, instead of grasping it in itself" (*Creative Evolution* 294). Bergson goes on to argue that the idea of negation has its origin in this process.

What I would like to focus on is the way this understanding of temporal perception locates as a foundational aspect of one's relation to existence a void that must constantly be deferred. One is unable to truly perceive the present, and instead perceives the past and interpolates it into the present through memory.[13] One looks into "what is" and, finding nothing, makes due instead with "what has been." Though the void is an illusion of perception, it, like existence, permanently remains. Just as one cannot, says Bergson, completely supress one's body and consciousness, so too can one not fill in the present with the past. For Bergson, time and perception move at the same speed, but time has had a head start.

"What is the Word" therefore proceeds quite logically when it abandons self-sufficient existence and instead reaches out for a co-existence, the form of "being-with" so well-articulated by Nancy. By fully engaging with this process of becoming through a poem constructed around literary composition itself, Beckett has left no internal existence to split, as with Mouth, leaving the speaker circling the drain toward an internalized Nothing which, *qua* Bergson, requires the emergence of an exterior observer in order to manifest. And yet the answer to the speaker's question fails to come, just like the ending of the sentence. Laura Salisbury has linked this perpetual incompleteness to the aphasia—a disruption of one's ability to understand written or spoken language—that Beckett briefly suffered after a neurological attack in 1988 (Beckett began writing the poem while in the hospital recovering from this attack). As Salisbury writes, "without the appearance of any personal pronouns [in the poem] ... aphasia resists localisation and the 'folly' involved in the hopeless search for the right word refuses to be bound in any straightforward way to the suffering transcendence that can be attached to self-expression. ... ["What is the Word"] is writing as an expression of pathology" (81).[14]

Whether or not we can completely accept the biographical half of Salisbury's argument, the "aphasic" nature of the poem is very clear. What we are left with is a continuous engagement with what linguists call the "tip-of-the-tongue" phenomenon, in which the speaker knows what they wish to say but is unable to retrieve the words with which to say it.[15] In "What is the Word," this failure of memory leads, similar to the radio plays, to a failure of selfhood, the inability to reach backward into time and rediscover who one supposedly is. The idiomatic French term for this phenomenon—*"presque vu"* or "almost seen"—could almost stand in as the poem's title, and certainly lends additional significance to the latter half of the poem's emphasis on seeing, "glimpsing," and the failure to do so. It is for this reason that I describe "What is the Word" as a *hypothetical* poem: its words and structure having been arranged around an unrealized possibility toward which it continuously gestures.

Just as Bergson argued, an engagement with Nothing invariably leads to a dialogic relationship. But the aphasic structure of the poem leaves no obvious avenues toward a "being-with." The speaker seems to lack utterly the internal divisions and self-fictionalizing that gives a character like Mouth stability, and the poem's continuous calls out for someone or something to answer its question, for a "seen" to arise from an "almost seen," go completely unanswered. The speaker risks a fate much like the Auditor, ignored out of existence. Though the poem seems to tend toward negation, a Nothing that would only be possible if its calls were answered, it instead takes on the role of the observer to an *external* Nothing, which it continually holds upon the tip of its tongue, but never speaks. And yet indecisiveness is generative; the poem continually goes back and forth as to how it ought to gesture toward incompleteness.

The first possibility is one we have already examined, which takes up most of the poem and involves simply implying the possibility of a naught outside grammatically, by continually posing pseudo-sentences. The other option is to simply ask "what is the word?", a phrase whose reoccurrence Van Hulle reads as "temporary deadlock[s]" and the culminations of distinct "failed attempts" at writing the sentence (189). But to simply pose the question leaves nowhere to go, for while it allows the speaker to impose a break in the composition and discard a line that was failing to come, it also makes an impossible demand of the Nothing around which the poem orbits—that it come forth on its own power and speak. Deferral, then, becomes necessary, and so we see the function not only of the continual drawing-out of the sentence to its grammatical limits but also the presence of dashes at the end of all lines but the last, implying the incompleteness of the line and the inevitability of a follow-up.

We can therefore begin to follow the logic of the poem's continuous fits and starts. It is a game of deferral, first by the extension of the sentence (always "almost seen") to greater and greater lengths and then, when that extension begins to fall to pieces, a reset with an explicit question, whose demand is undercut by the presence of the dash. In this way, the poem can maintain the double ontology that its engagement with Nothing demands while still continually placing *something* on the page. The speaker eventually finds that there is nowhere else to go. The last "what is the word" of the poem is also the first repetition of the phrase not buffered by the extension of the sentence, and the only one not accompanied by a dash. It is the last repetition before the speaker runs out of rope and ceases to exist. It should therefore be clear why Beckett chose this poem to close out his body of work: after a lifetime of wrestling with the poetics of failure, it is *with* failure that he saw his struggle to completion.

NOTHING ENDS

Nothing must happen twice if it is to happen once. It would seem that all three principal authors addressed in this essay in some way recognized that fact. Bergson, in *Matter and Memory*, described his work as "frankly dualistic" (*Matter and Memory* xi). He meant, in this case, the text's frequent invocation of mind/body dualism, but taken as a general declaration the term can easily apply across his major works, and his writing on ontology most definitely. He would, I think, concur with Nancy's argument that "being present and the present of Being does not coincide in itself, or with itself, inasmuch as it coincides or 'falls with' the other presence, which itself obeys the same law" (41). As such, the pursuit of Nothing is fundamentally doomed.

It is for this reason that the figure of the silent siren carries such potent force, whether that silence is literal, as in "What is the Word," or figurative, taking the form of a refusal of the unitary self and external relations, as in *Not I*. The problem that both texts face is that any call outward implies the possibility that it will not be answered, just like how beginning a sentence risks leaving it incomplete. Deferral, hedging, uncertainty, and doubles upon further doubles are strategies these texts employ to hold Nothing somehow away, to allow the pursuit of even further reduction and simplicity even in the face of the inescapability of at least bare existence. Locked in a state of continuous becoming that is also an un-becoming, these texts give Nothing what may be its only possible expression: both avoidance and pursuit, the success that occurs only as a side-effect of failure.

Notes

1. From Vivian Mercier's review of *Waiting for Godot*.

2. As my discussion of the concept of Nothing relies heavily on Bergson's analysis in *Creative Evolution*, I have elected to retain the capitalization of the word in those cases where I am referring to Nothing in that sense, and have used the lower-case version when using the word in any other way.

3. Previous examinations of the role of Nothing in Bergson have pointed out its essentially dialectical nature, with David H. Hesla's examination of the issue in the final chapter of *The Shape of Chaos* being an early, notable example. However, Hesla's contention that "the sum of even an infinite number of nothings is still Nothing, and that this is what [Beckett's] art comes to" (228), though seemingly commonsensical, misses the fact that in Beckett Nothing is *never actually reached*. It is precisely this mistake that I am trying to remedy by reading Beckett through Bergson, whose formulation of the concept of Nothing, though basically dialectical, evades this resolution.

4. For a summary of Proust's relation to Bergson, see Gunter, "Bergson and Proust: A Question of Influence."

5. It is notable that Bergson's thought, like Beckett's, emerges in part through a dialogue with pre-Socratic philosophy (see Weller). This overlap speaks, above all, to the intellectual affinity of the two authors on the subject. Indeed, the belief in the inaccessibility of knowledge attributed to Gorgias (328–29) would seem to say in general what Bergson says in specific relation to Nothing.

6. For an analysis of Bergson's work on Nothing as it relates to some of Beckett's earlier writing, and in particular *Watt*, see Gontarski, "'What it is to have been': Bergson and Beckett on Movement, Multiplicity, and Representation."

7. *Not I*, a phrase repeated five times throughout the text, with "she" instead of "we."

8. James Knowlson remarks on this section of the play: "It may be no accident that, when Beckett restored the figure of the Auditor to the April 1978 Paris production that he directed … the gesture of the Auditor at the end of the play … [was] an actual covering of the ears with the hands, as if the figure were unable to bear any longer the flood of sound issuing from Mouth" (814 n88). Knowlson goes on to compare this gesture to a figure in a painting by Caravaggio, but the change also acknowledges the Auditor's seeming acquiescence to Mouth's withdrawal.

9. As Thomson writes, "the process of reduction … does not stop at nothing; how could it? Something must be shown … even the impressive brutality of the sorts of torture device used to keep Mouth in place in *Not I* should not distract us from the fact that the lips do move" (75). Though on the topic of Mouth's refusal of the first person, Thomson notes that "this trial is not a diversion from a true existence, but the only existence this thing has" (75).

10. As Nancy observes: "not being able to say 'we' is what plunges every 'I'"—and it perhaps should be noted, every not-I—"whether individual or collective, into the insanity where he cannot say 'I' either. To want to say 'we' is not at all sentimental, not at all familial or 'communitarian.' It is existence reclaiming its due or its condition: coexistence" (42).

11. A similar passage occurs in lines 22–25.

12. For a more detailed reading on this relationship between speech and the presence of the speaker in Beckett, see Derval Tubridy.

13. Or, as David Hume writes in a similar vein, memory "discovers the identity" and "contributes to its production" (261).

14. While Beckett's engagement with aphasia in "What is the Word" seems tied to a specific incident late in his life, an interest in language pathologies can be found in his earlier work as far back as the 1920s and 30s (see Keatinge). For a more recent and more broadly focused examination of the role of aphasia in Beckett's work, see Natália Laranjinha's "L'Écriture aphasique de Samuel Beckett."

15. For a more detailed exposition on Beckett's engagement with the "tip-of-the-tongue" phenomenon, see Maria Kager. See also Bennett L. Schwartz and Alan S. Brown, eds., *Tip-of-the-Tongue States and Related Phenomena*. The study of the phenomenon goes back to the earliest days of modern psychology, appearing, for example, in William James's *Principles of Psychology* (1890) and Freud's *The Psychopathology of Everyday Life* (1901).

Works Cited

Addyman, David. "Different Spaces: Beckett, Deleuze, Bergson." *Deleuze and Beckett*, edited by S.E. Wilmer and Audrone Zukauskaite. Palgrave, 2015, pp. 137–151.

Beckett, Samuel. "Neither." *Samuel Beckett: The Complete Short Prose, 1929–1989*. Edited by S.E. Gontarski. Grove, 1995, p. 258.

———. *Not I. The Complete Dramatic Works*. Faber, 2006, pp. 373–383.

———. "What is the Word." *The Collected Poems of Samuel Beckett*. Edited by Seán Lawlor and John Pilling. Grove, 2012, pp. 228–229.

Bergson, Henri. *Creative Evolution*. Translated by Arthur Mitchell. Dover, 2013.

———. *Matter and Memory*. Translated by Nancy Margaret Paul and W. Scott Palmer. George Allen and Unwin, 1911.

Gontarski, S.E. "Introduction: Towards a Minoritarian Criticism—The Questions We Ask." *The Edinburgh Companion to Samuel Beckett and the Arts*, edited by S.E. Gontarski. Edinburgh UP, 2014, pp. 1–16.

———. "'What it is to have been': Bergson and Beckett on Movement, Multiplicity, and Representation." *Journal of Modern Literature*, vol. 34, no. 2, 2011, pp. 65–75.

Gunter, A.Y. "Bergson and Proust: A Question of Influence." *Understanding Bergson, Understanding Modernism*, edited by Paul Ardoin, S.E. Gontarski, and Laci Mattison. Bloomsbury, 2012, pp. 157–176.

Hesla, David H. *The Shape of Chaos: An Interpretation of Samuel Beckett*. U of Minnesota P, 1971.

Hume, David. *A Treatise of Human Nature*. Clarendon P, 1965.

Kager, Maria. "Comment Dire: A Neurolinguistic Approach to Beckett's Bilingual Writings." *L2 Journal*, vol. 7, no. 1, 2015, pp. 79–82.

Keatinge, Benjamin. "Beckett and Language Pathology." *Journal of Modern Literature*, vol. 31, no. 4, 2008, pp. 86–101.

Kenner, Hugh. *Samuel Beckett: A Critical Study*. U of California P, 1973.

Knowlson, James. *Damned to Fame: The Life of Samuel Beckett*. Bloomsbury, 1996.

Laranjinha, Natália. "L'Écriture aphasique de Samuel Beckett." *Samuel Beckett Today / Aujourd'hui: An Annual Bilingual Review / Revue Annuelle Bilingue*, vol. 22, 2010, pp. 449–462.

Maude, Ulrika. "Beckett and the Laws of Habit." *Modernism/Modernity*, vol. 18, no. 4, 2012, pp. 813–821.

Mercier, Vivian. "Review of *Waiting for Godot*." *Irish Times* (Dublin). 18 Feb. 1956, p. 6.

Milz, Manfred. "Echoes of Bergsonian Vitalism in Samuel Beckett's Early Works." *Samuel Beckett Today / Aujourd'hui: An Annual Bilingual Review / Revue Annuelle Bilingue*, vol. 19, 2008, pp. 143–54.

Nancy, Jean-Luc. *Being Singular Plural*. Translated by Robert D. Richardson and Anne E. O'Byrne. Stanford UP, 2000.

Salisbury, Laura. "'What Is the Word': Beckett's Aphasic Modernism." *Journal of Beckett Studies*, vol. 17, no. 1–2, pp. 78–126.

"Scholars Discover 23 Blank Pages That May As Well Be Lost Samuel Beckett Play." *The Onion* 26 April 2006. www.theonion.com/article/scholars-discover-23-blank-pages-that-may-as-well--1946.

Schwartz, Bennett L., and Alan S. Brown, eds. *Tip-of-the-Tongue States and Related Phenomena*. Cambridge UP, 2014.

Thomson, Stephen. "'A tangle of tatters': Ghosts and the Busy Nothing in *Footfalls*." *Beckett and Nothing*, edited by Daniela Caselli. Manchester UP, 2010, pp. 65–83.

Tubridy, Derval. "Words Pronouncing Me Alive: Beckett and Incarnation," *Samuel Beckett Today / Aujourd'hui: An Annual Bilingual Review / Revue Annuelle Bilingue*, vol. 9, 2000, pp. 93–104.

Uhlmann, Anthony. *Samuel Beckett and the Philosophical Image*. Cambridge UP, 2008.

Van Hulle, Dirk. *Manuscript Genetics: Joyce's Know-How, Beckett's Nohow*. UP of Florida, 2008.

Weller, Shane. "'Gnawing to be Naught': Beckett and Pre-Socratic Nihilism." *Samuel Beckett Today / Aujourd'hui: An Annual Bilingual Review / Revue Annuelle Bilingue*, vol. 20, 2008, pp. 321–333.

JEREMY COLANGELO is the author or editor of four books, including *Diaphanous Bodies: Ability, Disability, and Modernist Irish Literature* and the story collection *Beneath the Statue*. He is currently a sessional lecturer at the University of Western Ontario, and is working on a fiction project funded by the SETI Institute.

2 Beckettian Habit and Deictic Exhaustion

Shuta Kiba

Habit is a killjoy. It kills surprises and creates boredom, turning new and exciting events into tedious repetition. As Theodor Adorno points out, the modern artists are obsessed with the category of the "new."[1] Hence they dislike and avoid habit. The creative and aesthetic experience is often considered an extraordinary event that de-familiarizes our ordinary life—something that suspends and disrupts the inert force of habit. The pleasure of creative imagination is opposed to the boredom of tedious habit; as I sketch out this thematic dichotomy, however, I am conscious of my habit of critique, which always attempts to simplify and generalize things so that I can make *sense* of the world. This embarrassment turns my attention to Jacques Derrida's well-known remark on why he hesitates to write about Samuel Beckett:

> How could I write, sign, countersign performatively texts which 'respond' to Beckett? How could I avoid the platitude of a supposed academic metalanguage? [. . .] The composition, the rhetoric, the construction and the rhythm of his works, even the ones that seems the most 'decomposed', that's what 'remains' finally the most 'interesting', that's the work, that's the signature, this remainder which remains when the thematics is exhausted. (Derrida, *Acts* 60–61)

Beckett's work and signature are things that remain after the exhaustion of thematic possibilities. Any attempt we make to thematize the content of Beckett's works thus falls short of capturing his project, that is, what he *does* with his literature. The words "platitude" and "exhaustion" also indicate the sense of boredom and naivety ingrained in the habit of academic metalanguage.[2] Beckett's text is something beyond this naïve platitude. It exceeds the habit of academic discourse, thus causing the feeling of embarrassment and hesitance to thematically engage with his works.[3]

Following Derrida's lead, Derek Attridge suggests that we should first focus on the literal level of the text, namely, "the composition, the rhetoric, the construction and the rhythm" of Beckett's works: that is, what remains after the thematic exhaustion. He explains this by suggesting that we should read literary works not as "an object but an event" (10), focusing more on what happens in the text rather than its contents. Through the close reading of the textual forms and their affects, Attridge illuminates the "event-ness" of Beckett's literary works that we literally experience as the textual feeling. Given Beckett's obsessive engagement with the issue of repetition, movement, and motion, Attridge's argument is convincing and insightful.[4]

At the same time, however, it is my contention that the embarrassment entangled with the platitude of academic metalanguage (that is, our own habit of critique) is also part of the literary event that Beckett makes us experience through his works. In short, our thematic engagement comprises a part of Beckett's literary event.[5] In order to understand Beckett's literary event, therefore, we need to pay attention to the feedback loop between the form and the theme, or the language and the metalanguage. As the beginning of this introductory section rather blatantly demonstrated, habit is a helpful reference point here since it can work both formally and thematically: you can think and talk about habit while simultaneously reiterating your own habit of mind. As the following discussion will demonstrate, Beckett himself was very much interested in the theory and practice of habit. He thought and wrote about habit, but he was also writing with habit.

In what follows, I will elucidate Beckett's theory of habit and how it plays out in his formalistic experiments, especially in his use of disorienting and exhaustive deixis. I will first explore the theory of exhaustion developed by Gilles Deleuze and compare it with Beckett's early essay on Marcel Proust, where he illustrates his theory of habit. This will clarify how Beckett, in line with Deleuze, critically assesses the power of habit. Subsequently, I will delineate how the Beckettian theory of habit is both formally and thematically reflected in the first book of his trilogy, *Molloy*. To do so, I will look at his use of deixis by drawing upon Charles Sanders Peirce's semiotics, especially Peirce's account of an icon, an index, and a symbol (which is considered a linguistic convention produced by habit). In describing Beckett's relentless exhaustion as an affective accumulation of disorienting deixis, I will illuminate the way in which the Beckettian literary event resists the general tendency of the habituating process. At the same time, I will also demonstrate how his disorienting deixis gives readers a mixed sense of confusion and compulsion, which simultaneously propels and undoes the habit of teleological reading.

BECKETT'S EXHAUSTION AND THE THEORY OF HABIT

Deleuze begins his influential essay "The Exhausted" by distinguishing exhaustion from tiredness: "[t]he tired man has only exhausted realization, while the exhausted exhausts the whole of the possible [. . .] One gets tired of *something*, but exhausted of nothing" (116). Tiredness is entangled with its object (something), the causes of tiredness, and we usually know the thing that causes our tiredness (work, exercise, and so on). The causal relationship with objects is also tied to a teleological relationship with these objects. Our work tires us, but we keep working because the completion of our work means a realization of a certain goal (health, money, knowledge, and so on). Deleuze's account further clarifies the reason why this tiredness does not exhaust the whole of the possible: "the realization of the possible always proceeds through exclusion, because it supposes varying preferences and goals, always replacing the preceding ones" (116). The realization involves choosing one possibility over other possibilities; this process of choosing is highly dependent on one's disposition, preference, and teleological orientation, thus from the outset limiting the set of possibilities that one explores. As long as he tries to realize something, therefore, the tired man cannot exhaust the whole of the possible. He realizes one possibility at the cost of excluding the others.

In contrast, the exhaustion does not realize anything. It resists the exclusive impetus of the teleological, end-oriented *energeia*; thus, in the process of exhaustion, "one combines the set of the variables of a situation on condition of renouncing all preference, all organization according to end, all signification" (116). Deleuze calls this exhaustive process "inclusive disjunctions" when taking Beckett's characters as examples of the exhausted. For instance, in *Molloy*, the famous permutation of the sucking stones lets the eponymous character play with possibility without realizing anything. Molloy invents a system with sixteen sucking stones stored in four pockets so that every time he picks a stone from his pocket and sucks it, he sucks a different stone. If successfully executed, there will be neither preference nor prioritization of one specific stone, which allows Molloy to equally include all the disjunctive variables. Molloy's mathematically oriented system is the epitome of the inclusive disjunction whose primal drive is to exhaust the possible without realizing a specific possibility, and he describes this exhaustive process as "one after the other until their number was exhausted" (65). Deleuze compares Murphy's hesitation to choose and prefer one of his biscuits in *Murphy* to Bartleby's "I would prefer not to" and calls it Bartleby's Beckettian formula. This formula allows Beckett to neither choose nor prefer one possibility over others. It is a formula for the absolute non-commitment that allows us to tarry with the possible and exhausts it without realization.[6]

Deleuze's theory of Beckettian exhaustion indicates its sharp contrast with the general tendency of habit. Habit works against exhaustion; what is worse, it kills exhaustion twice. Firstly, habit works with the logic of realization: it cultivates a preference for one possibility and excludes others. For instance, the habit of walking excludes the possibility of crawling, rolling, skipping, jumping, or simply not walking. There are also different styles of walking: plodding, strutting, dragging, limping, and so on (which become more and more idiosyncratic if you consider other essential elements of walking such as posture, arm movement, and stride). Considering these limitless possibilities would turn us into Beckettian characters. Against this Beckettian exhaustion, habit kills all these possibilities by repeatedly choosing a specific possibility, cultivating a certain preference, thus enabling us to realize a preferable end. The familiar path made by habit thus teleologically orients us to preferable objects.

Secondly, habit alleviates tiredness by drawing on principles of identity and simplicity. Deleuze describes habit as a contractile power that creates an anticipatory circuit between two events, turning, for instance, the events of "A and B, A and B, A and B . . ." into "AB, AB, AB . . .".[7] According to the principle of identity, therefore, habit abstracts general rules (A→B as one set of the same event AB) from random events (A /B/ A /B/ . . .), establishing an energy-efficient circuit. Thus the contractile power of habit works as a generalizing force that simplifies the exhaustive process, alleviating the tiredness involved in making mental associations. In a similar vein, G.W.F. Hegel describes habit as the "soul's making itself an abstract universal being, and reducing the particulars of feelings (and of consciousness) to a mere feature of its being" (140). It is noteworthy that Hegel calls this abstractive process a soul's liberation from insanity. He sees this insanity in the state of "self-feeling" that is manically obsessed with particular details of corporeal feelings and ends up dissolving the sense of self in a myriad of feelings and sensations. Beckett's characters are the epitome of such a manic obsessive disorder. Habit, or what Hegel calls the "abstract realization" of the soul, cures the manic through generalization, allowing them to forget the exhaustive permutation of particular possibilities, thereby enabling them to become a simple being. It is, in a sense, a survival mechanism protecting against the fatigue of excessive sensations.

In his early essay on Proust, Beckett similarly theorizes about habit. For example, he depicts habit's contractive and simplifying power as a compromise that individuals have to accept in order to survive: "Habit is a compromise effected between the individual and his environment, or between the individual and his own organic eccentricities, the guarantee of a dull inviolability, the lightning-conductor of his existence" (*Proust* 18–19). Eccentric particularity is like a flash of lightning that shocks us with its overwhelming sensation, while habit is a "lightning rod," a defense mechanism deflecting any surprise. "Breathing is habit. Life is habit" (19). Habit foregrounds survival, but remains dangerously close to dull inertia.

Comparing habit to Proustian voluntary memory, Beckett argues that habit works with a false sense of realization that attains the "identification of the subject with the object of his desire" (14). Consequently, we end up thinking that "the actual seems the inevitable, and, all conscious intellectual effort to reconstitute the invisible and unthinkable as reality [is] fruitless" (14). Habit propels us to follow the well-trodden path toward the preferable object; the path becomes increasingly visible as we repeatedly take it, thus making the other possible paths invisible and unthinkable. Habit thus turns one path into an inevitable and necessary choice, making us prefer something against Bartleby's Beckettian formula.[8] As these passages indicate, Beckett was opposed to the "abstract realization" of habit that excludes eccentric particularities. The following passage illuminates how he regarded the particular eccentricity of objects as a source of enchantment as opposed to habit's abstract realization:

when the object is perceived as particular and unique and not merely the member of a family, when it appears independent of any general notion and detached from the sanity of a cause, isolated and inexplicable in the light of ignorance, then and then only may it be a source of enchantment. Unfortunately, Habit has laid its veto on this form of perception, its action being precisely to hide the essence—the Idea—of the object in the haze of conception—preconception. (Beckett, *Proust* 22–23)

This passage epitomizes the Beckettian (as well as the Deleuzian) critique of habit. The contractile power of habit kills exhaustion. It excludes the myriad possibilities of eccentric particularity, thereby incapacitating any inclusive disjunction, our capacity to say, "I would prefer not to." The exhaustive process is dangerous in that the flash of its lightning could bring us to the state of near madness, the insanity of self-dispossession. This is why "habit paralyses our attention, drugs those handmaidens of perception whose co-operation is not absolutely essential" (20). Nevertheless, this opioid also brings us to the state of dull detachment from the world, indifferent to the enchantment of reality. Enchanting reality is the world of eccentric particularity, but is considered inessential by habit's principles of identity and simplicity. Beckett's critique of habit teaches us how to pay more attention to this dangerous but enchanting world and exhaust the permutation of eccentric possibilities.[9]

BECKETT'S DISORIENTING DEIXIS

There are infinite possibilities, numerous paths we can take. The overwhelming number of possibilities can be intimidating, disorienting, and exhausting. Habit saves us from this exhaustion by simplifying the options.[10] It creates a one-way street by repeatedly identifying and choosing the same route, cultivating a preference for a specific option, thereby making a well-trodden path. In this way, habit helps us make *sense* of the world. This is why Hegel claims that our existence as a "thinking being" starts with habit: "habit is indispensable for the *existence* of all intellectual life in the individual, enabling the subject to be a concrete immediacy, an 'ideality' of soul—enabling the matter of consciousness, religious, moral, etc., to be his as *this* self, *this* soul" (143). Habit gradually forms in our minds a strong teleological disposition, the conceptual index that points at its preferred object and realizes that "*this* is me." This conceptual identification, as mentioned above, is what Beckett critically presented as a false sense of realization that achieves the "identification of the subject with the object of his desire" (14). Habit generates conceptual identification via the exclusive index that prefers one possibility over others. Against this exclusive index, Beckett advocates "inclusive disjunction," maintaining his vigilance against our habit of thinking that creates the above-mentioned "haze of conception" (23).[11]

This explains why Derrida hesitated to talk about Beckett within plain academic discourse. Derrida's concern was that our theoretical analysis of Beckett could fall into the habit of our own conceptual thinking, thereby missing Beckett's true accomplishment: his literary artistry that not only thematically criticizes habit but also performatively deconstructs our habits of mind. Derrida was thus reenacting Beckett's vigilance against the habit of conceptual thinking, which works as an exclusive index that constantly reproduces a simple and identical path, namely, academic metalanguage's platitudes.[12]

Beckett's writings performatively disrupt our habit of mind, or of teleological reading. This is most clearly exemplified in his use of the index. Unlike the exclusive index promulgated by the habit of our thinking, his exhaustive permutation, or inclusive disjunction, attempts to point out every possible detail of eccentric particularities, thus making his index disorienting and exhausting. The beginning of *Molloy* is a good example of this disorienting deixis:

> I am in my mother's room. It's I who live there now. I don't know how I got there. Perhaps in an ambulance, certainly a vehicle of some kind. I was helped. I'd never have got there alone. There's this man who comes every week. Perhaps I got here thanks to him. (Beckett, *Three Novels* 3)

The passage starts with a reference to the narrator's spatial location "here" (in my mother's room), while its simple declarative "I am" suggesting his temporal location of "now." It thus points to the narrator's spatiotemporal location: "here and now." But the next sentence disturbs this spatiotemporal relationship by grammatically shifting the subject position from "I" to "It," thereby splitting "I" into a narrated object "It" and narrative subject "I." As a result, at the descriptive level, the relative pronoun "who" separates space and time into "there and now": the same temporal location, but one is "here" and the other is "there." It is as if the "I am" in the first sentence had become the other in the second sentence. This split deepens in the next sentence when the narrative employs the past tense: "how I got there." Now, the spatial distance between "here" and "there" is transferred to the temporal distance between "now" and "then," denoting the spatiotemporal location as "there and then." Already in the third sentence, therefore, the narrative "I" seems entirely detached from the first declarative "I am." Since the spatiotemporal location is the only knowledge about the narrative "I" granted to us readers, its dislocation muddles the narrative sequence and disorients our reading experience. This dislocation and disorientation culminate when the narrator adds in the eighth sentence: "Perhaps I got here thanks to him." Now, the narrative denotes the spatiotemporal location as "here and then," thus exhausting the possible permutations of spatiotemporal indices. By committing himself to the exhaustive permutation of inclusive disjunction, therefore, Beckettian deixis becomes literally disorienting and exhausting.

In his semiotic theory, Charles Sanders Peirce argues that the demonstrative pronouns ("here" and "there") and the relative pronouns are pure indices. It is deixis, a pointing finger denoting a real physical connection between the sign and the object. Peirce's theory is relevant to my argument in that he emphasizes that the deictic connection between the sign and the object can happen independently of the mind because it "does not lie in a mental association" (1: 226). In short, an index can work independently of the habit of conceptual thinking. As Peirce argues, an index involves a mood that is "imperative, or exclamatory" (2: 16). The pointing finger is imperative: it literally and urgently turns our attention toward particular objects. Without the guidance of conceptual thinking, the Peircean index randomly impels us to look at things without a general guideline. Beckett's liberal use of deixis works exactly like this: unlike the exclusive index tied to the habit of conceptual thinking, Beckett's index tries to include all eccentric particularities, thereby dissolving the sense of orientation and the teleological disposition of our minds; it disorients our attention, frustrating our understanding and making our reading experience exhausting.[13]

Furthermore, Peirce's semiotic theory of the other two signs, *icon* and *symbol*, provides a comprehensive account of how Beckett's disorienting deixis plays with our habit of mind. An icon denotes a "resemblance" between the sign and the object, and as in the case of the pure index, an icon itself is independent of the mental association, which Pierce calls "degenerate" (1: 225). In mathematics, a degenerate case means a non-typical or non-generic case. This is in line with Peirce's descriptions of icon and index, which do not involve generalization by mental association; in short, they both denote a pre-conceptual relationship with their objects. This is why Peirce describes these signs as a sort of "mood" that precedes our conceptual thinking (2: 16). In contrast to an icon and an index, a symbol is a conventional and arbitrary sign that is developed by mental association. It is always abstract and general, and thus includes "all general words, the main body of speech, and any mode of conveying a judgment" (1: 226). Since symbol involves generalization and conceptualization via mental association and leads to a judgment, it has a propositional structure constituted by the relationship between the subject and the object. And here lies what makes Peirce's semiotics most crucial to my argument: he asserts that the transition from icons and indices to the general conception of a symbolic sign happens through habit. This is because, as Hegel pointed out, Peirce thinks that all conceptual thinking arises through habit: "intellectual power is nothing but facility in taking habits" (1: 291). Peirce's account thus offers a theory that connects the semiotic function of the index to the philosophy of mind regarding habit, while also enabling us to delineate the pre-habitual and pre-conceptual mood and affect of Beckettian deixis.

This allows us to delineate the nuanced transition from pre-conceptual index to habit of conceptual thinking in Beckett's writing without ourselves falling into the platitudes of academic metalanguage. In the process of explaining and making *sense* of Beckett's critique of habit, my argument was unable to entirely avoid the pitfall of simple oppositional thinking: the preference for exhaustion over habit, thus reproducing another metalanguage.[14] In contrast, Peirce is careful not to fall into the habit of oppositional thinking; he thus suggests that there cannot be an absolutely pure distinction among icons, indices, and symbols, since even at the early stage of incipient feelings, there is already some tendency toward uniformity, and "all things have a tendency to take habits" (1: 277). Keeping this in mind, I will try to illuminate this liminal space between pre-conceptual index and the habit of conceptual thinking in Beckett's works.[15]

In fact, the pre-formation of habit can be seen in the midst of Beckett's disorienting deixis. Going back to the opening of *Molloy*, for instance, the second sentence, "It's I who live there now," already involves a little bit of habituation. I have suggested that the indexicality of the relative pronoun "who" introduces a distance between the indexed "I" and the anaphoric gesture of the narrative "I," thus working as disorienting deixis. Yet this split also works as an abstract detachment of the narrative "I" from the actual event happening in the narrative sequence. This can thus be read as the narrator's act of generalization that historicizes his story, indicating the generalizing force of habit. The fact of habituation becomes more explicit in the seventh sentence: "There's this man who comes every week." It turns out that the man's habitual visit is related to Molloy's job, his habit of writing: "He [the man] gives me money and takes away the pages. So many pages, so much money. Yes, I work now, a little like I used to, except that I don't know how to work any more" (3). Molloy writes habitually. And perhaps, right now, we are reading the very text he has written. Again, this gives a sense of historicity to Molloy's writing and helps us figure out its spatiotemporal location.

Gradually, then, as the effect of Beckett's disorienting deixis dissipates, we start to make sense of the orientation of Molloy's writing. The repetition of "perhaps" and "I don't know" indicate the style of his writing, giving us not only the patterns and rhythms that we follow but also the indication of Molloy's disposition and character (for example, his forgetfulness, timidity, vulnerability, and so on). In short, we are getting habituated to Molloy's writing. The habit of his writing thus renders a teleological orientation to both his writing and our reading. After Molloy is given advice by the man who habitually visits his place, he even tries to rewrite the original opening of his text, thereby erasing the traces of his disorienting deixis: "It was he told me I'd begun all wrong, that I should have begun differently. He must be right. [. . .] Here's my beginning. It must mean something, or they wouldn't keep it. Here it is" (4). In this way, the index of "here and now" excludes the other possible permutation of the spatiotemporal indices, thereby successfully reopening the beginning of his story.

Despite Molloy's effort to set out a smooth narrative, however, his narration soon becomes muddled and disoriented again:

> All grows dim. A little more and you'll go blind. It's in the head. It doesn't work any more, it says, I don't work any more. You go dumb as well and sounds fade. The threshold scarcely crossed that's how it is. It's the head. It must have had enough. So that you say, I'll manage this time, then perhaps once more, then perhaps a last time, then nothing more. (Beckett, *Three Novels* 4)

The orientation of the narrative is theoretically mapped out with the indication of Beckett's trilogy: this time [*Molloy*], once more [*Malone Dies*], then a last time [*The Unnamable*]. The ultimate goal is described as "nothing." At the same time, the conceptual schema and its teleological orientation toward nothing is disrupted by the formal structure of the passage. Molloy says that he is close to nothing (that is, blind, dumb, and soundless), but the more he claims his impetus to nothingness, the more he piles up the heap of words and fills the passage with haunting murmurs, relentlessly claiming there is still something. In fact, almost all the indications toward nothingness are described with the word "more": a little more, more, more, once more, and more. The accumulation of words and sounds correspond with the multiple uses of pronouns: you, it, and I. Again, it is theoretically explained that they are all "in the head"; yet the multiple pronouns cannot but disorient our understanding through the obscurity of their origins. Contrary to Molloy's theoretical impetus to nothingness, the haunting murmurs get louder and louder.

As the Hegelian theory of habit illustrates, it is the contractile power of habit that simplifies these murmurs (you, it, and I) into "my" voice by conceptually and exclusively indexing the object as its own property: "*This* is me." In this way, habit establishes a propositional structure that binds the subject and the object-predicate (S is P). As my readings of the text so far have clarified, Molloy's contractile power is not yet strong enough to establish the higher genus of a unified subject (S) that subdues the chaotic murmurs and owns them as his object-predicate (P).[16] Without any stable propositional structures, therefore, Molloy cannot maintain his own subjectivity that vertically binds the horizontal accumulations of object-predicate. The generative power of habit thus constantly fails, degenerating into the lawless heap of barren objects.

As mentioned above, Peircean semiotics claim that icons and indices are "degenerate" by themselves. They do not generate any propositional structure: the iconic identification is just a dreamy mingling of two terms while the degenerate index can only denote a real connection of two terms without any generalization. Without the contractile power of habit, therefore, Molloy's world is full of degenerate icons and indices. They tantalize readers' mental associations with so many resemblances and indications, while ultimately frustrating and disappointing us by not providing any general or generative structure, or the "metalanguage" of the symbolic sign that teleologically orients our reading process.

In fact, *Molloy* is filled with *indications* of *resemblance*. At the beginning of the novel, for instance, its mirror structure is represented by travelers A and C who walk toward each other and look at each other "face to face" (5).[17] Molloy remembers that, while their appearances are different, "they looked alike" (5). The peasant-like appearance of C resembles Molloy and the gentlemanly appearance of A resembles Moran, the narrator of the second chapter. The resemblance of A and C becomes reenacted in the second chapter where Moran gradually transforms himself into Molloy. Because of the accumulations of these resemblances, it is tempting to formulate a theory: Molloy is C, Moran is A, and Moran becomes like Molloy at the end of the novel (A→C). Again, this theory fits the general schema of "mirroring" presented at the beginning of the book: "A and C going slowly towards each other" (4). It also becomes plausible if we think about what lies between A and C, that is, B or

Being. *Molloy* demonstrates an obsession with the question of being. The first chapter starts with "I am" and ends with "to be," indicating Molloy's journey to B [to be]. Moran is also intrigued by the mysterious language of bees, which he seems to understand at the novel's end when he finally transforms himself into a non-human being.

However, this sort of general proposition is doomed to be refuted by the particular differences within general resemblance. For instance, C carries "a stout stick" and wears "a cocked hat" (6) or a "town hat, which the least gust would carry far away" (9), while Molloy carries crutches and his hat is fastened to his buttonhole. Following the encounter and interaction with C, Moran decides to have a stick; yet finding out that he does not have a knife, he decides to use his umbrella as a stick. He also wears a hat, but it is a straw hat with an elastic. There are so many other indices of iconic resemblances throughout the narrative, yet because of Beckett's detailed description of the particular eccentricities, all these indices resist the generalizing force of habit, maintaining their "degenerate" status. "I apologize for these details, in a moment we'll go faster, much faster" (58), Molloy says in passing. Nevertheless, it turns out that *Molloy* never speeds up since, distracted by all these details, Molloy can never sway to the contractile power of habit. Habit would have given him the simplest, shortest path to his goal. Molloy is, however, too distracted to cultivate a simple habit.[18]

The only habit Molloy has acquired comes from mysterious "imperatives" that refer to his mother: "I knew my imperatives well and yet I submitted to them. It had become a habit. It is true they nearly all bore on the same question, that of my relations with my mother" (80–81). From the outset, his goal was "to get to [his] mother as quickly as possible" (25). As Peirce argues, an index involves a mood that is "imperative, or exclamatory, as 'See there!' or 'Look out!'" (2:16). It denotes a sense of urgency that forces our attention to the object pointed out. For Molloy, his mother was the primary object of his index, the ultimate goal to which the entirety of his story moves.[19]

However, even this privileged index loses its power and soon becomes "degenerate." Molloy tells us that "having set me in motion at last, they [the imperatives] began to falter, then went to silent, leaving me there like a fool who neither knows where is going nor why he is going there" (81). Even the exclusive index to his mother ends up becoming disorienting deixis. Molloy's subsequent confession emphasizes the fact that his index is always degenerate: "And every time I say, I said this, or, I said that [. . .] I am merely complying with the convention that demand you either lie or hold your peace. [. . .] In reality I said nothing at all" (82). All these degenerate icons and indices are pre-formations of habits and symbols; therefore, they tantalize us to assert something out of the accumulation of the degenerate signs. They incite our desire for knowledge and meaning, which in a sense motivates all genesis of symbolic signs. "Look, there!" The imperatives of index motivate us to create theories, propositions with metalanguage. As if to mock this desire, Beckett's disorienting deixis constantly degenerates, decomposes into a pile of barren dust, turning the sign of genesis into nothingness.

At the same time, this "nothingness" still accumulates like dust and creates some mood and affect as a literary event.[20] Deleuze calls it exhaustion, Derrida describes it as an implied embarrassment (*Acts* 60–61), Attridge senses it as a painful but pleasurable repetition (16, 21), and Sianne Ngai names it "stuplimity" (stupidity + sublime), which contains the contradictory feeling of boredom and surprise (262). At the center of all these feelings, we can see the imperative mood of the exclamatory index "Look!" It forcefully turns our attention to the eccentric particularities whose flash of lightning surprises us with its overwhelming sensation. This overwhelming sensation exhausts us with its infinite possibility; therefore, the imperatives of the index eventually turn into a habit, thereby simplifying our mental and physical operations. For the sake of protecting our life, habit kills surprise and drugs us into the boredom of dull inertia.

In sum, Beckett's disorienting deixis works at the threshold between the deictic imperative (involving surprise, exhaustion, stupidity) and the pre-formation of habit (involving embarrassment, boredom), situating his literary event at the intersection between pre-conceptual affect and conceptual metalanguage. The resulting effect upon readers is a strange amalgam of confusion and compulsion: we do not know where we are going, yet we feel and experience the imperative to go on. Beckett's literary event, in this way, turns us readers into Beckettian characters:[21]

> [. . .] perhaps they have carried me to the threshold of my story, before the door that opens on my story, that would surprise me, if it opens, it will be I, it will be the silence, where I am, I don't know, I'll never know, in the silence you don't know, you must go on, I can't go on, I'll go on. (*Three Novels* 407)

This is the end of the trilogy, *The Unnamable*, suggesting the failure of the ending presented at the beginning of *Molloy*: "I'll manage this time [*Molloy*], then perhaps once more [*Malone Dies*], then perhaps a last time [*The Unnamable*], then nothing more" (4). The teleology of habit ends up defeated by the imperatives of an index. Conceptually speaking, there is nothing left because the story ends and the murmur stops. Yet this "nothing" still means "something" as an index. The degenerate index asserts nothing, but its imperative mood points us toward the possibility we have not yet exhausted, propelling us to go on, exhausted, without a map.

Notes

1. Adorno argues that "[t]he category of the new has been central to art since the middle of the last century, if only in the context of the question of whether there ever was such a thing as a shift to modernism" (29).

2. The word "exhaustion" might remind us of Deleuze's famous essay on Beckett. However, the original publication of Derrida's interview precedes that of Deleuze's essay, thus Derrida is not alluding to Deleuze here. I will explore the Deleuzian theory of exhaustion in relation to the theory of

habit in the next section. Pedretti foregrounds Beckett's thematic as well as formalistic engagement with the sense of boredom, delineating Beckett's dialectic inversion and critique of the modernistic demand of the new.

3. Leslie Hill expresses a similar hesitation and vigilance against the naivety of metalanguage by saying: "But over several decades, in countless books and articles, the search for stable and satisfactory meanings in Beckett's writing has carried on unabated. Many different approaches have been tried. [. . .] To write on Beckett after all this implies rashness, obstinacy, even naivety. What remains to be said?" (ix) After expressing his dissatisfaction with critics who "seemed too willing to domesticate the author's texts and too ready to recuperate them within well-worn and reductive norms" (x), that is, the academic metalanguage, Hill announces that the concern of his project is "not with presumed authorial concepts, but with textual affect" (x), which is, as we will see, similar to the Attridge's project.

4. Attridge notes how readers become gradually familiarized with the voice of *The Unnamable*, while also paying attention to the momentum and the repetitive rhythm of Beckett's text that forms and plays with the reader's expectation. This analysis is insightful and resonant with my reading; as I explain in the final section, I read this familiarization as *habituation*. I also agree with Attridge's conclusion: "The literary force of the work, its singularity and inventiveness, the space of otherness it opens beyond our closed world of habitual thought and feeling, emerge only from the event of reading, and from the reader's painful, pleasurable experience of that event" (21).

5. Again, Attridge pays attention to the habituating process of our reading. His reading, however, foregrounds the literal level of textual feelings and neither delineates how these textual feelings lead to habituation nor demonstrates that this habituation always already involves the seeds of conceptual thinking.

6. Georgio Agamben discusses Bartleby in a similar vein in his "Bartleby, or On Contingency" (*Potentialities* §15). Žukauskaitė points out the similarity among Deleuze, Agamben, and Beckett, using the idea of the potentiality of life as an overarching theme. Fred Moten also sees exhaustion as "a mode or form or way of life" (738) embodied by Black life. Referring to Deleuze and Beckett, Moten describes the exhausted Black life as nothingness that folds the social (*not* political) biopoetics "animated by both lyric and *lysis*, continually driven toward new fields of exhaustion" (769). Moten also asserts the "relationship between teleological principle and sovereignty" (775).

7. See Deleuze, *Difference* 70. Deleuze's reference point here is David Hume, who contended that the human mind has a propensity toward "the same smooth and uninterrupted progress of the imagination, as attends the view of the same invariable object" (204). For Hume, habit works a generalizing force that abstracts the rule (for instance, the law of causation) out of the repetitions of random events. Deleuze, in contrast, foregrounds the *difference* within these repetitions that resists the seductive force of generalization. In this way, Deleuze illuminates that habit always already involves the repetition of *difference* amid its tendency toward the repetition of the same. In this respect, Deleuze's account becomes close to that of Gaston Bachelard who describes the individual being as "a fairly variable sum of untallied habits" (*Intuition* 41), reintroducing the dynamic and contingent variations into the concept of habit and reconceptualizing it as something spontaneous and creative. However, as *The Dialectic of Duration* suggests, Bachelard advocates the oppositional thinking of the Hegelian dialectic, and thus tends to prefer negation over difference. Despite the convergence, therefore, their accounts of habit eventually diverge. Deleuze's assessment of habit is more critical than Bachelard's.

8. Regarding positive accounts of Beckettian habit, see Maude (2012) and Bellini (2014). Drawing on Félix Ravaisson, Catherine Malabou, and others, Maude reads Beckettian habit as a compulsive disposition or an organic eccentricity that forms a residual subjectivity. Bellini describes the double-edged nature of habit in a similar way to Maude, referring to Maine de Biran and Ravaisson. As Maude notes, Ravaisson describes habit as both grace and addiction (i.e. illness), which nicely captures the Beckett's ambiguous description of habit in *Proust*. As Maude also points out, the account of habit as grace is in line with Heinrich von Kleist's theory on the graceful movement of

the marionette, which Beckett frequently quoted for his stage direction (Maude 819). Nonetheless, it is also noteworthy that Kleist never describes the automatic movement of a marionette as habit. In fact, we neither say "the habit of the computer" nor "the habit of my car"; we usually use "repetition" instead of "habit" to denote the activity of inorganic subjects. Thus, we should be cautious of the difference between organic habit and mechanical repetition. In my reading, Beckett's reference to Kleist leans toward the latter and he is generally more prone to criticize habit than Maude indicates; granted, the transition from repetition to habit is complex and nuanced. We will explore this nuanced transition in the final section.

9. Illuminating the association of habit with Irishness in Beckett's essay (both implicitly personified in the figure of D.P. Moran, whose name is also reminiscent of the narrator of the second chapter of *Molloy*), McKee argues that Beckett's critique of habit works in tandem with his desire to break the habit, custom, and tradition of Irishness. Despite Beckett's resistance to habit, however, Louar notes that Beckettian bodies are doomed to incorporate the habit and suffer the damnation of the life as a pensum: "[. . .] the politics of the Beckettian body is predicated on its inescapable organic and socio-political conditions: suffering and habit. [. . .] the theatrical statement 'breathing is habit' predicts the characters' somatic incorporation of the social environment, the forcefully taught lessons of a literally translated *savoir vivire* that constructs the Beckettian body as memory and its life as a pensum" (79).

10. Beckett thus states that "[t]he creature of habit turns aside from the object that cannot be made to correspond with one or the other of his intellectual prejudices, that resists the propositions of his team of syntheses, organized by Habit on labour-saving principles" (*Proust* 23).

11. Paul Saunders sees the ecological potential in Molloy's unnatural embodiment of nature, which, by resisting the conventional (thus habitual) representation of nature, gestures toward the ecology of negation that goes beyond the "rigid subject/object duality" and thereby "escape[s] a repressive reality principle" (59).

12. Hegel's theory of habit suggests that it is the contractile power of habit that starts our existence as a thinking being. "Breathing is habit. Life is habit" (*Proust* 19), said Beckett. We may as well add to this that "Thinking is habit." Given this, Derrida's vigilance is not surprising because Hegelian dialectics was the primary target of his deconstruction and other post-structuralist philosophers including Deleuze. We have already seen Deleuze's critique of the teleological force of habit with his theory of exhaustion. Deleuze criticizes the habit of dialectical thinking in a similar vein. In a sense, his *Difference and Repetition* was an attempt to formulate the theory of repetition that produces *difference* as opposed to the dialectical repetition of the same. Derrida's theory of *différance* was also developed against the teleological force of the dialectical thinking: "Such a *différance* would at once, again, give us to think a writing without presence and without absence, without history, without cause, without *archia*, without *telos*, a writing that absolutely upsets all dialectics, all theology, all teleology, all ontology" (*Margins* 67).

13. Moorjani argues that Beckett's "devious deictics" gestures toward "a *topos* outside the signifying practice of language, to which neither symbolic naming, indexical or deictic pointing, or iconic likeness can properly refer" (*Devious Deictics* 21). It thus constantly disrupts the logic of the narrative "I" with its "hysterical dispossession" (27). As explained below, I argue that the "disorienting deixis" still refers to *something* like an imperative mood, thereby simultaneously moving us to and against the habit of the narrative "I." Thus, disorienting deixis locates itself *within* the signifying practice of language and works in tandem with the habitual orientation toward the narrative "I."

14. At the same time, it is not just careless mistakes nor lack of analytical rigor that made me repeatedly create simple oppositions and blindly reenact the habit of mind. This is because, as mentioned above, habit works in tandem with our forgetfulness. As our habit of walking exemplifies, habit is fully active when it is automatic, when it is working in the back of our consciousness. If thinking is habit, that is, if habit is not the object of our thought but the condition of our thought, the contraction (i.e. generalization, simplification, identification) always happens with our thinking *without* our knowledge. The habit of our mind thus endlessly reproduces simple oppositions. It is no coincidence

that Hegel, who was strongly aware of this habit-mind connection, delineated the development of the mind with the repetitions of dialectics that progress with the endless struggle with the two opposing moments. Seeing habit at the core of Hegelian dialectics, Catherine Malabou argues that the contractile power of habit is analogous to Hegelian *Aufhebung*, which simultaneously *abolishes* and *preserves* the two contrary moments by lifting them up to a higher unity. Paying similar attention to the "forgetfulness" of human minds, Deleuze describes the dialectics in the following way: "Problems are always dialectical. This is why, whenever the dialectic 'forgets' its intimate relation with Ideas in the form of problems, whenever it is content to trace problems from propositions, it loses its true power and falls under the sway of the power of the negative, necessarily substituting for the ideal objectivity of the *problematic* a simple confrontation between opposing, contrary or contradictory, propositions. This long perversion begins with the dialectic itself, and attains its extreme form in Hegelianism" (*Difference* 164).

15. Positioning themselves against Hegel, post-structuralist thinkers share the same vigilance against the habit of the mind that unwittingly creates simple oppositions and blindly reproduces vulgar dialectics. They thus try to perform a critique of habit without falling into the same old habit. This is why Derrida argues that *différance* maintains "the relations of profound affinity with Hegelian discourse" while also working as "a kind of infinitesimal and radical displacement of it" (*Margins* 14). Deleuze also delineates the possibility of *difference* within the repetition congenial to habit (*Difference* 70–78). In this way, their critique of habit is performed not from outside but from *within* habit. Beckett's writings also work with a similar vigilance against the habit of dialectical thinking.

16. Will Broadway describes this as a "porous subjectivity." He argues that in *Molloy* "The distinction between top and bottom is flattened, and what emerges is a reconceptualization of the body as decentralized and of the embodied subject as decentralized, destabilized, and porous" (92).

17. This is an allusion to I Corinthians 13:12: "For now we see through a glass, darkly; but then face to face: now I know in part; but then shall I know even as also I am known." Michael Stewart elucidates the mirror-structure in *The Unnamable* and the gradual dissolving of identity in *Trilogy*, while referring to the Lacanian theory of the mirror stage.

18. Reading Molloy as a "semi-delirious travelogue" (27), Sheehan describes the "deviant journeying of Molloy and Moran" (27) as the expression of Beckett's nomadic modernism (in reference to Deleuze and Guattari's *A Thousand Plateaus*). Pedretti describes Molloy's distractedness as his indecisiveness, and calls it Beckett's "rhetoric of uncertainty," which undermines narrative authority and thereby disrupts the narrative teleology and readerly expectation. Perdetti explains: "It is not the elimination of narrative possibilities—the commonplace that 'nothing happens' in Beckett— but rather their over-inclusion which Beckett uses to frustrate traditional narrative expectation. In short, Molloy cannot decide in his account on what did or did not take place, so the act of narrative pruning never occurs" (593).

19. Kennedy describes Molloy's petty theft of cutlery as his expression of desire for his mother, referring to the object-relations theory of Donald Winnicott. While suggesting the phenomenon of dissolving self in the writing of Beckett, Derrida, and Deleuze, Sarah Gendron points out the similarity between Beckettian subjects and Deleuze's "virtual object" (Gendron 51), which Deleuze himself associates with Winnicott's transitional object, Melanie Klein's good and bad objects stemming from a child's relationship with their mother (*Difference* 101).

20. Boulter's depiction of the Beckettian subject as the "melancholy archive" (16) of history is insightful here. We can read it as a Benjaminian sense of historical materialism that works against the teleological movement of the history written by heroes and victors.

21. Boulter describes this in a similar way: "his characters—who at times become our surrogates, our uncanny doubles—express much the same confusion about their worlds as the reader; as such, the strangeness, because shared, becomes in a sense normalized" (17). I go on to describe this normalization as a habituation process.

Works Cited

Abbott, H. P. *The Fiction of Samuel Beckett: Form and Effect*. U of California P, 1973.

Adorno, Theodor. *Aesthetic Theory*. Translated by Robert Hullot-Kentor. Bloomsbury Academic, 2013.

Agamben, Giorgio. *Potentialities: Collected Essays in Philosophy*. Translated by Daniel Heller-Roazen. Stanford UP, 1999.

Attridge, Derek. "Taking Beckett at His Word: The Event of *The Unnamable*." *Journal of Beckett Studies*, vol. 26, no. 1, 2017, pp. 10–23.

Bachelard, Gaston. *The Dialectic of Duration*. Translated by Mary McAllester Jones. Rowman & Littlefield International, 2000.

———. *Intuition of the Instant*. Translated by Eileen Rizo-Patron. Northwestern UP, 2013.

Begam, R., and J. Soderholm. *Platonic Occasions: Dialogues and Literature, Art and Culture*. Stockholm UP, 2015.

Beckett, Samuel. *Proust*. Grove Press, 1957.

———. *Three Novels: Molloy, Malone Dies, The Unnamable*. Grove Press, 2009.

Bellini, Federico. "'DER MENCH [SIC] IST EIN GEWOHNHEITSTIER': Beckett and Habit." *Comparative Studies in Modernism*, vol. 5, 2014, pp. 91–101.

Boulter, Jonathan. *Beckett: A Guide for the Perplexed*. Continuum, 2008.

Broadway, Will. "Holes, Orifice, and Porous Subjectivity in Beckett's *Molloy*." *Journal of Beckett Studies*, vol. 27, no. 1, 2018, pp. 83–94.

Deleuze, Gilles. *Difference and Repetition*. Translated by Paul Patton. Colombia UP, 1994.

———. "The Exhausted." Translated by Christian Kerslake. *Parallax*, vol. 2, no. 2, 1996, pp. 113–135.

Derrida, Jacques. *Acts of Literature*. Routledge, 1992.

———. *Margins of Philosophy*. Translated by Alan Bass. U of Chicago P, 1982.

The English Bible: King James Version. Edited by Gerald Hamond and Austin Busch, vol. 2. W.W. Norton, 2012.

Gendron, Sarah. "'A Cogito for the Dissolved Self': Writing, Presence, and the Subject in the Work of Samuel Beckett, Jacques Derrida, and Gilles Deleuze." *Journal of Modern Literature*, vol. 28, no. 1, 2004, pp. 47–64.

Hegel, G.W.F. *Hegel's Philosophy of Mind*. Translated by A.V. Miller. Clarendon P, 1971.

Hill, Leslie. *Beckett's Fiction: In Different Words*. Cambridge UP, 1990.

Hume, David. *A Treaties of Human Nature*. Clarendon P, 1978.

Kennedy, Seán. "Mothering Molloy, or Beckett and Cutlery." *Journal of Beckett Studies*, vol. 28, no. 1, 2019, pp. 35–51.

Kleist, Heinrich von. "On the Marionette Theatre." Translated by Thomas G. Neumiller. *The Drama Review: TDR*, vol. 16, no. 3, The "Puppet" Issue, 1972, pp. 22–26.

Louar, Nadia. "Beckett's Bodies in the Trilogy, or Life as a Pensum." *Journal of Beckett Studies*, vol. 27, no. 1, 2018, pp. 69–82.

Malabou, Catherine. *The Future of Hegel: Plasticity, Temporality, and Dialectic*. Translated by Lisabeth During. Routledge, 2005.

Maude, Ulrika. "Beckett and the Laws of Habit." *Modernism/modernity*, vol. 18, no. 4, 2011, pp. 824–821.

McKee, Alexander. "Breaking the Habit: Samuel Beckett's Critique of Irish-Ireland." *New Hibernia Review*, vol. 14, no. 1, 2010, pp. 42–58.

Moorjani, Angela. "Beckett's Devious Deictics." *Rethinking Beckett: A Collection of Critical Essays*, edited by Lance Butler and Robin Davis. Palgrave Macmillan, 1990, pp. 20–30.

———. "Deictic Projection of the *I* and Eye in Beckett's Fiction and *Film*." *Journal of Beckett Studies*, vol. 17, no. 1–2, 2008, pp. 35–51.

Moten, Fred. "Blackness and Nothingness (Mysticism in the Flesh)." *The South Atlantic Quarterly*, vol. 112, no. 4, 2013, pp. 737–780.

Ngai, Sianne. *Ugly Feelings*. Harvard UP, 2005.

Pedretti, Mark. "Late Modern Rigmarole: Boredom as Form in Samuel Beckett's Trilogy." *Studies in the Novel*, vol. 45, no. 4, 2013, pp. 583–602.

Peirce, Charles S. *The Essential Peirce: Selected Philosophical Writings*. 2 Vols. Edited by Nathan House and Christian Kloesel. Indian UP, 1992.

Ravaisson, Félix. *Of Habit*. Translated by Clare Carlisle and Mark Sinclair. Continuum, 2008.

Saunders, Paul. "Samuel Beckett's *Trilogy* and the Ecology of Negation." *Journal of Beckett Studies*, vol. 20, no. 1, 2011, pp. 54–77.

Sheehan, Paul. "No Direction Home: Molloy, Travelogue, and Nomadic Modernism." *Journal of Beckett Studies*, vol. 26, no. 1, 2017, pp. 4–38.

Stewart, Michael. "The Unnamable Mirror: The Reflective Identity in Beckett's Prose." *Samuel Beckett Today / Aujourd'hui*, vol. 8, 1999, pp. 107–115.

Webb, Eugene. *Samuel Beckett: A Study of His Novels*. U of Washington P, 2014.

Žukauskaitė, Audronė. "Potentiality as a Life: Deleuze, Agamben, Beckett." *Deleuze Studies*, vol. 6, no. 4, 2012, pp. 628–637.

SHUTA KIBA is a PhD candidate in the Department of English at the University of Wisconsin-Madison. He is currently working on his dissertation on the biopoetics of the Romantic habit—its simultaneously regulative and liberatory operation as biopower in the writings of the British Romantics. His articles have appeared (or are forthcoming) in *Studies in Romanticism*, *Essays in Romanticism*, and *World Humanities Report*.

3 Glitches in Logic in Beckett's *Watt*: Toward a Sensory Poetics

Amanda M. Dennis

In 1953, Olympia Press published Samuel Beckett's *Watt*, written some ten years earlier and postponed, in part, because of the war. The other reason for the delay in the novel's publication was, we could say, the perceived absurdity of its style. Such absurdity might be, as the critic Michael Robinson suggests, a reaction to the absurdity of the Second World War. "Watt is a journey that ends in the discovery of non-meaning," he writes, where "all that is usually assumed true disintegrates into an ill-defined series of phenomena" (112). Yet this assessment may overshadow a more important feature of the novel—and the reason why it is so important in the landscape of experimental literature (important enough for Beckett, and particularly *Watt*, to be identified as the hinge between modernism and postmodernism).[1] Rather than a "discovery of non-meaning," the breakdown of habitual meaning structures, famously enacted in the pages of this experimental novel, is an intentioned interrogation into the processes by which meaning is produced. By mobilizing alternative modes of making sense—modes that involve the body—the novel lays bare the somatic foundations of meaning and the sources of its modification. The semantic disorientation we find in *Watt* is certainly *marked* by Beckett's experience of the war—he wrote the bulk of it while in hiding in the French countryside in Roussillon—but the novel is more than "daily therapy" or a way for its author to keep sane, as Deirdre Bair suggests in her biography of Beckett (348).[2] The novel might be said to limn the horrors of the Second World War via determinate negation, saying by not saying that historical circumstances require a renegotiation of what it means to mean.

On the page, wrestling with meaning becomes what the editors at Routledge, who rejected the novel for publication in 1945, describe as a "wild and unintelligible" text (Craig, et al. 14). We find musical notation, lists of objections and their solutions, croaking frogs, informational tables, poems, songs inventories, series, and phrases that repeat in obsessive loops. Certain repetitive passages make language appear to "glitch," as if it were a malfunctioning computer program or electronic device. (The word "glitch" comes from the Yiddish, *glitsh* or *glitshn:* a slippery place, to slide.) The aberrant quality of *Watt*'s prose has led Matthew Feldman to identify the novel as a pivot point in Beckett's oeuvre that heralds an increasingly experimental style (13). While Beckett's earlier novel, *Murphy* (1938), problematizes a Cartesian split between body and mind, *Watt* shifts the emphasis shifts to language, "dismantling coherence through language itself rather than through concepts" (Nixon 187). In order to critique language via literary style, the novel develops a peculiar poetics whereby it explores and expands the category of the meaningful.

The dominant critical response to *Watt* has been to read it as a mordant critique of rationality, and especially of systems that embrace a binary logic of either-or. Frequent glitches in *Watt*'s stuttering prose undermine the idea that language is primarily a conduit for information, and its excessive verbal and non-verbal sounds reveal the limitations of language conceived as a wholly rational system (an ideal of language dear to philosophers such as Bertrand Russell and Ludwig Wittgenstein as well as to the logical positivists). Various scenes in *Watt* dramatize the trumping of semantic meaning by pure sound, and the song sung by Watt's patron, Mr. Knott, is a good example. Mr. Knott's song was "either without meaning, or derived from an idiom with which *Watt*, a very fair linguist, had no acquaintance. The open a sound was predominant, and the explosives k and g." Sensation (sound) continues to dominate sense: Mr. Knott's speech is described as "wild dim chatter, meaningless to Watt's ailing ears" (208). As the novel troubles familiar hierarchies—intelligibility over sensation, mind over body—a "sensual poetics" emerges that foregrounds the importance of the physical body to the possibility of comprehension and communication. As it mocks language conceived as a rational system, *Watt* explores how language might operate differently through recourse to the body and the senses.

Six years after the novel's publication, an influential article by Jacqueline Hoefer set a precedent for reading *Watt* as a pastiche of logical positivism, which Hoefer links to Wittgenstein. Continuing in this vein, reading *Watt* as an "anti-logical" novel, John Mood argues that *Watt* signposts the end of rationalism, calling it a "devastating depiction of the cul-de-sac of modern Western rationalistic philosophy" (255). For Mood, *Watt*'s glitches are designed to show how easily rational systems such as logic and language can shift into their opposite, and he underscores the urgency of a critique of hyper-rationalism given the historical context of the novel's composition (259–62). The comparison Hugh Kenner draws between *Watt* and computer-programming code furthers readings of *Watt* as a pastiche of rational systems. Such readings convincingly demonstrate how *Watt* mocks a binary logic of either-or, and there is no doubt that criticism of hyper-rationality is necessary in the 1940's climate of fascism. But *Watt*'s critical gesture also proliferates possibilities for language, which emerge as the text disfigures and parodies predictable modes of expression.

In the late 1980's, Stephen Connor suggested that *Watt*'s repetitive language and logical glitches initiate alternative ways of meaning. Connor argues that the field of semantic, linguistic and sonorous possibilities grows larger in response to the dead ends and exhausted series in *Watt* (28). In similar spirit, John Wall contends that Watt's perception that "reality is deeply contradictory" spurs and sustains creative and imaginative activity (545). Most interesting of the attempts to elucidate how the strangeness of *Watt* constitutes an attempt to mean differently is Marjorie Perloff's suggestion that language in *Watt* is, literally, a "language of resistance." She derives the cryptic non-sequiturs of the novel's prose from code-languages used by the members of the resistance cell, Gloria SMH, for which Beckett volunteered during the war. Perloff suggests that *Watt*'s odd language alludes to the "cut-out" system according to which agents would identify each other via code phrases—often non sequiturs—so as to protect the identity of members of the resistance cell.[3] In the context of the resistance, Perloff observes, language was used to obfuscate as much as to convey information (122–125). She compares this to poetry, citing Wittgenstein's observation that "a poem, although it is composed in the language of information, is not used in the language-game of giving information" (qtd. in Perloff 177). Perloff expands this idea to draw a parallel between the non-conventional use of language among resistance operatives and the innovations of poetic language; language used for purposes *other* than to convey information becomes poetics.

Following this distinction between informational and poetic language, we may begin our attempt to distinguish a "sensual poetics" in *Watt* by assessing the novel's critique of language as a conduit for information. For Hoefer, *Watt* is a parody of the early Wittgenstein's ambition to create an "ideal language" that would enable one to live according to a completely rational system. Later, Jennie Skerl faults Hoefer for conflating Wittgenstein with the logical positivists, distinguishing Wittgenstein's critique of language from those of Russell, Feigl, Mach, and others involved with the Vienna circle (474). Both Jennie Skerl and Linda Ben-Zvi argue that it was neither Wittgenstein nor the logical positivists who influenced Beckett, but the Austrian philosopher, Fritz Mauthner, whose major work, *Beiträge zu einer Kritik der Sprache* (1901), Beckett is known to have studied.[4] In this work, Mauthner draws attention to the inescapability of language—the difficulty of waging a critique of language by means of language itself. (This problem accounts for much of the hilarity we find in *Watt*.) Yet while Mauthner advocates mystic silence and the destruction of language, the critique waged in *Watt* engenders a different mode of linguistic activity: a kind of experimentation akin to poetry (in Wittgenstein's sense).

It is easy to see how Hoefer arrived at her reading of *Watt* as a pastiche of logical positivism. The novel depicts the struggles of its hero to capture the vicissitudes of his world in language, and the failure of his enterprise, coupled with his dogged insistence, contributes to the novel's tragicomic humor. As a "hyperrational man in the face of an irrational world" (Mood 259), Watt finds in language—specifically in the act of naming—a means to control the chaos that assails: "Watt's need of semantic succour was at times so great that he would set to trying names on things" (83). Watt neutralizes disturbances by turning them into words, and he longs to hear a voice "wrapping up safe in words the kitchen space" (83). Further, he dreams of making "a pillow of old words" (117) and attributes apotropaic powers to explanation: "to explain had always been to exorcise, for Watt" (78). But the novel's anxious, exhaustive lists, series, and permutations undermine the dream of a world ordered by language and advertise the inability of ordinary, logical language to order chaos, protect from danger, or even express what is or can be known.

What can be known, the text tells us, lies outside the purview of language: "what we know partakes in no small measure of the nature of what has so happily been called the unutterable or ineffable, so that any attempt to utter or eff it is doomed to fail, doomed, doomed to fail" (62). The gong of the double "doomed" seems to underwrite (or overwrite) this insistence on the failure of language by showing that language can create (rather than represent) sensory experiences for a reader. On a semantic level, the passage suggests that representational language creates order precisely because it *cannot* represent in full what can be known, which would overwhelm discursive categories. Language, since it cannot capture the complexity of what is lived, neatly reduces the chaos of living to what can be said.

It seems the young Beckett would share with Mauthner the observation that, while knowing the world through language is perhaps inevitable, language necessarily changes, freezes, or obfuscates what it purports to know. For Mauthner, the only way to move beyond language and the deception to which it leads is to destroy it or shatter it. His *Beiträge* champions the critique of language as the most important business of humankind:

> He who sets out to write a book with a hunger for words, with a love of words, and with the vanity of words, in the language of yesterday or of today or of tomorrow, in the congealed language of a certain and firm step, he cannot undertake the task of liberation from language. I must destroy language within me, in front of me, and behind me step for step if I want to ascend in the critique of language, which is the most pressing task for thinking man; I must shatter each rung of the ladder by stepping upon it. (Qtd. in Ben-Zvi 183)

At times, Beckett's frustration with language expresses itself in similarly violent and defeatist terms, as when Molloy laments the death of a world "foully named" ("the icy words hail down upon me, the icy meanings") (31). In his oft-cited letter to Axel Kaun from 1937, Beckett expresses the hope that language might be used to indict itself, a sentiment similar to Mauthner's.[5] But unlike Mauthner, Beckett in *Watt* finds a way of working *within* existing language (rather than destroying or shattering it) to make it mean in unexpected ways. Despite Beckett's initial idea that language could lead to nothing nobler than its own destruction, *Watt* explores the sensory dimensions of language—sonority, consonance, repetition, and rhythm—rather than remaining strictly in the mode of critique.

Though Mauthner valorizes silence, this valorization is complicated by the existence of his *Beiträge*, which, far from laconic, goes on for thousands of pages. Skerl makes sense of this contradiction by characterizing the Austrian philosopher as a "supreme rational-empiricist [who becomes] a mystic by way of realizing the limitations of his philosophy" (478). In other words, Mauthner's all-too-rational critique of language leads him to embrace mystic silence. According to Skerl, it is in the spirit of Mauthner that *Watt* chronicles the "inevitable failure of one who attempts to know truth through language" (478). But Skerl also rightly identifies how Beckett's hero differs from Mauthner: "[Watt] revolts and fails again and again, clinging to logic and language" (478). Watt cannot remain silent, and the novel chronicles his attempts—perhaps also those of the novel's author—to render a deeply contradictory, polyvalent experience in language. These attempts generate innovations that begin with the erratic glitches and stammering permutations of *Watt*'s odd prose.

Play with sound and rhythm distracts from narrative chronology, frustrates intelligibility, and mocks rationalism's fondness for series and formulae. Exhaustive lists and permutations create patterns of sounds that establish an "order" in the text that is other than semantic. This can occur via graphic representations of sound that resemble musical notation, as in a well-known passage consisting of frog noises:

Krak!	—	—	—	—	—	—	—
Krek!	—	—	—	—	Krek!	—	—
Krik!	—	—	Krik!	—	—	Krik!	— [. . .] (137)

Nearly two pages of text are devoted to frog sounds followed by beats of rest. This interruption (or eruption) comes as Watt remembers "a distant summer night, in a no less distant land, and Watt young and well lying all alone stone sober in the ditch, wondering if it was the time and the place and the loved one already, and the frogs croaking at one, nine, seventeen, twenty-five, etc." (136). Watt's memory of the ardor he felt (for the fishwoman, Mrs. Gorman) overwhelms conceptual and discursive categories. Not only does the text give way to sound and rhythm—animal noises associated with sexual desire—but Watt, given his excessively rational temperament, imposes on the frogs' mating calls the regularity of a series. He observes that the terms, Krak!, Krek!, Krik!, occur on the first, ninth, seventeenth and twenty-fifth beats and so on (136). Watt's effort to discern patterns in the auditory ejaculations of amphibian desire is comical, but the reader understands, more deeply, that it is the erratic, unknowable nature of his own desire that incites Watt, as in a compulsion, to seek regularity—a version of meaning—in pure sensation. The difficulty of rendering desire in language is made manifest by the fact that the frog sounds appear in a chart and constitute a hiatus in the regular layout of the text.

In other passages, binary systems falter on the edge of absurdity, inviting, perhaps, a return of the irrational. A parlor maid named either Ann or Mary (there is some equivocation) is described "eating onions and peppermints turn and turn about, I mean first an onion, then a peppermint, then another onion, then another peppermint, then another onion, then another peppermint, then another onion, then another peppermint, then another onion, then another peppermint [. . .]" (51).[6] We've only to consult our bodily memory to grasp why onions (especially raw onions) and peppermints constitute the terms of an opposition. These terms, like the zero and one of binary code, or the "yes" and the "no," repeatedly alternate until Mary, who was dusting, forgot "little by little the reason for her presence in that place," and the "duster, whose burden up till now she had so bravely born, fell from her fingers, to the dust, where having at once assumed the colour (grey) of its surroundings it disappeared until the following spring" (51). Here, alternation between opposites, which is, incidentally, the basis for binary code, leads to a condition of gray where differentiation is difficult (the duster falls to the dust) and tasks are forgotten. Moreover, Mary's fantasies—"Erotic cravings? Recollections of childhood? Menopausal discomfort?" (51)—are allowed to "ravish" her from her task, thereby illustrating how a highly rational logic of binaries, taken to a humorous extreme, begets the resurgence of the irrational, or at least interferes with the *telos* of completing certain chores.

In instances such as these, repeated variously throughout the text, the language of *Watt* calls to mind the images and sounds of a machine short-circuiting. Here, the use of the word "watt" to denote a measurement of current may be at play.[7] In the example mentioned above, a system based on binary logic (onions and peppermints) stumbles into a glitch, repeating as if it were a computer program gone haywire that keeps performing its function even after the function has lost all meaning. The necessity of controlling closed systems (circuits, but also, more broadly, social systems) links to another allusion embedded in the novel's title. As Jean-Michel Rabaté points out, the novel's title alludes not only to the metaphysical question, "*What* is," but also to James Watt (1736–1819), inventor of the steam engine, one of the first automatic self-regulating devices (101).

Watt's steam engine included a feedback valve called a "governor" (the word shares an etymological link with cybernetics, since both derive from the ancient Greek word for "steering") that could control the speed of the engine. Cybernetic theory, which post-dates the writing of *Watt* by several years, transfers the necessity of auto-regulation into the domain of social systems, where individuals form closed feedback loops with their environments.[8] Looked at this way, aspects of *Watt* might be read as auto-regulatory devices for the communicative "system" of language. Erratic eruptions of sound may be necessary to ensure the proper functioning of language, purging it of excess (letting off steam). The theme of auto-regulation, in the background of *Watt*, reminds us that irrational excess emerges as a byproduct of any rational, machinic order that seeks to exclude it.

The verbal aberrations we find in *Watt* also resemble the surges in current that threaten the integrity of a system of (language, rationalism), except that these aberrations have a sonorous coherence and, like poetry, affect the senses. The excesses of language in *Watt*, like those in Lucky's speech in *Waiting for Godot*, are to be looked at and listened to, as well as read.[9] Watt's predecessor at the house of Mr. Knott, Arsene, creates sensory experiences by associating words on the basis of sound and rhythm—alliteration, rhyme, and meter—in his "brief" monologue of twenty pages: "Not a word, not a deed, not a thought, not a need, not a grief, not a joy, not a girl, not a boy [. . .]" (46). In an earlier manuscript draft of *Watt*, this passage and others like it were set out in verse and only later changed to prose (Ackerley 70). The following passage was initially set out in two quatrains: "The Tuesday scowls, the Wednesday growls, the Thursday curses, the Friday howls, the Saturday snores, the Sunday yawns, the Monday morns, the Monday morns [. . .]" (46). The homophonic relationship between "morn" and "mourn" gives those of us who read the passage on the basis of sound the option of anthropomorphizing the days of the week. In this way, we would make a sentence with a subject and a verb (*Monday mourns* is a grammatically correct sentence; *Monday morns* is not). Reading by sound allows a duality of sense—"mourns" and "morn"—to co-exist. More generally, by re-orienting language according to sensual, aural associations, the text exposes (and perhaps unsettles) our allegiance to linguistic norms, like a sentence comprised of a subject and verb, by which we orient ourselves in language.

The "singing alongside of" embedded in the word parody (*para + ode*) makes it appropriate that Watt's unsettling of linguistic norms comes through poetic attention to sound. However, more colloquial meanings of parody (pertaining to humor and imitation) are equally important in *Watt*, for the novel's most salient critique occurs via laughter. Mauthner, though he may aspire to absolute silence, writes that the only way to *articulate* the mystical state is through laughter: "Basically speaking, pure critique is merely articulated laughter. Each laughter is critique, the best critique [. . .] and the danger of this book [the *Beiträge*], the daring aspect of this attempt, lies in merely having put an articulated text to this laughter" (qtd. in Ben-Zvi 197).

This idea resonates in *Watt*, where there is great attention to the varieties of laughter:

> Haw! Haw! Haw! My laugh, [. . .] My laugh, Mr. Watt [. . .] Of all the laughs that strictly speaking are not laughs, but modes of ululation, only three I think need detain us, I mean the bitter, the hollow and the mirthless. They correspond to successive, how shall I say successive . . . suc . . . successive excoriations of the understanding. (48)

The laugh, as ululation or convulsion of the throat, creates eruptions of sounds that can, as the passage's stuttering "suc" and repeated "x" sounds (su*cc*ess and e*xcor*) show, excoriate the kind of understanding that relies too heavily on presupposition. Not only does the laugh peel the skin from the understanding, it also creates staccato breaks in the prose, interrupting narrative progress.

More importantly, perhaps, the three types of laugh—the bitter, the hollow, and the mirthless—correspond to and parody Aristotle's hierarchy of ethical, intellectual and dianoetic virtues, which lead to the perfection of the rational nature of man. Beckett copied out these virtues in his Philosophy Notes on Aristotle (Ackerley 75). *Watt* replaces the Aristotelian virtues with a typology of *laughter*—an involuntary bodily response born of emotion rather than reason. The highest, purest order of thought *(dianoesis)* finds its correlate in a laugh that goes "down the snout" or through the body of the human-animal: "the mirthless laugh is the dianoetic laugh, down the snout—Haw!—so. It is the laugh of laughs, the *risus purus*, the laugh laughing at the laugh [. . .]" (48). Aside from problematizing the kind of dualist thinking that would distance the thinking mind from the laughing body, the idea of a dianoetic or "pure" laugh that laughs at itself parodies the auto-critique of reason (Kant).[10] The laugh is derisive, "mirthless," full of irony. Where reason's critique of itself becomes laughable, reason and rationality may be trumped by forces outside their domain. And if laughter, which can erupt uncontrollably from the body, becomes a preeminent mode of critique, this further undermines the division between rationality and its opposite. *Watt* emphasizes serious faults in the foundations of rational understanding and provokes laughter at rationalism's attempts to save itself from crumbling.

Trumping (or flaying) the understanding through laughter indicates a theme of crucial importance in *Watt*: the relation between language and the body. Laughter is a convulsion of the speaking organs; it is felt in the stomach and in the face. It exemplifies one way in which language might short-circuit the understanding through an appeal to the body. Humor is an efficacious means of provoking bodily responses in one's readers; like sound and rhythm patterns, humor creates effects in excess of what the understanding can yield.

A reader sensitive to *Watt*'s brand of humor, J.M. Coetzee studies Beckett's manuscript revisions in an effort to determine how *Watt* was revised so as to create stylistic patterns that would produce effects in excess of conventional meaning structures. As an example, Coetzee takes the following sentence: "for Watt to get into Erskine's room, as they were then, Watt would have to be another man, or Erskine's room another room" (128). The crucial twist to what Coetzee calls a "comedy of the logical impasse" is the use of the conditional (*would* rather than *will*). Coetzee situates *Watt* within the "subgenre of logical comedy," reminding us how often humor is derived from substitutions of context (480). Things could be otherwise, and meanings depend upon one's position, one's angle of view. Comedy makes much out of meaning's context-dependence, as do poetic attempts to alter the manner in which language might mean. But humor in *Watt* also directly appeals to the bodies of its readers; it provokes affective responses by inciting us to laughter.

The role of the physical body in the transmission and comprehension of meaning is explored most explicitly late in the novel, when Watt creates a series of idioms that his interlocutor, Sam, begins, with some practice, to understand. This scene, on the grounds of a mental institution, occurs when Sam and Watt emerge from holes in their respective fences to meet in a zone between their gardens (60).[11] Sam observes, regarding the idioms that Watt invents to narrate his adventures in the house of Mr. Knott, "that the inversion was imperfect; / that the ellipse was frequent; / that euphony was a preoccupation" (164). Sam also points out that Watt's language, in addition to its concern with sound, involves talking just as he walked, from back to front. Watt's sentence asks to be read in reverse, following the back-to-front movement of his body: "*Day of most, night of part, Knott with now. . . .*" (164). Reading the phrase from back to front (right to left), we understand: *Now with Knott, part of night, most of day.*

Further idiomatic variations consist in Watt's inverting the order of the words in the sentence, the letters in the word, the sentences in the period or some combination of the three. Watt's penultimate idiom is as follows: "*Dis yb dis, nem owt. Yad la, tin fo trap. Skin, skin skin. Od su did ned taw? On. Taw ot klat tonk?* [. . .]" (We might hazard a translation: *Knot talk to Wat? No. Wat den did us do? Niks [Nichts], Niks, Niks. Part of nit[e], al day. Two men sid[e] by sid.*)[12] In order to better understand Watt's increasingly complex inversions, Sam mirrors Watt's way of walking: the two walk face to face, breast to breast, belly to belly, pubis to pubis, and finally "glued together" (168). By fitting himself to Watt's body, Sam grows "used to these sounds" (165). The text hints humorously that understanding may be predicated as much on the body as on the rational capacity to decode Watt's murmurings at the border of sense and nonsense.

But the correspondence of body parts does not, finally, yield complete communicative success. At first, the sounds of Watt's idiom, "though we walked glued together, were so much Irish to me" (169). Given the link between emotion, irrationality, and Irishness in Beckett's writing—in *Molloy*, tears and laughter are associated with the Gaelic language (37)—we wonder just what understanding might involve outside the strictly rational, informational, or logical. The "information" Watt transmits to Sam exceeds certain conventions of expression; language contorts and twists in grotesquely comic inversions as it attempts to convey what exceeds it. We glean as much from the pathos of its failure as we do from attempts to "translate" the idioms into comprehensible English. We know that whatever transpires between Watt and Sam is particularly relevant given that these questionably understood conversations are what generates this strange, antilogical novel we are in the process of reading: Watt's adventures in the house of Mr. Knott narrated by a certain Sam(uel Beckett). Language's appeal to the body, its poetic preoccupations (euphony and ellipsis), and the impossibility of complete linguistic accuracy constitute a commentary on the art of the novel, particularly the experimental novel we are reading—a *mise en abime par excellence,* and not without humor.

The physical body does not function as a key that would enable us to decode languages with which we are unfamiliar, but it may point toward novel means of communicating that overwhelm the strictly logical. In *Watt*, we find a vivid example of how a parody of the binary movement of back and forth becomes the basis for movement in new directions. This parody both ridicules systems of communication that limit themselves to binary alternatives and accents the flexibility of the body to move in ways that are unexpected and unpredictable within the frameworks of binary systems. Early in the novel, a passage details how Watt's body dramatically jerks between the poles of north and south in order to move east: "Watt's way of advancing due east, for example, was to turn his bust as far as possible towards the north and at the same time to fling out his right leg as far as possible towards the south, and then to turn his bust as far as possible towards the south and at the same time to fling his right leg as far as possible towards the north" (30). We have the image of Watt as a "headlong tardigrade," a microscopic organism moving jerkily on stubby "legs," swinging stiff limbs. This parody comes at the expense of a version of the dialectic: why move via alternation between north and south (yes and no, affirmation and negation) when one might simply turn to the east? The jockeying back and forth will surely culminate in exhaustion. And this movement is laughable insofar as we know that this back and forth laboring is unnecessary: sideways movement is easily achieved by simply turning the body.

The strangeness of Watt's walk becomes an interpretive dilemma for Lady McCann, who remembers a joke from her girlhood days. In the joke, medical students speculate about the stiff walk of a gentleman on the street. When they stop him to ask whether it is piles or the clap that is responsible for his stiff walk, he replies: "I thought it was wind myself" (31). The movement of the body, like language, can be the subject of interpretation and misinterpretation; misunderstandings in language thus parallel the way in which we might "read" body language askew, attributing false conditions or motives to the activities and gestures of the body.

Watt's mechanical walk, the "funambulistic stagger" that Lady McCann deems too regular and dogged to be attributable to the effects of alcohol, corresponds to a definition of the comic elaborated by Henri Bergson. Bergson's theory of laughter sets up a dichotomy between the body's natural grace—a vitality we associate with intellectual and moral life—and the jerky movements or automatism that we might associate with mechanized systems. For Bergson, comedy occurs when the rigidity of a machine is superposed upon the living: "The attitudes, gestures and movement of the human body are laughable in exact proportion as that body reminds us of a mere machine" (21). Bergson's earlier critique of language, in *Essai sur les données immédiates de la conscience*, faults language for its rigidity and describes it as a system that is inadequate to the fluid, flexible and ever-changing ideas it pretends to contain and convey. He recommends a poetic language for philosophy, which he aspires to in his own writing, and finds in the pitfalls of language a basis for comedy. The correlation between the rigidity of language and the comic is one to which *Watt* is particularly attuned, especially given that Bergson's meditations on the comic include sections devoted specifically to repetition and inversion (47–52).

In addition to Watt's jerky, mechanical walk and the tendency of language to "glitch" in ways that remind us of a machine malfunctioning, we also find in *Watt* a curious detachment from feeling, of which Bergson gives an account in his meditations on the comic. If we look at life as disinterested spectators, Bergson suggests, "many a drama will turn into a comedy." He gives the example of stopping one's ears to the sound of music in a room where people are dancing so that the dancers appear ridiculous. "How many human actions would stand a similar test?" he asks, "Should we not see many of them suddenly pass from grave to gay, on isolating them from the accompanying music of sentiment?" The comic is a temporary "anesthesia of the heart," a direct appeal to intelligence (Bergson, *Laughter* 10–11). In *Watt*, the "music of sentiment" is transposed into an atomized language in which emotions, such as Watt's sexual longing for the fishwoman or the parlor maid's daydreams, are transformed into aberrations or glitches in language: Krak! Krek! Krik! or the obsessive alternation between onions-and-peppermints. Language in *Watt* breaks down with the first suggestion of emotion, becoming a pattern of terms and sounds. It betrays its inadequacy in the face of the incalculable and transforms itself to comedy.

The bizarre automation of language in *Watt*, its repetitions and glitches, give us the image of a machine on the point of collapse. By parodying rational systems that operate according to a binary logic of either-or, the novel veers toward impasse, having declared it impossible that language might mean what it says. But in *Watt*, limitations of language are exhibited not only in the interest of critique. From the fragments of stalled out rational systems, the possibility of more vital, embodied ways of inhabiting language emerge. By undoing the oppositions that structure understanding in the conventional sense—divisions between rationality and irrationality, sensation and meaning—Beckett strives in *Watt*, as with many of his works, to create a language in which form and content blend so that, as he writes in "Dante . . . Bruno. Vico . . Joyce," sense is "forever rising to the surface of the form and becoming the form itself" (27). Such a language explicitly appeals to and involves the body—its sensitivity to sound, its possibilities for movement, and its capacity for laughter.

Notes

1. Brian Finney writes that Beckett, along with Borges, has "the distinction of inaugurating in literature what has come to be called postmodernism" (842).

2. Paul Stewart's *Zone of Evaporation: Samuel Beckett's Disjunctions* discusses why Bair's appeal to the historical Beckett explains away confusing aspects of the novel rather than confronting them as literary devices worthy of study (84–5).

3. For further consideration of the historical situation in 1940's France in in relation to Beckett's writing, see Gibson.

4. The date of Beckett's reading of Mauthner has been the subject of considerable debate in Beckett studies. Ben-Zvi dates Beckett's reading of Mauthner to 1929 and James Knowlson agrees that Beckett read Mauthner at the request of James Joyce around 1930 (327–328). John Pilling dates Beckett's reading of the *Beiträge* to 1938 and cautions that critics have overrepresented Mauthner's influence, looking for a "key" that would explain the enigmatic novel. For further discussion of Beckett's transcriptions of Mauthner in his "Whoroscope Notebook" (1938) and his marking up of his copy of the *Beiträge*, see Van Hulle and Nixon 169.

5. Mauthner illustrates the possibility of using language to indict itself by "placing language at the heart of the *Critique*, subsuming under it all knowledge, and then systematically denying its basic efficacy" (Ben-Zvi 183). Beckett writes in a similar tenor in his German letter: "language is best used where it is most efficiently abused" (518).

6. The names Mary and Ann may be an allusion to Lewis Carroll's *Alice's Adventures in Wonderland*. The white rabbit mistakes Alice for his housemaid, Mary Ann.

7. Evelyne Grossman points out the prevalence of electrical terminology in Beckett's texts, reminding us that the title of *Come and Go* in French (*va-et-vient*) pertains to circuits and switches (88).

8. The beginning of cybernetic theory dates to Norbert Wiener's *Cybernetics, or Control and Communication in the Animal and the Machine*, first published in 1948. On the relationship between cybernetic theory and Beckett with particular emphasis on *Watt*, see Seb Franklin, "Humans and/as machines: Beckett and cultural cybernetics."

9. Beckett's observation about James Joyce's prose pertains to *Watt* as well: "It is not to be read—or rather it is not only to be read. It is to be looked at and listened to. His writing is not *about* something; it is *that something itself*" ("Dante . . ." 27).

10. For a reading of *Watt* as a Kantian novel, see Murphy.

11. This garden scene has been read by critics as an (in)version of the garden of Eden. Richard Begam identifies what he terms a "lapsarian epistemology," explaining that if the garden is where "subject and object have broken apart" it is also where the self's encounter with the "not-I" becomes possible. He argues that the epistemological process transforms into a narrative one (73).

12. It is relevant that Watt's inversions operate upon the phonetic rather than orthographical versions of words: what we *hear* is more important than conventions of standard spelling (the German word *nichts* becomes *niks*, *Watt* becomes *Wat*, *Knott* becomes *Knot*, and *then* becomes *den*). For a full translation of the inversions, see Cohn 309–310 and Ackerley 47–158.

Works Cited

Ackerley, Chris. *Obscure Locks, Simple Keys: The Annotated* Watt. Edinburgh UP, 2010.

Bair, Deirdre. *Samuel Beckett: A Biography*. 2nd ed. Vintage, 1990.

Beckett, Samuel. "Dante . . . Bruno . Vico . . Joyce." *Disjecta: Miscellaneous Writings and a Dramatic Fragment*. Edited by Ruby Cohn. Grove Press, 1984, pp. 19–33.

———. *Molloy*. Grove Press, 1955.

———. *Murphy*. Grove Press, 1957.

———. *Waiting for Godot*. Grove Press, 1954.

———. *Watt*. Grove Press, 1953.

Begam, Richard. *Samuel Beckett and the End of Modernity*. Stanford UP, 1996.

Ben-Zvi, Linda. "Samuel Beckett, Fritz Mauthner, and the Limits of Language." *PMLA*, vol. 95, no. 2, 1980, pp. 183–200. *JSTOR*.

Bergson, Henri. *Laughter: An Essay on the Meaning of the Comic*. Translated by Cloudesely Brereton and Fred Rothwell. Arc Manor, 2008.

———. *Time and Free Will: An Essay on the Immediate Data of Consciousness*. Translated by F.L. Pogson. Dover Publications Inc., 2001.

Coetzee, J.M. "The Manuscript Revisions of Beckett's *Watt*." *Journal of Modern Literature*, vol. 2, no. 4, 1972, pp. 473–480.

Cohn, Ruby. *The Comic Gamut*. Rutgers UP, 1962.

Connor, Steven. *Samuel Beckett: Repetition, Theory and Text*. Basil Blackwell, 1988.

Craig, George, Martha Dow Fehsenfeld, Dan Gunn, and Lois More Overbeck, editors. *The Letters of Samuel Beckett: 1941–1956*. Vol. II. Cambridge UP, 2011.

Dow Fehsenfeld, Martha, and Lois More Overbeck, editors. *The Letters of Samuel Beckett: 1929–1940*. Vol. I. Cambridge UP, 2009.

Feldman, Matthew. "'But what was this Pursuit of Meaning, in this Indifference to Meaning?': Beckett, Husserl, Sartre and 'Meaning Creation.'" *Beckett and Phenomenology*, edited by Ulrika Maude and Matthew Feldman. Continuum, 2009, pp. 13–38.

Finney, Brian. "Samuel Beckett's Postmodern Fictions." *The Columbia History of the British Novel*, edited by John Richetti. Columbia UP, 1994, pp. 842–866.

Franklin, Seb. "Humans and/as machines: Beckett and cultural cybernetics." *Textual Practice*, vol. 27, no. 2, 2013, pp. 249–268.

Gibson, Andrew. "Beckett, de Gaulle and the Fourth Republic 1944–49: *L'Innommable* and *En attendant Godot*." *Limit(e) Beckett*, vol. 1, 2010, pp. 1–26.

Grossman, Evelyne. "Structuralism and Metaphysics." *Journal of Beckett Studies*, vol. 21, no. 1, 2012, pp. 88–101.

Hoefer, Jacqueline. "Watt." 1959. *Samuel Beckett: A Collection of Critical Essays*, edited by Martin Esslin. Prentice Hall, 1965, pp. 62–76.

Kenner, Hugh. *The Mechanic Muse*. Oxford UP, 1987.

Knowlson, James. *Damned to Fame: The Life of Samuel Beckett*. Simon & Schuster, 1996.

Mauthner, Fritz. *Beiträge zu einer Kritik der Sprache*. 1901. Felix Meiner, 1923.

Mood, John. "'The Personal System'—Samuel Beckett's *Watt*." *PMLA*, vol. 86, no. 2, 1971, pp. 259–62. *JSTOR*.

Murphy, P.J. "Beckett and the Philosophers." *The Cambridge Companion to Beckett*, edited by John Pilling. Cambridge UP, 1994, pp. 222–240.

Nixon, Mark. *Samuel Beckett's German Diaries 1936–1937*. Continuum, 2011.

Perloff, Marjorie. *Wittgenstein's Ladder: Poetic Language and the Strangeness of the Ordinary*. U of Chicago P, 1996.

Pilling, John. "Beckett and Mauthner Revisited." *Beckett after Beckett*, edited by S.E. Gontarski and Anthony Uhlmann. UP Florida, 2006, pp. 158–166.

Rabaté, Jean-Michel. "Unbreakable B's: From Beckett and Badiou to the Bitter End of Affirmative Ethics." *Alain Badiou: Philosophy and its Conditions*, edited by G. Riera. State U of New York P, pp. 87–108.

Robinson, Michael. *The Long Sonata of the Dead: A Study of Samuel Beckett*. Grove Press, 1974.

Skerl, Jennie. "Fritz Mauthner's 'Critique of Language' in Samuel Beckett's Watt." *Contemporary Literature*, vol. 15, no. 4, 1974, pp. 474–487. *JSTOR*.

Stewart, Paul. *Zone of Evaporation: Samuel Beckett's Disjunctions*. Rodopi, 2006.

Van Hulle, Dirk, and Mark Nixon. *Samuel Beckett's Library*. Cambridge UP, 2013.

Wall, John. "A Study of the Imagination in Samuel Beckett's 'Watt.'" *New Literary History*, vol. 33, no. 3, 2002, pp. 533–558. *JSTOR*.

Wiener, Norbert. *Cybernetics, or Control and Communication in the Animal and the Machine*. 1948. The MIT Press, 1965.

Wittgenstein, Ludwig. *Zettel*. Edited by G.E.M. Anscombe and G.H. von Wright. Translated by G.E.M. Anscombe. Blackwell, 1967.

AMANDA DENNIS is associate professor of comparative literature and creative writing at The American University of Paris. She is the author of *Beckett and Embodiment: Body, Space and Agency* (Edinburgh UP, 2021) and the novel, *Her Here* (Bellevue Literary P, 2021). She recently co-edited a special issue of the *Journal of Beckett Studies*, *Beckett and the Anthropocene*, and the volume, *Beckett and the Nonhuman*, a special issue of *Samuel Beckett Today/Aujourd'hui*. Now based in Paris, she has held fellowships and visiting lectureships in France, the US, the UK, and Spain.

4 Beckett's Vessels and the Animation of Containers

Hunter Dukes

> There was much talk at Hayden's of a bottle (it was empty), its curve of course, and then other unique peculiarities. I told him that he had never seen a bottle in his life. But it seems it is only poets that do not see bottles.
>
> —Samuel Beckett to Georges Duthuit
> (*Letters II* 117–8)

Just as Samuel Beckett describes the advent of a "no-man's land" between the subject and "the world of objects" in his essay "Recent Irish Poetry," his prose and plays often explore the gray area between the human and the nonhuman: objects that are almost human, humans that are almost objects (*Disjecta* 70). In most cases, where this type of thinking is present, we also find a vessel of some kind. While the bodies of Nagg and Nell might merely be hidden within *Endgame*'s ashcans, in *Play* the distinction is not so clear, for Beckett's stage directions describe "faces so lost to age and aspect as to seem almost part of urns" (*Dramatic Works* 307). While Molloy conceives of himself as a "sealed jar [...] well preserved," the Unnamable is actually contained within a jar, padded first with stone, then with sawdust (*Molloy* 48). Shortly after Watt begins to question if Mr. Knott's pot is, in fact, a pot, he also wonders if he himself is a container instead of a man.

> As for himself, though he could no longer call it a man, as he had used to do, with the intuition that he was perhaps not talking nonsense, yet he could not imagine what else to call it, if not a man. But Watt's imagination had never been a lively one. So he continued to think of himself as a man [....] But for all the relief that this afforded him, he might just as well have thought of himself as a box, or an urn. (*Watt* 69)

There is a historical Irish precursor for these images, which explicitly surfaces in *The Unnamable* through the figure of Billy in the Bowl. Noting that his next "vice-exister" will be a "billy in the bowl," the Unnamable imagines a man "with his bowl on his head and his arse in the dust" (26). "Billy," opaquely alluded to in *Rough for Theatre I*, which opens with the blind Billy sitting before his alms bowl, refers to a possibly apocryphal character from the streets of eighteenth century Dublin. A legless panhandler, "Billy in the Bowl" dragged himself about on his hands, his body embedded in a large cauldron fortified with iron. Rumored to be a particularly dangerous character, he would lie in wait for his victims behind a row of hedges on a lonely country road. As James Collins records in *Life in Old Dublin*, "[Passers-by], struck by his peculiar circumstances, stepped aside to view the strange sight—half man, half-bowl—and were soon undone in one way or another" (78). One has to wonder if the danger of Billy came not only from his violent temperament, but also a fear and distrust of his hybridity, a taboo against the comingling of bowl and body.

While "Billy in the bowl" was a phrase in circulation during Beckett's early years in Ireland, it also surfaces in a number of cultural artifacts with which he was likely acquainted, such as the well-known Irish street ballad of the early nineteenth century, "Johnny I Hardly Knew Ye," later rewritten as the American Civil War Ballad, "When Johnny Comes Marching Home." The verse of note reads:

> You haven't an arm and you haven't a leg,
> You're an eyeless, noseless, chickenless egg;
> You'll have to be put in a bowl to beg
> Johnny I hardly knew ye. (Blaisdell 53)

This unique image of an eyeless, noseless, chickenless egg—the amputee become effaced ellipsoid—serves as a template for *The Unnamable*'s narrator, who asks, "why should I have a sex, if I no longer have a nose?" and questions if he is not, in fact, a "medium egg" (15–6). The eighteenth and early nineteenth centuries were full of figures like Billy. Take, for instance, the sixth plate from William Hogarth's 1747 series *Industry and Idleness*, entitled "The Industrious 'Prentice out of his Time, & Married to his Master's Daughter." We do not find the Irish Billy in the Bowl, but rather an English figure referred to by some as Philip in the Tub, a man known for reciting epithalamiums in exchange for food and drink (Hogarth and Clerk 44). In the engraving, the legless man leans forward from a washbasin, proffering a poem titled "Jesse or the Happy Pair. A new Song." There is a French Billy as well, which Beckett may have encountered in Victor Hugo's *Notre-Dame de Paris*, where a *cul-de-jatte* (literally "bottom of a bowl" or "basin-arse") appears in a chapter aptly titled *La Cruche Cassée* [the broken jug] (124).[1]

While "Billy in the bowl," "Philip in the tub," and the *cul-de-jatte* serve as historical precedents for Beckett's figures, they do not elucidate the conceptual link: what does it mean to conceive of a body as a vessel, or, a vessel as a body? What is it about Beckett's containers that makes them seem at once so contently bound to their materiality and so keen to serve as emergent sites of subjectivity, at once so mundane and so almost human? I will pursue the latter question as a means of revealing an aspect of the former. I argue that vessels serve as melting pots, so to speak, through which Beckett can think through questions regarding the incongruity of the body and the self. Vital to this inquiry is André Breton's image of the communicating vessels, a visual metaphor Beckett revises in *The Unnamable*. By adopting material containers as surrogate bodies, or by projecting life into hollow vessels, Beckett's characters encounter the self beyond the body—a form of projective identification that anticipates psychoanalyst Wilfred Bion's theorizing of the "container-contained." Even Murphy, a character who fantasizes complete containment, eventually succumbs to this blending—as his body is cremated and irreversibly mixed with the object world.

MALONE AND THE HOMUNCULUS

In the spirit of The Unnamable, who orders us to "go through the motions of starting again," we must begin with a simple observation: vessels demarcate an interior and exterior (129). They enclose and contain an inner space cordoned off from the outer world—a metaphor often applied to the dualistic perception of an inner self enclosed within the body. Certain anthropologists (Gell, Gutherie) believe this notion of the body-as-container is an almost hard-wired human experience, similar to what linguists George Lakoff and Mark Johnson call The Container Metaphor in language (29). On the Beckett front, there has been a recent interest in notions of containment by scholars like David Foster, Ciaran Ross, Kathryn White, and a continued charting of the porous borderlines between the human and nonhuman by Ulrika Maude, Garin Dowd, and Yoshiki Tajiri. I contribute to these dialogues by suggesting that the two conversations are intimately intertwined—that, like the genie's bottle, the space offset by Beckett's vessels bridge worlds material and immaterial through a mechanism of container animation.

The theoretical underpinning for this approach to vessels can be found in Alfred Gell's writing on the homunculus. In *Art and Agency*, Gell describes what he calls the homunculus effect. Defining it simply, the homunculus is an enveloped subject. It is a way of describing Cartesian dualism, modeling how the "I" of consciousness is locked away in the body. Gell sees this relationship—between an inner, enclosed cavity and the outer, external world—as fundamentally human. Gell states, "the indexical form of the mind/body contrast is primordially *spatial and concentric*; the mind is 'internal' enclosed, surrounded, by something (the body) that is non-mind. Now we begin to see why idols are so often hollow envelopes, with enclosures" (132–3; emphasis in original). To enclose an icon is to give it life, to animate it through concealment, the way the human "I" is itself enclosed and concealed. For anthropologists like Gell, creating material homunculi is a way of animating the object world.

> Suppose, instead of drilling "eye" holes in [a] spherical idol, we leave it as it is, but place it in a box, an arc. At this moment it becomes possible to think of the spherical idol in a different way; we can easily suppose that the stone inside the box is the locus

of agency, intention, etc. and the ark is the sacred "vessel" which, body-like, contains and protects this locus of agency. (124)

Rather than reading the homunculus and its animus as some kind of diachronic symbol held up by a certain culture or ritualistic practice, Gell universalizes the claim and argues that "there is a certain cognitive naturalness of the idea of the mind or soul or spirit as a homunculus; that is, like a person but *contained within* a person" (131; emphasis in original). The homunculus becomes a visual corollary to the way in which we project and posit consciousness inside those around us, the way in which we visualize our own split between a life interior and exterior. By enclosing a small object—a stone, a marble, a piece of wood—in a hollow envelope, one can create a material representation of interiority. As Gell makes clear, widening his argument to include contemporary, secular examples, the "homunculus-effect" can be achieved wherever there is concentricity and containment.

Beckett would have been familiar with the notion of the homunculus from his reading of Descartes.[2] In *Malone Dies*, Malone even describes his "want of a homuncule" (56). Shortly after this passage, deprived of human company, Malone turns to the task of forming homunculi by creating small, emotional objects. Coming across the bowl of a smoking pipe in a field, he bends down to pick it up.

> Perhaps I thought [the pipe-bowl] pretty, or felt for it that foul feeling of pity I have so often felt in the presence of things, especially little portable things in wood and stone, and which made me wish to have them about me and keep them always, so that I stooped and picked them up and put them in my pocket, often with tears. (76)

What is behind Malone's pity? We should remember that "pity" and "piety" share the Latinate root *pietas*, meaning fulfillment of duties to family, country, and god. *Pietas* can also connote affection and compassion when applied to family members and friends (*OED*). This familial sense of pity surfaces again when Malone discusses his little objects as a surrogate society. "And but for the company of these little objects which I picked up here and there, when out walking, and which sometimes gave me the impression that they too needed me, I might have been reduced to a society of nice people" (76). Malone is able to avoid a society of nice people because his little objects approximate human companions, for he endows them with certain human capacities: agency and animism.

Tellingly, Malone seems only to feel this way about objects that enclose or are themselves enclosed. He reappropriates the pipe-bowl as what he calls a "receptacle" and goes as far as to fashion a "little cap" for it, as if it had a head (77). Other objects only become "treasures," after he begins to contain them within the cavities of his body, forming impromptu homunculi. He holds stones in his hands, buttons in his mouth, lies on top of scraps of papers, and places other objects deep in his pockets, "talking to them" and "reassuring them" (76). At any moment, Malone fears that these simple objects might get away, as if they are animate, semi-human agents. "I shall hold my photograph in my hand, my stone, so that they can't get away. [...] Perhaps I shall have something in my mouth, my scrap of newspaper perhaps, or my buttons, and I shall be lying on other treasures still" (79–80). Like the pipe-bowl, an object of enclosure that Malone believes needs him and his pity, the hard shapely objects come to need reassurance once enclosed in his deep pockets. By creating homunculi, Malone elevates these objects into an emotional register.

Malone not only conceives of these homunculi as emotional subjects, but—moving in the other direction—he himself begins to resemble an emotional object. Talking about the way he eats and excretes, for example, he writes: "When I want to eat I hook the table with my stick and draw it to me ... It is soup ... When my chamber-pot is full I put it on the table, beside the dish ... What matters is to eat and excrete. Dish and pot, dish and pot, these are the poles" (9). In this schema, Malone becomes the processing tube in a machine of digestion: the temporary holding chamber between two vessels. When, a page later, he says that his body is "what is called, unadvisedly perhaps, impotent," one cannot help but hear a pun (10). Malone might be impotent—he might lack the virility of his youth—but his body is also in-*potted*. It is one in a series of pots. In *Molloy*, Moran is similarly bounded, but by empty containers. On one side of a similar digestive assemblage are the pots in which Martha prepares his stew: "I peered into the pots. Irish stew. A nourishing and economical dish, if a little indigestible" (101). Shortly after this kitchen scene, Moran peers into another pot, this time at the opposite end of digestion: "We bent together over the pot which at length I took by the handle and tilted from side to side ... How can you hope to shit, I said, when you've nothing in your stomach?" (114). Nothingness pervades Moran's potty interest in digestion. The chamber pot is empty, his son Jacques's stomach is empty, even their indigestible food is empty, in a sense, for it becomes a container voided of its capacity to convey nutrition. Read in the larger context of Beckett's work, where bodies often blend and blur with urns, and men forget if they are not, in fact, containers, the distinction between cooking pots, stomachs, and toilets is more nomenclatural than ontological.

Beckett, then, offers a revision of Gell's system—showing that animism is bi-directional movement, and that the borderline between the animate and the inanimate can be crossed from both sides. That is, not only can homunculi be elevated through a network of social relations to the state of emotional quasi-subjects, human subjects can be reduced, through this very same network, to the state of quasi-object. Beckett collapses the distance between the human and the homunculus by enfolding them within each other. Malone's emotional objects become prosthetic extensions of his body, just as his body becomes a continuation of his dish and pot. Beckett's vessels expand notions of subjectivity, agency, and animism beyond the contours of the human form. If a well-wrought pot can emotionally affect a human subject to feel pity, need, and comfort, and if that human subject can find containment and enclosure in a non-biological body, the distinction between organic life and inorganic matter begins to break down.

COMMUNICATING VESSELS

This porosity between containers is what Beckett calls "communicating vessels" in a letter to Tonny Clerx on 11 April 1963:

> Communicating vessels. This was an experiment invented by Galileo Galilei, with interconnected vessels of different shapes, to carry out research into the conditions of equilibrium of liquids. Any change in one vessel (density, level) is felt throughout the whole system. (*Letters III* 536)

What Beckett is referring to is a simple scientific demonstration of Pascal's law or "the principle of transmission of fluid-pressure." Two vessels are connected by a tube or pipe; if liquid is added to one vessel, raising the fluid level, the other vessel adjusts to maintain equilibrium. While these containers surface in *Molloy* as "Galileo's vessels," they find a sustained treatment in *The Unnamable*, where communicating containers become the material conspirators feeding the narrator's paranoia (90). Wishing that that instead of having to speak, he had some sort of task to do with his "hands or feet, some little job, sorting things for example, or simply arranging things," the Unnamable imagines moving water from one vessel to another with a thimble (115).

The exercise quickly devolves into a procedural system reminiscent of Molloy's sucking stone circulations or Watt's walking permutations.

> I can see it from here, they would contrive things in such a way that I couldn't suspect the two vessels, the one to be emptied and the one to be filled, of being in reality one and the same, it would be water, water, with my thimble I'd go and draw it from one container and then I'd go and pour it into another. (115)

In the Unnamable's paranoid fantasy, when he draws water from one container and pours it into another, underground—unbeknownst to him—the containers are connected by an unseen pipe. "To be emptied, and filled, in a certain way, a certain order, in accordance with certain homologies, the word is not too strong, so that I'd have to think, tanks, communicating, communicating, connected by pipes under the floor, I can see it from here, always showing the same level" (116). When read next to Beckett's description in *Proust* of time as a decantation from one vessel to another, the Unnamable's imagined task becomes Sisyphean. "The individual is the seat of a constant process of decantation, decantation from the vessel containing the fluid of future time, sluggish, pale and monochrome, to the vessel containing the fluid of past time, agitated and multicoloured by the phenomena of its hours" (*Proust* 15). Rather than decanting time, the communicating vessels produce temporal stasis. The Unnamable goes as far as to imagine that his tormentors would create false hopes for him, using "pipes and taps" to temporarily adjust the water level and create the illusion of progress amidst his otherwise eternal torment (116). The communication between vessels always results in equilibrium, rendering all labor lost.

The connected vessels in *The Unnamable* are anticipated in *Murphy*, where "two buckets" become a metaphor for the state of humanity. "'Humanity is a well with two buckets,' said Wylie, 'one going down to be filled, the other coming up to be emptied'" (39). Curiously, examining the "Whoroscope" Notebook held at the University of Reading—in which Beckett first jotted down the quotation—I found it inverted: "a well with two buckets. While one goes up to be filled, another goes down to be emptied. Such is the state of all humanity" (MS3000/11).[3] While this might have been a transcriptional error on Beckett's part, the inversion of filling and emptying foreshadows the Unnamable's revision of *Proust*'s linear temporal decantation. We find a similar idea in *Waiting for Godot*, where Pozzo claims that "[t]he tears of the world are a constant quality. For each one who begins to weep, somewhere else another stops" (*Dramatic Works* 33). Communicating vessels create community, diffusing the suffering of an individual across a hodgepodge of interpenetrating bodies, to borrow a phrase from Deleuze and Guattari.

This communication between these containers is more than the movement of fluids; the word denotes intelligence, agency, and intention. While Malone's homunculi communicate pity, need, and comfort, the Unnamable's vessels communicate conspiracy. It is important to draw a distinction here between affective projection and phenomenological classification. Malone and The Unnamable are not mistaking inanimate containers for organic bodies; rather, when confronted with material representations of interiority through vessel-like forms, they project an affective response into and onto these containers, creating mirrored encounters with their fragmented selves. As such, communicating vessels and emotional homunculi are representations of the self beyond the body, external containers for an expanded conception of subjectivity. As Marta Figlerowicz writes in a study of character construction, "What Beckett seems most interested in are the affective reactions this instability of personal boundaries can cause" (79). By destabilizing the boundaries between the "I" and the "not I," to use one of his familiar tropes, Beckett's characters expand beyond their bodily delimitations, and in doing so, produce a need for semi-animate objects to contain these disembodied aspects of self.

Beckett's use of affective projection preempts Wilfred Bion's development of the psychoanalytic concept of the "container-contained." First discernable in Bion's *Elements of Psychoanalysis*, the relationship between the container and the contained rests upon Melanie Klein's notion of projective identification. In Bion's schema, objects in the external world can serve as containers for expelled psychic content—thoughts and feelings that the ego cannot contain. In an infant psyche, these containers correspond to a preservation function. "The container [*contenant*], properly so called, is still, stable, and forms a passive receptacle where the baby may store its sensations/images/affects, which in this way are neutralized and preserved" (Anzieu 101).

This function, at first preservative, becomes destructive in the unhealthy adult psyche. For the split schizophrenic, the expulsed contents of self take the form of now hostile objects. As Bion explains in *Second Thoughts*:

> In the patient's phantasy the expelled particles of ego lead to an independent and uncontrolled existence outside the personality, but either containing or contained by external objects, where they exercise their functions as if the ordeal to which they have been subjected has served only to increase their number and to provoke their hostility to the psyche that ejected them. (39)

The most curious (and cryptic) side-effect of schizophrenic projective identification is the subject's loss of ability to distinguish between figurative objects of thought and "real" objects in the world. Bion's schizophrenic is thinking with things in the most literal sense of the term. Unfortunately for the patient, having his materials of thought exist outside of his psyche's container is too much to withstand, and so the contents are often perceived as turning back, destructively, upon the original container (Bion, *Memoir* 38). At the beginning of Beckett's career, when he enigmatically writes in *Proust* about how "the whisky bears a grudge against the decanter" (21–22), he seems to anticipate similar unrest. Nowhere is this tension between the contained and the uncontained more palpable in Beckett's work than in *Murphy*, a novel that was written concurrently with his analysis by Bion. As Anzieu argues, *Murphy* stages the formative encounter between Beckett and Bion, and, as I will argue, their respective visions of containment (Schoolcraft 167).[4]

THE CONTAINER AND CONTAINED

Beckett probably first found the figure of the communicating vessels in André Breton's surrealist manifesto, *Les Vases Communicants* (Cohn 131). For Breton, the image of two vessels achieving relational equilibrium by means of a tube comes to serve as metonymic stand-in for surrealist thought.

> Everything I love, everything I think and feel, predisposes me towards a particular philosophy of immanence according to which surreality would be embodied in reality itself and would be neither superior nor exterior to it. And reciprocally, too, because the container would also be the contents. What I envisage is almost a communicating vessel between the container and the contained. (*Vessels* 46)

Breton's last sentence is rather difficult to envision. If the container and contained are configured as communicating vessels, what is communicated? What fills and flows between the chambers of container and contained?

These vessels might be best represented in the mathematical figure of the Klein bottle.[5] A non-orientable surface, the Klein bottle is a cousin of the Möbius strip without edges or bounds. Because the bottle dissolves the distinction between inside and outside, everything that contains the Klein bottle is also contained by it. Philosopher Michel Serres rightly describes the Klein bottle as a homunculus-like figure, for its contours model the paradoxical qualities of human consciousness.

[...] that the small, monstrous homunculus, each part of which is proportional to the magnitude of the sensations it feels, increases in size and swells at these automorphic points, when the skin tissue folds in on itself. Skin on skin becomes conscious [....] Without this folding, without the contact of the self on itself, there would truly be no internal sense, no body properly speaking [....] Klein bottles are a model of identity. We are the bearers of skewed, not quite flat, unreplicated surfaces, deserts over which consciousness passes fleetingly, leaving no memory. (22)

Just as Malone's homunculi approximate the self-interior, the Klein bottle's folding surface mimics the porous borderline of the skin and the internalized quality of perception. Like the mind of Murphy, which "excluded nothing that it did not itself contain" (*Murphy* 69), the Klein bottle is in the world, but, at the same time, the world resides within the Klein bottle. In fact, Beckett's double negatives obfuscate the statement, which can be rewritten as: "for everything, if Murphy's mind did exclude it, then Murphy's mind did not exclude it," or, in symbolic logic, $\forall x\ (Dx \rightarrow \sim Dx)$. This, of course, is a contradiction. If we are to take Beckett's claim about Murphy's mind seriously, which is a described as an "empty bottle" several pages later, the only solution to this paradox of simultaneous containment and exclusion is to conceive of Murphy's mind as a Klein bottle-like container: wrapping around into a fourth-dimension, excluding everything, while simultaneously containing everything (74). When Breton talks about a container that contains its contents, but whose contents are simultaneously the container itself, he is utilizing this same twisting logic.

Despite Murphy's Klein bottle mind, the novel is rife with an anxiety arising from porosity, and brims with a desire for the borders of the body to become rigid and impenetrable. It is not surprising that Beckett's most traditional novel features his most prosthetically conservative protagonist. Moving from the largest matryoshka-like container to the smallest, we find first the various cells and buildings that enclose Murphy throughout the novel—his mew in West Brompton, Celia's room on Brewery Road, and the garret in Magdalen Mental Mercyseat. These shelters serve as protective barriers to keep the inner world distinct from the outer. "Within the narrow limits of domestic architecture he had never been able to imagine a more creditable representation of what he kept on calling, indefatigably, the little world" (114). To make the big world—the outer, containing environment of his body—an extension of the little world—the empty psychic space of meditation—is the goal.

The ideal container for Murphy would be the padded cell of the psychiatric ward: "The pads surpassed by far all he had even been able to imagine in the way of indoor bowers of bliss. [...] The temperature was such that only total nudity could do it justice. No system of ventilation appeared to dispel the illusion of respirable vacuum" (113–4). The padded cell takes on the aspects of the skull, a respirable vacuum with an aperture, invoking the skull-like dimensions of the room in *Endgame* and Malone's haunting question—"And in the skull is it a vacuum?" (48). The justice of "total nudity" and the sexualized allusion to Spenser's "bower of bliss" also evokes intrauterine imagery, memories of the womb Beckett began to recover during his writing of *Murphy* (Knowlson 171). As if to further underscore the possibility of airtight containment within the padded cell, a hypomanic is described as bouncing "off the walls like a bluebottle in a jar" (*Murphy* 154). Here we find a reiteration of *Murphy*'s nested containment. The bluebottle, a common housefly, becomes a blue bottle through phonetic association—offering an image of a bottle within a jar, a container contained.

Between domestic architecture and Murphy's body, there is his suit. The jacket, "a tube in its own right," exhibits "an autonomy of hang" that contains his body like "the mouth of a bell" (47). This bell-like suit anticipates Malone's hat, which "has lost its brim, [and] looks like a bell-glass to put over a melon" (78). The "corkscrew effect" that betrays the fatigue of Murphy's trousers conjures associations of corked bottles and sealed containers. The material of his suit is even described "holeproof" by its makers. "This was true in the sense that it was entirely non-porous. It admitted no air from the outer world, it allowed none of Murphy's own vapours to escape" (47). Like the padded cell in which Murphy is most at home, his hole-proof suit becomes a fantastic non-porous membrane, an ideal skin to quarantine his body from the rest of the world.

Moving a further layer of containment inward, we encounter Murphy's body—a container for his mind. In order to gain a satisfying level of consciousness, he must first quiet his body, "for it was not until his body was appeased that he could come alive in his mind" (4). In fact, Murphy even fantasizes about surrendering control of his body's inhalation—one of the nervous system's most ingrained and unconscious functions—in order to better think. "'The last time I saw him,' said Neary, 'he was saving up for a Drinker artificial respiration machine to get into when he was fed up breathing'" (33). Another second skin of sorts, the Drinker method of artificial respiration (also known as the iron lung) was invented by Harvard engineer Philip Drinker in 1928, and involves placing the body in a pressurized container, leaving only the head exposed (Rothman 42). The iron lung becomes a visual precursor for the mound in *Happy Days*, the ashcans in *Endgame*, and the urns in *Play*, as well as the mechanical telos of Murphy's rocking chair—a machine that, in a cyborg-like fashion, rhythmically regulates the body so the mind can wander free.

The most understudied communicating vessel in *Murphy* could be the Leyden Jar, a container rich with historical and technical associations. "The development of what looked like collusion between such utter strangers remained to Murphy as unintelligible as telekinesis or the Leyden Jar, and of as little interest" (71). Developed in 1745 by Pieter van Musschenbroek, the Leyden jar was the proto electric capacitor, a device allowing scientists to "accumulate for the first time large amounts of electricity in a storage container" (Sconce 30). The technology was later appropriated by Italian scientist Luigi Galvani, the father of galvanism (31). While it is unclear whether Beckett was directly acquainted with Galvani's work, he certainly was exposed to the name and some associated concepts through his reading of James Joyce's *A Portrait of the Artist as a Young Man*, which borrows "the enchantment of the heart" from Galvani (192). In *Murphy*, the narrator's statement that the jar is as "unintelligible" as telekinesis is a claim about the jar's ability to communicate charge through a seemingly impermeable glass jar, a transmission very much akin to the almost telekinetic communication between the Unnamable's vessels. It is also a device that threatens the desired non-communicability between Murphy's closed spheres.

Despite Murphy's desire for complete enclosure, his nested world is continually undermined. The novel ends with a comic disavowal of containment when Murphy is cremated and his ashes scattered across the floor of a pub. "By closing time the body, mind and soul of Murphy were freely distributed over the floor of the saloon; and before another dayspring greyened the earth had been swept away with the sand, the beer, the butts, the glass, the matches, the spits, the vomit" (171). In a novel obsessed with quarantine and non-porosity, there could not be a more fitting disavowal of containment than scattered ashes—the contained (body, mind, and soul) reduced to its most elemental form. This is in direct contrast to Beckett's recurrent "womb-tomb" motif (Ricks 40–1), to use a phrase that he will later develop to emphasize the continuity of containment between birth and the grave. As Anzieu writes in relation to this scene, "the empty breast, i.e. the failure of the containing function, cannot be better imagined" (Schoolcraft 164). Beckett may have found inspiration for this scene in "Hydriotaphia," Sir Thomas Browne's well-known essay on urn burial, which he read at Trinity College (Byron 223). The mixing of Murphy's ashes with sand, butts, glass, matches, spit, and vomit reads as an ironic reinterpretation of the mixing of familial ashes together in the same urn (Browne 25). This comingling of human ashes with object matter is a fitting end for Murphy, "who was not tied by interest to a corpse-obedient matter and whose best friends had always been among things" (119).

CONCLUSION

This irretrievability of Murphy's ashes from surrounding matter would later find itself redoubled in Beckett's life, when he inquired—on behalf of Maria Jolas—about exhuming James Joyce's body in Zurich and moving it to Ireland. As Knowlson recounts: "'Seven years already,' the undertaker told Beckett, putting on a troubled expression, like a doctor who is being consulted too late: 'Do you think there will be anything left to transport?'" (334).

In addition to the mixing of the ashes with the pub detritus, Murphy's decision to be cremated in the first place might have been a final gesture toward protecting his vision of complete containment, to prevent his body and mind from becoming the container of something undesired. According to Browne, this anxiety is latent in burial: "To be gnawed out of our graves, to have our skulls made into drinking-bowls, and our bones turned into pipes, to delight and sport our enemies, are tragical abominations escaped in burning burials" (30). Without cremation, Murphy's skull and mind, which excluded nothing that it did not itself contain, could be forced to contain something that it would rather exclude.

It seems Beckett's fascination with vessels might be substituted for Breton's concern with surreality. That is, rather than the subject being superior or exterior to the object, Beckett envisions an immanent network of intercommunicating vessels. Like Malone's homunculi, which are formed within the contours of his body, and like his body itself, which is mechanized within a series of vessels, the container, as Breton says, is also the contents. The borderline between subject and the object begins to dissolve, as each mutually constructs and contains the other. Even Murphy, a character who quests for complete containment, is fated for complete enmeshment with the object world. Perhaps Billy in the Bowl marks the midpoint of this gathering between the "container-contained"—not a subject reduced to object, nor an object elevated to subject, but body and bowl together in Beckett's no-man's land.

Notes

1. It is uncertain how much of *Notre-Dame de Paris* Beckett actually read. In letter written on 18 September 1951 to Mania Peron, Beckett writes "J'essaie de lire *Notre-D. de Paris*. Impossible" (*Letters II* 297).

2. Descartes frequently uses the metaphor of the homunculus to describe the subject as the seat of consciousness. In "Of Vision," the sixth discourse of the *Optics*, he writes: "Now although this picture, in being so transmitted into our head, always retains some resemblance to the objects from which it proceeds, nevertheless, [...] the picture causes us to perceive the objects, as if there were yet other eyes in our brain with which we could apprehend it" (101). As Matthew Feldman has shown, Beckett studied L. Debricon's *Descartes: Choix de Textes*, which contains excerpts and summaries of the *Optics*, making familiarity with the content of this passage likely (47–8). Descartes neatly demonstrates the infinite regression implied by dualism—that eyes require an additional set of eyes that require an additional set of eyes ... *ad infinitum*. Homunculi seem to insist upon their own homunculi. "Psychology *without* homunculi is impossible," writes Daniel Dennett in a discussion of this infinite regression, "but psychology *with* homunculi is doomed to circularity or infinite regress, so psychology is impossible" (119–22; emphasis in original). The homunculus model leaves us with a vision of Pyre Gynt's onion—layer upon layer, membrane upon membrane, always differentiating, but organized around an absent center. It should be noted that Beckett does not solely source his homunculi from Descartes. Dirk Van Hulle has traced Beckett's interest in homunculi back to his *Faust* notes, as well as an article by Herbert Silberer entitled "Der Homunculus" (*Genetics* 167, 171).

3. Chris Ackerley annotates the passage in *Demented Particulars*, attributing the phrase to John Marston's *The Malcontent*, which Marston in turn drew from Richard II (2579–2594). It also seems to have connections to an opaque phrase in George Berkeley's *Commonplace Book*, which Beckett underlined with his infamous green pencil: "When we imagine 2 bowls v.g. moving in vacuo, 'tis onely conceiving a person affected with those sensations" (qtd. in Van Hulle and Nixon 133).

4. Samuel Beckett began therapy with Wilfred Bion shortly after Christmas 1933 (Knowlson 168). While the therapy was difficult and both men occasionally found themselves at odds with each other, there seems to have been some benefit, as the analysis continued for almost two years. Curiously, while both surely remembered their work together, Bion avoids referring explicitly to Beckett in his later writings, and Beckett hardly ever spoke about their encounter after it concluded. For this reason and others, Bion—who famously took Beckett to the Tavistock clinic to see C.G. Jung speak—has been relatively understudied in relation to Beckett's work (Miller and Souter 3–21). Due to a scarcity

of records regarding Beckett's time with Bion, and the fact that most of Bion's well-known concepts were developed after the treatment ended, it is difficult to trace a direct connection between their therapeutic sessions and either man's writing. By implying that Bion may have found inspiration for the "container-contained" in *Murphy*, I am following Steven Connor, who suggests that we need to read Beckett into Bion as much as Bion into Beckett, and that doing so might reveal "an example of the most long-range and delayed-action countertransference on record" (13).

5. Elizabeth Klaver argues that *Quad*, *Ohio Impromptu*, and *How It Is* all construct three-dimensional Klein bottles, "a system that offers no real beginning, ending, or exit" (378). S.E. Gontarski adds to Klaver's reading, suggesting that the Klein bottle structure of *Quad* is an attempt to represent four dimensions in three dimensions, much like Beckett's recurring crucifixion motif (175).

Works Cited

Ackerley, Chris, and Samuel Beckett. *Demented Particulars: The Annotated Murphy*. Edinburgh UP, 2010. Kindle edition.

Anzieu, Didier. "Beckett and Bion." *The International Journal of Psychoanalysis*, vol. 16, 1989, pp. 163–8.

Beckett, Samuel. *The Complete Dramatic Works of Samuel Beckett*. Faber and Faber, 2006.

———. *The Complete Short Prose, 1929–1989*. Edited by S.E. Gontarski. Grove, 2002.

———. *Disjecta: Miscellaneous Writings and a Dramatic Fragment*. Edited by Ruby Cohn. Grove, 1983.

———. *The Letters of Samuel Beckett*. Vol. 2, 1941–1956. Cambridge UP, 2011.

———. *The Letters of Samuel Beckett*. Vol. 3, 1956–1963. Cambridge UP, 2014.

———. *Malone Dies*. Faber & Faber, 2010.

———. *Molloy*. Faber & Faber, 2009.

———. *Murphy*. Faber & Faber, 2009.

———. *Proust and Three Dialogues with Georges Duthuit*. John Calder, 1999.

———. *The Unnamable*. Faber & Faber, 2010.

———. *Watt*. Faber & Faber, 2009.

———. "Whoroscope Notebook." June 1936. Manuscript 3000, Folder 11. Samuel Beckett Collection, University of Reading, Reading, UK.

Bion, Wilfred R. *Elements of Psycho-Analysis*. Karnac, 1984.

———. *A Memoir of the Future*. Karnac, 1991.

———. *Second Thoughts; Selected Papers on Psychoanalysis*. Heinemann, 1967.

Blaisdell, Bob, ed. *Irish Verse: An Anthology*. Courier Dover Publications, 2012.

Breton, André. *Communicating Vessels*. Edited by Mary A. Caws. U of Nebraska P, 1990.

Browne, Thomas. *The Works of Sir Thomas Browne*. Faber & Gwyer Ltd., 1928.

Byron, Mark. "English Literature." *Samuel Beckett in Context*. Edited by Anthony Uhlmann. Cambridge UP, 2013, pp. 218–28.

Cohn, Ruby. *A Beckett Canon*. U of Michigan P, 2001.

Collins, James. *Life in Old Dublin*. Tower of Cork, 1978.

Connor, Steven. "Beckett and Bion." *Journal of Beckett Studies*, vol. 17, no. 1–2, 2008, pp. 9–34. *Chadwyck-Healey Literature Collections*. Accessed 8 Sept. 2015.

Dennett, Daniel C. *Brainstorms: Philosophical Essays on Mind and Psychology*. Harvester, 1979.

Descartes, René. *Discourse on Method, Optics, Geometry, and Meteorology*. Hackett, 2001.

Dowd, Garin. *Abstract Machines: Samuel Beckett and Philiosophy after Deleuze and Guattari*. Rodopi, 2007.

Feldman, Matthew. *Beckett's Books: A Cultural History of Samuel Beckett's "Interwar Notes."* Continuum, 2006.

Figlerowicz, Marta. "Bounding the Self: Ethics, Anxiety and Territories of Personhood in Samuel Beckett's Fiction." *Journal of Modern Literature*, vol. 34, no. 2, 2011, pp. 76–96.

Foster, David. "Between Beyonds: Play's Urns and Their Exhabitants." *Samuel Beckett Today/Aujourd'hui*, vol. 25, 2013, pp. 211–23. *ProQuest Literature Online*. Accessed 8 Sept. 2015.

Gell, Alfred. *Art and Agency: An Anthropological Theory*. Clarendon, 1998.

Gontarski, S.E. *A Companion to Samuel Beckett*. Wiley-Blackwell, 2010.

Guthrie, Stewart. *Faces in the Clouds: A New Theory of Religion*. Oxford UP, 1995.

Hogarth, William, and Thomas Clerk. *The Works of William Hogarth (including the 'Analysis of Beauty')*. London: Printed for R. Scholey, 1810.

Hugo, Victor. *Oeuvres*. Vol. 1. Furne, 1840.

Hulle, Dirk Van. *Manuscript Genetics, Joyce's Know-how, Beckett's Nohow*. U of Florida P, 2008.

———. and Mark Nixon. *Samuel Beckett's Library*. Cambridge UP, 2013.

Joyce, James. *A Portrait of the Artist as a Young Man and Dubliners*. Barnes and Noble Classics, 2004.

Klaver, Elizabeth. "Samuel Beckett's *Ohio Impromptu, Quad*, and *What Where*: How It Is in the Matrix of Text and Television." *Contemporary Literature*, vol. 32, no. 2, 1991, pp 366–82. *JSTOR*. Accessed 8 Sept. 2015.

Knowlson, James. *Damned to Fame: The Life of Samuel Beckett*. Grove, 1996.

Lakoff, George, and Mark Johnson. *Metaphors We Live By*. U of Chicago P, 1980.

Maude, Ulrika. *Beckett, Technology and the Body*. Cambridge UP, 2009.

Miller, Ian S., and Kay Souter. *Beckett and Bion: The (Im) Patient Voice in Psychotherapy and Literature*. Karnac Books, 2013.

Nixon, Mark. *Samuel Beckett's German Diaries 1936–1937*. Continuum, 2011.

"pity, n." *OED Online*. Oxford University Press, June 2015. www.oed.com.

Ricks, Christopher. *Beckett's Dying Words*. Oxford UP, 1993.

Ross, Ciaran. *Beckett's Art of Absence: Rethinking the Void*. Palgrave Macmillan, 2011.

Rothman, David J. *Beginnings Count: The Technological Imperative in American Health Care*. Oxford UP, 1997.

Schoolcraft, Ralph. "Beckett Et Le Psychanalyste." *SubStance*, vol. 22, no. 2/3, Nov. 1993, pp. 331–34. *JSTOR*. Accessed 8 Sept. 2015.

Sconce, Jeffrey. *Haunted Media: Electronic Presence from Telegraphy to Television*. Duke UP, 2000.

Serres, Michel. *The Five Senses: A Philosophy of Mingled Bodies*. Continuum, 2009.

Tajiri, Yoshiki. *Samuel Beckett and the Prosthetic Body: The Organs and Senses in Modernism*. Palgrave Macmillan, 2006.

White, Kathryn. *Beckett and Decay*. Continuum, 2009.

Hunter Dukes is the managing editor of *Cabinet* magazine and *The Public Domain Review*. Formerly, he held a lectureship at Tampere University and a research fellowship at Peterhouse, University of Cambridge. He is the author of *Signature* (Bloomsbury, 2020) and several academic articles about Irish literature.

5 Blanchot in Infinite Conversation(s) with Beckett

Arleen Ionescu

ON THE NECESSITY TO WRITE ON NOTHING

In 1997 Gerald Bruns was the first critic to point out an affinity between Samuel Beckett and Maurice Blanchot. In *Maurice Blanchot: The Refusal of Philosophy* he mentions an apparent "shameless pilfering" (20) in Beckett's description of the condition of the artist in his 1949 dialogues with the art critic and historian Georges Duthuit on Matisse and Tal Coat, a description that is quite similar to Maurice Blanchot's statements from "From Anguish to Language," the introduction to his 1943 collection of essays *Faux pas*, later on included in *The Gaze of Orpheus*. Consider the works side by side:

> Blanchot: "The writer finds himself in the increasingly ludicrous condition of having nothing to write [*de n'avoir rien à écrire*], of having no means with which to write it, and of being constrained by the utter necessity of always writing it" (*Faux Pas* 3) / "The writer finds himself in this more and more comical condition—of having nothing to write, of having no means of writing it, and of being forced by an extreme necessity to keep writing it." (*The Gaze of Orpheus* 5)

> Beckett: "The expression that there is nothing to express, nothing with which to express, nothing from which to express, no power to express, no desire to express, together with the obligation to express." (*Proust and Three Dialogues* 103; "Three Dialogues" 139)

Indeed, if we compare the two accounts, they are strikingly similar, and "perhaps no mere coincidence" (Willits 257); they both express what Blanchot called the "'naïve calculation' of the nihilist" (*Faux pas* 6–7). According to Bruns, Blanchot's "Nothing is [the writer's] material" (*Faux pas* 3; *The Gaze of Orpheus* 5) was neither as in Flaubert's or Mallarmé's case "a statement of principle" nor did it mean "a pure refusal" (21, 22). It was rather an indication that "[w]riting belongs to the space (or say the *entre-temps*) of the neither/nor (what Blanchot will later call *le Neutre*—neither this nor that, 'the pure and simple no' or difference in itself, unopposed by identity)" (Bruns 22). Or, in other words, it was a claim that

71

"impossibility lies not in the writer's being unable to find something to write, but precisely in his being unable to write the nothing in its purity" (Weller, *Literature, Philosophy, Nihilism* 88).

It is clear that, as Shane Weller rightly observes in *Language and Negativity in European Modernism: Toward the Literature of the Unword*, "both Blanchot's and Beckett's conceptions of the artist's predicament echo, in their insistence upon necessity and impossibility" (127) were close, a fact also demonstrated after the publication of Beckett's *Letters* where the Irish writer's comments on Blanchot's *Lautréamont et Sade* (1949) have made us become aware of how important Blanchot was for him (See *Letters 2* 210, 211 and 219). In his book *Beckett and Sade*, Jean-Michel Rabaté reviews in great detail Beckett's letters testifying also to his "temporary friendship with Bataille and his appreciation of the critical work of Blanchot" (9). According to Rabaté, while Beckett "was trying to move beyond the impasse of Watt" (32), Beckett read Blanchot and agreed with his criticism of Pierre Klossowski's interpretation of Sade from "À la rencontre de Sade" (*Temps Modernes*, 1947).

In "Beckett/Blanchot: Debts, Legacies, Affinities," Weller draws our attention to the complete absence of Blanchot in Bair's and Knowlson's biographies on Beckett. Weller refers to a letter (25 May 1951) written by Beckett's partner, later on his wife, Suzanne Déschevaux-Dumesnil, who confessed to Jérôme Lindon (Beckett's publisher at Minuit) about Beckett's admiration for Blanchot (also confirmed by Bident 431). According to Weller, one more report of Beckett's connection with Blanchot is the testimony of Patrick Bowles (the co-translator of *Molloy* into English) who remembered a conversation with Beckett that took place in November 1955 on Blanchot's belief that "every philosophy of non-meaning rests on a contradiction as soon as it expresses itself." (qtd. in Weller, "Beckett/Blanchot" 27)

Noting that Blanchot critically engaged mainly with Beckett's prose, Weller remarks that Beckett never resorted to the thematic of the neuter as a form of reduction, yet a prevailing, nameless tone of voice is repeatedly heard as the hallmark of all his works. This tone can be linked to Blanchot's concept of the Neuter, "a voice that bears no name and is not the voice of any identifiable, properly nameable subject," which both writers used in their "belief that the essence of literature lies in an impersonal, depropriating, and deterritorialising voice" ("Beckett/Blanchot" 29). Rabaté's "How Beckett Has Modified Modernism" reveals that such a voice came to add to Sartre's and Camus's existentialism a "missing element" is "the constitution of subjectivity by language, a theme that came to prominence with Maurice Blanchot in the late 1950s" (28). Rabaté concludes that Beckett expanded modernism "to include Bataille's theory of excess and his parallel critique of the human, Levinas's ethics of the Other, Blanchot's main concept of the Neuter, Lacan's debunking of the self or ego taken as a stable basis for thinking deeply, and Derrida's philosophy of writing as generating an endless divisibility of the subject that he called *différance*" (35).

In all his works, Blanchot strove to build upon impossibility, paradox, and set himself the task "to write without writing, to bring literature to that point of absence where it disappears," a point that he coins as "'writing degree zero,' the neutrality which every writer deliberately or unwittingly seeks, and which leads some to silence" (*The Blanchot Reader* 147–8). For Blanchot, "writing degree zero" connects to his view on how literature and death are both experienced as anonymous passivity, an experience he calls the *Neuter*. As in his definition "to write without writing," to+verb+without+to+verb, as well as noun+without+noun are specific Blanchotian formulas marking the Neuter. As I argue elsewhere, "Blanchot's formula *X without X* is not purely privative but points to a duplicity in the *pas-de* (*le pas au-delà*), which makes passivity a pre-critical notion, an arch-passivity on the side of the divide passivity/activity" (Ionescu, "Pas-de-noms" 65). The same passivity is a distinctive feature of many Beckettian characters who act without acting, such as in the plays when the stage directions indicate that the characters assert they would do something, yet they never actually do it. Because of space limitations, I cannot investigate in detail what Ardoin characterizes as "paralysis in motion" (146), so I will simply point to the many instances in which Estragon, Vladimir, Clov, or Hamm propose to perform different activities, followed by stage directions that indicate their lack of movement.

Curt G. Willits, in his study on the connection between Blanchot and Beckett—primarily based on Blanchot's critical study "Where Now? Who Now?" (originally published as "Où maintenant? Qui maintenant?" in *La Nouvelle Revue Française*, October 1953)—interprets the essence of the "void" that becomes the empty voice of a human being "disappearing into it," a condition that preoccupied both writers. Blanchot's essay on Beckett impressed Beckett so much that, in a letter to Barbara Bray from 1959, Beckett recommends it be translated (*Letters 3* 222). In "Where Now? Who Now?", Blanchot asserts that Beckett's text narrates an "experience lived under threat of the impersonal, the approach of a neutral speech that speaks itself alone" (213). Jonathan Boulter establishes how the two writers inhabited the "shared philosophical space" of the neutral; he brings together what Blanchot calls the Neuter in *The Step Not Beyond* and what Beckett calls "neither" throughout his whole creation (203).

Blanchot appears to have been looking for "a double, a companion for his own solitude" (Weller, "Beckett/Blanchot" 35), which he found in Beckett, who was ready to acknowledge his kinship to the French thinker. Thus, in a short text commemorating Beckett shortly after his death, "Oh All to End," which became the preface to the August-September 1990 issue of *Critique*, Blanchot claims that Beckett "was willing to recognize himself" in a passage from *Awaiting Oblivion*, since his work could be best defined as "an attempt to keep within the limits of literature that voice or rumble or murmur which is always under threat of silence" (*Blanchot Reader* 299). This was the reason why, in Blanchot's opinion, Beckett neither refused nor accepted the Nobel Prize he was given. The fragment from *Awaiting Oblivion* reads:

> This even speech, spaced without space, affirming beneath all affirmation, impossible to deny, too weak to be silenced, too docile to be contained, not saying something, only speaking, speaking without life, without a voice, in a voice lower than any other: living among the dead, dead among the living, calling to die, to come back to life in order to die, calling without appeal. (82)

Beckett's short prose often resorts to the voice of narrators who do not say anything but rather "speak without life" about an experience of the impossible. Blanchot emphasizes in his essay that Beckett's plays express a need for "a double, a companion for solitude" (*Blanchot Reader* 299). Blanchot pointes out that Beckett's masterpiece was yet "his epic in three cantos entitled *How It Is*, in which, from verse to verse as though from stanza to stanza, the vast stretch of time of his life makes itself heard, from childhood and from even before childhood (…)" (*Blanchot Reader* 299). As I will demonstrate through a close reading of several fragments from *The Infinite Conversation*, the speech "without a voice" calls the narrator of *How It Is* without appeal into the body of Blanchot's *The Infinite Conversation*, not letting Beckett's narrator continue his trip in his own solitude, but rather hand in hand with Blanchot's narrator.

Commenting on Blanchot's concept of "night writing" requiring the experience of the nocturnal that Blanchot proposed in his essay "The Outside, The Night," included in *The Space of Literature* (163–70), Nicholas Royle calls night writing "the very experience of the impossible" (115). Royle's "uncanny" re-enacting the gesture of the impossible through his own critical study was meant to discover "what comes out of the darkness" (108), an assertion coming in the shade of Paul de Man's "to make the invisible visible is uncanny" (49).

In the following two parts, in a similar gesture, I am going to peer through what comes out of the darkness of night writing in several Blanchotian and Beckettian texts, also following Blanchot's advice that "between being and nothingness" we could "reserve" one "possibility of a discrete reasoning" (*Infinite Conversation* 342). However, since with Beckett and Blanchot we are surrounded by an infinity of nothing(ness)(es) and negation(s), bringing the invisible to the level of the visible means striving to comprehend the incomprehensible in a different act of reading through unseen, nihil-seen things.

FROM *ZERO NEIGHBOR* TO THE WRITER OF OBLIVION

In *Negative Dialectics*, Theodor Adorno terms the Beckettian space of literature a "fissure of inconsistency" that lies between his emphasis on "a lifelong death penalty" and his "only dawning hope (…) that there will be nothing any more" (380–1). He insists on reading Beckett's texts as an "image world of nothingness as something" (381). More recently, Hélène Cixous calls Beckett "Zero's Neighbour" for his attempt to maintain "the being to faint in the vicinity of zero" (8), the number that paradoxically represents nothingness, void, yet is represented by the figure 0, which is actually a sign, thus something. In a thought-provoking study on nothingness, Rotman reveals that

> the void, emptiness, that which has no being, the non-existent, that which is not—is a rich and immediate source of paradoxical thought: the sign "nothing" either indicates something outside itself and thereby attributes the condition of existence to that which has none, or the sign has no referent, it does not ostend, it points to nowhere, it indicates and means no more than what it says—nothing. (58)

For Cixous, Beckett's work is a series of "[t]he Almost-Nothings of the whole that make up the Whole" (xiv). In "Kafka and After," Weller engages with Adorno's approach to Beckett's work from *Negative Dialectics* as well as with other commentators who, like Cixous, do not believe in Beckett's nihilism. Beckett maintaining himself in the vicinity of zero through creating what Ruben Borg calls "disembodied voices, and utterly finite beings, whose compulsive logorrhea is dramatized as an inability to die completely" (168) is similar Blanchot's speaking in order to say nothing. A possible definition of this type of speech can be found in his essay "Literature and the Right to Death" where he writes:

> "a nothing demands to speak, nothing speaks, nothing finds its being in speech, and the being of speech is nothing. This formulation explains why literature's ideal has been the following: to say nothing, to speak in order to say nothing. That is not the musing of a high-class kind of nihilism" (324). Blanchot makes sure he differentiates between literature and nihilism, or, as Weller put it, that "it is a certain nothing (*rien*) that speaks in literature, but that this speaking of the nothing is not to be confused with nihilism" (*Literature, Philosophy, Nihilism* 93).

Layering a framework on the series of absolutes that Ramona Cormier and Janis L. Pallister establish in an early classic book entitled *Waiting for Death*—"absolute silence in Lucky, absolute blindness in Pozzo, absolute immobility in Estragon and Vladimir" (93) over Blanchot's *récit Awaiting Oblivion*, we can easily notice the two characters' absolute anguish, which confers a curious vacuity to their full conversation. The two protagonists aspire to retain "nothing in forgetting," thus absolute forgetting that corresponds to Beckett's disbelief in a humanity that he portrays as exhausted and with no ultimate purpose.

Daniel Watt tackles several similarities in the experience of reading *Awaiting Oblivion* and *Waiting for Godot*. For Watt, "the abundance offered by the waiting" in Blanchot's *récit* was capable of generating a "language of its own," emerging "only in the night of writing" that was dealt with in a previous section of this article, a writing that language can no longer express, because it would lack both value and object (69). Blanchot's *Awaiting Oblivion* is infused with a language consisting of negative absolutes, which are repeated continuously, and suffixes that suggest void: "traceless murmur" (4), "flawless memory" (6), "lawless" (17), "endlessness of waiting" (23), "countless population of emptiness" (26), "the restlessness of hope" (27), "dreamless night" (32), "effortlessness of attraction" (32), "power of powerlessness" (74), "split nonetheless" (74), "lifeless" (79), "measureless evenness" (80). The male character starts writing his own emptiness, realizing his writing will focus on sparseness, failure and oblivion: "To begin with, he would know nothing (and he could see how much he had wanted to know); moreover, he would never perceive at what moment he would be on the verge of finishing. What a serious, frivolous existence with no resolution, with no perspective, would result" (6–7).

It is my contention in "Waiting for Blanchot" that *Awaiting Oblivion* can be interpreted as an exhausted form of extending Beckett's waiting into a third act, and written in a polyphonic dialogue with both Beckett and Martin Heidegger (fragments from *Awaiting Oblivion* were published in the *Festschrift* honoring Heidegger's seventieth anniversary). Blanchot aspired to "solitary waiting," one "that was within us and has now passed to the outside, waiting for ourselves without ourselves, forcing us to wait outside our own waiting, leaving us nothing more to await." (*Awaiting Oblivion* 14). In my view,

> Vladimir and Estragon have been waiting for Godot so passionately that their waiting becomes absolute and could be said to outlive them once the curtain has fallen. As they have found themselves 'blathering' about nothing in particular 'for about half a century,' they can prolong their waiting *ad infinitum*, defying the temporality of their *Dasein*, getting close to eternity, as Blanchot envisages about his male character in *Awaiting Oblivion*: 'Waiting made him eternal, and now he has nothing more to do than to wait eternally' (27). (Ionescu, "Waiting" 82)

Awaiting Oblivion reveals that the male protagonist, whose name we never find out and who is a simple "he," is a writer knowledgeable about the meanings of waiting. He therefore can be regarded as a projection of Beckett, the playwright who wrote the first play ever about waiting:

> He attempts to lead this even speech, while letting himself be led by it, toward this measure of evenness, light in the daylight, tension in attention, justice in death.
>
> He knows that waiting participates in such a measure: in waiting entering the evenness of waiting, even if waiting always exceeds waiting in its evenness with itself. (82)

Blanchot saturates waiting to the point of neutralizing oppositions, adding to Beckett's modes of waiting for Godot, thus, someone (in Act 1), followed by waiting without an object (in Act 2), a third mode and Act that is defined in the last line of the quoted paragraph: "waiting exceeding waiting in its evenness with itself." In this way, waiting makes way for oblivion, that form of reduction which Blanchot calls the neuter deriving "from a negation of two terms: *neuter*, neither one nor the other. Neither nor the other, nothing more precise" (Blanchot, *The Step not Beyond* 74). Beginning from the neuter, the French thinker displaces "first the subject, then identity in general, and finally the present itself" (Nelson, Preface to *The Step not Beyond* ix), hence the lack of identity of the characters and the lack of any time setting in *Awaiting Oblivion*.

THE INFINITE CONVERSATION: FROM BLANCHOT TO BECKETT

The relation between Beckett and Blanchot becomes much more complex once we open Blanchot's *The Infinite Conversation*, a whole compendium of almost 500 pages, mostly written from 1953 to 1965. The book ends on a note equating it with a "nearly anonymous" work, whose purpose was "to designate in vain" "the absence of the book" (435).

Such a puzzling self-proclaimed posthumous note can be also connected to the name without name: "In the neuter—the name without name—nothing responds, except the response that fails, that has always just missed responding and missed the response, never patient enough to 'go beyond,' without this 'step / beyond' being accomplished" (Blanchot, *The Step not Beyond* 118). Hence, when shutting the book, we remain with an unresolved question: who is then speaking in *The Infinite Conversation*? In a similar way to some of the scholars interested in the relation between Blanchot and Beckett mentioned at the beginning of this article, I propose that this investigation starts from "Where Now? Who Now?" in which Blanchot asks a quadruple question: "What is this tireless 'I' that seemingly always says the same thing? Where does it hope to come? What does the author, who must be somewhere, hope for? What do we hope for, when we read?" (210). As can be seen, Blanchot places "hope" in his interrogations, giving a positive meaning to the intentions of the author who designates his narrator as a first-person protagonist. Moreover, the readers also need to maintain a positive attitude about the authorial intention: there is something to be hoped for in the experience of reading. Two pages later, Blanchot reiterates his questions and seems to be able to provide the readers with an answer on the nameless "I" of the Irish-born writer: "Who is speaking here? What is this I, condemned to speak without rest, the one who says: 'I am forced to speak. I will never be quiet. Never?' By a comfortable convention, we answer: it is Samuel Beckett" (212).

Indeed, Beckett speaks through Blanchot's prose in several fragments from *The Infinite Conversation* and Blanchot offers only acknowledgement of the titles of Beckett's texts incorporated in his book, using a dialogic narrative practice that forces the reader to trace where exactly these fragments come from. The plurality of voices in *The Infinite Conversation* can also be seen as an echo of *The Unnamable* that Blanchot considers "rather something much more than a book: the pure approach of the impulse from which all books come, of that original point where the work is lost, which always ruins the work, which restores the endless pointlessness in it, but with which it must also maintain a relationship that is always beginning again, under the risk of being nothing" ("Where Now? Who Now?" 213). According to Blanchot, *The Unnamable* is "condemned to exhaust infinity" ("Where Now? Who Now?" 213), which is also the fundamental desideratum of *L'entretien*[1] *infini* translated as *The Infinite Conversation*. Perhaps in the context of Blanchot's thoughts on how Beckett's exhausts infinity, a short reference to Gilles Deleuze's "The Exhausted" is needed. "Being exhausted," Deleuze tells us, "is much more than being tired" (152) and hence the French philosopher's consistent search for exhaustive series in Beckett's texts, a search that could have been also influenced by Blanchot's interpretation of *The Unnamable* from "Where now? Who Now?"

Vainity, void, and nothingness are certainly the subject matter of Beckett's plays, trilogy of novels and short stories that Blanchot summarizes in "Where Now? Who Now?" as follows:

> I have nothing to do, that is to say nothing in particular. I have to speak, that's vague. I have to speak, having nothing to say, nothing but the words of others. Not knowing how to speak, not wanting to speak, I have to speak. No one forces me to, there is no one, it is an accident, it is a fact. Nothing could ever relieve me of it, there is nothing, nothing to discover, nothing that diminishes what remains to be said […]. (213–14)

This Nothing brings, as Blanchot claims in *The Space of Literature*, the *désœuvrement* of the writer that refers to the absence of the work: "It is a region anterior to the beginning where nothing is made of being, and in which nothing is accomplished. It is the depth of being's inertia [*désœuvrement*]." ("Where Now? Who Now?" 45). In his essay on Beckett, Blanchot reiterates that the writer does not find in his work a shelter from the difficulties of life but, on the contrary, he exposes himself to a more menacing danger, that of remaining outside his work: "The work demands that, demands that the man who writes it sacrifice himself for the work, become other-not other than the living man he was, the writer with his duties, his satisfactions, and his interests, but he must become no one, the empty and animated space where the call of the work resounds" ("Where Now? Who Now?" 215–16). For Blanchot, Beckett's *The Unnamable* becomes *désœuvrement*, since it is "floating eternally between being and nothingness, incapable henceforth of dying and incapable of being born, shot through with ghosts, his creatures, in which he does not believe and which tell him nothing" ("Where Now? Who Now?" 216).

In *The Space of Literature*, Blanchot endeavors to find out when Orpheus becomes a poet and concludes that it was after Orpheus' failure to bring Eurydice to the visible. In a similar movement in "Where Now? Who Now?" (216), Blanchot attempts to get to the origin of Beckett's work in the last section of his essay which he titles "Neutral Language." That is the answer, the origin of Beckett's work is when language becomes "neutral language," where everything both ends and starts again:

> There, language does not speak, it is; in it nothing begins, nothing is said, but it is always new and always begins again. It is this approach of origin that always makes the experience of the work more threatening, threatening for the one who has it, threatening for the work. But it is also this approach that alone makes art an essential search, and it is because it made it obvious in the most decisive way that *The Unnamable* has much more importance for literature than most of the "successful" works that literature offers. ("Where Now? Who Now?" 216)

Hence, Blanchot urges to the reader to hear the voice, to give it credit since it makes the reader come close to the neutral:

> Let us try to hear "that voice that speaks, knowing it is lying, indifferent to what it says, too old perhaps and too humiliated ever finally to be able to say the words that will make it stop." And let us try to go down into that neutral region where someone has sunk, given over to words, someone who, in order to write, has fallen into the absence of time, there where he must die from an endless death. ("Where Now? Who Now?" 217)

The way Blanchot hears Beckett's voice and lets it be heard in his essay anticipates the gesture of mirroring his voice in Beckett's voice in *The Infinite Conversation*. Blanchot's essay ends without any critical conclusion but with a long quotation from *The Unnamable*. Interestingly, Leslie Hill wonders whether the voice of *The Unnamable* is the voice of literature itself, although he could not answer only positively. Hill concludes: it is the voice of literature due to its self-referentiality pointing out the limitations of language and the difficulty of the creative process but it also illustrates Beckett's philosophy (72). Therefore, we can see that the dialogic stage between Blanchot and Beckett is set up as early as his critical essay on Beckett.

Contrasting the fragment from Beckett's *The Unnamable* with Blanchot's last page of his essay on Beckett, one can find the key to why Blanchot juxtaposed Beckett's voice to his own in *The Infinite Conversation*. By the time Blanchot was writing his "Where Now? Who Now?", he would have recognized himself in Beckett. There is thus no surprise that in *The Infinite Conversation*, Blanchot's and Beckett's voices are distinguishable from each other only via the mere formatting convention (italics) that Blanchot uses in his text. Before starting inserting quotations from *How It Is* and *Texts for Nothing*, Blanchot explains that these texts are meant to be heard rather than read (*Infinite Conversation* 329). Blanchot briefly announces the title of what he calls "our epic" (329), *How It Is*, thus overlapping his voice on Beckett's and becoming "we" instead of "I." Blanchot reiterates part of his definition of *How It Is* from the short essay "Oh All to End": "a narrative of the first citation in three parts, with stanzas and verses, the back and forth that by nearly regular interruptions gives us a sense of the necessity of this uninterrupted voice" (*Infinite Conversation* 329).

From this point onward, Beckett's voice starts speaking through Blanchot's text. Italics are used instead of quotation marks.

> To begin with, this panting keeps the voice from being heard; thus *this breath token of life must die down* so that life can be heard, so this being can say *I hear my life*. And it is always with a certain happiness that he says it, as though hearing remained the ultimate passion even if, or because, it interrupts life.
>
> —To hear, simply hear: *my life a voice without quaqua on all sides words scraps then nothing then again more words more scraps the same ill-spoken ill-heard then nothing vast stretch of time then in me in the vault bone-white if there were a light bits and scraps*

ten seconds fifteen seconds ill-heard ill-murmured ill-heard ill-recorded my whole life a gibberish garbled six-fold
—But what is this voice?
—That is the question not to ask, for the voice is already present in one's hearing of the question one asks about it. (*Infinite Conversation* 329–30; fragment in italics from Beckett, *How It Is* 134)

In the first review of *How It is*, published in *Express* (1961), Maurice Nadeau asserts that Beckett's "last" voice is progressing in a state of nothingness to such an extent that at the end of the "strange ascetic exercise" it would be transformed into "silence, death and nothingness without sentences" (qtd. in Graver and Federman 249). Three years after *How It Is* was published, an anonymous reviewer regards the novel as a "de-creation" of a "great poetic energy" (qtd. in Graver and Federman 22). In his review from *Book Week* (1964), John Simon argues that in such a hermetic work there is an emphasis on neither-here not-there but rather on "murmurs, cries of pain, ghastly laughter" that should be encountered "in the form which achieves greatest scope with the least sacrifice of coherence" (qtd. in Graver and Federman 23).

After the first decade of the twenty-first century, scholars slightly diversified their interpretations of this text. In 2011 C.J. Ackerley proposes a possible annotation of the text, assuming that "[t]he art of annotation, by this definition, is an aesthetic of failure, and the only plausible outcome is the resolution to fail better" (792). In 2015, Michelle Rada, reading *How It Is* from the perspective of reader response criticism, interprets the text by looking into the relation between actor and spectator; according to her, it "becomes that of a reader who silently takes in the words dictated by an unnamable voice to an unnamed narrator attempting to reproduce them" (153). In 2018 Boulter considers Blanchot's reading of *How It Is* an "expression of neutrality" (204). In 2019, in an attempt to "move beyond the old cliché according to which the work is about the meaninglessness of human experience" (143), Emilie Morin regards this text as summoning "a specific strand of war memory, tied to a long history of French military losses and defeats" (141). She rightly observes that the narrator of *How It Is* "crawls through sullied mud, out of which other bodies and things emerge; he chokes on mud, and speaks in, through, and to mud" (Morin 141).

Returning to Blanchot's fragment, we can remark that he bans the question "what is this voice?" and replies, "That is the question not to ask" (*Infinite Conversation* 329). Unlike the early reviewers of *How It is*, Blanchot does not see the novel opening onto nothingness but to a certain extent anticipates contemporary readings of *How It Is*, formulating hypotheses:

—At the end there is a kind of hypothesis: it is perhaps the voice of all of us, the impersonal, errant, continuous, simultaneous and alternating speech in which each of us, under the false identity we attribute to ourselves, cuts out or projects the part that falls to him or to her: *rumor infinitely transmissible in both directions,* a procession, not stopping, that holds in reserve a certain possibility of communication: *there he is then at last not one of us there we are then at last who listens to himself and who when he lends his ear to our murmur does no more than lend it to a story of his own devising ill-inspired ill-told and so ancient so forgotten at each telling that ours may seem faithful that we murmur to the mud to him*

—*and this life in the dark and mud its joys and sorrows journeys intimacies and abandons as with a single voice perpetually broken now one half of us and now the other we exhale it pretty much the same as the one he had devised*

—*and of which untiringly every twenty or forty years according to certain of our figures he recalls to our abandoned the essential features.* (Blanchot, *Infinite Conversation* 330; italics, qtd. from Beckett, *How It Is* 139 with two breaks added)

In order to decipher Blanchot's text, we will look into *How It Is*, where these words belonged to the narrator who was alone, in the dark, lying face-down on an endless plain of mud, crawling from west to east with his sack of tins of fish and a tin opener. Yet the voice of that narrator, Beckett claims, is someone else's coming from elsewhere. The narrator would act like a sort of medium who would recite someone else's voice that possessed him. Similarly, Blanchot's voice quotes from someone else (Beckett) coming from elsewhere (*How It Is*). In Part 2 of *How It Is*, the reader encounters Pim carrying his own sack across the mud. He is tortured by the narrator who forces him to speak by scratching him with his fingernails until he bleeds and gouging him with his tin opener. Pim would sing (quote) the words that were carved into his skin by the narrator:

how it was I quote before Pim with Pim after Pim how it is three parts I say it as I hear it

voice once without quaqua on all sides then in me when the panting stops tell me again finish telling me invocation

past moments old dreams back again or fresh like those that pass or things things always and memories I say them as I hear them murmur them in the mud in me that were without when the panting stops scraps of an ancient voice in me not mine

my life last state last version ill-said ill-heard ill-recaptured ill-murmured in the mud brief movements of the lower face losses everywhere[.] (7)

Blanchot attempts to sketch in a few words the contents of *How It Is* and, apart from "two or three images of childhood and adolescence [...] affirmed in the beginning," he thinks the reader of the text can retain also images, in spite of the fact that s/he sees "almost nothing" (330). What the reader can see are "*the sack the tins the mud the dark*" (330). There is a regression in vision in this sequence that Blanchot carefully arranges in descending order from the visible to the invisible: first, a big object (Pim's sack); second, small objects (the tins); third, while the vision becomes blurred, mud; and last, dark. Hence, vision is turned into an impossibility (we may as well at this point wonder: how can one see the "dark" that Blanchot includes in his list?).

Darkness as a vision is also what characterizes Beckett's late "novels," where narrative conventions are broken, going beyond meaning by reduction. If Edmund Husserl imagined reduction as a process whereby empirical subjectivity was deferred in such a way that pure consciousness could be delineated in its essential and Supreme Being, Beckett imagined reduction linguistically in such a way that language strips itself of its function as a speech act and is "deadened by human habit" (Kearney 173). As William S. Allen remarks, in Beckett's text there are three elements that make the text hard to construct: the lack of punctuation leading to ambiguities, which forces the reader "to adapt to the rhythm of the text," the non sequiturs that "disrupt the progress" and the "thorn-like words or phrases that do not seem to be part of the whole" (226). The ending of the book—"good good end at last of part three and last that's how it was end of quotation after Pim how it is" (*How It Is* 129)—may suggest that even after everything ends, hence his narrative stops and even quoting from another narrative stops, there is still something: "how it is." The narrator finds himself "[e]xhausted by the massive exercise of imagining and trying to make sense of" this how it is and "comes to a point of resolution: 'to have done with this voice namely this life,' and so he reaches out for 'a solution,' 'a formulation that would eliminate him completely and so admit him to that peace at least while rendering me in the same breath sole responsible for this unqualifiable murmur'" (Allen 229). The definitive distinction between the narrator's voice (the inside) and the quoted one (the outside) is extremely intricate because the quoted voice "offers the solution for its own elimination," but "it also places pressure on determining the positions of 'him' and 'me' in the subsequent formulation of elimination and responsibility" (Allen 229).

This is exactly what Blanchot keeps in his following quoted fragment where he insists on Beckett's text (the quoted voice—marked as "he," "him") taking such an authority on Blanchot's narrated voice (marked as "me"), that it becomes its own *Bible*:

> This is biblical speech: extending from generation to generation, it runs on.
>
> Only here the duty is not to prolong it but to put an end to it, to bring the movement to rest; and in order to do this, the solo reciting voice asks himself if there would not be *a formulation that would eliminate* him *completely and so admit* him *to that peace at least while rendering* me *in the same breath sole responsible for this unqualifiable murmur of which consequently here the last scraps at last very last—responsible for this unqualifiable murmur*, responsible for this irresponsibility. (Blanchot, *The Infinite Conversation* 330; italics, qtd. from Beckett, *How It Is* 144; emphasis added)

In this fragment, Blanchot adds the echo "— *responsible for this unqualifiable murmur*" that he copies from the middle of the fragment and completes with his own words "responsible for this irresponsibility."

On the next page, another Beckettian work, *Texts for Nothing*, becomes the "murmur" transcribed in a voice that Blanchot quotes, acknowledging his source as a passage towards "becalmed moments" (331):

> *Yes, I was my father and I was my son, I asked myself questions and answered as best I could, I had it told to me evening after evening, the same old story I knew by heart and couldn't believe, or we walked together, hand in hand, silent, sunk in our worlds, each in his worlds, the hands forgotten in each other. That's how I've held out till now. And this evening again it seems to be working. I'm in my arms, I'm holding myself in my arms, without much tenderness, but faithfully, faithfully.*
>
> *Sleep now, as under that ancient lamp, all twined together, tired out with so much talking, so much listening, so much toil and play.* (Blanchot, *Infinite Conversation* 331; italics, qtd. from Beckett, *Stories and Texts for Nothing* 79)

Beckett's fragment suggests that while holding hands, father and son (or son and father) know each other's stories by heart. The characters are both silent and apart, their respective worlds and thoughts are different, but the simple act of holding hands keeps them together.

In *Damned to Fame*, Knowlson speaks about his first interview with Beckett in which he could not agree with Beckett that a separation between his life and his work is possible: "I then adduced some of the images of his childhood in Ireland that appear often in his work, even in his late prose texts: a man and a boy walking hand in hand over the mountains; a larch tree turning green every year a week before the others; the sounds of stonecutters chipping away in the hills above his home" (21). Indeed, Beckett's work shows the recurring image of a father and a son holding hands. That recurrence was, according to Beckett, almost "obsessional" (21).

Clearly this is a biographical reference to Beckett's walks with his own father, as stated by Weller in "Orgy of False Being Life in Common: Beckett and the Politics of Death." He alludes to a letter in which Beckett describes the bliss of spending time with his father who was growing old (42). Weller adds that the fragment quoted by Blanchot belongs to "Text 1" from *Texts for Nothing* that unfolds the story of a boy whose mother is dead as follows: the story is told by the father "with whom the son would join (in the mother's absence) in the 'hand-in-hand' [...] locked into their solitudes" (42–43). Such a solitude was transformed into *Worstward Ho* into "the radically paradoxical community without community or relation without relation, of what Beckett terms the 'as one'" (Weller, "Orgy of False Being" 43). The fragment from *Worstward Ho* is a variation of the father-son fragment from "Text 1." This time, however, we cannot be sure that the two characters are father and son; the father has become an old man while the child looks young:

> Bit by bit, an old man and child. In the dim void bit by bit an old man and child. [...] Hand in hand with equal plod they go. [...] The child hand raised to reach the holding hand. Hold the old holding hand. Hold and he held [...] Joined by held holding hands. Plod as one. (12–13)

In "The Politics of Body Language: The Beckett Embrace," Weller offers us a second thought-provoking interpretation of the same father-son fragment in relation to other texts (especially in *Worstward Ho* and *Company*): the image of father-son holding hands suggests "an act of textual self-embracement" (151). The critic notes the paradox between this "valorised all-male hand-in-hand" and the "irremediable solitude" to which Beckett recurred in *How It Is* and *Company* "in the affirmation of being-alone," adding that "Beckett's community without community of father and son is akin to the 'communauté inavouable' theorised by Maurice Blanchot" (Weller, "Body Language" 152).

Indeed, Beckett and Blanchot read each other, and thus kept each other company in a community without community, telling stories to get rid of their anxieties. Blanchot's insertion of this particular fragment from Beckett at the end of his engagement with Beckett's work from *The Infinite Conversation* suggests a life circle that is repeated ad infinitum, an *infinite conversation* between two writers who travel hand in hand.

When commenting on Beckett, Blanchot points out that the playwright combines two movements, writing and reading; their combination places Beckett close to a non-heard or unheard speech that brings him "on an equal footing with the reader." It then leads to "a neutral affirmation, equal-unequal, eluding all that would give it value or even affirm it" (*Infinite Conversation* 329). Beckett's work is "the disappearance of every sign that would merely be a sign for the eye" which manifests itself in a reduction "to the essential, but rejecting only words that are useless to listening, with a simplicity that at times divides and redoubles itself" (*The Infinite Conversation* 329). This voice is eventually incorporated by the other one, replacing its silence in a prolonged and parallel moment of waiting (*Waiting for Godot* echoing with *Awaiting Oblivion*). Waiting brings them together again through a series of negations:

> — Then at times the voice would fall silent?
>
> —'And were the voice to cease quite at last, the old ceasing voice, it would not be true, as it is not true that it speaks, it can't speak, it can't cease. And were there one day to be here, where there are no days, which is no place, born of the impossible voice the unmakable being, and a gleam of light, still all would be silent and empty and dark, as now, as soon now, when all will be ended, all said, it says, it murmurs."
>
> —So we must still wait. And in waiting what is there to be done?; what do we do?
>
> —Well, waiting, we chat.[2] (Blanchot, *Infinite Conversation* 331; italics, qtd. from Beckett, *Stories and Texts for Nothing* 140)

The technique that Blanchot uses is not foreign to Beckett. Richard Kearney calls this feature of Beckett's work "infinite regress of language (towards some non-existent origins)," a concept that he imported from the notion of *palimpsest*, through which "behind every text lies another that has been erased or written over, and behind that yet another etc." (172). Like Vladimir and Estragon or Clov and Hamm who do not seem able to part in spite of threatening each other continuously with leaving, Beckett and Blanchot become bound to each other in their attempt to transform words into murmurs.

Notes

1. One of the meanings of *entretien* in French is « conversation suivie avec une ou plusieurs personnes; entrevue » (https://www.larousse.fr/dictionnaires/francais/entretien/30081), a reason why the translator must have opted for "conversation" in the translation of the title.

2. Among the many other significances of "to chat" *OED* lists "to converse familiarly and pleasantly" ("chat"). That is to "make conversation," or to paraphrase Estragon, to "make a little conversation," is something that Beckett's character proposes to Vladimir in order to "pass the time" in *Waiting for Godot*. Blanchot augments Beckett's "to make a little conversation" to his own "to make an *infinite* conversation."

Works Cited

Ackerley, C.J. "'Primeval mud impenetrable dark': Towards an Annotation of *Comment c'est/ How It Is.*" *Modernism/modernity*, vol. 18, no. 4, Nov. 2011, pp. 789–800.

Adorno, Theodor W. *Negative Dialectics*. Translated by E.B. Ashton. Routledge, 2000.

Ardoin, Paul. "Deleuze's Monstrous Beckett: Movement and Paralysis." *Journal of Modern Literature*, vol. 38, no. 2, 2015, pp. 134–49.

Bair, Deirdre. *Samuel Beckett: A Biography*. 1978. Simon and Schuster, 1990.

Beckett, Samuel. *How It Is*. Translated by Samuel Beckett. Grove Press, 1964.

———. *The Letters of Samuel Beckett, vol. 2: 1941–1956*. Edited by George Craig, et al. Cambridge UP, 2011.

———. *The Letters of Samuel Beckett, vol. 3: 1957–1965*. Edited by George Craig, et al. Cambridge UP, 2014.

———. *Nouvelles et Textes pour rien*. Minuit, 1958.

———. *Proust and Three Dialogues*. John Calder, 1965.

———. *Stories and Texts for Nothing*. Grove Press, 1967.

———. "Three Dialogues." *Disjecta: Miscellaneous Writings and a Dramatic Fragment*. Edited by Ruby Cohn. John Calder, 1983, pp. 138–45.

———. *Worstward Ho*. John Calder, 1983.

Bident, Christophe. *Maurice Blanchot: partenaire invisible*. Champ Vallon, 1998.

Blanchot, Maurice. *Awaiting Oblivion*. Translated by John Gregg. U of Nebraska P, 1997.

———. *The Blanchot Reader*. Edited by Michael Holland. Blackwell, 1995.

———. *Faux Pas*. Translated by Charlotte Mandell. Stanford UP, 2001.

———. *The Gaze of Orpheus and Other Literary Essays*. Translated by Lydia Davis. Station Hill Press, 1981.

———. *The Infinite Conversation*. Translated by Susan Hanson. U of Minnesota P, 2003.

———. "Literature and the Right to Death." *The Work of Fire*. Translated by Charlotte Mandell. Stanford UP, pp. 300–44.

———. *The Space of Literature*. Translated by Anne Smock. U of Nebraska P, 1989.

———. *The Step Not Beyond*. Translated by Lycette Nelson. SUNY Press, 1992.

———. "Where Now? Who Now?" *The Book to Come*. Translated by Charlotte Mandell. Stanford UP, 2003, pp. 210–17.

Borg, Ruben. "Putting the Impossible to Work: Beckettian Afterlife and the Posthuman Future of Humanity." *Journal of Modern Literature*, vol. 35, no. 4, 2012, pp. 163–80.

Boulter, Jonathan. "Neutral Conditions: Blanchot, Beckett, and the Space of Writing." *Understanding Blanchot, Understanding Modernism*, edited by Christopher Langlois. Bloomsbury Academic, 2018, pp. 203–18.

Bruns, Gerald L. *Maurice Blanchot: The Refusal of Philosophy*. Johns Hopkins UP, 1997.

"chat, intrasitive verb." *Oxford English Dictionary*, CD-ROM, 2nd ed., v. 4.0.0.2. Oxford UP, 2009.

Cixous, Hélène. *Zero's Neighbour Sam Beckett*. Translated by Laurent Milesi. Polity, 2011.

Cormier, Ramona, and Janis L. Pallister. *Waiting for Death: The Philosophical Significance of Beckett's* En attendant Godot. Alabama UP, 1979.

de Man, Paul. *Resistance to Theory*. Foreword by Wlad Godzich. 6th edition. U of Minnesota P, 2002.

Deleuze, Gilles. "The Exhausted." *Essays Critical and Clinical*. Translated by D.W. Smith and M.A. Greco. Verso, 1998, pp. 152–74.

Graver, L., and R. Federman, editors. *Samuel Beckett: The Critical Heritage*. Routledge, 2005.

Hill, Leslie. "Poststructuralist Readings of Beckett." *Palgrave Advances in Samuel Beckett Studies*, edited by Lois Oppenheim. Palgrave Macmillan, 2004, pp. 68–87.

Ionescu, Arleen. "Pas-de-noms/ Plus de noms: Derrida and Blanchot." *Word and Text—A Journal of Literary Studies and Linguistics*, vol. 1, no. 1, 2011, pp. 59–69.

———. "Waiting for Blanchot: A Third Act for Beckett's Play." *Partial Answers: Journal of Literature and History of Ideas*, vol. 11, no. 1, 2013, pp. 71–84.

Kearney, Richard. *Navigation: Collected Irish Essays 1976–2006*. Lilliput, 2006.

Knowlson, James. *Damned to Fame: The Life of Samuel Beckett*. Simon and Schuster, 1996.

Morin, Emilie. "Beckett, War Memory, and the State of Exception." *Journal of Modern Literature*, vol. 42, no. 4, 2019, pp. 129–45.

Rabaté, Jean Michel. *Beckett and Sade*. Cambridge UP, 2020.

———. "How Beckett Has Modified Modernism: From Beckett to Blanchot and Bataille." *Beckett and Modernism*, edited by Olga Beloborodova, Dirk Van Hulle and Pim Verhulst. Palgrave Macmillan, 2018, pp. 19–35.

Rada, Michelle. "The Illusionless: Adorno and the Afterlife of Laughter in How It Is." *Journal of Modern Literature*, vol. 38, no. 2, 2015, pp. 150–67.

Rotman, Brian. *Signifying Nothing: The Semiotics of Zero*. The Macmillan Press, 1987.

Royle, Nicholas. *The Uncanny*. Manchester UP, 2003.

Watt, Daniel. *Fragmentary Futures Blanchot, Beckett, Coetzee*. InkerMen Press, 2009.

Weller, Shane. "Beckett/Blanchot: Debts, Legacies, Affinities." *Beckett's Literary Legacies*, edited by Matthew Feldman and Mark Nixon. Cambridge Scholars, 2007, pp. 22–39.

———. "Beckett among the Philosophes: The Critical Reception of Samuel Beckett in France." *The International Reception of Samuel Beckett*, edited by Mark Nixon and Matthew Feldman. Continuum, 2009, pp. 24–39.

———. "Kafka and After." *Modernism and Nihilism*. Palgrave Macmillan, 2011, pp. 102–36.

———. *Language and Negativity in European Modernism*. Cambridge UP, 2019.

———. *Literature, Philosophy, Nihilism: The Uncanniest of Guests*. Palgrave Macmillan, 2008.

———. "Orgy of False Being Life in Common: Beckett and the Politics of Death." *Beckett and Death*, edited by Steven Barfield, Matthew Feldman, and Philip Tew. Continuum, 2009, pp. 31–49.

———. "The Politics of Body Language: the Beckett Embrace." *The Flesh in the Text*, edited by Thomas Baldwin, James Fowler, and Shane Weller. Peter Lang, 2007, pp. 141–59.

Willits, Curt. G. "The Blanchot/Beckett Correspondence: Situating the Writer/Writing at the Linen of Naught." *Colloquy: Text, Theory, Critique*, vol. 10, 2005, pp. 257–68.

ARLEEN IONESCU is senior researcher at West University of Timișoara. She has published on James Joyce, Maurice Blanchot, Samuel Beckett, trauma studies, and related aspects of modernism in *James Joyce Quarterly, Memory Studies, Oxford Literary Review, Parallax, Partial Answers, Joyce Studies Annual*, and *Style*. She is joint-editor-in-chief (with Laurent Milesi) of *Word and Text*. Her books include *Romanian Joyce: From Hostility to Hospitality* (2014), *The Memorial Ethics of Libeskind's Berlin Jewish Museum* (2017). She co-edited with Maria Margaroni *Arts of Healing: Cultural Narratives of Trauma* (2020) and with Simona Mitroiu an issue of *Parallax* on *Holocaust Narratives in the Post-Testimonial Era* (2023).

II. Art and History in the Context of Posthumanism

6   Beckett, Painting and the Question of "the human"

Kevin Brazil

Ce qui veut dire que le visage humain n'a pas encore trouvé sa face et que c'est au peintre à lui donner.

Antonin Artaud,
"Le Visage Humain"
(*Œuvres* 1534)

Which means that the human face has not yet found its face and that it's up to the painter to give it one.

Antonin Artaud,
"The Human Face"
(*Watchfiends & Rack Screams* 277)

Artaud's declaration of the task of the painter, with its untranslatable distinction between the human *visage* and and its *face*, was written to accompany an exhibition of his paintings and drawings held at the Galerie Pierre in Paris from 4–20 July in 1947. This declaration proved prophetic. In 1982, the Barbican Centre in London titled a survey of post-war French painting: "Aftermath France, 1945–1954: New Images of Man," thereby retrospectively discerning that the question of the human was one that was explored in the work of artists as stylistically diverse as André Fougeron, Pablo Picasso, Nicolas de Staël, Bram van Velde, and Wols. The post-war concern with the human was not confined to the visual arts. The philosophical debate around humanism was perhaps the central debate in post-Liberation France. Jean-Paul Sartre's *Existentialism is a Humanism* (1946), Maurice Merleau-Ponty's *Humanism and Terror* (1947), and Martin Heidegger's *Letter on Humanism* (1949) were published in this period. And in the political sphere, the electorally triumphant Parti Communiste Française framed its mission in terms of a utopian Marxist humanism. The question of the human was one that traversed the boundaries of the spheres of aesthetics and politics in such a manner as to suggest the inadequacy of their conceptual separation. Following the logic of Jacques Rancière, we can understand both spheres as being engaged in a battle over "the distribution of the sensible" (*The Politics of Aesthetics* 12) over what can or cannot be disclosed to the subject as being in common—in this period figured as the "human" and the differing forms of political subjectivity available within these configurations of community.

Such was the field in which Samuel Beckett wrote three essays of art criticism that were his major contributions to the genre: "Le peinture des van Veldes ou le monde et le pantalon" (1946); "The New Object/Peintres de l'Empêchment" (1948); and "Three Dialogues" (1949) co-authored with George Duthuit. Given that this period from 1945–1949, what he later called "his frenzy of writing" (Knowlson 358) was one in which major works were written—the *Nouvelles*, the *Trilogy*, *Waiting for Godot*—Beckett's art criticism has rightly been seen as offering a critical companion to those works, although discussions of the "Three Dialogues" have tended to exclude the equally rich critical commentary of the previous two essays. Beckett's criticism also positions itself in the post-war humanist debate, for Beckett concludes his first essay on the van Velde brothers by declaring "parlons de l' 'humain'" ("let us speak of the 'human'") (*Disjecta* 131). Thomas Trezise was one of the first critics to explore the ways in which Beckett's work "radically questioned the foundations of humanism" (ix) by exploring his "affinity" with figures such as Bataille, Blanchot, Deleuze, and Derrida (5). David Houston Jones also explores the encounters between "Beckettian testimony and recent rethinkings of human epistemology" (15), drawing parallels with the work of Agamben and Lyotard.

It was precisely through a dialogue with painting that Beckett chose to "speak of the 'human.'" Beckett's place within the debates is contextualized by the journals in which his work was being published: *Cahiers d'Art*, *Les Temps Modernes*, *Fontaine* and the post-war version of *Transition*.[1] Publication in those journals situates Beckett within what Anna Boschetti has analyzed as "the field of intellectual journals" in post-war France (3). Understanding Beckett's works within a dynamic critical field allows a more politicized understanding of his works to come into focus, works that were marked by a pervasive if apathetic hostility towards the promises of post-war Marxist humanism. After contextualizing Beckett's art criticism, I will turn to the moments in which this questioning of the human appears in his fiction and drama, most pointedly in "The End," *Eleutheria*, and *Molloy*. This is not to say that questioning the human is limited to those texts; rather, they provide the most specific points of intersection between the concerns of Beckett's criticism and that of its wider historical context.

"LE PEINTURE DES VAN VELDES OU LE MONDE ET LE PANTALON"

Beckett's first work of published art criticism, "Le peinture des van Veldes ou le monde et le pantalon,"("The painting of the van Veldes, or the moon and the trousers"), was written in January 1945 and published in the October 1946 issue of *Cahiers d'Art*, which Beckett describes in a letter to George Reavey as the "2nd post-liberation number of the Cahiers" (31 October 1945, *Letters 2* 24).

"Postliberation" is an apt description of the concerns of the issue, in which the editor, Christian Zevros, had included a dossier of texts by Lenin and Stalin on the political role of the artist and writer (341–342). In his introduction, Zevros writes that in reading these texts, "l'imagination et les libertés de la future condition humaine brouillent nos yeux de leur rosée" ("the imagination and the freedoms of the future human condition will cloud our eyes with their glow") (341).

It is precisely such a vision of the future human condition that Beckett attacks in his essay. In discussing the work of Bram and Geer van Velde, Beckett writes that what unites their different approaches is an interest in "la condition humaine" ("the human condition)" (*Disjecta* 129). For a painter, this interest in the human condition means to be condemned to strive to paint the impossible, since for the painter, Beckett writes, "le chose est impossible" ("the thing is impossible") (*Disjecta* 129). This impossible thing is both the object of representation and the task of the painter himself. For both artists, it is the inescapable condition of time that makes it impossible the perceive, and thus represent, the object. In the work of Bram van Velde, this inescapable condition leads him to turn to the "champ intérieur" ("interior field") (125) in order to paint "la chose morte . . . [l]a chose immobile dans le vide" ("the dead thing . . . the thing immobile in the void") (*Disjecta* 126). This striving after the impossible thing is contrasted with the rational "médetations plastiques" ("plastic meditations"; 127) of Georges Braque, whose work Beckett considers as giving the impression of a "hypothèse qui s'en dégage" ("a hypothesis that has disengaged itself") (127). Geer van Velde's work, in contrast, is discussed as being entirely turned towards the outside in an attempt to capture time. Yet this is described as being as futile an effort as representation of Heraclitus' river, in which no one can step twice, and his work thus appears as a second form of a "*memento mori*" (*Disjecta* 129). In fact, in this essay, Beckett defines the entire history of painting in regard to this problematics of time: "A quoi les arts représentatifs se sont-ils acharnés depuis toujours? A voulouir arrêter le temps, en le représentant" ("For what have the representative arts always thirsted? To want to stop time by representing it") (*Disjecta* 126).

In an earlier letter to Thomas McGreevy dated 8 September 1934 on the work of Cézanne, Beckett criticizes those painters such as the Impressionists who ignored this "discrepancy between that which cannot stay still for its phases & that which can," praising Cézanne for being the first to understand "the dynamic intrusion to be himself & so landscape to be something by definition unapproachably alien," thus marking the beginning of "the deanthropomorphizations of the artist" (*Letters 1* 223). That such a realization of painting's inability to depict the inescapable condition of time is linked to a critique of anthropomorphism is underlined in "Le peinture des van Veldes" when Beckett refers to a jet of sheep's urine in the paintings of Paulus Potter as the "symbole par excellence de la fuite des heures" ("the symbol *par excellence* of the flight of the hours") (*Disjecta* 126). In a recurring trope in Beckett's work, a scatological image of animality is used to mark out the limits of human capacity to represent time.

Beckett concludes the essay by returning to the subject of this impossible human condition by turning to question the very concept of the human itself. "Pour finir, parlons d'autre chose, parlons de l'"humain'" ("To finish, let us speak of something else, let us speak of the 'human'" (*Disjecta* 131). Beckett declares that this is a word that has returned today with "une fureur jamais égalée" ("a fury never before equaled") (*Disjecta* 131), hence Beckett is highly cynical about its presence in contemporary debate, calling it "un vocable, et sans doute un concept aussi, qu'on réserve pour les temps des grand massacres" ("a word, and no doubt a concept also, that is reserved for times of great massacres") (*Disjecta* 131). Furthermore, it is a word that he sees as abundantly appearing in artistic debate. For Beckett, it is "épouvantable" ("appalling") that an artist should have anything to do with "the human," for its reintroduction to the sphere of art is capable of destroying poetry, music, painting, and thought for the next 50 years (*Disjecta* 131). Against the humanist painter who declares that all men are brothers, Beckett proposes his own mordant aesthetic manifesto:

> L'espace vous intéresse? Faisons-le craquer.
> Le temps vous tracasse? Tuons-le tous ensemble.
> La béauté? L'homme réuni.
> La bonté? Étouffer.
> La vérité? Le pet du plus grand nombre.
>
> You are interested in space? Make it crack.
> You are tormented by time? Let's kill it together.
> Beauty? Man re-united.
> Goodness? Suffocate.
> Truth? The fart of the greatest number. (*Disjecta* 132)

The tiniest part of this kind of painting would ironically contain more humanity than what he calls "leurs processions vers un bonheur de mouton sacré" ("their processions for the happiness of the sacred sheep") (*Disjecta* 132). Once more, an image of the animal is used to mock the achievements of humanity. Beckett does not deny that there are "conditions éternelles de la vie" ("eternal conditions of life") (*Disjecta* 132), but states that "il y a son coût" ("they have their price") (132). These conditions of life that Beckett wishes to see realized on the painted canvas have ultimately little to do with the "human."

HUMANISM:
"A WORD RESERVED FOR TIMES OF GREAT MASSACRES"

Beckett was correct in his cultural diagnosis: humanism had returned with a vengeance to post-war French debate. Discussion of this context must attend to the term's notorious nebulosity. As early as October 1945, in his response to Sartre's lecture "Existentialism is a Humanism," the Surrealist Pierre Navaille complains that:

Today, unfortunately, the term humanism is used to designate philosophical schools of thought, not according to two meanings, but according to three, four, five, or six. Nowadays, everybody is a humanist. Even certain Marxists, who pride themselves on being classical rationalists, are humanists in a diluted sort of way, stripped of the liberal ideas of the previous century—embracing instead a liberalism refracted through the current crisis. If Marxists can claim to be humanists, then followers of the various religions—Christians, Hindus and many others—can also claim to be humanists, as do existentialists, and in general all philosophers. (Qtd. in *Existentialism is a Humanism* 62–23)

As Denis Kamboucher comments, given this confusion, "[a] systematic history of the 'humanist' theme in twentieth-century Europe and notably in post-war France should one day be written" (19). Similarly, in his account of the emergence of an "an atheism that is not humanist" in mid-century French philosophy, Geroulanous Stefanos describes the post-war period as witnessing a "short lived humanist reconciliation" (210), prompting a series of critiques by Maurice Blanchot, Martin Heidegger, and Jean Hyppolite. The kind of history sought by Kamboucher will not be attempted here; rather I wish to show what Beckett's distinct contribution to the histories of humanism and anti-humanism might be. And to do so, I will adopt the approach suggested by Beckett's skeptical observation that the "human" is "a word, and no doubt a concept also, that is reserved for the times of the greatest massacres" (*Disjecta* 131). There is a gap, a "without a doubt" between the deployment of the word "human" and its correlate "humanist," and the concept denoted, leading to the proliferation of humanisms described by Navaille. In contextualizing Beckett's questioning of "the human," my intent here is not to adjudicate the competing theoretical claims of Sartre, Ponge, Merleau-Ponty, and Heidegger. Instead, I wish to draw attention to how proclaiming allegiance to the human is used discursively to relate philosophy and aesthetics to the "great massacres" of history (*Disjecta* 131).

As Navaille observes, the Marxist version of humanism that became prominent after the war resulted from two related developments. The first was the prestige and moral authority that the P.C.F. enjoyed as a result of its leading role in the Resistance, earning it the title of the "parti des fusillées" ("party of the shot") (Rioux 54). This was accompanied by electoral success, with the P.C.F. winning the largest share of the vote in Assembly Elections on 21 October 1945 and 10 November 1946, a dominance which lasted until the crisis of 1947, when the Communists were expelled from government on 5 May 1947 (Rioux 112–132). The second was a resurgent interest in the humanism of the early Marx, particularly as developed in the 1844 "Economic and Philosophical Manuscripts" in which the theory of alienation and communism's overcoming of alienation was outlined. As Marx writes: "Communism as completed naturalism is humanism and as completed humanism is naturalism" (97). As Mark Poster notes, French editions of this text "did not appear until 1937 and even then it was ignored until after the Liberation . . . [thus] for political and textual reasons, which were interconnected, no real reading of Marx was possible in France until after the Second World War" (42).

In the case of Sartre and Merleau-Ponty, however, a second important philosophical source for presenting their thought as a form of humanism is what Vincent Descombes terms "the humanist interpretation of Hegelian idealism" (52) developed by Alexandre Kojève in his course on Hegel given at the École des Hautes Études in Paris from 1933 to 1939. In Descombes's account, Kojève's replacing of the Spirit with Man in his *"anthropological version* of Hegelian philosophy" (27; italics original) ultimately requires "[t]he identity of subject and object . . . [and that] man (subject) would encounter nothing outside of himself (in the object) to impede the realisation of his projects" (28). Descombes summarizes this interpretation of Hegel as an inverted theology: "Humanist atheism reclaims [divine attributes] for the human subject, who in this way becomes the true God. It is precisely this substitution, whereby everywhere the word "Man" is written to replace the word "God," which defines *humanism"* (29; italics original). Judith Butler also stresses the anthropological nature of Kojève's reading, writing that "Kojève went so far as to claim that Hegel's entire theological speculations ought to be understood as a theory of human action" (65). In relation to *Being and Nothingness*, Butler writes that "[t]he effort at anthropogenesis elaborated by Kojève finds existential transcription in the Sartrian contention that all human desire is a function of the desire to become God. But for Sartre, this desire is bound to fail" (95).

This negating desire can only be resolved in the realm of the imagination, leading to Sartre's privileging of literary works, which "manifest the 'desire to be' through creating an embodiment—the text—which reflects the self that is its author" (Butler 96). In his introduction to the inaugural issue of *Les Temps Modernes*, Sartre links his privileging of literature to a theory of humanism. By virtue of the fact that each writer is situated in his era, the practice of an engaged literature will discover aspects of a human condition that for Sartre is absolute, but "il l'est à son heure, dans son milieu, sur sa terre" ("but is it in his [man's] hour, in his milieu, on the earth") ("Présentation" 7). This "engaged literature" was the praxis of Sartre's existentialist humanism, which was launched into public consciousness with the lecture "Existentialism is a Humanism" in October 1945, marking a catalyzing moment in the post-war humanist debate.

SARTRE, PONGE, AND THE FUTURE OF MAN

In an article entitled "A propos de l'existentialisme: Mise au point," published in *Action* on 29 December 1944, Sartre outlines the key elements of his argument that existentialism was a humanism. As was the case for the October lecture, the article is a response to Communist critiques of Sartre's existentialism, and his response is to claim that, in fact, his refusal to "grant man an eternally established human nature . . . isn't too far from the conception of man found in Marx" ("A More Precise Characterization of Existentialism" 157). After stating the central tenet of his existentialism, that "[e]xistentialism, on the contrary, maintains that in man—and man alone—existence precedes essence" (156), Sartre concludes: "[h]ave I said enough to make it clear that *existentialism is no mournful delectation but a humanist philosophy of action, effort, combat, and solidarity?*" (160; italics original). These points are reiterated in "Existentialism is a Humanism." In the lecture, Sartre rejects the idea of a human nature in favor of a "universal human condition" (*Existentialism is a Humanism* 42), grounded in a subjectivity attained in the presence of the Other, which leads to existing in the world with the "absolute freedom of choice" (*EH* 43) to define one's projects. Concluding the lecture, Sartre stresses the transcendental core of human subjectivity in relation to the world outside oneself: "since man is this transcendence, and grasps objects only in relation to such transcendence, he himself is the core and focus of this transcendence" (*EH* 52). For Sartre, the human defines himself precisely in his domination of the objects of the world.

As an example of a writer who opposes "mournful delectation" with a vision of man in a constitutive and dominating relation to the objects of the world, in both the *Action* article and his lecture Sartre refers to "Notes premiers de l'Homme" by Francis Ponge, which was published in the inaugural issue of *Les Temps Modernes*. In this aphoristic text, written between 1943 and 1944, Ponge prophesies a future deification of man:

> [Man] has developed from himself the idea of God. It is necessary to reinstate this back into himself . . . It is necessary to replace the idea of God with the idea of man. And simply live. ("Notes" 70, 73)

The text ends with the phrase quoted by Sartre: "*Man is the future of man*" (75). Ponge was a member of the P.C.F. at this time, and this conception of man as a future to come is heavily indebted to the early Marx. This can be seen in Ponge's art criticism, particularly on Georges Braque.[2] In "Braque ou l'art moderne comme événement et plaisir," published in *Action* in January 1947, Ponge forcefully states the relations between his politics and aesthetics, declaring solidarity with "the political realists, whose disciple and friend I flatter myself I am" ("Braque, or Modern Art as Event and Pleasure" 43) with "realists in politics," here denoting the P.C.F. The Marxist influence is evident in this text when Ponge paraphrases the "Theses on Feuerbach" to define the artist: "He is one who *in no wise* explains the world, but changes it. You recognise the formula, more or less" ("Braque" 45). By not simply representing objects in the world, but also creating new forms of viewing them, Braque "presents the future" in two related forms: "[t]he future of nature and the future of man" (Ponge, "Braque" 138). Thus, with this attempt to depict an increasing sense of man's perceptual understanding of the world, Ponge praises Braque's depictions of objects, "which pull us out of the darkness of our night, from the old version of man (and its so-called humanism) to reveal to us, Man, the Order to Come" ("Braque" 140). In "Le peinture des van Veldes," Beckett criticizes Braque's work giving the impression "d'hypothèse qui s'en degage" (a hypothesis that disengages itself) (*Disjecta* 127) from the attempt to depict the relation to the impossible object. But Beckett also translates this text by Ponge for *Transition Forty-Nine*, and his comments to the journal's editor, Georges Duthuit, are revealing:

> *Ponge on Braque* It is revolting. "Braque is now over 60 and the world is beginning to fit into his groove"!!. What oft was thought. For someone who is a pupil of the realists in politics he is pretty unsteady on his feet. . . . What a relief to know that we are back for good and all from the fête galante, and pitched, naked once more, in front of the dead fish (and the lumps of coal)." (1 March 1949, *Letters 2* 122)

The distance from Ponge's interpretation of Braque could not be clearer. But what is also clear is Beckett's understanding of the political implications of Ponge's visual aesthetics: that they make him a pupil of the realists in politics, or the Parti Communiste Français. This link between realist aesthetics and Communist political humanism permeated the discourse surrounding painting in post-war France. And this link is presumed in a second Beckett essay on the van Velde brothers, published in 1948, in which he develops an understanding of the future of the visual arts, and the history of the relations between subject and object, in ways diametrically opposed to Ponge.

"PEINTRES DE L'EMPÊCHMENT," CÉZANNE, AND MERLEAU-PONTY

Beckett's second essay on the work of the van Velde brothers was commissioned to accompany an exhibition of their work: *Introducing Two Modern French Painters: Geer van Velde, Bram van Velde*, held from 8–27 March 1948 at the Samuel Kootz Gallery in New York. The text was composed in French in March 1947 and Peter Fifield convincingly argues that Beckett himself translated the text into English (874). The French version was published as "Peintres de l'Empêchement" in the June 1948 issue of *Derrière le miroir*, the journal of the Galerie Maeght in Paris. The New York exhibition was one half of an exchange with the Galerie Maeght, with the exhibition in Paris being the first exhibition of post-war abstract American art in Paris. As Serge Guilbault writes, this exchange program, coming in the wake of France's acceptance of the Marshall Plan, was widely perceived by French critics as "part of a wide-ranging and all but unstoppable cultural offensive against France" (151), and furthermore, that this exchange program with Galerie Maeght was indirectly funded by the American Embassy in Paris (150–151; 236 n.174). Beckett's essay is thus positioned within the wider post-war struggle over the perceived shift of the center of the visual avant-garde from Paris to New York.

The English version of the essay opens with an explicit acknowledgement of this battle: "We are now freely informed . . . that the Paris school, whatever that means, is finished, whatever that means" ("The New Object" 878). In contrast, Beckett argues that it is in the art of Bram and Geer van Velde that the School of Paris has its future, and does so by outlining their place within a theory of the history of painting. Beckett writes that "[t]he history of painting is the history of its relation to its object, a relation evolving, necessarily, in terms first of extension, then of penetration" ("New" 878). But, as Beckett continues, "the object of representation is at all times in resistance to representation" ("New" 879). Developing this history of the object's necessary "resistance" to consciousness and representation—the "empêchement" of the essay's French title—Beckett locates a contemporary "crisis": "For what remains to be represented if the essence of the object is to elude representation?" ("New" 879). His answer is that "[t]here remains to be represented the conditions of that elusion" ("New" 879). And this is what Beckett states the art of the van Veldes achieves, realizing an "art of confinement" ("New" 880). As Beckett writes in the French version of this essay, their work promises a "bel avenir" ("great future") because 'le même deuil les mène loin l'un de l'autre, de deuil de l'objet." ("the same mourning carries them away from each other, the mourning of the object") (*Disjecta* 135). Significantly, as Peter Fifield observes, in the typescript for this essay, Beckett had originally written "recherche" instead of "deuil," and "search" is what appears in the English version. But this was replaced with "deuil" in Beckett's hand, leading to a far more contextually aware allusion to a future in which painting will carry out an endless work of mourning for an irrecoverable object (Fifield 874). This undercuts and ironizes the rhetoric of the future of painting and of Man that Beckett perceived in Ponge's essay on Braque, and this change to the essay for a Parisian context indicates a conscious critique of the post-war humanist discourse surrounding the visual arts.

It was in the work of Cézanne that Beckett locates the beginnings of the historical crisis whereby the subject began to be alienated from the object. Of Cézanne's treatment of landscape, Beckett writes to McGreevy that "Cézanne seems to have been the first to see landscape & state it as material of a strictly peculiar order, incommensurable with all human expressions whatsoever" (8 September 1934, *Letters 1* 222). In Cézanne's self-portraits Beckett sees that this alienation from the world also leads to an alienation from one's own self. Cézanne, Beckett writes, "has the sense of his incommensurability not only with life of such a different order as landscape but even with life of his own order, even with the life... operative in himself" (16 September 1934, *Letters 1* 227). Cézanne was central to Beckett's interpretation of modern art, one in which the "deanthropomorphizations of the artist" led to a wider questioning of the human. Cézanne came to occupy a similar position in the post-war thought of Merleau-Ponty, and in tracing the differences between their respective interpretations of Cézanne, Beckett's art criticism can be further positioned within the politics of post-war humanism.

Merleau-Ponty's "Cézanne's Doubt" was published in *Fontaine* in December 1945, between the appearance of his *Phenomenology of Perception* (1945) and *Humanism and Terror* (1947). In this essay, Cézanne's painting acts as bridge to link the phenomenological subjectivity of the former with the political philosophy of the latter. This is made explicit in the preface to the essay collection *Sense and Non-Sense* published in 1948: while "today's citizen is not sure whether the human world is possible" the fact that "Cézanne won out against chance" shows that "men, too, can win provided they will measure the dangers and the task" (5). The means by which the "human world is possible" are developed by Merleau-Ponty in

Humanism and Terror, which grew out of a series of articles on Arthur Koestler's *Darkness at Noon* entitled "Le Yogi et le Prolétaire" which appeared in *Les Temps Modernes* between October 1946 and January 1947. Beckett's "Poèmes 38–39" appeared alongside the second part in the November 1946 issue, and his observation to George Reavey that "[t]he boys are very cross with Koestler" (15 December 1946, *Letters 2* 49) indicates his awareness of Merleau-Ponty's sustained attack on Koestler's criticism of the Moscow Show Trials in *Darkness at Noon*.

Yet Merleau-Ponty admits that "the book poses the problem of our times" (*Humanism and Terror* 2)—the role of violence in politics. Drawing on Kojève's interpretation of the Master-Slave dialectic in Hegel, Merleau-Ponty argues that given that "[a]ll we know is different kinds of violence . . . we ought to prefer revolutionary violence because it has a future of humanism" (*H&T* 107). For Merleau-Ponty, this humanism is to be found in the Marx of the "Economic and Philosophical Manuscripts," and the "real question" that *Darkness at Noon* raises is whether "communism [is] still equal to its humanist intentions?" (*H&T* xviii). The answer here is a cautious yes, so long as one takes Marxism as a theory of "subjectivity and action committed within a historical situation" (*H&T* 22). Revolutionary violence can lead to a future of humanism through the recognition of the "mission in the proletariat," which moves through history towards "the recognition of man by man" (112). The historical proletariat is key for Merleau-Ponty: it is "the sole authentic intersubjectivity because it alone lives simultaneously the separation and union of individuals" (116–117). Thus, "[t]he theory of the proletariat as the vehicle of history's meaning is the humanist face of Marxism" (118).

Humanism and Terror ends by comparing the political philosophy outlined to "a view which like the most fragile object of perception—a soap bubble—or like the most simple dialogue, embraces indivisibly all the order and all the disorder of the world" (189). Along with the description of the proletariat as the "sole authentic intersubjectivity," this indicates that Merleau-Ponty is developing the political implications of his *Phenomenology of Perception*. The basic phenomenological premise of the *Phenomenology of Perception*, that "[w]e are caught up in the world and do not succeed in extricating ourselves from it in order to achieve consciousness of the world" (5), implies the historicity of the subject: "there is history only for a subject who lives through it, and a subject only in so far as he is historically situated" (200).

In the *Phenonemology of Perception*, Merleau-Ponty uses Cézanne's work to illustrate an exemplary, historically situated model of phenomenological perception. In discussing the patient Schneider, whose coordination between his visual and tactile perception is impaired and who can only coordinate tactile and visual perception through linguistic description, Merleau-Ponty contrasts this with Cézanne's description of his "motif" falling into place (*PP* 152 n. 71). This structural unity between modes of perception is described as "this subject-object dialogue, this drawing together, by the subject, of the meaning diffused through the object, and, by the object, of the subject's intentions—a process which is physiognomic perception" (*PP* 152–153). Cézanne's foregrounding of the "immanent or incipient significance in the living body" (*PP* 230) makes his work an example of the future overcoming of human self-alienation, and in "Cézanne's Doubt," this is presented as victory of the human over the inhuman.

At first sight, Merleau-Ponty admits that "the inhuman character of his paintings" could be seen to "only represent a flight from the human world, the alienation of his humanity" (*Sense and Non-Sense* 10–11). And this too could be an alienation from the landscape that "itself is stripped of the attributes which make it ready for animistic communions" (*S&N* 16). But for Merleau-Ponty, this doubt is overcome: "But indeed only a human being is capable of such a vision which penetrates right to the root of things beneath the imposed order of humanity... one sees how Cézanne was able to revive the classical definition of art: man added to nature" (*S&N* 16). This is achieved as a result of Cézanne's perception of the world, which makes "a basic distinction not between 'the senses' and 'the understanding' but rather between the spontaneous organization of the things we perceive and the human organization of ideas and sciences" (*S&N* 13). This is Cézanne's "intuitive science," by means of which alienation is overcome, and Merleau-Ponty quotes Cézanne's statement that: "'The landscape thinks itself in me,' he said, 'and I am its consciousness'" (*S&N* 17).

In an ironic inversion of Merleau-Ponty's comparison of Cézanne with a psychiatric patient, Beckett writes to McGreevey that as a consequence of his treatment of landscape, "Cézanne leaves landscape maison d'aliénés [a lunatic asylum] & a better understanding of the term 'natural' for an idiot" (8 September 1934, *Letters 1* 222). For Beckett, Cézanne's work reveals the alienation of man from man, with "[e]ven the portrait beginning to be dehumanised as the individual feels himself more & more hermetic and alone & his neighbour a coagulum as alien as a protoplast or God" (*Letters I* 223). Cézanne's painting is thus the site of an essential difference between Beckett and Merleau-Ponty, one that is not without political implications. In Cézanne's work, Merleau-Ponty sees the occurrence of the subject-object dialogue that is central to his phenomenology and his politics. In contrast, in "Recent Irish Poetry" (1934) written a few months before his letters to McGreevy on Cézanne, Beckett declares that "the new thing that has happened, or the old thing that has happened again" was "the breakdown of the object... [and] the breakdown of the subject," what he calls the "rupture of the lines of communication" (*Disjecta* 70). Years later, when Beckett engages in a correspondence with the art critic Georges Duthuit on the work of Bram van Velde that would form the basis of the published "Three Dialogues," Beckett writes to Duthuit: "I remember coming out, the regulation 20 years ago, being at that time a little less than now, with an angry article on modern Irish poets, in which I set up, as a criterion of modern poetry, an awareness of the vanished object. Already!" (2 March 1949, *Letters 2* 131). And it is in the "Three Dialogues" that Beckett makes a final attempt to define how this "awareness of the vanished object" might be realized in painting, in ways that once again show that this involves a questioning of the human.

"THREE DIALOGUES" AND *RÉALISME SOCIALISM*

"Three Dialogues: Samuel Beckett and Georges Duthuit," published in *Transition Forty-Nine*, number 5, in December 1949, was not Beckett's first contribution to *Transition*. (This new *Transition*, edited by Georges Duthuit, was a short-lived attempt to revive the spirit of Eugene Jolas's more well known pre-war magazine *transition*.) As John Pilling and Séan Lawlor document, Beckett helped to translate approximately thirty articles or poems published in *Transition* between 1948 and 1950 (88–89), and was as such central to the journal's project. This was defined in the inaugural issue as to "to assemble for the English-speaking world the best of French art and thought, whatever the style and whatever the application" (Duthuit 5), although advertisements in later issues for periodicals such as *Direction* (no. 3), *The Hudson Review* (no. 5), and *The Partisan Review* (no. 5) indicate that this English-speaking world was primarily an American one. *Transition*, then, acted as a conduit by which a certain image of French art and thought was produced for an American audience. And with its combination of presenting developments in French art alongside works of literary theory by Georges Bataille and Sartre, the journal can be seen as a part of the prehistory of the creation of what François Cusset calls the "textual American object of *theory*" (ix). It was as a participant in such critical debates that Beckett's critical was presented to an American audience.

In *Transition Forty-Nine*, the central topic of debate Duthuit presents in the "Documents" section is the relationship between a work of art and the wider political community. Reproductions of the paintings by Tal-Coat, Masson, and Bram van Velde discussed in the "Three Dialogues" are interspersed among statements by Braque, Léger, Matisse, Miro, and Fourgeron on the relationship between the artist and his community, inviting an interpretation of the position of the "Three Dialogues" on this topic. "B's" comments in "Three Dialogues" address this question by repeating his previous criticisms of Marxist aesthetics and their attendant humanism, and valorizing instead the work of Bram van Velde. In the third dialogue, "B" claims Bram van Velde's work is of a new order to all previous great artists. Of these, "B" claims:

> Among those whom we call great artists, I can think of none whose concern was not predominantly with his expressive possibilities, those of his vehicle, those of humanity. The assumption underlying all painting is that the domain of the maker is the domain of the feasible. (*Disjecta* 142)

As in his criticism of Ponge, Beckett connects a concern with the expressive possibilities of painting—its ability to represent the object—with a philosophy of humanism. Beckett's claim that Bram van Velde's painting has moved beyond the "misapprehension . . . that its function was to express, by means of paint" (*Disjecta* 143), therefore marks a move beyond a concern with the human. Beckett also comments on the relationship between art and politics when he states that "[t]he realisation that art has always been bourgeois, though it may dull our pain before the achievements of the socially progressive, is finally of scant interest" (*Disjecta* 144). The type of "socially progressive" art that Beckett dismisses here is exemplified in *Transition* by what is referred to as "the Fougeron case" ("Documents" 110). This scandal was caused by the exhibition of the painting *Parisiennes aux Marché* by André Fougeron at the Salon d"Automne in 1948, which graphically depicted the food shortages still endemic in Paris after the war. Beckett had in fact already encountered this painting. In his letter attacking Ponge's essay on Braque that he translated for this issue, Beckett concludes his diatribe by sarcastically writing: "What a relief to know that we are back for good and all from the fête galante, and pitched, naked once more, in front of the dead fish (and the lumps of coal)" (*Letters 2* 122). As Serge Guilbault shows, the dead fish in this painting became a metonymic reference point for debating the political and aesthetic implications of *réalisme socialisme* in what became known as "La Bataille réalisme-abstraction" in the immediate post-war years (*Reconstructing Modernism* 44). The claims that Beckett makes in the "Three Dialogues" for an art of "invalidity, of inadequacy, of existence at the expense of all that it excludes, all that it blinds to" (*Disjecta* 145) has as its paratextual opposite the "réalisme socialisme" of an artist like Fougeron. And what this art excludes is the concern with humanity that Beckett attempts to claim that Bram van Velde's work has moved beyond. Yet the "Three Dialogues" ends with B. abruptly breaking off, admitting that "I am mistaken, I am mistaken" (*Disjecta* 145). There is a sense that the questioning of humanity that Beckett demands from the art of Bram van Velde had not been realized. However, this was a task which Beckett took up in his own work at this time along lines set out in his art criticism. With this shift to exploring this questioning in literature and drama a final set of intersections of Beckett's work with those of his contemporaries can be traced.

"NEGATIVE ANTHROPOLOGY," HEIDEGGER AND THE ANIMAL

In contextualizing Beckett's art-criticism amid a resurgent Marxist humanism, it would of course be reductive to claim that this was only factor that determines the political stakes of Beckett's work. As dramatized by the behavior of the narrator of the "The End," which was composed in early 1946, triumphalist Marxist humanism was something against which Beckett's attempted reaction was indifference to the point of self-destruction, rather than direct opposition. As the narrator of "The End" lies begging on a street corner, pissing, shitting, and scratching himself, he witnesses a "strange scene," a man bellowing: "Union . . . brothers . . . Marx . . . capital . . . bread and butter . . . love" (*Expelled* 52). Accused that his begging is "a crime, an incentive to stultification and organised murder," the narrator pockets his pennies and heads on his way, with a closing quip that parodies the deification of man central to the Marxism of writers such as Ponge:

> He must have been a religious fanatic, I could find no other explanation. Perhaps he was an escaped lunatic. He had a nice face, a little on the red side. (*Expelled* 52)

In *Eleutheria*, which Beckett wrote in January-February 1947, the utopian dreams of post-war Marxist humanism also come in for comic assault. The text of the play makes knowing comments on the contemporary post-war situation. Madame Piouk's inquiry after Madame Meck's husband: "How is the general?" (25), and Madame Meck's response that "[h]is dying breath was for France" (*Eleutheria* 26) raises up the image of de Gaulle, who dramatically departed from the political scene in January 1946. After de Gaulle's departure, the Fourth Republic came into being, and Paul Ramadier became its first prime minister on 22 January 1947, leading a coalition of Socialists and Communists, an event alluded to when Jacques asks M. Krap "What does monsieur think of the new government?" (*Eleutheria* 61). For as Dr. Piouk reminds the audience: "We are no longer living in the Third Republic" (*Eleutheria* 113). Indeed, it is in the character of Dr. Piouk, "who loves humanity" (*Eleutheria* 19), that the play explicitly attacks post-war discourses of humanism. Within *Eleutheria* at least, Piouk's love of humanity is associated with Marxism, for so effuse is his love of humanity that Madame Krap suspects: "You wouldn't be a Communist?" (43). Yet when pressed to solve the problem of humanity, he suddenly proposes abortions, euthanasia, enforced homosexuality, and the "death penalty to any woman guilty of giving birth" (*Eleutheria* 44). In contrast to Piouk, Victor Krap, the failed writer at the center of the play, can only offer what the Spectator calls a "negative anthropology," only defining life by "what it isn't" (147). The drama ends with a performative enactment of this "negative anthropology," with stage directions indicating Victor crawling into bed and "turning his emaciated back on humanity" (170).

This taste for "negative anthropology" also appears in *Molloy*, the work that Beckett wrote after *Eleutheria*, beginning it in May 1947 and completing it that November. Thinking back on his past learning, Molloy recalls:

> The next pain in the balls was anthropology and the other disciplines, such as psychiatry, that are connected with it, disconnected, and reconnected again, according to the latest discoveries. What I liked in anthropology was its inexhaustible faculty of negation, its relentless definition of man, as though he were no better than God, in terms of what he is not. But my ideas on this subject were always horribly confused, for my knowledge of men was scant and the meaning of being beyond me. (37–39)

While Molloy's "negative anthropology" gestures back to *Eleutheria*, his linking of the definition of man with the "latest discoveries" and the "meaning of being" also gestures outwards to another negative anthropology that appeared in 1947: the publication of a fragment of Martin Heidegger's *Letter on Humanism* which had appeared as "Lettre à Jean Beaufret" in the November 1947 issue of *Fontaine*.[3] The letter is Heidegger's rejection of Sartre's claim that "Existentialism is a Humanism." For Heidegger, "[e]very humanism is either grounded in a metaphysics or is itself made to be the ground of one" (*Basic Writings* 157), and to this extent Heidegger states his thinking is against humanism. In his detailed account of the composition of this text, Anson Rabinbach argues that it can be read as "an allegory of the author's attempt to remove himself from all ethical considerations or demands of responsibility" (11).

Here "humanism" functions discursively, as it does for Sartre, as a way in which the philosophical thinking of Being is played out in the historical actuality of a social world from which, for tactical reasons, Heidegger wished to extricate himself. As early as 1940, Rabinbach shows, Heidegger used a critique of humanism as a mode of nihilism and metaphysics in order to distance his thinking from the Nazi regime (19–20). In the *Letter* itself, this attempt to disregard recent history is part of an effort "to create the impression of a philosophical continuity from the pre-Rectorate period to his post-war thinking" (Rabinbach 7), one in which, for Heidegger, "man is the being whose Being as ek-sistence consists in his dwelling in the nearness of Being" (*Basic Writings* 167). However, the human species maintains a privileged relation in this nearness to Being. Heidegger insists that through the capacity for language, man remains distinct from the animal: living creatures remain "separated from our ek-sistent essence by an abyss" (*Basic Writings* 156).

It is by way of the transgression of this border between man and animal in *Molloy* that Beckett's questioning of the human assumes a more radical nature than that proposed by Heidegger. Despite his taste for "negative anthropology," Molloy initially believes that "I am human, I fancy" (78). But Molloy is haunted by his "lust to kill" (67). This lust is consummated when he murders a solitary stranger whom he cannot understand: "seeing that he had not ceased to breathe I contented myself with giving him a few warm kicks in the ribs, with my heels" (85). The relish Molloy takes in murder moves him beyond the pale of the human, for shortly afterwards he hears a murmur and "pricks up [his] ears, like an animal I imagine" (89). And his narrative ends with him "abandoning erect motion, that of man" (*Molloy* 90). Jacques Derrida writes how throughout Heidegger's work, whenever the question of difference between human and animal is broached, "Heidegger's discourse seems . . . to fall into a rhetoric which is all the more peremptory and authoritarian for having to hide a discomfiture . . . [and that] in these cases it leaves intact, sheltered in obscurity, the axioms of the profoundest metaphysical humanism" (11–12). What we see in *Molloy*, then, is the different paths that Beckett and Heidegger take in their contemporaneous responses to post-war French humanism. Heidegger attempts to place man in a privileged relation to Being, one that is based on difference from the animal. Molloy's violence undermines any such claims for an essential difference between the human and the animal. Indeed as Beckett sarcastically observed in "Les peintures des van Veldes," it is precisely in times of great massacres that the claim for the human is most loudly heard. And just as in that essay, where the flow of sheep's urine was a symbol of the limits of the human capacity to represent time, in *Molloy* the return to animality symbolizes the limits of the human capacity to resist the urge towards violence. Only in moving beyond such oppositions, *Molloy* suggests, and by accepting the limited capacity of the human animal, could such violence be potentially overcome.

CONCLUSION

Molloy's descent into the mud of animality is the beginning of a long process of decomposition that the voice of *How It Is* will look back on, remembering "I was young I clung on to the species we're talking of the species the human" (39). The phrasing here almost exactly recalls the text of "Le peinture des van Veldes," with its call "let us speak of the human." This textual echo points to how it was in Beckett's engagement with painting that he first developed this questioning of the human, showing the centrality of the visual arts to Beckett's work in ways that go beyond iconographical and textual references. This engagement with painting also enabled Beckett to participate, however obliquely, in the wider political, philosophical, and aesthetic debates of post-war France. And given that Beckett's contemporaries in these debates were figures such as Sartre, Merleau-Ponty, and Heidegger, it is in Beckett's engagement with painting that historicist and theoretical approaches to Beckett's work can be reconciled (see Rabaté 699–702), for it indicates that Beckett's work belongs to the history *of* theory. For Beckett in "Le peinture des van Veldes," a painting begins as a "non-sens" ("non-sense") (*Disjecta* 119) into which a whole history of interpretation, criticism and desire is inscribed, and for the Beckett writing in post-war France, what he chose to see on the canvas was, as he wrote of his experience working with the Red Cross in Saint-Lô, "a vision of a time honoured conception of humanity in ruins" ("The Capital of the Ruins" 279).

Notes

1. In addition to his art criticism, Beckett's journal publications from 1945 to 1949 were: "Suite," *Les Temps Modernes* 1.10 (July 1946): 107–119; "Poèmes 38–39," *Les Temps Modernes* 2.14 (Nov. 1946): 288–293; "L'Expulsé," *Fontaine* 10.57 (Dec. 1946–Jan. 1947): 685–708; "Trois poèmes—Three poems." *Transition Forty-Eight* 2 (June 1948): 96–97.

2. In her account of Ponge's art criticism, Shirley Ann Jordan observes: "it is worth considering that whatever reverence Ponge may have for the humble object, and however novel his description of its relationship to himself, the external world is still employed in his work as key to the condition of humanity" (116).

3. The text published in *Fontaine* corresponds, with some textual variants to pages 168–181 in the English version published in *Basic Writings*.

Works Cited

Artaud, Antonin. *Œuvres*. Edited by Evelyne Grossman. Gallimard, 2004.

———. *Watchfiends & Rack Screams: Works from the Final Period*. Translated by Clayton Eshleman. Exact Change, 1995.

Barbican Art Gallery. *Aftermath France, 1945–54: New Images of Man*. Barbican Center, 1982.

Beckett, Samuel. "The Capital of the Ruins." *Samuel Beckett: The Complete Short Prose 1929–1989*. Grove Press, 1995, pp. 275–278.

―. *Disjecta: Miscellaneous Writings and a Dramatic Fragment*. Edited by Ruby Cohn. John Calder, 1983.

―. *Eleutheria*. Translated by Barbara Wright. Faber, 1996.

―. *The Expelled / The Calmative / The End / First Love*. Edited by Christopher Ricks. Faber and Faber, 2009.

―. *How It Is*. Edited by Edouard Magessa O'Reilly. Faber, 2009.

―. *The Letters of Samuel Beckett Volume 1: 1929–1940*. Edited by Lois More Overbeck and Martha Dow Fehsenfeld. Cambridge UP, 2009.

―. *The Letters of Samuel Beckett Volume 2: 1941–1956*. Edited by Gordon Craig, et al. Cambridge UP, 2011.

―. *Molloy*. Edited by Shane Weller. Faber and Faber, 2009.

―. "The New Object." *Modernism/Modernity*, vol. 18, no. 4, 2011, pp. 878–880.

Boschetti, Anna. *The Intellectual Enterprise: Sartre and Les Temps Modernes*. Translated by Richard McCleary. Northwestern UP, 1988.

Butler, Judith. *Subjects of Desire: Hegelian Reflections in Twentieth-Century France*. Columbia UP, 1987.

Cusset, François. *French Theory: How Foucault, Derrida, Deleuze, & Co. Transformed the Intellectual Life of the United States*. U of Minnesota P, 2008.

Derrida, Jacques. *Of Spirit: Heidegger and the Question*. Translated by Geoffrey Bennington and Rachel Bowlby. U of Chicago P, 1989.

Descombes, Vincent. *Modern French Philosophy*. Translated by L. Scott-Fox & J.M. Harding. Cambridge UP, 1980.

"Documents." *Transition Forty-Nine*, vol. 5, 1949, pp. 110–126.

Duthuit, Georges. "Introduction." *Transition Forty-Eight*, vol. 1, 1948, p. 5.

Fifield, Peter. "Introduction to Samuel Beckett, 'The New Object'." *Modernism/Modernity*, vol. 18, no. 4, 2011, pp. 873–877.

Geroulanos, Stefanos. *An Atheism That Is Not Humanist Emerges in French Thought*. Stanford UP, 2010.

Guilbaut, Serge. *How New York Stole the Idea of Modern Art: Abstract Expressionism, Freedom, and the Cold War*. Translated by Arthur Goldhammer. U of Chicago P, 1985.

―. *Reconstructing Modernism: Art in New York, Paris, and Montreal, 1945–1964*. MIT Press, 1990.

Heidegger, Martin. *Basic Writings*. Routledge, 2011.

―. "Lettre á Jean Beaufret." *Fontaine*, vol. 11, no. 63, 1947, pp. 787–804.

Jones, David Houston. *Samuel Beckett and Testimony*. Palgrave Macmillan, 2011.

Jordan, Shirley Ann. *The Art Criticism of Francis Ponge*. W.S. Maney for the Modern Humanities Research Assn., 1994.

Kambouchner, Denis. "Lévi-Strauss and the question of humanism; followed by a letter from Claude Lévi-Strauss." *The Cambridge Companion to Lévi-Strauss*. Cambridge UP, 2010. 19–38.

Knowlson, James. *Damned to Fame: The Life of Samuel Beckett*. Bloomsbury, 1996.

Lawlor, Sean, and John Pilling. "Beckett in Transition." *Publishing Samuel Becket*. Edited by Mark Nixon. British Library, 2011, pp. 83–97.

Marx, Karl. *Karl Marx: Selected Writings*. 2nd ed. Edited by David McLellan. Oxford UP, 2000.

Merleau-Ponty, Maurice. *Humanism and Terror: The Communist Problem.* Translated by John O'Neill. Transaction Publishers, 2000. Cited as *H&T.*

———. *Phenomenology of Perception.* Routledge, 2002. Cited as *PP.*

———. *Sense and non-sense.* Northwestern UP, 1964. Cited as *S&N.*

Ponge, Francis. "Braque, or Modern Art as Event and Pleasure." Translated by Samuel Beckett. *Transition Forty-Nine*, vol. 5, 1949, pp. 43–47.

———. "Notes premiers de l'Homme." *Les Temps Modernes*, vol. 1, no. 1, 1945, pp. 67–75.

Poster, Mark. *Existential Marxism in Postwar France: from Sartre to Althusser.* Princeton UP, 1977.

Rabaté, Jean-Michel. "Beckett's Three Critiques: Kant's Bathos and the Irish Chandos." *Modernism/Modernity*, vol. 18, no. 4, 2011, pp. 699–719.

Rabinbach, Anson. "Heidegger's Letter on Humanism as Text and Event." *New German Critique*, vol. 62, 1994, pp. 3–38.

Rancière, Jacques. *The Politics of Aesthetics: the Distribution of the Sensible.* Trans. Gabriel Rockhill. Continuum, 2004.

Rioux, Jean-Pierre. *The Fourth Republic, 1944–1958.* Cambridge UP, 1987.

Sartre, Jean-Paul. "A More Precise Characterization of Existentialism." *The Writings of Jean-Paul Sartres.* 2 vols. Northwestern UP, 1974, pp. 155–160.

———. *Existentialism is a Humanism.* Trans. John Kulka. Yale UP, 2007.

———. "Présentation." *Les Temps Modernes*, vol. 1, no. 1, 1945, pp. 1–21.

Trezise, Thomas. *Into the Breach: Samuel Beckett and the Ends of Literature.* Princeton UP, 1990.

Zevros, Christian, ed. "Des problèmes de la creation littéraire et artistique d'après quelques texts de Lénine et de Staline." *Cahiers d'art*, vol. 20–21, 1946, pp. 341–342.

KEVIN BRAZIL is an associate professor of English literature at the University of Southampton. He is the author of *Art, History, and Postwar Fiction* (Oxford UP, 2018) and the essay collection, *What Ever Happened to Queer Happiness?* (Influx Press, 2022).

7 Art of Impoverishment: Beckett and *arte povera*

Erika Mihálycsa

But the body, to get there with, where's the body? It's a minor point, a minor point.

—Samuel Beckett, Texts for Nothing (*CSP* 139)

"Does there exist, can there exist, or not, a painting that is poor, undisguisedly useless, incapable of any image whatever, a painting whose necessity does not seek to justify itself?" Beckett asks in a June 1948 letter in exasperated response to his friend Duthuit's advocacy for the art "of those who, having, want more, and having the ability, want more still" (*Letters II* 166, 165). His dismissal of those artists who, as he would put it in "Three Dialogues with Georges Duthuit," are merely "straining to enlarge the statement of a compromise" (*Disjecta* 138), goes beyond questions of form. For him, the aesthetic and epistemological quandaries that triggered such painting are mere "crises, to be overcome, bad times to be lived through, not even, substance of heroic struggle" (*Letters II* 166). Painting—especially the abstract art of the van Velde brothers, heirs to the interwar modernism of the École de Paris—served as a pitch where Beckett could articulate his post-humanist poetics of radical impoverishment in a "numberless, valueless, achievementless world" (*Letters II* 103).

While the van Veldes continue to be his reference points well after he stops collaborating with the revived *Transition* and puts an end to what might be termed his art criticism, new developments on the European art scene approximate his poetics and can be characterized with Beckett's retrospective assessment of his work: "Aesthetically the adventure is that of the failed form (no achieved statement of the inability to be)" (*Letters II* 596).[1] Such a parallel to Beckett's essays on art and his writing degree zero from the 1940s and early 1950s suggests itself in one of the most radical departures in postwar art, the early work of Alberto Burri, emerging at the crossroads of prewar Surrealism, and postwar abstraction and Informel, that constitutes a premise to *arte povera* but also became a decisive influence on the palimpsestual art of salvage of Rauschenberg, Cy Twombly, or Tápies.

Both Beckett and Burri respond to the breakdown of European culture and the attempt to redeem it in the form of Marxist existentialist and phenomenological-inspired humanism, by transgressive practices of exposing and undoing the foundational conventions and underlying philosophical frameworks of their domains of art—the continuity of the (Cartesian) self, of space and time, narrative, even the referent in Beckett's case; the idea of the two-dimensional canvas as the repository of mimesis, but above all, painting as the extension of the authorial self, stylistic coherence seen as a rhetorical practice of the language of art. Both turn their backs on formalism, aligned with postwar abstraction and especially Abstract Expressionism in painting. Their works embody, rather than represent, the impoverishment and "wounding" of art, by holing writing/painting with pauses; egregious, devouring gaps; torn crevices; discontinuities; procedural writing; and handling of plastic material. In moving from prewar modernist models toward an embodied aesthetic of finitude, the two artists working in their different media privilege a material imagination of indigence grounded in detritus, which is singularly able to stage the ongoing disaster of contemporary history.

Beckett's exchange with Duthuit that leads to "Three Dialogues" is coeval with the completion of *Malone meurt*, *Godot* and starting work on *L'Innommable*, and documents Beckett's rejection of the illusion of a therapeutic, liberating art, together with "those closed, achieved worlds that give off a grinding of solitudes, prides. And at the same time of a possible totality of being" (*Letters II* 131). This radical poetics of negativity, indigence, and finitude is founded on the ethical obligation toward the text's creaturely life, "a wretchedness to defend," as Beckett writes to Simone de Beauvoir on behalf of the protagonist of his 1946 short story "Suite" (*"La Fin"*/"The End"; *Letters II* 42). In the closure of *"La peinture des van Velde ou le Monde et le Pantalon,"* in which he provocatively adopts the stance of the amateur *"cochon"* (pig) with no authority of expertise, Beckett launches a mordant attack on humanism, noting that "human" is a word and concept "reserved for the time of great massacres" (*Disjecta* 131). Kevin Brazil comprehensively discusses the enmeshedness of Beckett's writings on art with the critical and ideological debates of the immediate postwar years in France, where philosophical humanism of a Marxist-existentialist orientation merged with a phenomenological humanism of a Bergsonian hue (Brazil 34–41), to respond to momentous changes such as the reconfiguring of Paris's role in the art world with the rise of the New York School and the Greenbergian narrative of modernism, and, most importantly, the complex and often contradictory attempts to renew the ethos of prewar modernism with its formalist aesthetic.

Under Duthuit's editorship, *Transition* became one of the important venues of these debates, showcasing Sartre's existentialism and new French non-figurative painting to an Anglophone audience. The legacy of the Fauves, advocated by Duthuit, was epitomized by a group of non-figurative painters, including Pierre Tal Coat and André Masson, propelled to the center of the Paris art scene by criticism tributary to vitalism (see Carville 182–213). On the other hand, the most poignant aesthetic proposal to come from postwar France was Sartre's existentialism as a new humanism, which substituted God with the humanist subject endowed with inalienable freedom. Beckett's writings on art fly in the face of both; the "art of confinement" (Beckett, *Disjecta* 137) he envisions counters the existentialist framing of the subject to the point where his stance converges with Lévinas's ethics of nonrelation, both contesting the Sartrean, totalizing vision of literature born out of absolute freedom, and placing the artwork in the realm of the nonconceptual, non-transparent, non-knowable, at the limit of the human (see Fifield 23–42).

Beckett's essays on art are also radically negative answers given to the (putatively universalist) subjectivism and doctrine of the autonomy of art that constituted the underlying assumptions of the New York School and Greenberg's aesthetic, which were starting to be promoted as part of Cold War cultural policies. The English version of *"Peintres de l'empêchement"* was published in the catalogue of Bram van Velde's New York exhibition at the Samuel Kootz Gallery (8–27 March 1947) as "The New Object," addressed to an American audience, and sarcastically refutes the claim, made by the American critic preceding the piece, that the École de Paris is finished and buried.[2] In the French essay Beckett characterizes the art of the van Veldes as driven by the "mourning for the object"(*"Peintres de l'empêchement," Disjecta* 135)[3]—a mourning that is interminable, since for Beckett the subject-object relationship cannot be sutured in coalescing the two in coenaesthesia (Duthuit's position in "Three Dialogues"). How far Greenberg advocated humanistic values is illustrated by his critique on Dubuffet and the new French art scene in the summer 1946 issue of *Les Temps Modernes* (where the first part of Beckett's short story "Suite," the future *"La Fin"/*"The End," appeared that same year): he warns that American artists will not produce major art "unless American art reconciles itself with the minimum of positivism on which rests, in my view, the continuity and force of modern art in France, unless we integrate our poetry into our art's immediate physical dimensions" (Greenberg 350).

In the polemic between Beckett and Duthuit, considerations of form take on powerful political overtones in the context of postwar angst when the social role of art and its relation to formal mastery became again a pressing question.[4] In his exemplary rehistoricization, David Lloyd shows how Duthuit's phenomenologist endorsement of the painting of Masson and Tal Coat as examples of "Byzantine" space, not based on geometric perspective, touch on the continuity of spatial (pictorial) representation and social relations—implicitly, on the question of the communal relevance of art (Lloyd 107). Of particular interest is Beckett's key term (*peintre de*) *l'empêchement / coincement* (impediment, "stuckness"), featuring in both *"La peinture des van Velde ou le Monde et le Pantalon"* [1945] and *"Peintres de l'Empêchement"* [1948] (*Disjecta* 118–131, 133–137), which Lloyd traces back to an earlier review of Bram van Velde's painting by critic Jan Greshoff, who used it in the sense of a visual barrier between the painting's and the spectator's space, that thwarts linear perspective's illusion of spatial continuity and contributes to a sense of visual disorientation (118).[5]

In addition to the undecidability of inner/outer space, which denies the comfort of unitary perspective, van Velde's vestigial figuration plays on the face/mask/eyes taken to their componenets, so the painting's allusive figure becomes "of figure itself, of the face or mask that is the prototype of all figuration" (Lloyd 115). This hesitancy between figuration and the non-figurative stems from the image's capacity to evoke a (pictorial) space for a gaze that is not represented but created, almost as a discontinuity: van Velde decomposes the figure, subjecting it to visual operations that stage, in the words of Beckett's painter friend Avigdor Arikha, "the difficulty of seeing" (qtd. in Lloyd 118). The term also has a political subtext. As Emilie Morin shows, at a time of intense debates around fictionalized accounts of the camps, some novels harnessing the form of testimonial writing were denounced by Jean Cayrol as exploitative concentration camp romances, against which a *"littérature d'empêchement"* was asked for, of voluntary impoverishment and radical disorientation of the rationalist order (Cayrol 535, qtd. in Morin 181–182)—the very kind of literature Beckett was engaged in writing in *Watt, Molloy*, and *Texts for Nothing*, a performative rupturing of forms of closure. However much Bram van Velde's abstraction relinquished the possession of the object and such vestiges of traditional aesthetic enjoyment to which his contemporaries Masson and Tal Coat were still tributary, the radicalism of his art falls short of Beckett's statements, which, as Uhlmann among others warns, have predominantly been exploited as a blueprint to Beckett's own writing.

The pool of contemporary artists Beckett seriously engaged with does not include Alberto Burri or representatives of early *arte povera*.[6] However, Burri's art suggests itself as a close visual parallel to Beckett's aesthetics of impoverishment, for which *"arte povera"* has been used as a metaphor, without referencing the artistic practices of the Italian artistic movement. Burri's work is contingent with several major developments in postwar art—Informel, minimalism, and *arte povera*, which itself spills over into minimalism, conceptual art, and performance art (see Barilli 40–54)—but cannot be inscribed into any of these. His status continues to be treated as a side alley of postwar European late modernism in mainstream post-Greenberg histories and accounts of twentieth century art. Informel, to which Burri was loosely connected, was framed by its chief theorist, Michel Tapié, as an attempt to rethink modernism from the foundations by privileging the material, pre-formed, pre-organized, and the spontaneous, capitalizing Bataille's transgressive *informe*.[7] Informel with its central figure Dubuffet, and to a lesser extent the Roman Gruppo Origine, was also inscribed from the beginning within the philosophical framework of Marxist humanist existentialism,[8] which saw in their practices a verification of humanistic values and a reaffirmation of the artist's control over inchoate material processes. During the second half of the fifties, however, when Burri's work had its first major exhibitions in America, existentialism became enmeshed with Cold War politics and eventually came to be the label passed around for any figurative art.[9]

Burri's revolution coincides with the turning inside out, in the work of Jackson Pollock and Lucio Fontana, of painting as two-dimensional, mimetic window on the inner/outer world. But Burri subjects the painting-object and its illusion of mimetic space to more radical critique than either of the above, and with it, the dogma of the artwork's autonomy and the position of the author as central signifying presence—ultimately, an understanding of art as the extension of the authorial ego, visible in the New York School's residual expressionism and unshaken faith in its self-affirming autographic gesture (Danto 57). In Burri's works, matter protrudes from an ostentatiously inefficient structure, including the material framing of the object-image, often jutting out from the image's abstract space (the series *Gobbi—Hunchbacks*—uses tacks to stretch the canvas or metallic sheet, rendering them three-dimensional); his burlaps (implicitly metaphors of the canvas) are holed, tattered, charred, and stitched from both sides. Burri performs the meta-gesture earlier and in a more embodied, material form than Fontana's *Concetti spaziali* that slash the monochrome, homogeneous canvas, opening the painting's two-dimensional space in violent, aestheticized gestures. In place of Pollock's easel, drippings, paint-throwing—sublimated autograph handlings of the artist as controller, amounting to a celebration of formalism and of the valorization of the peculiarity of the medium[10]—one finds in the *Sacchi* "an adventure of failed form": the collage of stitches, the affirmation of (waste) matter, the tentative lacerations and coagulations of heterogeneous materials on the image.

One way in which the *Sacchi* perform the crisis of modernist painting is by their obstinate referencing of the grid, the utopian structure of Cubism/Constructivism/De Stijl, by shredding it, only to stitch it together—enacting both a "ravaging debasement of Mondrian and a reaffirmation of the Dutch artist's Apollonian control" (Hamilton 45). As Rosalind Krauss argues, the longevity of the grid in visual modernism was guaranteed by the fact that it displays and hides matter, abstracting it into structure, and by extension, by the fact that it hides and in the same act displays the relation, embarrassing in modern thought, between art and spirituality ("Grids" 54). The grid, as a myth of modernist formalism, extends well beyond the chronological confines of prewar modernism and beyond the visual arts, into serial music, Minimalism, and performance (Krauss, "Grids" 64). The emblematic grid has a narrative equivalent in structuralist analysis in the redeployment of a story's sequential elements into spatial relations, and thus acquires a capacity to serve as "a paradigm or model for the antidevelopmental, the antinarrative, the antihistorical" (Krauss, "Grids" 64).

In Burri's case the gesture points in the opposite direction, of violently subverting the (cognitive, aesthetic) structure that is no longer sovereign and toward affirming the primacy of low matter, of detritus, of the finite. The wound, the low, the "thing" becomes the degree zero of plastic art-making, the foundation from where to rethink painting. Burri's alleged surgeon's stitches,[11] read as therapeutic suturing of the wounds of (modernist) painting and of a traumatic history by existentialist-inspired criticism in the 1950s–60s, especially by Fairfield Porter and James Johnson Sweeney, are manifestly botched, often hanging loosely off the frayed edges or hesitantly embroidering areas of intact burlap where they hold nothing together; more than their function, they perform failure. This fact alone shows the limits of reparative humanist readings and commends Burri's inclusion in ethical postwar late modernism, a category where Beckett's texts also belong.

At the same time, Burri's practice is also a performance of an ontological crisis in addition to the epistemological one captured in the fates of the subject-object relation, grounded in Kantian phenomenology, with which Beckett grapples in his 1940s essays on art. Its recasting of collage also suggests an abolishing of figure-ground, object-subject distinctions and a deployment of the (subject's) gaze as one, material object among the other objects, indistinguishable from them, not represented but incorporated. The classical avant-garde collage, according to Krauss's seminal analysis of Picasso's 1912 experiments with newspaper cut-outs, playfully substitutes signs for the illusion of spatial depth, figure and ground—for instance, in having two sides of the same newspaper stand for "figure" and "ground" in the 1912 *Violin*, where "the circulation of the sign produces this very same condition, but semiologically, on the level of the sign: front, solid, shape: behind, transparent, surround" (*The Picasso Papers* 25). With Burri's burlap collages, not only is the painting's plane ripped open, but in abolishing "figure" and "ground," the artwork embodies the failing attempt to set apart these categories and, implicitly, the failure of all attempts to suture the gap between image and world, signifier and signified.

At the same time, Burri's *Sacchi* and collages of other discarded materials also surrender space to the archival memory stored in (waste) matter, to a space of witnessing. These discreet memories of things act as countersignatures, rival repositories of memory and testimony, especially with historically and politically imbricated materials. In addition to rupturing the subject-object relation, Burri's non-gestural artworks also discard conventional expectations of self-expression, the turning of the psychological I into a formed visual image. Revealing in this respect is Burri's 1952 collage *Self-Portrait* [Fondazione Alberto Burri, Città di Castello], whose small dimensions (8x10 cm) contrast with the monumental *Sacchi* from the same year, appearing rather like a collection of fabric samples with different weaves of burlap in infinite regress. In what corresponds to perspectival vanishing point there is a blot of black paint—the sole painterly sign of the image, to stand for the autograph brushwork (see Recalcati 55–58). The image both invites and subverts perspectival interpretation, where perspective presupposes a transcendental position and localizes the spectator's gaze in a continuation of its illusionistic space. *Self-Portrait* performs the disjunction of subject and object, as well as the coalescing of matter and shaped form. It doesn't depict, not even gesturally, while directing an allusive gaze at the onlooker while refusing to accept "the old subject-object relation" ("The New Object" 880). It is neither "I" nor "not-I," both material and disembodied, making its residual subject one with the collage's material objects.

It is instructive to consider late 1940s works of a trial-and-error quality, which preceded the *Sacchi* and the first *Combustioni*, as stages of impoverishment and breaking with formal closure—images that withdraw from a tradition of painting understood as progressive possession of its object that could be fruitfully described as "*malfaçon créatrice voulue*" 'willed creative mismaking' (Beckett, *Disjecta* 122). After the small-dimension series *Neri* of the immediate postwar years, tributary to Dubuffet's experiments with tar but as remote from the latter's residual ideologism and neo-primitivism as from the expressionistic tendencies of the Informel (Wols, Fautrier), Burri starts experimenting with collages.[12] The 1949 *SZ1* opens the way to the *Sacchi*, assembling fragments of burlap labeled with the abbreviations of the food aid destined for Europe as part of the Marshall Plan and fragments of the US flag, in a way that is symptomatic of both breaking with modernist aesthetic principles and reaffirming them. It adheres to the avant-garde form of the collage, distributing heterogeneous materials delineated with thick black contours in a Miróesque arabesque. The shared white painted ground renders the flat, eclectic materials and their structuring outlines "figure," belonging to a common pictorial space that situates the object—the equivalent of a unifying narrative framework; the non-painterly, politically imbricated materials sit uneasily in this formalist composition.

Following on Maurizio Calvesi's observations, Jaimey Hamilton cogently analyzes the materials of the *Sacchi* and *Combustioni–Plastiche*—leftover packaging material of Marshall Plan food aid on which fragments of upholstery are sewn, tatters of a once-flourishing Italian textile and brocard tradition, and the plastic that first arrived in Italy as packaging for US military aircraft and weapon shipments in the 1950s. The political underside of these relief transports was America's "accursed share"—an outlet for domestic overproduction and creating a foreign market for that surplus produce the first step toward the gradual extension of America's economic (and implicitly cultural and pop-cultural) power over Western Europe during the Cold War (Hamilton 46–2). *SZ1* thus prefigures the later *Sacchi*'s exposure of discourses of humanism premised on political economy, the putatively universal subjectivism that underscores existentialist work and thought in this decade. In the same years when Pollock's works are presented in *Vogue* as backdrop of fashion photographs, raising the uncomfortable question of the public use of art in postwar capitalism,[13] the space from which Burri's paintings speak is not that of the abstract utopia, more and more indistinguishable from the triumphalist capitalism of the International Style, to which not only the works of the New York School but also of most of European abstraction, tachisme first and foremost, lend themselves with singular ease. Their space is delineated by the ruins of a utopian political, economic promise—the future grown old.

In 1950 Burri completed *Rosso*: of the same dimensions, featuring a similar distribution of painted surfaces of varying thickness of impasto on a uniform cadmium ground, including the use of pumice and gold leaf, this painting gives up the delimiting contours. In between the small 1948 *Neri*, *SZ1*, and *Rosso* the aesthetics of the *Sacchi* and *Combustioni* aggregates: a gradual relinquishing of formal control with the disappearance of the contours, allowing the different surfaces—brittle, lacerated matter worn off by time—to introduce a note of finitude.

BATHETIC MATERIALITIES

The first of Beckett's four 1946 short stories speaks acutely of Beckett's alternative pitted against *de rigueur* postwar reconstruction optimism and the positive accounts of recasting consciousness by art: a degree zero of the human condition in "this universe become provisional" ("The Capital of the Ruins," *CSP* 278), to be rethought as embodied in the abject, impotent body and in leftover matter, here first in the form of reach-me-downs marking the lineage and progress of dying:

> The clothes [they gave me]—shoes, socks, trousers, shirt, coat, hat—were not new, but the deceased must have been about my size. That is to say, he must have been a little shorter, a little thinner, for the clothes did not fit me so well in the beginning as they did in the end, the shirt especially, and it was many a long day before I could button it at the neck, or profit by the collar that went with it, or pin the tails together between my legs the way my mother had taught me. (*CSP* 78)

As Emilie Morin shows, "The End" is shot through with material references and allusions to the plight of survivors returning from the camps, including a stay at the converted hotel Lutetia and release with clothes and a small sum of money (166–69). One of the castoffs the protagonist receives is a tie whose pattern is suggestive of the US flag imprinted on the packaging of food aid shipped to Europe between 1945–1946, even before the Marshall Plan: "It seemed a pretty tie to me, but I didn't like it . . . It was blue with kinds of little stars" (*CSP* 79). Together with the other objects and garments, especially the bowler—relic of respectability and social conformism caricatured in all Beckett's work and the attribute of the narrator's son, "the insufferable son of a bitch" (87)—the tie subsumes the moralizing, policing discourses of an unspecified "them," at whose mercy the narrator finds himself in a manner that prefigures the Unnamable's predicament of self-utterance. The blank detailing of the narrator's progress toward a *Muselmann*-like state[14] is all the more ethically incisive as it is set in a vaguely post-liberation topography, whose indeterminacy is heightened by repetitive phrases, "The general impression was the same as before" (81).

In addition, the narrative hesitantly meanders in an indefinite time between incongruous locations; Beckett's earlier theoretical preoccupations with the figure-ground relation are paralleled here by the obliteration of the distinction between plot and description (Cohn 129). The story's temporality is not produced by the complex operations of consciousness that expand or contract the time experience, as in high modernist models, but by the impaired body that is subject to the slow disaggregating action of time, resulting in a "weak" narrative form. The body is pervasively assimilated to objects and indifferent (often scatological) matter. Its end, prefiguring the closing affirmation of *The Unnamable*, further exposes the contiguity of matter as bodily discharge and consciousness, as the closing vision is experienced in an act of excretion:

> To contrive a little kingdom, in the midst of the universal muck, then shit on it, ah that was me all over. The excrements were me too, I know, I know, but all the

same. Enough, enough, the next thing I was having visions, I who never did, except sometimes in my sleep, who never had, real visions, I'd remember, except perhaps as a child, my myth will have it so. (*CSP* 98)

The fruitful friction between earlier poststructuralist framings of Beckett and the findings of the archival turn, of posthumanist and new materialist explorations has led to an emphatic rereading of Beckett's text-world as writing where "an ethic that is also a bathetic" takes precedence over aesthetic (Rabaté 158), and as writing that struggles with the ethical and implicitly aesthetic predicament of bearing witness to something Beckett didn't have a first-hand experience of, a situation impossible for testimony.[15] As veteran Beckett director Herbert Blau warns, when Clov speaks of "death" outside, it is "something other than the death of him, something more brutally lethal, the untold numbers dead, not in a text, no text for nothing, but in the brutal material world" (49). Agamben's framing of impossible testimony in *Remnants of Auschwitz*—the survivors' inevitably ethically impaired speaking on behalf of the absent dead who alone could testify—and his theorizing of shame have been adduced to the Beckettian figure of unsayability, the aporia that the Unnamable inhabits and from where the *Texts for Nothing* start ("I can't go on, I must go on, I'll go on"), as alternatives to the exteriorized Blanchotian neuter.[16] Even in their voiding of referents and shredding of narrative functions, Beckett's texts assimilate untenable narrative positions to recurring images of impaired, exterminated bodies and the illegible traces left by the "lost ones" populating them:

> Whose voice, no one's, there is no one, there's a voice without a mouth, and somewhere a kind of hearing, something compelled to hear, and somewhere a hand, it calls that a hand, it wants to make a hand, or if not a hand something somewhere that can leave a trace, of what is made, of what is said, you can't do with less, no, that's romancing, more romancing, there is nothing but a voice murmuring a trace. (*CSP* 152)

As much as the passage dismantles narrativization with its corollaries, the textual projection of a referential world, the conventions of subject, the psychological self, space, time, or memory, the charge of "romancing" levelled at the potentially violent, unethical narrative imposing of a voice also appears an oblique allusion to the (conventional, catharsis-oriented, humanist) fiction taking on the form of testimonial writing, set in the camps, that Cayrol labeled "concentration camp romances" (see Morin 181–182). The impossible narrative position staged in *Texts for Nothing* has an embryonic occurrence already in "The End" in the form of corrosive language skepticism, in the problematic narratorial voice's failing attempts to produce traditional object descriptions: "Only the ground floor windows—no, I can't. The estate seemed abandoned. The gates were locked and the paths were overgrown with grass. Only the ground-floor windows had shutters" (*CSP* 95). This hesitancy enacts not only the failure to differentiate subject and object, where the subjective voice's freedom of utterance is measured on its capacity to control and distribute objects, but also the failure to produce traditional narrative with a humanistic scaffolding. Most incisively of the *Nouvelles*, "The End" exposes the ethical indistinction and continuity of the times before and after its eclipsed event, and the work on language that literature needs to pass through in the wake of Auschwitz, of which Paul Celan speaks: "[language] had to go through its own lack of answers, through terrifying silence, through the thousand darknesses of murderous speech" (34).

The ethical pressure of witnessing cracks open most of the humanist and formalist literary and visual aesthetic proposals and interpretive grids of the 1940s–50s. One of the questions left largely unaddressed by the intellectual debates of the immediate postwar years in which Beckett marginally participated addressed the ethical nature of the relationship between abstraction, the unsayable, and forms of testimony, especially since abstract and non-figurative art in the 1940s became synonymous with the ideology of aesthetic autonomy, seen as the apex of modernism in the Greenberg/Fried narrative; the impact of these pressures is well illustrated by the trajectory of Beckett's close friend and camp survivor Avigdor Arikha, who eventually abandoned abstraction for drawing after life (cf. Lloyd 154–220).

Probably the best illustration of this dilemma was voiced by Francis Ponge, whose Marxist-informed celebration of Braque's art as a valiant recasting of the language of art and through it, of remodeling consciousness Beckett had translated for *Transition* and privately lampooned to Duthuit (see Brazil 38–39). In a preface to Informel artist Jean Fautrier's October 1945 exhibition *Otages* [Hostages] at Galerie Drouin, Ponge voices the uncomfortable question raised by Fautrier's richly allusive paintings—putatively transposing into image the sounds of fusillation and the cries of tortured political prisoners and hostages overheard while hiding from the Gestapo—if painting under the sign of traditional aesthetic enjoyment, producing images of a "serene beauty" (10), is an ethically tolerable artistic response to torture and extermination.[17] Burri's material abstraction makes this very ethical conundrum visible, and embodies the pressure under which formalism is fissured, its totalizing aesthetic and formal closure lacerated.

In several respects Burri's deskilling, use of poor materials sit uneasily with both the residual existentialist humanism of the Informel as theorized by Tapié and best exemplified by Wols and Fautrier, and with those Informel artistic practices that entirely adhere to Bataille's concept of the *informe*. The curt treatment Burri receives in Bois and Krauss's seminal *Formless* testifies to this gap: for them, the *Plastiche* series "demolish[es] the myth of plastic as infinitely transposable substance, as alchemical miracle, by burning it," presenting it as "wholly other," yet eventually amounts to an aestheticizing of "low" matter—structuring and reabsorption by the image being the principal motive why in their judgement most representatives of the Informel fall short of uncompromising fidelity, pitted against the bolder experiments with kitsch and "base" matter of Fontana and Piero Manzoni (*Formless* 58). This ultimately formalist reading covers up the ethical and political stakes of Burri's works from the *Sacchi* onward, glossing over their palimpsestual quality, their polysemic incorporation of an archive of images in their use of "things"—sack-cloth, wood veneer, plastic foil, gold foil, shirts. In this respect they also intersect with the work of memory and the work *on* memory in their staging the effacement by time but also, of what is remembered and how, and how the discreet things themselves construct memories, reverberations and visual echoes across recent historical events and across the history of the visual arts. Burri's incorporated matter is also "re-collection," collected material remnants, the debris of history, which participate in a theatre of memory; these works belong in the same lineage with contemporary artists such as Anselm Kiefer of William Kentridge, whose artworks embody the image as ruin, immersed in, rather than seeking to represent, the ongoing catastrophe of contemporary history. There is a direct line of descent from the shirts incorporated in the monochrome *Two Shirts* (1957) or *Rosso* (1956), to Kiefer's layered assemblage-paintings (cf. Arasse 69–97); Burri's shirts also allude to the unrepresentable by substituting things—clothing, throwaway rags—for the subject, and thus participate in an essentially modernist critique of the power and validity of representation, performing and voiding figuration. By virtue of their paradoxical indeterminacy and overdetermination, these images, as well as the coeval *Sacchi* can short-circuit the meta-gesture of laying bare the "body" of the image, canvas, with food and shortage of it, ingrained in the sack-cloth packaging material, while also empowering a series of interpretations, including a figuration of Franciscan ascesis and political-economic inequality of overproduction vs. devastation.

Burri's *Sacchi*, *Legni*, *Combustioni* stage, embody the thing in time, with the marks and scars of finitude: even the gold leaf applied is consumed with use, in addition to being "wounded" in the course of the creative process. If capturing the object in time by means of painterly techniques was one of the themes Beckett's visual aesthetic obstinately circles in "La Peinture des van Velde," and what du Bouchet and Duthuit saw in(to) Tal Coat's paintings,[18] Burri does it by subjecting his work to the thing's finitude: from the choice of the weathered materials to the modes of their belaboring. The materials of these artworks are things subtracted from the realm of objecthood—that is, from use-value: they are surplus material, non-recuperable waste produced in the course of fulfilling functions of commodification and circulation (packaging), slipping out of the preserve of use.[19] They are what is left behind, exhausted, emptied of human presence and of their use-value, the thing in ruin, which therefore can become a particularly poignant metonymy for the body's endingness, and the ruin as condition in the present. Time is inscribed in their thing-ness, in their passage from sacks to rags, from the miraculously versatile, universally transposable packaging material—plastic—to non-recuperable waste and technological fossil. All the more so since some of the *Combustioni-Plastiche* have trapped insects among their layers. The material can also be concrete as in *Grande Cretto di Gibellina*, Burri's monumental memorial artwork encasing the ruins of the Sicilian town Gibellina, destroyed in a 1968 earthquake. In all these, time literally devoured their fabric, leaving them holed, cracked, charred, chafed thin and fragile, frayed. These are ruins but as Beckett puts it, ruins that nevertheless offer a refuge: "ruins true refuge" ("Lessness," *CSP* 197).

This traumatic treatment to which Burri subjects the modern technological wonder, plastic, and the par excellence modernist building material, concrete, inscribing them with the scars and cracks of the disastrous, irruptive event that coincide with the scars of finitude, suggests a highly critical attitude to the positivity of postwar capitalism and the utopia of modernist architecture. It also exudes a sense of lateness enmeshed with the unsayable that has been framed, in the wake of Adorno, as characteristic of the late modernist sublime, an aesthetics of sublimity at the point of exhaustion that, as Lecia Rosenthal writes, operates with a sense of belatedness that "intermixes with the suspension of totality, closure, and the reassurance of a coming or achieved rupture with the past. The late sublime emerges out of an exhaustion that is not exhaustive, an iterative lessening and draining effect, the repetition of a threat or promise to end, particularly to bring the end of all, a repetition that does not fail to fail to come to fruition" (21).

The distribution of shredded upholstery, gold leaf (richly evocative of a long tradition of devotional painting) and other materials in Burri's *Sacchi* and *Combustioni* show certain similarities with the treatment of textual matter as residue, *caput mortuum* in Beckett's texts, even more than with the thematic investment in errant cast-offs and miscellaneous waste. Like the last remaining possessions of Winnie or the contents of Malone's pockets insightfully analyzed by Julie Bates, such "things" presuppose a work of salvage or gleaning and "provide the means for isolated characters to continue telling themselves stories about their worlds and themselves" (18)—implicitly, ill seen, ill said stories about culture and (visual) tradition. In *Watt*, whose text foregrounds at every step a manuscript stitched together of heterogeneous materials with egregious gaps, the Addenda's miscellaneous textual figments are pronounced rejects by an intrusive authorial footnote: "Only fatigue and disgust prevented [their] incorporation" (Beckett, *Watt* 205). These fragments, ranging from musical scores and multilingual quotes to aborted ekphrastic scenes, resist any possible recuperation within the novel's text, which is thus rendered incomplete.

The obvious model that Beckett's text disassembles is *The Waste Land*, already a target of Beckett's recreative critique in his early poem *Whoroscope*: but whereas Eliot's "heap of broken images" ("The Waste Land" 58) relies on a scaffolding of myth and a practice of renovating tradition, and is pronounced by Eliot's notes a single soliloquy in Tiresias' brain, Beckett's use of Kant or the *Divine Comedy* doesn't allow such aesthetic recuperation into a coherent system. Though "*Parole non ci appulcro*" (*Watt* 205)—Virgil's statement of unwillingness to embellish his words in an Italian superscribed with Latin (*Inferno*, Canto VII.60)—may seem a programmatic refusal to aestheticize the word surface, any attempt to integrate it into however precarious a grid of significances with the other textual figments, noises, and "descant" necessarily founder among the Addenda's resistant gaps. No solace of form or, in Lyotard's terms, nostalgic aesthetic of the sublime compensates for the impossibility of representation, and at no point does any "philosophically informed, religiously underpinned 'cultural unity'" emerge (Davies 112). Fragments of disjointed tradition are treated as detritus, of the same order that litters Beckett's stages from *Happy Days* to the "miscellaneous rubbish" of *Breath*.

The works of Burri, emerging in the aftermath of a disaster seen as continuous, perform a laceration, splintering, ruining of their medium with a radicalness comparable to Beckett's narratricidal texts. In progressively impoverishing painting, stripping it of the vestiges of expressionism, of gesture, in embodying the failure of the attempt at suturing the subject-object relation and at reasserting the sovereignty of structure, his art can be said to perform what Beckett's writings on art in the 1940s called for—"an art unresentful of its insuperable indigence" (*Disjecta* 141).

Notes

1. The van Veldes would in fact have integrated well into the pool of European abstract painters who constituted the bulk of the 1955 MOMA show "The New Decade" where Burri first exhibited in the US, mostly continuous with prewar abstraction, in spite of the statement opening the catalogue, by Jean Bazaine, that the "naïve epithets 'modern' or 'avant-garde'" were merely "signs of a guilty conscience, a need for self-justification" (Ritchie 16).

2. David Cunningham tantalizingly considers Beckett's stance in *Three Dialogues* in the context of Greenberg's nascent (re)definition of modernism, and of Greenberg's and Fried's dilemmas faced with the tendency that seemed to take to its logical extreme their version of the dialectic and self-critical, self-questioning nature of modernism: the post-Abstract Expressionist Minimalism of Frank Stella or Sol LeWitt. This reading implicitly gives a minimalist inflection to Beckett's position in "Three Dialogues" and leaves open the question, whether that aesthetic is essentially formalist (Cunningham 39).

3. Peter Fifield shows how Beckett changed the word "récherche" for "deuil" ("Introduction to Samuel Beckett, 'The New Object,'" 874). In "The New Object," the "search for an object" characterizes the van Veldes' art (878).

4. On the contexts of "Three Dialogues" see Lloyd 87–109; Uhlmann 146–52; Carville 182–213. On Beckett's ethical rejection of André Masson and Bataille see Rabaté 76–91.

5. Jan Greshoff, "Deux peintres hollandais à Paris: A.G. et Gérard van Velde," *La Revue de l'Art* 30 (Jan.-June 1929).

6. Of the artists associated with Burri in different periods, there is only one passing reference to a missed 1965 Rauschenberg exhibition in Beckett's notebooks and letters (*Letters III* 654–655); only Jasper Johns's tangential relation to Burri can be styled up into a nexus of sorts to Beckett.

7. Michel Tapié, *Observations*, 23; cf. Hamilton 35–38. On how Tapié's theorizing and Dubuffet's practice reinstate a structure or pattern, aesthetically sublimate waste and thus contradict Bataille's radical concept of the *informe*, which is characterized precisely by its resistance to conceptual formulations and (epistemological, aesthetic) structuring, see Bois and Krauss, "A User's Guide to Entropy," 47–55.

8. Tapié, "The necessity of an *autre* aesthetic" [1953] (*Observations* 22). Burri participated in the first major international group show that offered an overview of Informel, "The New Decade" (MOMA, 1955). On the politics of the postwar Rome avant-garde circles of Enrico Prampolini and the pressures to address and overcome the pro-Fascist credentials of prewar Italian avant-garde see Celant 2–31 and Vetrocq 20–27.

9. See the description of the groundbreaking 1959 MOMA exhibition, "New Images of Man," in Foster, Kraus, Bois, and Buchloh 421. On the use of European existentialism and American Abstract Expressionism in Cold War cultural diplomacy see Guilbaut and Barnhisel.

10. See T.J. Clark's discussion of the pathos of Pollock's *Number 1* (1948), the first of the thrown paintings that still retains the proportion of easel painting and generates a flatness of the image that becomes, on the edges, consubstantial with the canvas surface, while acting as a foil to Malevich's abstraction, as "high moments of modernism ... when the physical limits of painting are subsumed in a wild metaphysical dance" (310–311).

11. Burri volunteered in the 1935 Abyssinian colonial war, later served as a surgeon in the Libyan campaign, where he lost a brother, was captured by American troops in 1942 and taken to a PoW camp in Hereford, Texas; it was there that he first took up painting on burlap and on his release in 1946, he brought back several of these sacks to Italy. However, as Judith Rozner saliently points out, the stitches used by Burri are actually basic embroidery stitches, such as the running or the mattress stitch (87), their framing as surgeon's stitches being a product of pervasive biographical approaches to Burri's art.

12. The *Neri*, especially the 1948 *Nero* that Burri himself chose to be the opening piece of the permanent collection at the Collezione Burri, Città di Castello, have been interpreted in terms of a lifelong preoccupation with Caravaggio that leads to *Grande Nero Plastica* and its allusiveness to the *Conversion of St. Paul*, and as "a statement of artistic theory": see Calvesi 7; Sarteanesi 29–30; di Capua and Mattarella 19.

13. T.J. Clark draws attention to the "bad dream of modernism" transpiring in the March 1951 fashion photographs for *Vogue*, with Pollock paintings as a backdrop, as well as in the naturalness with which these paintings blend into the Miesian architectural spaces of the International Style: the possibility that the modernist utopia might be, in the Cold War West, "not much more than the idealization of capitalism and its representations" (306).

14. The *Muselmann* was the denomination of those prisoners in the camps who in an extremity of suffering came to a liminal state of living death, beyond human interaction and beyond eliciting others' compassion. Described by Primo Levi and Jean Améry (*Jenseits von Schuld und Sühne* 39), the *Muselmann* is a centrepiece of Agamben's *Remnants of Auschwitz*, "absolute biopolitical substance" (85) and the figure for the lacuna of testimony.

15. Already Adorno reads Beckett's work as a response to the unrepresentable and unassimilable in Auschwitz in "Notes on Beckett." Dominick LaCapra includes Beckett in a tradition of "testimonial art"—a "witing of terrorized disempowerment as close as possible to the experience of traumatized victims without presuming to be identical to it" (*Writing History, Writing Trauma* 105–6). On the historical and political subtexts of Beckett's work see especially Gibson; Morin; McNaughton; Anderton.

16. See Russell Smith's and David Houston Jones's use of Agamben's philosophy of impossible testimony as a fulcrum for reading the voice in Beckett. Smith in particular offers Agamben as an ethical counterpart to Blanchot's and Foucault's theoretical appropriations of the ethics of enunciation in Beckett, since their tendency to overcome the aporias performed by Beckett's texts inevitably reifies the texts' ethical stakes. Blanchot's 'ventriloquistic' model of enunciation in particular offers an exteriorized, undifferentiated, transcendental speech dissociated from the agency of a speaker, thus from enunciation as such: "if there is an occasion but no artist, a representee but no representer, then there can be no 'ferocious dilemma of expression'" (Smith 345).

17. Fautrier's haute-pâte paintings, of an expressionistic style continuous with the painter's prewar genre painting and of an ostentatiously "candy-colour" palette, are framed as a defiant, subversive employment of kitsch in Foster, Krauss, Bois, and Buchloh (341–342).

18. David Hatch shows how the *Dialogues* respond to a critique, published in the same issue of *Transition* 1949, of critic André du Bouchet who celebrates Tal Coat's ability to capture objects in time and that of Masson to have overcome the impediments of expressing the void—a view partly

echoed by "D" in the *Dialogues*, and passionately rejected by "B," along with a whole rhetoric of possession, cognitive/technical mastery, and aesthetic recuperation of the processes of creation and undoing (57–71).

19. See Heidegger's differentiation between "object"—the tool, functional, known and knowable thing, defined through use—and "thing"—the no longer functional object, the object broken down, mostly reduced to waste, in "The Thing." Material studies generally attribute no agency to the discarded object; cf. Steven Connor, "Thinking Things."

Works Cited

Adorno, Theodor. "Notes on Beckett." Translated by Dirk Van Hulle and Shane Weller. *Journal of Beckett Studies*, vol. 19, no. 2, 2010, pp. 157–178.

Agamben, Giorgio. *Remnants of Auschwitz: The Witness and the Archive.* Trans. Daniel Heller-Roazen. Stanford UP, 1998.

Améry, Jean. *Jenseits von Schuld und Sühne.* Klett-Cotta, 2000.

Anderton, Joseph. *Beckett's Creatures: Art of Failure after the Holocaust.* Bloomsbury, 2016.

Barnhisel, Greg. *Cold War Modernists: Art, Literature and American Cultural Diplomacy.* Columbia UP, 2015.

Barilli, Renato. *Informale Oggetto Comportamento. La ricerca artistica negli anni '70.* 3rd ed. Feltrinelli, 2016.

Bates, Julie. *Beckett's Art of Salvage: Writing and Material Imagination, 1932–1987.* Cambridge UP, 2017.

Beckett, Samuel. *The Complete Short Prose: 1929–1989.* Edited and Introduction by S.E. Gontarski. Grove, 1995. Cited as *CSP*.

———. *Disjecta. Miscellaneous Writings and a Dramatic Fragment.* Edited by Ruby Cohn. Grove Press, 1984.

———. *The Letters of Samuel Beckett. Volume II: 1941–1956.* Edited by George Craig, Martha Dow Fehsenfeld, Dan Gunn, and Lois More Overbeck. Cambridge UP, 2011.

———. "The New Object." *Modernism/modernity*, vol. 18, no. 4, Nov. 2011, pp. 878–880.

———. *The Unnamable.* Edited and Introduction by Steven Connor. Faber and Faber, 2010.

———. *Watt.* Grove, 2003.

Blanchot, Maurice. *The Step Not Beyond.* Translated by Lycette Nelson. SUNY P, 1992.

Blau, Herbert. "Apnea and True Illusion: Breath(less) in Beckett." *Beckett at 100. Revolving It All.* Edited by Linda Ben-Zvi and Angela Moorjani. Oxford UP, 2008. 35–53.

Bois, Yves-Alain and Rosalind E. Krauss. *Formless: A User's Guide.* Zone, 1997.

———. "A User's Guide to Entropy." *October*, vol. 78, Autumn 1996, pp. 38–88.

Braun, Emily, Megan Fontanella, and Carol Stringari. *Alberto Burri: The Trauma of Painting.* Guggenheim Museum Publications, 2015.

Brazil, Kevin. *Art, History, and Postwar Fiction.* Oxford UP, 2018.

Calvesi, Maurizio. *Alberto Burri.* Fabbri, 1971.

Carville, Conor. *Samuel Beckett and the Visual Arts.* Cambridge UP, 2018.

Cayrol, Jean. "D'un Romanesque concentrationnaire," *Esprit*, vol. 159, September 1949, p. 535.

Celan, Paul. "Speech on the Occasion of Receiving the Literature Prize of the Free Hanseatic City of Bremen." *Collected Prose*. Translated by Rosmarie Waldrop. Sheep Meadow P, 1986, pp. 33–36.

Celant, Germano. "In Total Freedom: Italian Art, 1943–1968." *The Italian Metamorphoses, 1943–1960*, edited by Germano Celant. Guggenheim Museum, 1995, pp. 2–31.

Clark, T.J. *Farewell to an Idea: Episodes from a History of Modernism*. Yale UP, 1999.

Cohn, Ruby. *A Beckett Canon*. U of Michigan P, 2002.

Connor, Steven. *Beckett, Modernism and the Material Imagination*. Cambridge UP, 2014.

Connor, Steven. "'On such and such a day . . . in such a world': Beckett's radical finitude." *Borderless Beckett/Beckett sans frontières: Samuel Beckett Today/Aujourd'hui* 19. Edited by Minako Okamuro et al. Rodopi, 2008, pp. 36–50.

Connor, Steven. "Thinking Things." *Essays at Cultural Phenomenology* (2009), www.stevenconnor.com/thinkingthings/ thinkingthings.pdf.

Cunningham, David. "Ex Minimis. Greenberg, Modernism and Beckett's *Three Dialogues*." *Samuel Beckett Today / Aujourd'hui*. vol. 13, 2003, pp/ 29–41.

Danto, Arthur C. *The Wake of Art. Criticism, Philosophy, and the Ends of Taste*. Edited and Introduction by Gregg Horowitz. Tom Huhn. G&B, 1998.

Davies, William. "'A new occasion, a new term of relation': Samuel Beckett and T.S. Eliot." *Beckett and Modernism*, edited Olga Beloborodova, Dirk Van Hulle, and Pim Verhulst. Palgrave Macmillan, 2018, pp. 111–128.

di Capua, Marco, and Lea Mattarella. "Palazzo Albizzini." *Fondazione Burri*, edited by Chiara Sarteanesi. Skira, 1999, pp. 17–73.

Eliot, T.S. "The Waste Land." *The Annotated Waste Land, with Eliot's Contemporary Prose*. Edited by Lawrence Rainey. Yale UP, 2005., pp. 57–74.

Fifield, Peter. "Introduction to Samuel Beckett, 'The New Object.'" *Modernism/modernity*, vol. 18, no. 4, 2011, pp. 873–877.

———. *Late Modernist Style in Samuel Beckett and Emmanuel Levinas*. Palgrave, 2013.

Foster, Hal, Rosalind E. Krauss, Yves-Alain Bois, and Benjamin Buchloh. *Art Since 1900: Modernism, Antimodernism, Postmodernism*. Thames & Hudson, 2004.

Gibson, Andrew. *Samuel Beckett*. 2010. Reaction, 2013.

Gontarski, S.E., editor. *The Edinburgh Companion to Samuel Beckett and the Arts*. Edinburgh UP, 2014.

Greenberg, Clement. "L'Art américain du XXe siècle," *Les Temps Modernes* vol. 2, no. 11–12, Aug.-Sept. 1946, p. 350.

Guardamagna, Daniela, and Rossana M. Sebellin, editors. *The Tragic Comedy of Samuel Beckett*. U of Rome Press OnLine, 2009.

Guilbaut, Serge. *How New York Stole the Idea of Modern Art: Abstract Expressionism, Freedom, and the Cold War*. Translated by Arthur Goldhammer. U of Chicago P, 1983.

Hamilton, Jaimey. "Making Art Matter: Alberto Burri's *Sacchi*." *October*, vol. 124, Spring 2008, pp. 31–52.

Hatch, David. "'I am mistaken': Surface and Subtext in Samuel Beckett's *Three Dialogues*." *Samuel Beckett Today / Aujourd'hui*, vol. 13, 2003, pp. 57–71.

Heidegger, Martin. "The Thing." *Poetry, Language, Thought*. Translated by Albert Hofstadter. Harper & Row, 1971, pp. 161–184.

Jones, David Houston. "From Contumacy to Shame. Reading Beckett's Testimonies with Agamben." *Beckett at 100. Revolving It All*, edited by LindaBen-Zvi and Angela Moorjani. Oxford UP, 2008, pp. 54–67.

Krauss, Rosalind E. "Grids," *October*, vol. 9, Summer 1979, pp. 50–64.

———. *The Picasso Papers*. Farrar, Strauss and Giroux, 1998.

LaCapra, Dominick. *Writing History, Writing Trauma*, rev. ed. Johns Hopkins UP, 2014.

Levi, Primo. *Se questo è un uomo*. Einaudi, 2014.

Lloyd, David. *Beckett's Thing: Painting and Theatre*. Edinburgh UP, 2018.

McNaughton, James. *Samuel Beckett and the Politics of Aftermath*. Oxford UP, 2018.

Morin, Emilie. *Beckett's Political Imagination*. Cambridge UP, 2017.

Okamuro, Minako, Naoya Mori, Bruno Clément, Sjef Houppermans, Anjela Moorjani and Anthony Uhlmann, editors. *Borderless Beckett/Beckett sans frontières. Samuel Beckett Today/Aujourd'hui*, vol. 19. Rodopi, 2008.

Oppenheim, Lois. *The Painted Word. Samuel Beckett's Dialogue with Art*. U of Michigan P, 2000.

Ponge, Francis. "Notes sur les *Otages*." *L'Atelier contemporain*. Paris: Gallimard, 1977. Reprinted in «Le Peintre à l'étude», *Œuvres complètes*, vol. I, by Francis Ponge, edited by B. Beugnot. Bibliothèque de la Pléiade, 1999, pp. 98–100.

Porter, Fairfield. "Alberto Burri." *Art News*, vol. 52, no. 8, December 1953. pp. 40–41.

Rabaté, Jean-Michel. *Think, Pig! Beckett at the Limit of the Human*. Fordham UP, 2016.

Recalcati, Massimo. *Il mistero delle cose. Nove ritratti di artisti*. Feltrinelli, 2016.

Ritchie, Andrew Carnduff, editor. *The New Decade: 22 European Painters and Sculptors*. With statements by the artists. MOMA, 1955.

Rosenthal, Lecia. *Mourning Modernism. Literature, Catastrophe, and the Politics of Consolation*. Fordham UP, 2011.

Rozner, Judith. "Alberto Burri: The Art of the Matter." PhD thesis. University of Melbourne, 2015. https://minervaaccess.unimelb.edu.au/bitstream/handle/11343/54617/W1,%20Volume%201%20-%20BurriThesis-Final.pdf.

Sarteanesi, Nemo. "Una visita guidata alla collezione Burri." *La Collezione Burri*. Edited by G. Bonomi. Gesp, 1995.

Serafini, Giuliano. *Burri. Art Dossier* 62. Giunti, 1991.

Smith, Russell. "'The acute and increasing anxiety of the relation itself': Beckett, the Author-Function, and the Ethics of Enunciation." *"All Sturm and No Drang": Beckett and Romanticism. Samuel Beckett Today/Aujourd'hui*, vol. 18, edited by Dirk Van Hulle and Mark Nixon. Rodopi, 2007, pp. 341–353.

Sweeney, James Johnson. *Alberto Burri*. Galleria Obelisco, 1955.

Tapié, Michel. *Observations*. Edited and translated by Paul and Esther Jenkins. George Wittenborn, 1956.

Uhlmann, Anthony. "Beckett, Duthuit and Ongoing Dialogue." *The Edinburgh Companion to Samuel Beckett and the Arts*, edited by S.E. Gontarski. Edinburgh UP, 2014, pp. 146–152.

Vetrocq, Marcia E. "Painting and Beyond: Recovery and Regeneration, 1943–1952." *The Italian Metamorphoses, 1943–1960*, edited by Germano Celant. Guggenheim Museum, 1995, pp. 20–31.

Erika Mihálycsa teaches modern and contemporary British and Irish literature at Babeș-Bolyai University, Cluj. Author of the monograph *"A wretchedness to defend": Reading Beckett's Letters* (2022), with Jolanta Wawrzyczka she co-edited *Retranslating Joyce for the 21st Century* (2020) and, with Carmen Borbély and Petronia Petrar, *Temporalities of Modernism* (2022). She edited Rareș Moldovan's new, annotated Romanian translation of Joyce's *Ulysses* (2023) and has translated works by Beckett, Flann O'Brien, Patrick McCabe into Hungarian, and a handful of modern and contemporary Hungarian authors into English.

8 Beckett, War Memory, and the State of Exception

Emilie Morin

Many things bear Samuel Beckett's name or have been adorned with his portrait. The world has seen Beckett beer bottles, Beckett coins, and Beckett stamps come and go, as well as a Beckett bar and a Beckett gastro-pub, Beckett boots and luxury bags, a Beckett public square, a Beckett bridge, and, last but not least, a ship: the Irish military vessel LÉ Samuel Beckett. At the ship's naming and commissioning ceremony in 2014, Taoiseach Enda Kenny paid tribute to Beckett's life choices and the military honors he had received for his involvement with the French Resistance. "I want to remember Samuel Beckett," Kenny said, "not just the literary and dramatic genius but the uncompromising man whose insight into life and his decisions in how to live it are so instructive for us today and always" (Kenny). Since then, the rescue and humanitarian missions conducted by the LÉ Samuel Beckett in the Mediterrean Sea have been described in some detail in the press, along with its state-of-the-art military equipment, its deployment at international arms fairs, its recent services to the *Star Wars* film cycle, and its interior decoration, which includes a photograph of Beckett in a Parisian café.

Like the decision to name a Dublin bridge after Beckett, this episode was met with a mixture of amusement and irritation, particularly in Ireland. Fintan O'Toole, notably, has marvelled at the irony of naming the ship after "one of the greatest enemies corporate culture has ever had" (12). The response of the Beckett Estate to the tribute was warm and appreciative, contrasting with the virulent opposition manifested by Stephen Joyce to the naming of the LÉ James Joyce (a "disingenuous and presumptuous" idea, he wrote to Alan Shatter, the parliamentarian who had issued the initial proposals) (McCarthy 7). For Shatter, the ship naming campaign, which diverged from the custom of using Irish mythological female figures, was a diplomatic enterprise that would "facilitate greater recognition for [Irish] naval services when they visit foreign ports" (McCarthy 7).

It is difficult to know what to make of this tribute to Beckett. Indeed, few writers have scrutinized states of suspension and aftermath as closely, and few writers have granted to political history and political symbols such direct and immediate articulations. We might also wonder what the refugees who have boarded the LÉ Samuel Beckett have made of this: under what circumstances can a connection between a military ship and a famous exile who only ever wrote about suffering and waiting become comforting, or indeed appropriate? Nonetheless, the anecdote illustrates the ways in which Beckett's name, life, and work remain tied to war and emergency, and to protean and confused forms of political memory. To those who have been forcibly displaced, or seen their rights threatened or withdrawn, Beckett's writing portrays situations that are all too recognizable and concrete. The coordinates—ruins, ashes, mud, and stones—deployed in many of his texts are not simply the coordinates of terror, suffering, and devastation, but remnants of a type of warfare that resonates with conflicts past and present. Just like the author, the work wears its political knowledge lightly. Yet it stands firmly on the side of the powerless and is borne out of a deep awareness of what happens in situations of emergency in their dual sense: when one's life is under threat, and when the law has been lawfully suspended.

In what follows, I evaluate what Beckett's postwar work owes to the memories and legacies of military states of emergency, to the aftermaths of the law's legal abrogation, and to those situations that arise when state powers are no longer answerable to the customary rule of law. The type of political situation that Beckett pondered most consistently and fully over the course of his career, I argue, remains connected to the state of exception—what Giorgio Agamben defines as the locus not of an execution of the law, but of its undecidability and inexecution. In his influential book, *State of Exception*, Agamben sketches the contours of a modern history that coincides with the history of martial law, rule by decree, and states of emergency, states of siege, and states of war. This history, in turn, is deeply pertinent to Beckett's own political knowledge and experiences. As I demonstrate here, the Beckett writing to and within states of emergency is a compelling thinker of power and subjugation, and has few affinities with the lonely prophet of doom commonly proffered by modern literary studies. His texts, strewn with bodies trapped in, swallowed by, and choking on political symbols, nurture a relation to political history that becomes strikingly literal once considered against the long history of states of exception.

Agamben certainly points us in this direction when he summons Beckett in his recent book *Means Without End*, in which he returns to ideas central to *State of Exception*. Power, he argues, "no longer has today any form of legitimization other than an emergency, and [...] power everywhere and continuously refers and appeals to emergency as well as laboring secretly to produce it" (Agamben, *Means* 5). In this sequel, Agamben seeks "genuinely political paradigms" in commonly depoliticized experiences and phenomena extending to the sphere of pure gesture (ix). This endeavor leads him to conclude that politics "*is the sphere of pure means, that is, of the absolute and complete gesturality of human beings*" (59; emphasis in original). Beckett briefly enters into this reflection: for Agamben, a capacity for political emancipation surfaces, and new configurations of politics become possible, when a literary text—and the few texts he cites include Beckett's television play *Nacht und Träume*—offers a synthesis of the literal and the experiential (55).

The kind of emancipation that Beckett's work might ignite, however, remains murky, here as elsewhere. Theodor Adorno gave a compelling articulation to this problem in *Negative Dialectics*, where he described the "fissure of inconsistency" between Beckett's emphasis on "a lifelong death penalty" and his "only dawning hope [...] that there will be nothing any more" (380-1). The "legacy of action" that Adorno discerns in Beckett's "image world of nothingness as something" is defined in powerful terms, pertinent to the subject of this article—as "a carrying-on which seems stoical but is full of inaudible cries that things should be different" (381).

In the definition that Agamben offers in *State of Exception*, the state of exception encompasses a wide range of situations closely tied to "civil war, insurrection, and resistance" (2). The state of exception is also "the legal form of what cannot have legal form"—a legal state that lies at the limits of political fact and public law itself, and at the same time "binds [and] abandons the living being to law" (1). Agamben's commentary owes much to Théodore Reinach's 1885 study of the French state of siege, which highlights the significance of emergency legislation to a broader legal system. For Reinach, the exceptional measures that enable the proclamation of the *état de siège* are the public law equivalent of legitimate defense and derive from "a principle anterior and superior" to all other legislation (Reinach 7). Bringing Reinach's views in dialogue with arguments advanced by Walter Benjamin and Carl Schmitt, Agamben outlines a space located at the boundary of the law and at the boundary of life, "the no-man's-land between public law and political fact, and between the juridical order and life" (*State* 1).

In different terms, Walter Benjamin and Hannah Arendt have also pointed to the enduring significance of emergency law. For Benjamin, the state of emergency is the constitutional state that became "not the exception but the rule" in the long "tradition of the oppressed" culminating in pre-war Nazi Germany; in order to be effective, he argues, the struggle against fascism must create a "real" state of emergency and free itself from aghast naivety and amazement (257). The state of emergency marks the moment at which, for Arendt, "thinking ceases to be a marginal affair" and gains its true moral and political significance (445). "When everybody is swept away unthinkingly by what everybody else does and believes in," she observes, "those who think are drawn out of hiding because their refusal to join is conspicuous and thereby becomes a kind of action" (445-6).

These observations resonate with many of Beckett's own experiences and recollections, and with many facets of his writing practice. There are few degrees of verbal and physical violence, and few forms of subjugation and suffering, that do not find representation in Beckett's texts, just as there are few states of being that do not chime in some way with a suspension of the law. The state imagined by Beckett is not lawless, but suffers simultaneously from an excess of the laws regulating customary practice and from their sudden suspension. Even Beckett's early hero Belacqua—the archetype of political complacency—has internalized the terminology of emergency: in *More Pricks Than Kicks*, he refers to his carefully-orchestrated walks around Dublin as "raids" (44). Later texts present characters haunted by visions of lynchings, trials, long sentences, and mass graves. "I wasted my time, abjured my rights, suffered for nothing," says the narrator of *The Unnamable* (308). Here as elsewhere, the French text is richer in political dread than its English counterpart and mentions a botched prison sentence or a forced labor sentence: "j'ai perdu mon temps, renié mes droits, *raté ma peine*" (32; emphasis added), which translates literally as 'I have wasted my time, abjured my rights, made a mess of my sentence.' There are similar episodes in *Malone Dies*, *Mercier et Camier*, and "Suite," as well as in *En attendant Godot*, *Fin de partie*, and their English counterparts. These works diffusely recall border zones, battlefields, penal colonies, and internment camps, and feature characters who seem to know much about homelessness, displacement, and survival—those circumstances when a suitcase is also the promise of a lifeline.

It is rare to glimpse the shadow of common law in Beckett's work: all too often, the law has been replaced by a hodgepodge of archaic rules and authoritarian practices that are as powerful as they are absurd. An emblematic episode in *Molloy* involving Molloy's negotiations with a police officer reveals a law that fulfils many functions, none of which have anything to do with protection or justice. Agreeing to dismount one's bicycle when entering a town, as the law requires, does not mean that one can rest on the handlebars, for example. The police officer who arrests Molloy explains that "[his] way of resting, [his] attitude when at rest, [...] [his] head on [his] arms, was a violation of [...] public order, public decency" (20). Physical limitations mean nothing: indeed, "there are not two laws, [...] one for the healthy, another for the sick, but one only to which all must bow, rich and poor, young and old, happy and sad" (20). Molloy's brief stay at a police station featuring a gallery of lawyers, policemen, priests, and journalists offers further insights into a law misapplied and misappropriated. Anything, particularly summary execution, is possible at any moment, and Molloy feels "trapped" and "visible," at the mercy of forces that are continually making and remaking their own laws: "All these righteous ones, these guardians of the peace, all these feet and hands, stamping, clutching, clenched in vain, these bawling mouths that never bawl out of season" (35).

In *En attendant Godot*, Estragon's question—"We've lost our rights?"—and Vladimir's answer—"We got rid of them" (20)—mark one of the many points at which the familiar predicament of Beckett's characters, with nowhere to go and little to remember beyond faint memories of a past or continuing "combat," becomes indexed to a multiplicity of possible and confusedly familiar situations (9). Read along the grain of its "inaudible cries that things should be different," to borrow Adorno's phrase (381), the postwar work offers a startling reflection on the relation between political passivity and political awareness, which chimes with philosophical preoccupations prevalent at the time of its writing.

These subjects are central to Karl Jaspers's controversial study of guilt, *Die Schuldfrage* (published in French translation by the Editions de Minuit in 1948, the year after its German publication). The philosophical and political ramifications of guilt, for Jaspers, are tied to the new emergency military government established by the Allied forces, which renders the possibility of a return of democracy in Germany as a distant prospect. Distress and failure—concepts that Beckett scrutinized closely—rank high in Jaspers's investigation. Noting that most people only understand the kind of distress that affects them personally, Jaspers warns against the extreme social divisions that have arisen in the war's aftermath and calls for a better recognition of distress and failure as key forces within the body politic. He differentiates between the many criminal, political, moral, and metaphysical forms that guilt can take, and asks all German citizens to recognize the part that they have played in supporting Nazism. "No one is guiltless," he warns (16). His arguments resonated with those advanced by others such as Martin Niemöller, whose celebrated song of resistance, popularized later, summarizes all too well the consequences of failing to stand up for the socialists, the trade unionists, and the Jews: finding that there is no one left to stand up in one's defense when one's turn comes.

Beckett was probably aware of Jaspers's work from an early point: during the late 1940s and early 1950s, their work was published in the same three French periodicals: *Fontaine*, *Deucalion*, and *Les Temps Modernes*. There are many affinities between Jaspers's reflection on the political experience of ordinary citizens and the characteristic mixture of passivity, cowardice, small-scale courage, and fortitude displayed by many of Beckett's characters. Notably, Moran—who perceives himself as "the faithful servant [...] of a cause that is not [his]" (*Three Novels* 132)—is one of many narrators who are complicit with the indescribable state of affairs that reduces others to fearful servitude and possibly death. He attends to mysterious missions that include "see[ing] about" Molloy (*Three Novels* 92)—or, in the French text, "*s'occuper*" (*Molloy* 125) ('taking care of,' suggesting an assassination or some form of brutality)—and he describes these tasks as mere attempts to follow the "reasonings and decrees" issued by a voice that "exhorts [him] to continue to the end" (*Three Novels* 132). Affirming his readiness to follow orders, he vouches to continue even if "the whole world, through the channel of its innumerable authorities speaking with one accord, should enjoin upon me this and that, under pain of unspeakable punishments" (132).

Beckett knew much—more than most—about the laws and constitutional amendments through which governments have administered colonial rule, war, the aftermaths of war, and challenges to sovereignty, and he was intimately aware that states of emergency bring mass arrests, forced internment, and detention camps. Notably, a petition he endorsed in the early 1980s against Jaruzelski's proclamation of martial law in Poland and the detention of political dissenters was phrased as a proclamation of solidarity with dissenters and civilian victims in a time of fear, uncertainty, and threat ("Appel"). His own exposure to war and conflict was unusually extensive for someone of his privileged social class, and made accessible to him a direct political knowledge that few of his contemporaries shared.

The rhythms of his writing were often attuned to the rhythm of political history: in late 1946, for example, the "siege in the room"—the phrase he used to designate the period of prolific writing that began in the war's aftermath—replaced life under the wartime state of siege, just as a new French Constitution celebrated "the victory won by free peoples over the regimes that have attempted to reduce to servitude and degrade human beings" ("Préambule"). Even the earliest first-hand accounts of Beckett's artistic ambitions collected during the 1960s (which overwhelmingly present metaphysics as his principal preoccupation) tentatively suggest a political knowledge that exceeds the limits of common experience. In the magazine *Encore*, Charles Marowitz admitted that he had found himself "frightened in [Beckett's] presence as [he] might be in the presence of a man who came within a hairsbreadth of death and survived" (43). Likewise, in the *New York Herald Tribune*, John Gruen did not linger on his impressions but described Beckett as a "somewhat terrifying," "constrained and diffident" figure (31).

Beckett's life and travels exposed him to different types of emergency legislation—for example, to the effects of the Irish Emergency when he returned to Ireland in 1945 and 1946 and, during the following decade, to the emergency legislation passed to curb the colonial war spreading across Algeria and France. During the 1930s and early 1940s, those whose status, nationality, and belongings came under threat in Nazi Germany and in occupied Paris included some of Beckett's relatives, friends, and acquaintances—in particular, his Jewish uncle, William "Boss" Sinclair and his family; Lucie Léon, the Russian-born wife of James Joyce's collaborator Paul Léon, who spent much of her adult life categorized as "stateless"; and the Jewish artists Jankel Adler and Otto Freundlich, whom Beckett had met in Paris prior to the war (Morin 73, 52, 159).

Emergency law was for him a political reality from a young age: his school years coincided with the deployment of the 1914 and 1915 Defence of the Realm Acts, which granted to the British military the power to arrest, detain, try in military courts, and execute Irish civilians perceived as a threat (Campbell 8-27). From his childhood, he remembered "the unhappiness" and "the troubles" (Knowlson 20-1) that made it necessary to "get [...] away" to school in Enniskillen (Gordon 10). Lois Gordon emphasized Beckett's proximity to the political events that shaped the modern Irish state, remarking on his likely political literacy from an early age (7-31), while W.J. McCormack stressed that Beckett entered Portora Royal School when unilateral partition was imposed, and that he traveled between Enniskillen and Dublin during the worst times of the Irish War of Independence and the Irish Civil War (380). Later, these events became enshrined in literary records with which Beckett was familiar: Ernie O'Malley, with whom be became friends in the mid-1930s, published in the Spring of 1936 a memoir entitled *On Another Man's Wound* (his friendship with Beckett seems to have begun shortly after the book's publication). In this highly significant book (Morton 46), O'Malley offers a detailed portrayal of the state of exception, describing the curfews, night raids, armed patrols, torture, interrogation, hunger strikes, public meetings, and demonstrations, as well as the dangers that came from using certain words or whistling certain tunes.

Beckett's journey through Nazi Germany in 1936 and 1937, widely perceived as a turning point in his adult life, marked another moment at which he was exposed to lives spent under the shadow of unrepealed emergency legislation. The Germany where he was once fined for wandering in a "dangerous fashion," as he reported (*Letters 1* 394-5), was a country where civil rights had been suspended since the 1933 emergency Decree for the Protection of People and State. He records indirect responses to this state of affairs in the diaries he kept of his journey. While pondering a sort of memoir, for example, he entertained the prospect of writing an article about Hamburg's Ohlsdorf cemetery, in a "cold elegiac" tone bearing similarities with the Code Napoléon (Nixon 113)—the legal text that defines the modalities according to which French nationality and civic rights can be enjoyed and withdrawn. While in Germany, he had numerous conversations about the dangers of Nazism. His interlocutors included the art historian Will Grohmann, whom he met in Dresden, and who offered his own poignant observations: "it is more *interesting* to stay than to go, even if it were feasible to go. They can't control *thoughts*" (qtd. in Nixon 139; emphasis in original).

The idea that even in the most oppressive and terrifying circumstances, something in the human spirit remains free and indomitable haunts many of Beckett's later texts, and chimes with reflections offered by others. Hans Magnus Enzensberger (whose early political essays Beckett deeply appreciated) argues that, while there have been many kinds of totalitarian societies, "there are no societies of total control. [...] Some little worlds, some little niches subsist. This came true under Nazism and in Stalin's USSR. There is always a space in which one is able to maintain a certain dignity and is not obliged to capitulate, without becoming a hero" (qtd. in Semo 3; my translation). Beckett, for his part, appears to have been fascinated by figures whose repertoire supports such a proposition—for example, the clowns Bim and Bom, whose act endured from the late tsarist period through to the late Stalinist years.

The manner in which Beckett's work invokes the darker side of history is so prevalent that it has become common to see him feature alongside Kafka in discussions of the capacity of literature to reflect on, and sometimes anticipate, regimes of exception. The predilection that Adorno, for example, expressed for Beckett and Kafka comes across strongly in his reflections on Nazism and authoritarian rule. Beckett's writing held similar significance for a lesser-known figure: Charlotte Beradt, one of Arendt's postwar friends, who published in the 1960s a remarkable collection of dreams collected in Berlin between 1933 and 1939, at a time when she was affiliated with the German Communist Party. Beradt discerned important truths in the dreams of ordinary Germans. At the other end of the political spectrum, others felt the same: Robert Ley, the Nazi-era leader of the German Labor Front whom she cites in her epigraph, once stated that "The only person in Germany who still leads a private life is the person who sleeps" (qtd. in Beradt 8). Beckett emerges in her study as a writer who, like Kafka, displays unusual intuition and gives uncanny forms to the political nightmares experienced by others. Notably, Beradt relates the words of a Jewish lawyer who once dreamt that he was sitting on a yellow bench reserved for

Jews next to a rubbish bin in Berlin's Tiergarten Park, and that he had put a sign around his neck that read, "I Make Room for Trash If Need Be" (134-5). For Beradt, this dream chimes with the situation portrayed in *Endgame*, with its characters already trapped in bins, who have lost everything except their physical place in the world (135). One wonders what Beradt would have made of *Eleutheria*—Beckett's first full-length play, published posthumously—where Victor Krap's nightmare ("towers ... circumcised ... fire ... fire ...") functions as a prelude to his denunciation of the passivity displayed by all those who "come across an infinite number of mysteries every day, and [...] pass by on the other side," greeting with horror, pity, and relief any "solution which is not that of death" (144-5).

It is not in Nazi Germany but in wartime France, split between a German-occupied zone and a 'free' zone administered by the Vichy regime and controlled by a fiercely anti-republican far right, that Beckett was most directly exposed to the realities of emergency law. The state of siege—proclaimed from September 1939 to October 1945—provided legal frameworks for a succession of regimes: for the 'phoney war' of 1939-1940, for the Vichy government headed by Philippe Pétain and Pierre Laval, and for Charles de Gaulle's Provisional Government (Simonin 365-90). The moments at which Beckett used the privileges conferred by his Irish passport to assist others and serve resistance cells are well known. He occasionally found himself in some difficulty—particularly after crossing the demarcation line in September 1942 (the 'free' zone was to remain under the control of the Vichy regime for only another month before passing into German hands). He sought refuge in the Vaucluse region, in a village called Roussillon; he was suspected of having forged papers, his movements were restricted to the village and its surrounding area, and he was fined for crossing the demarcation line illegally. His difficulties with the local authorities continued the following year. What little remains of his wartime correspondence conveys the manner in which he was both exposed to and preserved from the anti-Semitic and xenophobic logic of the Vichy regime. "They can't believe that I can be called Samuel and am not a Jew," he wrote to the First Secretary of the Irish Legation in Vichy (*Letters 2* xvii).

Emergency law throughout this period had an extraordinary reach and an extraordinary constitutional brutality. In July 1940, the state of siege made it possible for Pétain to replace republican proclamations of liberty, equality, and fraternity with "the rights of work, family, and fatherland," and to pass constitutional legislation transferring to himself as head of state all executive powers formerly assumed by the Chambers of Parliament, paving the way for the suppression of parliamentary powers (Azéma 152-79). The powers ordinarily exercised by civil authorities were transferred to the army, and numerous measures were taken as part of Pétain's National Revolution to reshape the fabric of the state beyond the realms of justice and public order. Four years later, in August 1944, the state of siege enabled de Gaulle to re-establish the French Republic, to declare as void all the constitutional acts and legislation passed after July 1940, and, thereafter, to categorize as ineligible to public office any parliamentarian who had previously passed Pétain's constitutional amendments ("Ordonnance du 9 août 1944"; "Ordonnance du 20 novembre 1944").

The texts Beckett composed in the war's immediate aftermath feature historical details recalling the extended period covered by the state of siege. Mercier and Camier's journey, for example, begins with an altercation involving a veteran of the Great War, who has been appointed by a mysterious body to implement law and order around the parking of bicycles and the ownership of dogs (unlike the episode relating Molloy's arrest, bicycle rules are not invoked clearly). The French original lingers on the encounter, but the episode is abbreviated in the English version. In the French text, Mercier and Camier are all too aware that the dogs mating nearby contravene a specific decree, if not the law as a whole, like the locked bicycle that can't be moved (*"Ils contreviennent à l'arrêté, dit Mercier, au même titre que la petite reine"* [*Mercier et Camier* 20-1]; 'they breach the decree, said Mercier, in the same way as the bicycle'). The identity of the *"gardien"*—a "ranger" in the English text—is unmistakable: he is there to keep watch, threaten, and denounce. Everything about his manner, outfit, and obsessions suggests a satire of the laws and constitutional amendments through which Pétain sought to implement his National Revolution. War veterans were at the forefront of Pétain's agenda: notably, a 1940 decree instating a new *Légion Française des Combattants* (French Legion of Combatants), and dissolving all previous veterans' associations, conferred a range of civic, social, and moral roles upon a new federation gathering veterans of the Great War and of the 1939-1940 war (*"Loi portant création"*). The legion, which was deployed across the Vichy zone and banned from the German-occupied zone, soon gave rise to another corps, the *Service d'Ordre Légionnaire* (the Legion's Order Service), conceived to act as "the Marshal's eyes and mouth" (Ferro 224-46). Beckett's characters mock the veteran's credentials, recalling the time when he was "crawling in the Flanders mud, shitting in his puttees. […] Will you look at that clatter of decorations, said Mercier. Do you realise the gallons of diarrhoea that represents?" (16).

The memory of war, in Beckett's work, is the memory of states of exception; it is also the memory of the symbols through which states have claimed their power to abrogate the law. The texts written and translated over the course of the Algerian War of Independence (1954-1962) are the most striking in this respect, and feature numerous details invoking the emergency politics of the *raison d'état* that shaped perceptions of legality and sovereignty throughout this period. The state of emergency, first declared in Algeria in 1955, was framed as applicable to metropolitan territory as well, building on prior war legislation created in 1938. Emergency law gave public authorities the power to control public spaces and movement—in practice, this permitted them to orchestrate the mass internment of civilians, declare a curfew, create special security zones, assign people considered as "suspects" to their residence, forbid any meetings in public places including bars and cafés; and, last but not least, to "take all measures necessary to keep control" over publications, the press, radiophonic broadcasts, cinematic projections, and dramatic performances ("Loi no. 55-385"). The following year, another decree extended powers of censorship to "all means of expression," as part of a body of "exceptional measures" giving "special powers" to the government and the army in order to maintain public order and "safeguard" the national territory in Algeria ("Décret no. 56-274").

Initially, the state of emergency was only applied for a few months; however, the "special powers" remained in force throughout the war years, and soon became synonymous with torture, disappearance, imprisonment without trial, and summary execution. Emergency legislation was deployed on French metropolitan territory at key turning points, such as May and June 1958; the law was modified in 1960, at the time of the "Week of the Barricades" in Algiers, and was applied again in France at the time of the Generals' Putsch and thereafter, from April 1961 to May 1963 (Thénault 63-78). The extended shadow of the state of emergency looms large in Beckett's portrayals of the war; his correspondence reveals the attentiveness with which he followed events in Algiers and in Paris.

Torture and the consequences of emergency legislation, such as internment without trial and summary execution, are situated at the center of texts such as *Comment c'est* and *How It Is*, *Fin de partie* and *Endgame*, *Happy Days* and *Oh les beaux jours*, *Pochade radiophonique* and *Rough for Radio II*, *Fragment de théâtre II* and *Rough for Theatre II*. The comments Beckett made about *Fragment de théâtre II*, with which he had great difficulties, convey his attempt to harness the legal rhetoric at work around him: he referred to the unnamed protagonist who stands at the window, seemingly ready to jump, as the "*prévenu*"—the accused—who may eventually regain his freedom (*Letters 3* 167 n2). *Pochade radiophonique* revolves around another victim: Fox, the tortured, whose situation recalls Algerian war testimonies published by the Editions de Minuit, as well as other accounts of torture such as those Ernie O'Malley published two decades previously. In *On Another Man's Wound*, O'Malley described being "blindfolded, handcuffed, kicked down the lane and into a motor car and driven away," then "seated [...] on a wooden form" (218). "They tied my hands and legs as before. I felt trussed; they put a cloth across my eyes. [...] Blood dribbled down my buttocks and legs. [...] I could not walk when I was told to move on. The guard lifted me, carried me along and flung me into a room. My head struck the stone floor and I was dazed" (222-3).

Beckett's texts from the Algerian war years present worlds in suspension, in which the main priority is survival, and the desert is often deployed as an explicit setting and as an ideal tied to the promise of escape. This is not an innocuous choice: in the late 1950s and early 1960s, the Algerian desert was an overdetermined political space, which made desertion a permanent possibility and a permanent threat. It was also a site impacted by wider geopolitical tensions: the Algerian Sahara was depicted by de Gaulle, during an unofficial trip in March 1957, as "an immense chance" that should not be lost under any circumstances (Abramovici 53). Control of the Sahara Desert, where considerable oil resources were discovered in 1956, influenced the conduct of the Algerian war and its outcomes, and the desert became a strategic site providing opportunities for nuclear testing as well as oil drilling.

Actes sans paroles I or *Act Without Words I*—"the desert mime," as Beckett called it (*No Author* 12)—invokes the political topography of Algeria at war, with its lone protagonist thrust into a "[d]esert," submitted to "[d]azzling light" and a regime of thirst administered by a mysterious force offstage (*Complete Dramatic Works* 203). In 1957, at a time when many French people knew at least one conscript who had been sent to Algeria, a French performance of the mime came across as a political allegory about desertion (Jacquemont). The piece was conceived to accompany *Fin de partie / Endgame*, another play invoking the desert, in which desertion fleetingly emerges as the last possibility for survival. In *Endgame*, Nell's last word to Clov is "Desert!"; it is both the final instalment in her extended recollection of Lake Como and an injunction whose meaning can undergo subtle variations depending on which syllable is stressed. Clov understands her pained utterance as a recommendation to "go away, into the desert" (103). In *Fin de partie*, Nell's line is whispered, subversive; she says to Clov, "*Déserte*" (37). This is an order unconnected to her recollections of youth (the final e puts her line in the imperative mood, and removes any possible connection to her fractured description of Lake Como). Her murmur comes across as her last wish: that her disappearance might lead to his desertion.

At other key moments, the play invokes the long history of conquest, war, and empire. Notably, Hamm's descriptions of his manor and former grounds, which once suffered from varying levels of fertility and rapidly changing yields, resonate with accounts of the colonization of Algeria: the colonial emphasis on farming led settlers to lands that proved difficult to cultivate, breeding severe food shortages, epidemics, and crisis. Beckett's characters speak and act like colonial settlers in texts written long before the beginning of the Algerian war: Moran, like Clov, wears "*babouches*" at home (160). The narrator of *L'Innommable* relishes the odd colonial reference: he compares, for example, the color of dawn to a "Tunis pink" ("*ce rose de Tunis, c'est l'aurore*" (189); "Look at this Tunis pink, it's dawn" (404)), and he occasionally resorts to words tied to the colonization of Algeria such as "*barouf*" for racket and "*sabir*" for gibberish (86, 65). *Sabir*, a pejorative term, originally designated the Arabic inflected by Italian, Spanish, and French spoken in Algeria and other parts of North Africa after the 1830 conquest of Algeria.

In a manner similar to *Act Without Words I* and *Endgame*, *Happy Days* replays war anxieties through motifs that function as powerful political referents recalling the topography of war and colonial conquest. The setting—"scorched grass" in "[b]lazing light" (*Complete Dramatic Works* 138)—evokes the aftermath of forcible removal and perhaps plunder. In the French text, Winnie speaks of a world ruled by sinister forces when she drops her guard and loses courage, and she insults the desert—"*ce fumier de désert*"; 'this muck of a desert' (51). She finds solace, she admits, in thinking about having her throat cut—a guerrilla method favored by the Algerian National Liberation Front; the line "*Ça que je trouve si réconfortant quand je perds courage et jalouse les bêtes qu'on égorge*"; 'that's what I find so comforting when I lose courage and become jealous of the animals who get their throats cut' (24) appears only in the French translation. The play began to find form in

October 1960, and a particularly intense period of writing followed in early 1961 (Pilling 152-3), at a time marked by great uncertainty over the referendum on Algerian self-determination and the birth of the Organisation Armée Secrète (Secret Army Organization), a terrorist organization defending the interests of the *pieds-noirs*, the French living in Algeria. Considered in this context, the position of Winnie and Willie, stranded settlers who pretend to continue as normal, left alone in a hostile land that only wishes to see them disappear, becomes a literal illustration of the tensions Beckett witnessed around him.

Many among the *pieds-noirs* felt betrayed by de Gaulle and profoundly resented his attempts to resolve the conflict through political means. Their fate was clear long before the 1962 Evian Accords: as early as May 1961, a State Secretariat was created to investigate the eventuality of mass departures from Algeria to France (Scioldo-Zürcher 564-9). At the end of that year, the French National Assembly passed a law designed to set up infrastructure and support for mass repatriation ("Loi no. 61-1439"). Suzanne Beckett—who was, like her husband, a child of empire (she had spent part of her youth in colonial Tunisia)—would have been sensitive to the fragility of their situation. Beckett, for his part, seems to have been deeply concerned about the impact of emergency legislation and about the war's broader political stakes. When he began work on *Happy Days*, a wider Cold War context rattled by the Algerian war was on his mind: early notes from 1956 featured allusions to nuclear strikes, and a male protagonist who wore striped pyjamas (Gontarski 49, 40)—a costume recalling the Nazi prisoner of war camps and concentration camps. Beckett's speculative play with a powerful symbol of war memory resonated with the perception shared among many in France that the methods employed by the army to quell the Algerian conflict had Nazi precedents.

Beckett's choice of readings during this period conveys an ambition to understand the breadth of the legislative measures supporting the Algerian war. In 1959, from the Editions de Minuit, he bought a copy of Henri Alleg *La Question* (Morin 201), a testimony in which Alleg shows how his arrest, torture, and detention directly arose from the law granting to the army the power to take "exceptional measures" in order to control the Algerian conflict. Another book published by the Editions de Minuit, which Beckett acquired in May 1960, offered a detailed investigation of the legislation on "special powers." This was *Le droit et la colère*, co-authored by Jacques Vergès, Michel Zavrian, and Maurice Courrégé, the three lawyers who defended FLN militants in the courts and prisons (Morin 201-2). Insurgent Algeria, the authors assert, is a country characterized by an "absence of rights," at the mercy of an emergency legislation incompatible with the human rights conventions endorsed by the French government (Vergès, Zavrian, and Courrégé 63-72). Vergès, Zavrian, and Courrégé describe how a series of decrees restricting individual rights were gradually implemented and expanded the powers of the army; they pay close attention to the prevalence of summary execution and the rise of unexplained disappearances and, reproducing many letters and documents, relate the arrests of the lawyers defending Algerian prisoners and the censoring of their correspondence with their clients. The book pays close attention to a February 1960 decree that assigned all matters related to the Algerian war to military tribunals operating under military orders, creating a distinctive loophole that placed Algerian political prisoners beyond the protection of the Geneva Conventions and beyond the guarantees offered by common law (130-1).

Beckett's concern with states of exception resonates in *Comment c'est* (or *How It Is*) and throughout the drafts that preceded its completion. The manuscripts developed around familiar coordinates of conquest, war, and emergency: passages gradually elided in drafts of this arduous experimental text reveal a narrator vainly attempting to fulfil the semblance of military orders and canvassing a hostile territory. The deaths and births of empires, together with the joys and sorrows of the living, surface as recurrent motifs across drafts. The published text, however, summons a specific strand of war memory, tied to a long history of French military losses and defeats. The narrator crawls through sullied mud, out of which other bodies and things emerge; he chokes on mud, and speaks in, through, and to mud.

Dredging through mud, eating mud, and sinking in mud are common tropes in war novels relating journeys through the French and Flemish Ardennes: notably, Louis-Ferdinand Céline's *Voyage au bout de la nuit* (which Beckett admired greatly) and Claude Simon's *La route des Flandres* (which Beckett had less regard for; he nonetheless read it upon its publication in 1960, while struggling with *Tout Bas*, the text that would subsequently become *Comment c'est* [*Letters 3* 360]). Céline's and Simon's novels share the same coordinates as Beckett's text: mud, tinned rations, vigils, patrols. They summon the battles fought in the north of France, from the 1870s Franco-Prussian War to the First World War to—in Simon's case—the defeat of 1940. Céline's hero, Bardamu, professes his dislike for "those endless fields of mud, those houses where nobody's ever home, those roads that don't go anywhere," concluding: "And if to all that you add a war, that's completely unbearable" (11). To impending death on the battlefield, he would infinitely prefer "[his] own kind of death, the kind that comes late"; war, after all, is nothing but "eating Flanders mud, my whole mouth full of it, fuller than full, split to the ears by a shell fragment" (17). Likewise, Simon's *The Road to Flanders*—which anticipates both the subject matter of Beckett's text and its experiments with punctuation—begins with an anecdote involving dogs eating mud. Here mud submerges even the possibility of war: Simon's narrator discovers that his brigade "no longer existed; had been not annihilated, destroyed according to the rules—or at least what he thought were the rules—of war" (124), but had been "so to speak absorbed, diluted, dissolved, erased from the general-staff charts without his knowing where nor how nor when" (125), "somehow evaporated, conjured away, erased, sponged out without leaving a trace save a few dazed, wandering men hidden in the woods or drunk" (126). Beckett's text goes a few steps further: the world is mud, and swallowing mud or being swallowed by it are the two alternatives that circumscribe all all actions. Lines elided from a previous draft ask profound questions about war memory: the narrator ventures a guess that the present era, "which even to [him] seems characterized by unrivalled abjection," may "seem heroic in its own way, eventually, seen from the future" (*Comment* 221; my translation).

For Beckett, political history was synonymous with war, and its representation raised deep and troublesome questions about form and about responsibility. In conversation, he had a tendency to portray the political shifts taking place around him by means of plain euphemisms, and to push political experience beyond the realm of articulation: in 1955, he spoke of a "malaise," "loss of spirit," and "blackout," for example (Bowles 28). In a later interview, he drew attention to his texts as reflections of a "mess" and "distress" that he had not invented, but that he, and anyone else sensitive to the world, could witness everywhere (Driver 242). He said to his interviewer, Tom Driver, that he placed his own hopes in an art form that "admits the chaos and does not try to say that the chaos is really something else" while continuing to honor the very function of form: to "[exist] as a problem separate from the material it accommodates" (244-245, 243). The Algerian war, unnamed, looms large in his meditations on form in the early 1960s, just as it looms large in his declarations about a world reduced to the most utter "confusion," so much so that "our only chance now is to let it in […], open our eyes and see the mess" (Driver 242). "It is not a mess you can make sense of," he concluded (Driver 242). To another interlocutor, he offered a similar argument about a literary form situated in a state of exception, deprived of the customary adornments and comforts. He confided to Lawrence Harvey that "Being is constantly putting form in danger," and that "he knew of no form that didn't violate the nature of being 'in the most unbearable manner'" (435).

These declarations about an art of writing built on desolation and hindered expression are commonly interpreted in the second, third, or fourth degrees, as renewed affirmations of the bottomless metaphysical despair to which Beckett's work gives free rein. A different reading is possible: as Alain Badiou suggests, we should take the author himself "at his word" (39-40) (*"au pied de sa lettre"* [9]) in order to understand the nuances of his writing. To read Beckett in the first degree is to move beyond the old cliché according to which the work is about the meaninglessness of human experience; it is also a step toward recovering a sense of its political immediacy and the rawness of its ties to war memory.

Works Cited

Abramovici, Pierre. *Le putsch des généraux: De Gaulle contre l'armée (1958-1961)*. Arthème Fayard, 2011.

Adorno, Theodor W. *Negative Dialectics*. Translated by E.B. Ashton. Routledge, 2000.

"Appel des intellectuels européens pour la Pologne." *Libération*, 30 Dec. 1981, p. 36.

Arendt, Hannah. "Thinking and Moral Considerations: A Lecture." *Social Research*, vol. 38, no. 3, 1971, pp. 417-46.

Azéma, Jean-Pierre. "Le régime de Vichy." *La France des années noires, vol. 1: De la défaite à Vichy*, edited by Jean-Pierre Azéma and François Bédarida. Seuil, 2000, pp. 151-79.

Agamben, Giorgio. *Means without End: Notes on Politics*. Translated by Vincenzo Binetti and Cesare Casarino. U of Minnesota P, 2000.

———. *State of Exception*. Translated by Kevin Attell. U of Chicago P, 2005.

Badiou, Alain. *Beckett: L'increvable désir*. Hachette, 1995.

———. *On Beckett*. Edited by Alberto Toscano and Nina Power. Clinamen, 2004.

Beckett, Samuel. *Comment c'est/How It Is and/et L'Image: A Critical-Genetic Edition*. Edited by Edouard Magessa O'Reilly. Routledge, 2001.

———. *The Complete Dramatic Works*. 1986. Faber, 2006.

———. *Eleutheria*. Translated by Barbara Wright. Faber, 1996.

———. *En attendant Godot*. Editions de Minuit, 1952.

———. *Fin de partie*. Editions de Minuit, 1957.

———. *The Letters of Samuel Beckett, vol. 1: 1929-1940*. Edited by Martha Dow Fehsenfeld and Lois More Overbeck. Cambridge UP, 2009.

———. *The Letters of Samuel Beckett, vol. 2: 1941-1956*. Edited by George Craig, et al. Cambridge UP, 2011.

———. *The Letters of Samuel Beckett, vol. 3: 1957-1965*. Edited by George Craig, et al. Cambridge UP, 2014.

———. *L'Innommable*. 1953. Editions de Minuit, 2004.

———. *Mercier and Camier*. 1974. Calder, 1999.

———. *Mercier et Camier*. Editions de Minuit, 1970.

———. *Molloy*. 1951. Editions de Minuit, 1982.

———. *More Pricks Than Kicks*. 1934. Calder, 1993.

———. *Oh les beaux jours, suivi de Pas moi*. Editions de Minuit, 1963.

———. *Three Novels: Molloy, Malone Dies, The Unnamable*. 1959. Calder, 1994.

Beckett, Samuel, and Alan Schneider. *No Author Better Served: The Correspondence of Samuel Beckett and Alan Schneider*. Edited by Maurice Harmon. Harvard UP, 1998.

Benjamin, Walter. *Illuminations*. Edited by Hannah Arendt. Translated by Harry Zohn. Schocken, 1969.

Beradt, Charlotte. *The Third Reich of Dreams: The Nightmares of a Nation 1933-1939*. Translated by Adriana Gottwald. Aquarian Press, 1985.

Bowles, Patrick. "How to Fail: Notes on Talks with Samuel Beckett." *PN Review*, vol. 20, no. 4, 1993, pp. 24-38.

Campbell, Colm. *Emergency Law in Ireland, 1918-1925*. Oxford UP, 1994.

Céline, Louis-Ferdinand. *Journey to the End of the Night*. Translated by Ralph Manheim. Alma Classics, 2012.

"Décret no. 56-274 du 17 mars 1956 relatif aux mesures exceptionnelles tendant au rétablissement de l'ordre, à la protection des personnes et des biens et à la sauvegarde du territoire de l'Algérie." *Journal officiel de la République française*, 19 Mar. 1956, p. 2665.

Driver, Tom. "Beckett by the Madeleine." *Samuel Beckett: The Critical Heritage*, edited by Lawrence Graver and Raymond Federman. Routledge, 1979, pp. 241-7.

Ferro, Marc. *Pétain*. Fayard, 1987.

Gontarski, S.E. *Beckett's Happy Days: A Manuscript Study*. Ohio State University Libraries, 1977.

Gordon, Lois. *The World of Samuel Beckett, 1906-1946*. Yale UP, 1996.

Gruen, John. "Beckett: Rare Playwright, Rare Interview." *New York Herald Tribune*, 19 July 1964, p. 31.

Harvey, Lawrence. *Samuel Beckett: Poet and Critic*. Princeton UP, 1970.

Jacquemont, Maurice. "Acte sans paroles." Theater programme, Paris Studio des Champs Elysées, 1956-1957, n.pag.

Jaspers, Karl. *The Question of German Guilt*. Translated by E.B. Ashton. Fordham UP, 2000.

Kenny, Enda. "Speech by the Taoiseach, Mr. Enda Kenny, T.D., on the Occasion of the Naming and Commissioning of the New Naval Offshore Patrol Vessel LÉ Samuel Beckett," 17 May 2014, Irish Department of Defense. www.defence.ie/WebSite.nsf/Speech+ID/9BA47AA140E2B99D80257CDB00340EFF?. Accessed 3 Jan. 2018.

Knowlson, James and Elizabeth, editors. *Beckett Remembering/Remembering Beckett*. Arcade Publishing, 2006.

"Loi no. 55-385 du 3 avril 1955 instituant un état d'urgence et en déclarant l'application en Algérie." *Journal officiel de la République française*, 7 Apr. 1955, p. 3479.

"Loi no. 61-1439 du 26 décembre 1961 relative à l'accueil et à la réinstallation des Français d'outre-mer." *Journal officiel de la République française*, 28 Dec. 1961, p. 11996.

"Loi portant création de la Légion Française des Combattants." *Journal Officiel de la République Française*, 30 Aug. 1940, p. 4845.

Marowitz, Charles. "Paris Log." *Encore*, Mar.-Apr. 1962, pp. 37-46.

McCarthy, Justine. "*Ulysses* Heir Doesn't Want Joyce at Sea." *Sunday Times*, 8 Sept. 2013, p. 7.

McCormack, W.J. *From Burke to Beckett: Ascendency, Tradition and Betrayal in Literary History*. Cork UP, 1994.

Morin, Emilie. *Beckett's Political Imagination*. Cambridge UP, 2017.

Morton, Stephen. *States of Emergency: Colonialism, Literature and Law*. Liverpool UP, 2013.

Nixon, Mark. *Samuel Beckett's German Diaries, 1936-1937*. Continuum, 2011.

O'Malley, Ernie. *On Another Man's Wound*. 1936. Anvil Books, 1979.

"Ordonnance du 9 août 1944 relative au rétablissement de la légalité républicaine sur le territoire continental." *Journal officiel de la République française*, 9 Aug. 1944, pp. 7-8.

"Ordonnance du 20 novembre 1944 portant adaptation aux territoires relevant du Ministère des Colonies des dispositions de l'ordonnance du 21 avril 1944 sur l'organisation des pouvoirs publics en France après la libération." *Journal officiel de la République française*, 21 Nov. 1944, pp. 1404-5.

O'Toole, Fintan. "Beyond Belief—Why Did We Grant Disney's Skelligs Wish?" *Irish Times*, 1 Sept. 2015, p. 12.

Pilling, John. *A Samuel Beckett Chronology*. Palgrave Macmillan, 2006.

"Préambule de la Constitution du 27 octobre 1946." www.legifrance.gouv.fr/Droit-francais/Constitution/Preambule-de-la-Constitution-du-27-octobre-1946. Accessed 11 July 2017.

Reinach, Théodore. *De l'état de siège et des institutions de salut public*. Cotillon, 1885.

Scioldo-Zürcher, Yann. "La loi du 26 décembre 1961: Une anticipation du rapatriement des Français d'Algérie." *Histoire de l'Algérie à la période coloniale, 1830-1962*, edited by Abderrahmane Bouchène, Jean-Pierre Peyroulou, Ouanassa Siari Tengour, and Sylvie Thénault. La Découverte, 2014, pp. 564-9.

Semo, Marc. "'Il n'y a pas de sociétés de contrôle total': Entretien avec Enzensberger." *Libération*, Book Supplement, 1 Apr. 2010, p. 3.

Simon, Claude. *The Road to Flanders*. Translated by Richard Howard. Oneworld Classics, 2010.

Simonin, Anne. *Le déshonneur dans la République: Une histoire de l'indignité, 1791-1958*. Grasset, 2008.

Thénault, Sylvie. "L'état d'urgence (1955-2005). De l'Algérie coloniale à la France contemporaine: Destin d'une loi." *Le Mouvement Social*, vol. 218, no. 1, 2007, pp. 63-78.

Vergès, Jacques, Michel Zavrian, and Maurice Courrégé. *Le droit et la colère*. Editions de Minuit, 1960.

EMILIE MORIN is professor of modern literature at the University of York, UK. She has published widely on Samuel Beckett. Her recent books include *Beckett's Political Imagination* (Cambridge UP, 2017) and *Early Radio: An Anthology of European Texts and Translations* (Edinburgh UP, 2023).

9 Putting the Impossible to Work: Beckettian Afterlife and the Posthuman Future of Humanity

Ruben Borg

One of the defining critical issues in posthuman studies today is the problem of grasping (and properly articulating) the historical character of our current posthuman condition—in other words, of situating the posthuman moment in human history. Is posthumanity to be interpreted as a mere phase in the history of human subjectivity? Does it come about in response to ethical and epistemological challenges inherited from the experience of human subjects? Or is it rather an altogether new paradigm that renders the very use of words like "subjectivity," "history," and "experience" anachronistic? This essay seeks to address these questions by analyzing strategies of historical self-definition at work in a number of texts dealing with the "posthuman future of humanity." Drawing on Beckett and Derrida (and implicitly on Hegel), I will argue that an experience of the impossible informs the moment of posthuman self-reflection; and consequently, that the challenge of theorizing a point of contact between human and posthuman being (or human and posthuman history) calls for a new, ad hoc interpretation of the concept of "impossibility."

The scope of this argument allows for no more than a brief survey of the posthuman canon. But as we look at some representative texts, two hypotheses suggest themselves right away: first, that posthumanity is always co-implied with humanity, that from the outset it was a constituent part of the human character, possibly a function of the eminently human faculty of self-transcendence; and second, that a posthuman epoch set in, with historic consequences, once human history reached its saturation point.

Neil Badmington spells out the first hypothesis in *Alien Chic*, where he reads the figure of the alien in contemporary culture as a symptom of human anxieties vis-à-vis the posthuman within:

> Posthumanism, as I see it, is the acknowledgement and activation of the trace of the inhuman within the human. In the end, absolute difference is abducted by différance (with an "a"). In the end, "Man" secretes the other within. In the end, close

encounters are constitutive, and invasion is inescapable. In the end, humanism finds itself a little alien. (155)

The relationship between posthumanism and human experience obeys a peculiar logic here. Let us note, first of all, that the posthuman is defined through an act (or a series of acts) by which "humanism finds itself. . . ." It is a moment of self-discovery and "acknowledgement," where what needs to be acknowledged is mankind's inherent other, an alien that differs from human beings no more than "humans differ from themselves" (Badmington 129). Accordingly, self-difference is viewed as a predicate of human nature, perhaps even a defining potentiality of the species. But there is no indication that it might be anything more than an abstract, immutable character trait, save for the anaphoric insistence that *acknowledgement* and *self-discovery* must necessarily occur "in the end."

It is of course significant that over the past fifteen to twenty years posthumanism has acquired an unprecedented historical self-consciousness, an ability to speak of itself as an evolving discipline and an intellectual project. Introducing a special issue of *Comparative Literature Studies* devoted to Posthumanism, Katherine Hayles notes that

> [t]aken as a group, the essays point not so much to consensus as to common sites where contestations to determine the future of humanity are especially intense. [. . .] It is too soon to say where these engagements will end. Perhaps the only clear conclusions are that the future of humans will increasingly be entangled with intelligent machines, and that embodiments will still matter in some sense, however virtual or cyborgian they become. ("Refiguring the Posthuman" 316)

The briefest of summaries will suffice, here, to identify an overwhelming temporal contradiction at the heart of the debate: the posthuman is already with us, even as it is yet to come. In other words, the currency and the futurity of the posthuman are one and the same. An important implication of Hayles's argument is that the variety of contexts in which posthumanism plays itself out coincides with a variety of possible futures. It is by focusing on the future as a site of multiple possibilities that the posthuman begins to be thought. The task is all the more urgent when we observe that Hayles is speaking here not of a posthuman future but, more precisely, a "future of humanity" in which the posthuman ought to become increasingly recognizable, that is to say, more and more like itself.

ETHICAL PROBLEMS, POSTHUMAN SOLUTIONS

This anachronism lies at the heart of any discourse on the posthuman: viewed as part of an evolutionary continuum, posthumans share a genetic past with human beings. In a very concrete sense, they emerge from within a human world. But they must leave that world behind. To theorize the historicality of the posthuman, to comprehend the place of the posthuman in human history, is also to come to grips with this logic of evolutionary supersession.

Intuitively, evolutionary discourse may be seen to compete with the postapocalyptic imagery prevalent in numerous posthuman myths. But in fact, the historical character of the posthuman compels us to think of evolution and apocalypse as co-implied. Evolutionary discourse affirms temporal continuity and privileges versions of becoming—myths of gradual genetic reprogramming—over the sense of an irreparable rupture in time. And here too, the notion of a "possibility" to be fulfilled or transgressed is key. Bruce Clarke, for example, concludes *Posthuman Metamorphoses* with the observation that "humanity [. . .] will earn its continuation only by metamorphic integration into new evolutionary syntheses" (196). Within this narrative, the posthuman fits the role of a "human metamorphosed by reconnection to the worldly and systemic conditions of its evolutionary possibility" (Clarke 196). Thomas Foster, in turn, speaks of "contemporary posthumanist impulses to intervene in and direct what would have once been a process of natural selection, in order to accelerate human potential for differentiation and (self)modification" (6). Note that the phrase pits two types of evolutionary work against each other: *natural selection* takes evolutionary possibilities as given in advance (in nature), whereas the *human potential for differentiation*, itself a given, opens the field to some degree of indeterminacy in the exercise of human agency. Only a third term, *acceleration*, registers a disruption of the natural order that, in effect, coincides with the posthuman event.

Where it intervenes in evolutionary processes, the posthuman event marks an uncanny intersection of technology and nature. It introduces difference not from within a field of given possibilities, but in excess of that field. Nature becomes more than natural, the organism more than merely organic. Most importantly, for my purposes of here, the event makes the very realization of genetic possibilities dependent on the workings of the impossible. H.G. Wells provides the argument with a powerful illustration:

> It often seems to be tacitly assumed that a living thing is at the utmost nothing more than the complete realization of its birth possibilities, and so heredity becomes confused with theological predestination. [. . .] We overlook only too often the fact that a living being may also be regarded as raw material, as something plastic, something that may be shaped and altered, that this, possibly, may be added and that eliminated, and the organism as a whole developed far beyond its apparent possibilities. (*Early Writings* 36)

Here, technological invention is found to be inherent in natural selection, a constitutive factor and a guarantee of the plasticity of living forms. To be sure, technology's role in this process is not reducible to any practical application, to this or that particular instance of technological use. Rather, the power of technology and the significance of a technological experience emerge in precisely the kind of event that folds nature and the impossible together. As Callus and Herbrechter have argued, the posthuman does not need technology, though it remains a technological formation through and through. It is simply "that which reconfigures the actual and the possible once human potential is reengineered and new orders instituted (whether by technology or otherwise)" ("Introduction: Cy-Borges" 35).[1] Or, if you will, it is what puts the impossible to work as human possibilities are reengineered—and therein lies the key feature of its technological determination.

By this last definition, the evolutionary character of the human/posthuman relation may be conceived alongside the sheer irruptive power of the posthuman turn. The rhetoric approximates that of Foster's argument (quoted above). Here, however, the emphasis lies on the inventive thrust of the *now*, on the moment's future origin, rather than its position in an evolutionary continuum. If the posthuman can indeed be understood as an acceleration of human potential—and we are able to adopt this definition without qualms—it is because we recognize an original impossibility at work in reality, in nature, and in the possible itself.

But the folding in of human and posthuman histories belies another, more serious issue—one that goes to the heart of the debate on early cybernetic fantasies of disembodiment. As Hayles observes, in the ideology that sustains these fantasies "[t]he contrast between the body's limitations and cyberspace's power highlights the advantages of pattern over presence. As long as the pattern endures, one has attained a kind of immortality" (*How We Became Posthuman* 36). Hayles goes on to trace a vague, causal link between the cultural bias towards disembodiment and posthumanist myths of ecological disadaptation and of being ill-at-ease in the world:

> In a world despoiled by overdevelopment, overpopulation and time-release environmental poisons, it is comforting to think that physical forms can recover their pristine purity by being reconstituted as informational patterns in multidimensional computer space. A cyberspace body, like a cyberspace landscape, is immune to blight and corruption. It is no accident that the vaguely apocalyptic landscapes of films such as *Terminator*, *Blade Runner*, and *Hardware* occur in narratives focusing on cybernetic life-forms. The sense that the world is rapidly becoming uninhabitable by human beings is part of the impetus for the displacement of presence by pattern. (*How We Became Posthuman* 36–37)

Dematerialization is contemplated, here, as an evolutionary response to a biological and ecological threat. But the scenario, Hayles argues, is at best naive—and at worst corrupt. It threatens a return to the dichotomy of "mind" and "body" that props up the liberal humanist project. It is a reversion from the gains of historical materialism. Most damningly, it labors under the misguided assumption that the Mind (or some version of it) is the true site of identity, that it has natural primacy over matter, and that the body is merely its accessory for being in the world—a tool that can be exchanged should a more efficient (or more fashionable) one become available. Robocop and Terminator were never far from being repossessed as parables on human agency or metaphors for the endurance of human resolve. So too, the posthuman subject viewed as a pure sequence of information, as the translation of thought into digital form, stakes its survival on the idea that technological instantiation is incidental to being—that some material form enables truth's circulation in the marketplace, but doesn't affect its nature. Hayles goes on to say:

> [O]ne could argue that the erasure of embodiment is a feature common to *both* the liberal humanist subject and the cybernetic posthuman. Identified with the rational mind, the liberal subject *possessed* a body but was not usually represented as *being* a body. [. . .] If my nightmare is a culture inhabited by posthumans who regard their bodies as fashion accessories rather than the ground of being, my dream is a version of the posthuman that embraces the possibilities of information technologies without being seduced by fantasies of unlimited power and disembodied immortality. (*How We Became Posthuman* 4–5)

A great deal hangs on the implied association between immortality and unlimited power. For Hayles, the stakes are, first and foremost, ethical. Dreams of disembodied immortality are *ethically* objectionable because they deny the finitude of the subject. In other words, they afford the subject a megalomanic illusion of coinciding with the whole of being. To have unlimited power is to attain an absolute perspective. It is to hold the entire history of being in a single act of memory. It is also to eliminate difference and to preclude the possibility of a properly challenging experience, or any sort of encounter with the unexpected. In the long run, disembodied immortality neutralizes *virtuality* itself, *viz.*, the operations of a modal verb, the power of a technological invention or of an unforeseen event to affect reality.

By inference, an ethically valid posthumanism would need to be attuned to the idea of its own finitude. More importantly, it would know itself to be *empowered* by its finitude. It would find, in the full acceptance of its mortality, a certain self-defining potential. (Indeed, if this were not so, Hayles's argument might reduce to a mere call for technological self-censorship). To embrace "the possibilities of information technologies without being seduced by fantasies of unlimited power" is to promote a new understanding of death—death as a source of power, or at the very least, as an empowering agency.

The last ten years have witnessed a sustained effort to theorize this version of the posthuman. Yet the significance of "death" for the project—the relation between death and power—remains largely unexplored. Hayles's insistence on posthuman embodiment has the indubitable merit of grounding posthuman identity-politics in a concrete and highly particularized reality. Her attention to the material processes underlying informational exchange continues to guard against universalizing and homogenizing tendencies in posthumanist thought. But the approach has had the additional effect of reclaiming the posthuman for the history of subjectivity. The posthuman is made thought-friendly and history-friendly, as its apocalyptic sting is strategically removed. As Hayles herself notes, it is only a "fraction of humanity" that should be threatened by this version of the posthuman, since it effectively critiques only one of many possible models of subjectivity. In the last analysis, "the posthuman does not really mean the end of humanity. It signals instead the end of a certain conception of the human [. . .]

Located within the dialectic of pattern/randomness and grounded in embodied actuality rather than disembodied information, the posthuman offers resources for rethinking the articulation of humans with intelligent machines" (Hayles, *How We Became Posthuman* 286–287).

It is probably unnecessary to point out that this version of posthumanism remains at bottom a politics of human identity. It features the posthuman as a propitious moment in the history of the human subject—a new ideological configuration of the old form—rather than an alternative paradigm. Once again, the suspicion here is that posthumanity's ethical gains are not really its own—that embodiment and mortality are in fact borrowed criteria underwriting a borrowed ethics.

Thomas Foster seems to be grappling with this very issue when he speaks of a "key antinomy or unbridgeable gap that posthumanism has trouble thinking through" (xxvii). He analyzes this gap as an impasse "between the argument that posthumanism [. . .] can be part of struggles for freedom and social justice, and the argument that posthumanism dismisses such struggles or even makes them obsolete" (Foster xxvii).

THE RHETORIC OF DEATH-IN-LIFE IN BECKETT

Possibly more than any other writer in the twentieth century, Beckett has labored to articulate this condition of self-externality. The strange sense of being historically obsolete yet unsurpassable is shared (and in a sense explicated) by a host of narrators from Beckett's fiction—disembodied voices, and utterly finite beings, whose compulsive logorrhea is dramatized as an inability to die completely.

Beckett's preoccupation with the overlap of death and life is evident even in his early fiction. The protagonist of the stories collected in *More Pricks than Kicks*, Belacqua Shuah, bears the name of Dante's flute-maker in *Purgatorio* IV, a figure of supreme idleness, and the *Comedy*'s arch-example of a negligent soul. Several features of his character would have appealed to Beckett's sensibility. Chief among these is Belacqua's indolence, which is not merely sloth, but moral inertia—a flat and self-contented passivity with respect to all impulses, be they good or bad. It is this inertia that first draws Beckett's interest in the overlap of life and death. Like many of the souls Dante encounters in Purgatory, Belacqua inhabits a space between the animate world and the inanimate. But Belacqua is uniquely at home in the middle-ground. Indeed the most striking expression of his inertia is a tendency to merge with his surroundings. When Dante comes upon him at the foot of Mount Purgatory, he is leaning against a rock, motionless. Dante hears his voice, but sees only the mountain.

> Una voce di presso sonò, Forse
> Che di sedere in prima avrai distretta.
> Al suon di lei ciascun di noi si torse,
> E vedemmo a mancina un gran petrone,
> Del qual ne io ne ei prima s'accorse.

> [. . .] A voice from nearby sounded, "Perhaps
> You may be obliged to sit down, first."
> At the sound of it both of us turned
> And we saw to the left a great boulder
> That neither he nor I had noticed previously.
>
> (Alighieri, *Purgatorio* IV, ll. 98–102; translation modified.)[2]

The irony of Belacqua's character (and a further sign of his at-homeness in Purgatory) is that he is in no hurry to be redeemed. Relishing the opportunity for a verbal duel, he mocks Dante's eagerness to move forward, and gladly embraces his divine punishment—waiting at the foot of the mountain for a period equal to the length of his sinful life. Dante's Belacqua wields irony as a rhetorical device selfconsciously adopting it as a moral stance: while he waits out his penance, he enjoys the pleasures of repartee and one-upmanship with Dante, to whom he concedes the moral high-ground. By contrast, his Beckettian counterpart is the *unknowing subject* of a broader irony, the irony of a self-ironizing moral universe that would have us laugh at both human weakness and divine judgment at the same time.

To appreciate this dynamic we might compare Beckett's treatment of Belacqua with T.S. Eliot's use of another moral exemplum from Dante's Purgatory: the Provencal poet Arnaut Daniel. According to Eliot, Daniel is the quintessential purgatorial soul insofar as he embraces his punishment, eagerly immersing himself in the fire that refines him.[3] His desire for redemption is emblematic of a redemptive potential in human nature, a power of self-transcendence to which Eliot's poetry always aspires.

Beckett's Belacqua is a parodic subversion of the same principle. He, too, submits willingly to his sentence, and in so doing, represents the modern Everyman as a purgatorial creature. But in his case, the willing acceptance of punishment—the diagnosis it implies—only makes a mockery of the desire to be redeemed. Within this interpretative framework, Dante's encounter with Belacqua may be seen to function as a meta-discursive moment that makes of the pilgrim's whole journey—life and afterlife—a purgatorial experience, precisely that "limbo purged of desire" announced in Beckett's *Dream of Fair to Middling Women* (44), and dramatized in all of his later works.

The implication is that in Beckett's work, reality itself—reality as a whole—is suspended in a state of in-betweenness. The idea is first suggested in the essay on Joyce, where Beckett speaks of "this earth that is Purgatory, Vice and Virtue" ("Dante . . . Bruno" 21). Here Purgatory represents not only the point of contact between opposing moral determinations, but also the space in which those determinations collapse. Identified with "this earth," it stands for the full breadth of human experience, a space in which all distinctions and determinations are undone.

The opening scene of "Dante and the Lobster" strikes the same note. As Daniela Caselli observes, the scene sets up a subtle game of identifications.

"Belacqua moves—although he is 'stuck'—from the Dante to the Beckett text [. . .] a subtle use of the pronouns merges Belacqua Shuah—the reader of *Paradiso* II—with Dante's Belacqua of *Purgatorio* IV, and with Dante the protagonist of the *Comedy*" (Caselli 59). The Dantean reference thus provides an opportunity to blur boundaries not only between different identities, but also between the world of the book and the world of the reader.

Furthermore, the scene conflates Purgatory with Hell and Heaven, as if to abolish all topographic, ethical and ontological distinctions. In the absence of human desire, all three stages of Dante's spiritual journey fold into each other. Time (*lived* time, that is; the time of human experience) loses its thrust, and a passive waiting replaces Dante's heroic will-to-redemption as the universe's ethical norm.

It is important to clarify that this passive waiting is not merely a negative determination of action. It precedes the distinction between action and passion. It is neutral to both terms, and in fact may be said to hold them in reserve; hence its irreducibility to the order of subjective experience. Beckett's "limbo" is in this sense a peculiar conjunction of existential and ontological states (being-dead or being-alive; being-actual or being-virtual), a meeting of dialectical opposites, but without any possibility of a workable synthesis. Nor is the dominant tone here one of disgust, as Martha Nussbaum might argue, but rather, one of ironic reflection that is symptomatic of this state of being-in-between.

THE REALITY OF DEATH-IN-LIFE

I have argued elsewhere that this rhetoric of death-in-life in Beckett offers an ironic take on vitalist models of time and subjective experience.[4] Beckett at once adopts and overturns the Bergsonian view of time as a continuous evolutionary movement, a process that is neither ideal nor strictly speaking material. Here I would like to elaborate on the logic of in-betweenness implied in that strategy, and the sense of unsurpassable finitude it calls into play.

Aside from the connotations of Belacqua's name, Beckett mobilizes the motif of death-in-life in a number of images and verbal echoes recurring throughout the text of "Dante and the Lobster." Readers will recall the ending of the short story on a note of "quick death" (*More Pricks* 22). In turn, that note reverberates with a Dantean pun that had preoccupied Belacqua earlier in the day: "*qui vive la pietà, quand'è ben morta*" ("Here pity is alive when it is dead" [*Inf.* XX, 28]; or in Beckett's own poetic translation: "Pity is quick with death").[5] Once we are alerted to this thematic cluster, it is easy to see that it permeates Belacqua's consciousness. His lunch revolves around the purchase of a "rotten lump of Gorgonzola cheese," that ought to be "sweating" and "alive," but instead turns out to be a "cadaverous tablet" giving off a "faint fragrance of corruption" rather than "a good stench" (*More Pricks* 14). In preparation of his meal, he takes care that the toast be "done to a dead end" (12) and looks forward to "the anguish of pungency, the pang of spices, as each mouthful die[s] scorching his palate" (13).

The irony of these passages has been duly noted by critics: Belacqua's horror at the thought of boiling the lobster alive contrasts with the pleasure he takes in consuming the rotting cheese and metaphorically doing the toast to death. It is a short-lived horror, to be sure. But it registers, for a moment at least, an awareness of the difference between *literal* and *figurative* determinations of life and death. A genuine experience of finitude seizes Belacqua precisely at this point. In the fleeting instant, it is harder than ever to sustain the illusion that there might be such a thing as "life in the abstract" (*More Pricks* 114). The reality of life and death is brought home as immediately and undeniably as this sudden surge of emotion. Nor can life itself be reduced in this case to an ideal process unfolding in time towards an abstract limit. Yet the earnestness of that conclusion is soon dissipated, and Beckett's ironic pun on "quick death" suggests that Belacqua's pity is in fact little more than easy piety.

References to Cain also fit into this thematic network. As Takeshi Kawashima shows, the biblical figure is an essential part of the intertextual setup of Belacqua's character, adding a mythical element to the pattern of doubles and identifications in the text, and branding Belacqua himself with an accursed lineage.

> Belacqua shares a stigma with Cain, who is destined for exile and dispossession. The sinner's lineage is extended when "Dante and the Lobster" mentions McCabe, a real prisoner sentenced to death, whose execution is scheduled for the following day. When Belacqua deploys an old *Herald* on the table, he finds the "rather handsome face of McCabe the assassin" staring up at him. Afterwards, Belacqua's mind is haunted by McCabe's image, and every time Belacqua sets eyes on it, a subliminal effect is added to his secret sympathy for the condemned. Belacqua, Cain, and McCabe all share the negative legacy of sin and punishment, in which the lobster of the title too is enmeshed. (Kawashima 332)

"Seared with the stigma of God's pity, that an outcast might not die quickly" (*More Pricks* 12), Cain embodies a paradox of divine justice, and exemplifies the irony of being sentenced to a quick death. His mark protects him from harm, condemning him to a life (traditionally, an eternity) of wandering. Typologically associated with the killing of Christ, this exemption from death is a negative inversion of the glory of eternal life reserved for Jesus and his disciples. It represents a variation on the idea of resurrection, a reversal, as it were, of immortality. Thus, on the one hand, the piety of wishing the condemned man a mercifully quick death resonates with the mercy of God's decree that no one lay a hand on Cain. Yet the pun also implies a divine judgment—a curse visited upon the outcast, who is suspended for eternity in living-death.

Cain's brand of afterlife, in short, is one of those forms of impotence, of total dispossession, that Beckett himself has identified as a key to his artistic project: an afterlife that registers, not the soul's triumph over the finite realities of the flesh, nor the power of revealed knowledge in the presence of God, but an inability to die, or to die completely.[6] Once again, we must take note here of a state of being that short-circuits dialectical oppositions. Like Belacqua's passivity, which, as we have seen, is not merely a negative determination of action, Cain's impotence is also not quite death and not quite life. It exceeds the one and falls short of the other.

This idea informs Beckett's later fiction. In the opening scene of *Molloy*, for instance, the title character expresses a desire "to speak of the things that are left, say [his] goodbyes, finish dying" (*Three Novels* 7), while in *Malone Dies*, the lead character is obsessed with the thought that if he were dead, he would have no way of knowing it—or that once dead he might not be able to notice any change.[7] The eponymous character of *The Unnamable*, yearning for the passage of time, wonders why the hour itself seems so inert: "the question may be asked, off the record, why time doesn't pass, doesn't pass from you, why it piles up all about you, instant on instant, on all sides, deeper and deeper, thicker and thicker, your time, others' time, the time of the ancient dead and the dead yet unborn, why it buries you grain by grain neither dead nor alive" (*Three Novels* 389).

What is particularly striking about this last image is that it disables the distinction between subjective and objective time—between duration and chronology—projecting the experience of death-in-life onto yet another stage, the threshold between internal consciousness and material reality. Time is never more real than at this point. Having acquired a solid density, its effects are felt in the flesh, all around one's body, in measures of thickness and depth. Yet the experience could not be further removed from the living present. Time doesn't pass because it is already wholly past—a time of "the ancient dead and the dead yet unborn" (*Three Novels* 389). We graduate, here, from the idea of paralysis, understood as a restriction of one subject's motor function, to that of impassivity, intended as a predicate of time itself as a whole.

The obverse of that image returns us to Belacqua in a short story that was intended as the coda to *More Pricks than Kicks*. "Echo's Bones" shows Beckett's fictional alter-ego sitting on his gravestone watching his grave being robbed. The scene ideally pulls together various thematic threads from the passages analyzed earlier. Like the Unnamable, Belacqua is neither quite dead nor quite alive. He awakens to an afterlife in excess of his own mortality, cheated of more than just his resting place. Instead of finding himself buried in an impassive time, he is deprived of his own death—his grave, not the thickness of the past but the excessive, unlimited presence of a consciousness that has overrun (life) itself. The object of the allegory is the very same impotence implied in Molloy's hopeless urge to "finish dying" and in Belacqua's earlier identification with Cain: namely, an impotence-unto-death, a draining of power that withholds even the freedom to die completely.

Such an experience of afterlife parodies the very idea of transcendence. In the perverse simultaneity of being-already-dead and being denied one's death, actuality and virtuality collapse into each other; death and mourning become indistinct. Indeed death itself is mourned for having become impossible.

FINITUDE, SELF-EXTERNALITY AND ETHICAL FREEDOM

It is my contention, here, that posthumanism and Beckett studies overlap on the question of finitude.[8] To be more precise, they share a concern with the *ethics* of the limit. In Beckett studies, the treatment of this theme has developed along three broadly defined lines of enquiry:[9]

a. A refutation of Martha Nussbaum's charge that Beckett's art is one of unredeemable guilt and disgust at the finitude of human existence (see especially Simon Critchley and Robert Eaglestone);
b. A study of the Cartesian and anti-Cartesian implications of Beckett's fiction, mainly inspired by Beckett's response to the work of Arnold Geulincx (especially Matthew Feldman, and Anthony Uhlmann); or
c. A discussion of Badiou's powerful, if somewhat eccentric analysis of figures of love and infinity in Beckett's later work (most notably, in Andrew Gibson).

There is little, if any, dialogue among the three strands. For Badiou, Beckett is a thinker of alterity at its most essential. His art is a methodical and progressive refinement of the forms of encounter, a constant attuning to the minimal conditions required of a relation with an Other, pushing past nihilistic solutions to affirm the barest possibility of such an event. This is the basis of what Badiou terms "Beckett's paradoxical optimism" (Badiou 25), an uncompromising philosophical experiment conducted under the aegis of love: "The numericality of love—one, two, infinity—is the setting for what Beckett rightly calls happiness. Happiness also singularises love as a truth procedure for happiness can only exist in love. Such is the reward proper to this type of truth. In art there is pleasure, in science joy, in politics enthusiasm, but in love there is happiness" (33).[10]

By contrast, Nussbaum argues that the negative emotional charge of Beckett's writing ultimately reduces it to an ethically bankrupt pessimism: "There is a peculiar movement in Beckett's talk of emotions [. . .] from a perception of human limits to a loathing of the limited, from grief to disgust and hatred, from the tragedy and comedy of the frail body to rage at the body, seen as covered in excrement" (Nussbaum 251).[11]

Finally, the Geulingian camp returns to the themes of ignorance and powerlessness in Beckett in an effort to rethink the possibility of ethical freedom beyond the framework of Descartes's Mind-Body dualism. Ethics, in this context, begins with an emptying of the will, a divestiture of consciousness from the trappings of knowledge. For Geulincx, this is the way of humility, a cardinal virtue which allows one to acknowledge God as the ultimate cause of all things. Beckett's Geulingian intuition is to view *nescience* as a plausible way (perhaps the only one still available) to put the certainty of human finitude in contact with an experience of the infinite.[12]

I should make clear that my sympathies fall squarely with this last interpretation. As I understand them, Beckett's philosophical parables put traditional models of being-in-the world to the test by staging the exhausted, impracticable afterlife of that enduring Enlightenment ideal—the self-determined subject. The sense of being not only mortal, but in excess of one's own death, corresponds to a state of *infinite passivity*—precisely that "limbo purged of desire" in which Beckett's characters are always suspended.[13] Time itself is pressed into a state of pure hesitation; and on this hesitation, on the utter indeterminacy of the *now*, is staked the possibility of an ethical future.[14]

Yet it is Nussbaum's article that provides the most direct clue to Beckett's posthumanism. "Beckett's people," Nussbaum writes, "are heirs of a legacy of feeling that shapes them inexorably. They cannot help being shaped in this way, and they feel like 'contrivances,' like machines programmed entirely from without" (Nussbaum 250). The simile is telling; Nussbaum is right in suggesting that Beckettian ethics has much to do with the idea of a machine-like being facing the evidence of its own unsurpassable finitude. Significantly, this finitude is associated with a sense of being externally determined.

Drawing on that image, I would like to repurpose the theme of unsurpassable finitude by examining it against the recurrent Beckettian motifs of death-in-life and seeing-oneself-dead.[15] I read these motifs allegorically, as figures of a peculiarly modernist experience of finitude and liminality, in order to argue that Beckett's narratives dramatize an over-extended moment in human consciousness—a moment we might more generally describe as *impossible*.

This reference to the impossible gives Beckett's treatment of finitude its ethical purchase. A death that is actualized and mourned at the same time is not only an impossibility, but also the very matrix of an impossible event taking effect in reality. By making the reality of the impossible a central concern of his fiction, Beckett puts his finger on a paradoxical moment in the history of subjectivity, a historical impasse that calls for the invention of ad hoc ethical solutions.

To be sure, the association of ethical freedom with a space of pure subjective interiority forms a defining principle of modern philosophy—a foundational notion without which modernity itself becomes unthinkable. Nothing is more alien to the rights of the individual in a modern secular state than the idea of one's innermost thoughts being probed, judged and censored before they are expressed or put into action. Even allowing for the constructedness of social realities and experiences, the notion of mind control signals an ultimate invasion of privacy, the stuff of Orwellian dystopias and cold-war paranoid scenarios. In this context, consciousness is typically identified with a human potential for infinity. The (interiorizing) work of consciousness makes possible the transcendence of one's own finitude—as when the past is recollected and borne into the present, or the finality of every passing moment is overcome and rendered virtual.

The dread Beckett's characters feel at waking to a state of death-in-life is symptomatic of a subjectivity that has been turned inside out. The work of consciousness goes on, but without the benefit of interiority, it can only realize itself as an extreme form of impotence; an awareness of oneself as machine. To grasp the ethical import of Beckett's treatment of finitude, we needn't look further than this allegory of life at an impasse, this figurative identification of a machine-like existence with an excess of consciousness. Beckett consistently provides the criteria for a continued ethical thinking in the face of this impasse. His images of afterlife affirm both finitude and indeterminacy, and maintain them in a non-dialectical relation.

We return by this route to the critical issue of posthuman ethics identified by Hayles: namely, the problem of thinking through the virtualization of bodies, the co-implication of organic life with informatics, and the dream/nightmare scenario of a pure downloadable consciousness utterly divorced from its material substratum, without reducing posthuman subjectivity to a megalomaniac parody of its liberal humanist counterpart. The impotence-unto-death experienced by Beckett's characters and narrators offers a model by which to configure the relation between human life and a posthuman supersession of the finitude that characterizes human life—and it does so without lapsing into grand narratives of omnipotence and absolute knowledge.

MOURNING ONE'S OWN DEATH AND THE RUIN OF REALITY

In invoking such a concept of finitude (through the Beckettian tropes of death-in-life and of a consciousness that mourns its own death), I take my cue from Derrida, who speaks of "two experiences of mourning," one turned towards preserving the past, and one towards forgetting. These two experiences must eventually denote a single operation, namely, the work "of an *originary* mourning, of a possible mourning as that which is impossible" ("Preface" xxxix).

For our purpose, the main interest of this Derridean formula is in the way it exposes, at the heart of the Hegelian metaphorics of interiority (and organicity), a deep-seated concern with the *impossible* as a historical force. Crucially, what Derrida terms "impossible mourning" is not a mourning that never happens. Nor indeed should an impossible event be mistaken for an unreal one. Rather, any attempt to put the impossible to work must think of it as lacking nothing of reality. For if the impossible *did* lack something of reality, it could never be thought of as an event. Indeed it might be dismissed as a mere flight of fancy (an act of the imagination); as such, it would only reinforce, by way of simple subtraction, the order of pre-established possibilities. This kind of view would foreclose human history to the experience of whatever is not already inscribed in its program. It would cancel out the very condition in which new technologies emerge and unforeseen futures are created.

On this score, Derrida invites us to explore "the place of a thinking that ought to be devoted to the virtualization of the event by the machine" (*Without Alibi* 135). Note how the strange symmetry of this sentence mutually enfolds the task of *thinking* and the work of *virtualization* in order to endow the machine with enormous philosophical responsibility. Such a task, then, would correspond "to a virtuality that, in exceeding the philosophical determination of the possibility of the possible [. . .] exceeds by the same token the classical opposition of the possible and the impossible" (Derrida, *Without Alibi* 135). At stake in this formulation is precisely a posthumanist view of technology as that which opens the Hegelian dialectic to a space of utter indeterminacy. On this reading, *virtualization* opens reality to the workings of the impossible. It forms the very entry point of the impossible into the field of total possibility.

Virtuality, technology, and the machine: no serious treatment of the posthuman can avoid engaging with these concepts. Yet I suspect if certain versions of posthumanism downplay the radical nature of the posthuman turn, it is because they fail to see how an impossible event can operate in history: they mistake the impossible for the unreal. In so doing, they misunderstand the roles of futurity and technology in theorizing the posthuman condition. The counter-argument is simple enough: impossibility characterizes any event in which reality (as a whole) diverges from itself. We see its mark whenever history veers towards an unexpected future, or when nature is reprogrammed through technological invention. From a posthuman perspective, such events constitute reality's inaugural moments—they are *conditions of possibility*. History is always being thrown off course, and the natural state is never given.

THE RIGHT TO BE SHOWN IMPOSSIBLE

My conclusion, then, is that an experience of the impossible (such as might be allegorized in the act of mourning one's own death, or in the extreme passivity of a "limbo of purged of desire") is integral to posthuman self-consciousness and posthuman self-understanding; and consequently, that a Beckettian interpretation of the concepts of "impossibility" and "finitude" effectively recalibrates some of the most important issues in posthuman thought. These include, most notably, the problem of theorizing a point of contact—a measure of overlap or translatability—between human and posthuman being, human and posthuman history, human and posthuman ethics, and so forth. The issue here is never whether the posthuman is a being of the future. Even when historicized, or spoken of in the past tense, posthumanity retains an unmistakably futural character in relation to human history. The moot point is whether a posthuman future was always a possibility for human beings—whether man always had it in him, as it were, to turn out this way.

Beckett intervenes in this debate by insisting on what the Unnamable calls "the right to be shown impossible" (*Three Novels* 375). The figure of a "limbo purged of desire," and the recurrent motif of death-in-life, charge the Beckettian narrative with the power of an impossible event, a state of suspension that cannot be reabsorbed into the economy of any ideal history. Germane to both nature and culture, no less real to one than to the other, the "impossibility" I am referring to here short-circuits the dialectical setup that sustains modern versions of subjectivity—in particular, that old straw man the liberal humanist subject. Suspended between death and the inability to finish dying, Beckettian subjects (if we are to call them that) must relinquish any form of internal teleology. In other words, they must face up to their own self-externality.

The reality of our posthuman future emerges in precisely this kind of liminal existence, this sheer indeterminacy into which the field of given (predetermined) possibilities and the impossible are folded together. It falls to the posthuman to reflect on the conjunction between, on the one hand, the power of a living organism to carry itself past its inherent limit, and on the other, the embeddedness of objects in the actuality of that limit. Embracing hesitation as an ethical imperative, the posthuman becomes actual just as it understands itself to be impossible. Its lot, in this sense, is to experience the in-between of Spirit and Nature, to inhabit "the limit" as an opening in which reality plays itself out whole.

Notes

1. Elsewhere, a propos of Derrida's discourse on apocalypse, Callus and Herbrechter observe that "the disparities between the humanly possible and the inhumanly and dehumanizingly impossible have significantly altered and narrowed" ("Latecoming"). See also their "Critical Posthumanism, or, The Inventio of a Posthumanism without Technology."

2. While I greatly admire Robert Durling's translation, I modify it here in order to keep Dante's use of "forse" (perhaps) at the end of the line. The importance of the word "perhaps" in Beckett's work is well known, and the fact that Dante gives it prominence within Belacqua's speech was no doubt significant for the Irish writer.

3. 'Poi s'ascose nel foco che li affina' (Alighieri, *Purg.* XXVI, 148). Eliot famously quotes this line at the end of "The Waste Land" (ln. 427), and again, more obliquely in "Little Gidding" (ln. 145). But the encounter between Dante and Daniel is also alluded to in Eliot's dedication of "The Waste Land" to Ezra Pound, and in the title of Eliot's collection of poems *Ara Vos Prec*.

4. See Borg, "Ethics of the Event."

5. For a commentary on this translation, which appears in the early poem "Text," see Ruby Cohn (11–12), Christopher Ricks (29–32) and Sam Slote (22–23). See also Daniela Caselli (esp. 58–61) for an analysis of the significance of Dante's pun throughout Beckett's career. As Caselli shows, "quick" is repeatedly used by Beckett in its archaic form, as a synonym of "living." For instance in "What a Misfortune," Belacqua bestows his pity not on the dead, but on "the nameless multitude of the current quick" (qtd. in Caselli 68); and in "Echo's Bones," he is said to have departed "from among the quick" (qtd. in Caselli 75).

6. See the Interview with Israel Shenker: "The kind of work I do is one in which I'm not master of my material. The more Joyce knew the more he could. He's tending towards omniscience and omnipotence as an artist. I'm working with impotence, ignorance" (Shenker 3).

7. Compare this to Victor Krap's statement in *Eleutheria*: "If I was dead, I wouldn't know I was dead. That's the only thing I have against death. I want to enjoy my death. That's where liberty lies: to see oneself dead" (150).

8. On this point, see Jonathan Boulter's analysis of Beckett's treatment of human finitude in terms of the figure of the ghost and the logic of postcorporeality (12–15).

9. For a more exhaustive summary of the ethical strands in Beckett criticism, see Russell Smith's "Introduction" to *Beckett and Ethics*. Smith reflects on the phrase "Beckett's 'ethical undoing'" to suggest (a.) "an undoing of ethics through a disintegration of each term of the ethical relation"; (b.) an ethical insistence even in the face of this undoing; and (c.) a form of "not doing" that takes on ethical value, in other words, a "principled rejection of an ethics of [. . .] action" (Smith 3).

10. To clarify what is meant by the "numericality of love," we must remember that Badiou develops his notion of "the encounter" in terms of a highly formalized procedure, tracing the passage from the One of the solipsistic *Cogito* to the Infinite (identified with the multiplicity of beings and an opening of subjective experience onto the sensible world), by way of the figure of the Two, which is proper of the encounter. Badiou's bias is clearly in favor of the figure of the Two, which mediates the other terms and, at the same time, constitutes them in relation to each other: "Happiness is not in the least associated with the One, with the myth of fusion. Rather, it is the subjective indicator of a truth of difference, of sexual difference, a truth that love alone makes effective" (Badiou 34). Hence, the focus on Beckett as a writer "who gives voice to the gift and the happiness of Being" (29).

11. To this day, Nussbaum's critique continues to provide the momentum for a re-evaluation of Beckett as a counter-intuitively ethical thinker. A recent international conference ("Samuel Beckett: Out of the Archive," York 2011) saw two keynote lectures framed as a direct response to Nussbaum's argument: namely, Jean-Michel Rabaté, "Beckett's Three Critiques"; and Linda Ben Zvi, "Beckett and Disgust: The Body as 'Laughing Matter.'"

12. As Anthony Uhlmann points out, Beckett's encounter with Geulincx's *Ethics* may be seen to produce "an image of thought, with thought imagined as involving or being 'grounded' upon the extremely unstable foundation of ignorance. Whereas the ancient imperative was "Know Thyself," this image of thought (at least as it is adapted from Geulincx by Beckett) affirms that the self, which nevertheless remains the ground for all subsequent knowledge, cannot be known" (Uhlmann 92).

13. The philosophical background to this claim, particularly as it pertains to modernism and twentieth-century theories of time, is presented in Borg, "Ethics of the Event."

14. With regard to this last point, we must rehearse at least two senses in which the discourse of futurity becomes important in twentieth-century thought: first, as the far side of a horizon of experience; and second, as an index of indeterminacy in history. The two ideas are of course related. But where the former emphasizes the field of experience itself (the relation of the world to its limit), in the latter we look to the future as an ethical force. We identify the future with the new and the unforeseeable, indeed with any aspect of reality that escapes pre-determination.

15. For the purpose of this essay, "death-in-life" and "living death" are used interchangeably to signify any overlap between the two states. The notion of "afterlife" will also serve as a shorthand label for all tropes in which the boundaries between the life and death appear to have been transgressed.

Works Cited

Alighieri, Dante. *La Divina Commedia*. [*La Commedia secondo l'antica vulgata*.] Società Dantesca Italiana. Mondadori, 1966–68.

———. *The Divine Comedy. Volume 2: Purgatorio*. Edited and translated by Robert M. Durling. Introduction and notes by Ronald L. Martinez. Oxford UP, 2003.

Badiou, Alain. *On Beckett*. Translated by Alberto Toscano and Nina Power. Clinamen Press, 2003.

Badmington, Neil. *Alien Chic: Posthumanism and the Other Within*. Routledge, 2004.

Beckett, Samuel. "Dante . . . Bruno.Vico..Joyce." *Our Exagmination Round His Factification for Incamination of Work in Progress*. By Saumel Beckett et al. Faber and Faber, 1961, pp. 3–22.

———. *Dream of Fair to Middling Women*. Arcade Publishing, 2006.

———. *Eleutheria: A Play*. Translated by Barbara Wright. Faber and Faber, 1996.

———. *More Pricks than Kicks*. Grove Press, 1972.

———. *Three Novels: Molloy, Malone Dies, The Unnamable*. Grove Press, 1958.

———. "Text." *The European Caravan: An Anthology of the New Spirit in European Literature*. Brewer, Warren and Putnam, 1931, pp. 478–480.

Borg, Ruben. "Ethics of the Event: The Apocalyptic Turn in Modernism." *Partial Answers: Journal of Literature and the History of Ideas*, vol. 9, no. 1, 2011, pp. 188–201.

Boulter, Jonathan. *Beckett: A Guide for the Perplexed*. Continuum, 2008.

Callus, Ivan, and Stefan Herbrechter. "Critical Posthumanism, or, The Inventio of a Posthumanism without Technology." *Subject Matters*, vol. 3, no. 2/vol. 4, no. 1, 2007, pp. 15–29.

———. "Introduction: did someone say Cy-Borges." *Cy-Borges: Memories of Posthumanism in the Work of Jorge Luis Borges*. Eds. Stefan Herbrechter and Ivan Callus. Bucknell UP, 2009, pp. 15–38.

———. "The Latecoming of the Posthuman, Or, Why 'We' Do the Apocalypse Differently, 'Now'." *Reconstruction: A Journal of Interdisciplinary Culture*, vol. 4, no. 3, 2004.

Caselli, Daniela. *Beckett's Dantes: Intertextuality in the Criticism and Fiction*. Manchester UP, 2005.

Cohn, Ruby. *A Beckett Canon*. U of Michigan P, 2001.

Clarke, Bruce. *Posthuman Metamorphoses: Narrative and Systems*. Fordham UP, 2008.

Critchley, Simon. *Very Little . . . Almost Nothing*. Routledge, 1997.

Derrida, Jacques. "Preface. A Time for Farewells: Heidegger (read by) Hegel (read by) Malabou." *The Future of Hegel*. Translated by Joseph D. Cohen. Routledge, 2005.

———. *Specters of Marx*. Translated by Peggy Kamuf. Routledge, 1994.

———. *Without Alibi*. Translated by Peggy Kamuf. Stanford UP, 2002.

Eaglestone, Robert. *Ethical Criticism: Reading after Levinas*. Edinburgh UP, 1997.

Eliot, T.S. "Little Gidding." *Four Quartets*. Faber and Faber, 1944, pp. 35–44.

———. "The Waste Land." *Selected Poems*. Faber and Faber, 1961, pp. 49–74.

Feldman, Matthew. "'A Suitable Engine of Destruction'? Samuel Beckett and Arnold Geulincx's *Ethics*." *Beckett and Ethics*, edited by Russell Smith. Continuum, 2008, pp. 38–56.

Foster, Thomas. *The Souls of Cyberfolk: Posthumanism as Vernacular Theory*. U of Minnesota P, 2005.

Freud, Sigmund, "Fixation to Traumas—The Unconscious." *The Standard Edition of the Complete Psychological Works of Sigmund Freud*. Vol. XVI. Edited and translated by James Strachey and others. Hogarth Press, 1963, pp. 73–85.

Gibson, Andrew. *Beckett and Badiou: The Pathos of Intermittency*. Oxford UP, 2006.

Hayles, Katherine N. *How We Became Posthuman: Virtual Bodies in Cybernetics, Literature, and Informatics*. U of Chicago P, 1999.

———. "Refiguring the Posthuman," *Comparative Literature Studies*, vol. 41, no. 3, 2004, pp. 311–316.

Kawashima, Takeshi. "'What Kind of Name is that?' Samuel Beckett's Strategy of Naming." *Borderless Beckett / Beckett sans frontiers*, edited by Minako Okamuro, et al. Rodopi, 2007, pp. 327–337.

Malabou, Catherine. *The Future of Hegel: Plasticity, Temporality, Dialectic*. Translated by Lisabeth During. Routledge, 2005.

Nussbaum, Martha. "Narrative Emotions: Beckett's Genealogy of Love." *Ethics*, vol. 98, no. 2, 1988, pp. 225–254.

Ricks, Christopher. *Beckett's Dying Words*. Oxford UP, 1995.

Shenker, Israel. "'Moody Man of Letters': Interview with Samuel Beckett." *The New York Times*, 6 May 1956, section 2, pp. 1, 3.

Smith, Russell. "Introduction: Beckett's Ethical Undoing." *Beckett and Ethics*, edited by Russell Smith. Continuum, 2008, pp. 1–20.

Slote, Sam. "Stuck in Translation: Beckett and Borges on Dante." *Journal of Beckett Studies*, vol. 19, no. 1, 2010, pp. 15–28.

Uhlmann, Anthony. *Samuel Beckett and the Philosophical Image*. Cambridge UP 2006.

Wells, H.G. *Early Writings in Science and Science Fiction*. Edited by Robert M. Philmus and David Y. Hughes. U of California P, 1975.

Wolfe, Cary. *What is Posthumanism?* U of Minnesota P, 2010.

RUBEN BORG is chair of the English department at the Hebrew University of Jerusalem. His work has appeared in *Journal of Modern Literature, Modern Fiction Studies, Poetics Today, Modernism/modernity*, and numerous other journals devoted to twentieth-century literature and film. He has also contributed chapters to collaborative volumes on Deleuze, Beckett and Posthumanism. Borg is the author of *The Measureless Time of Joyce, Deleuze and Derrida* (2007), and of *Fantasies of Self-Mourning: Modernism, the Posthuman and the Finite* (2019), and co-editor of three volumes on Flann O'Brien: *Contesting Legacies, Problems with Authority*, and *Gallows Humour*. His current project is a study of emotions in the work of James Joyce.

10 Dogging the Subject: Samuel Beckett, Emmanuel Levinas, and Posthumanist Ethics

Karalyn Kendall-Morwick

The late-modernist fiction of Samuel Beckett figures the human as having a tenuous grasp on its species identity—as "[clinging] on to . . . the human," in the words of one narrator (*How* 47). This theme, visible in Beckett's early work, comes to the forefront in the novels written in the wake of the dehumanizing atrocities of World War II. The eponymous protagonist of *Watt* is "troubled . . . by this indefinable thing that prevented him from saying, with conviction, and to his relief, of the object that was so like a pot, that it was a pot, and of the creature that still in spite of everything presented a large number of exclusively human characteristics, that it was a man" (82–83). As the pun on Watt/What indicates, the ontological status of the human is a central concern in this and subsequent novels—especially the trilogy of *Molloy*, *Malone Dies*, and *The Unnamable*, whose narrators, Paul Sheehan notes, share a "relationship with their species [that] is provisional and under constant renegotiation" ("Zoomorphism" 663). Molloy, for instance, "abandon[s]" the "erect motion . . . of man" in the course of his narrative and makes only qualified assertions about his species identity: "I am human, I fancy . . ." (*Three* 89, 78).

Beckett's work has thus been invoked in recent debates concerning the demise or persistence of humanism. Richard Begam reads the trilogy as mapping a "shift from a humanist discourse, centred on man, to an antihumanist discourse, centred on language" (302). Conversely, Gilbert Yeoh insists that Beckett's work affirms humanism by conveying the "genuine despair of human subjects overwhelmed by the growing darkness, obscurity and impenetrability that result from the proliferating negative textuality" (115). Jonathan Boulter deems Beckett's stance posthumanist, but adds that "the persistence of the human even in its most denuded form . . . essentially collapses the opposition 'human-posthuman'" (15). The slippage between "posthumanist" and "posthuman" in Boulter's analysis warrants attention, as theorists like Cary Wolfe hold that posthumanism "isn't posthuman at all—in the sense of being 'after' our embodiment has been transcended—but is only posthumanist, in the sense that it opposes [humanist] fantasies of disembodiment and autonomy" (*What* xv). Indeed, particularly perplexing for Beckett's human is the fact that he remains recognizable as such.[1] Despite his "loss of species," he exhibits reason, free will, and language, making him "all too human" in the words of Moran, the detective who narrates the second half of *Molloy* (*Watt* 85, *Three* 107). Sheehan thus characterizes Beckett's stance as an "apostasised humanism" that "reopens the possibility of value renewal" within the category of the human while rejecting the "overconfident critical orthodoxy" of the humanist tradition (*Modernism* 184).

Until recently, despite rigorously examining Beckett's relationship to humanism, scholars have paid scant attention to the presence of animals in Beckett's oeuvre—a notable omission considering the centrality of the human/animal binary to humanist delineations of the subject by thinkers as diverse as Aristotle, Descartes, Kant, Heidegger, Lacan, and Levinas. Early studies tended to read Beckett's animals as metaphors for the dehumanized modern subject, but a number of critics have begun to take seriously Beckett's interest in animals as such.[2] Shane Weller notes that Beckett repeatedly presents animals "as suffering beings," collapsing "the strict Cartesian distinction between human and animal" (214, 216). Martin Puchner similarly contends that Beckett blurs the human/animal boundary through a "decentering of the human" (21). Puchner situates Beckett's animals within debates about animal rights, a perspective that Wolfe critiques as "essentially humanist" in its goal of extending a more or less Kantian subjectivity to animals, "thus effacing the very difference of the animal other that it sought to respect" (*Animal* 8). In contrast, Weller argues that Beckett's insistence on animals' radical alterity—even as he troubles the Cartesian binary—precludes a simplistic response to animal suffering. Beckett's stance, he proposes, is best understood as "anethical": "a double movement both towards and away from any ethical position" (219).

We can start to make sense of this apparent ambivalence by examining how Beckett troubles not just the human/animal distinction, but the very idea of "the animal." Derrida takes this concept to task in *The Animal That Therefore I Am*, denouncing the "asinanity" (31)—translator David Wills's approximation of Derrida's "*bêtise*"—of grouping "every living thing that is held not to be human" into a single category without regard for "the infinite space that separates the lizard from the dog, the protozoon from the dolphin, the shark from the lamb," and so on (34). Beckett's resistance to this homogenizing gesture is particularly evident in his representations of dogs. Of the nonhuman inhabitants of the Beckettian landscape, dogs are the most conspicuous and, arguably, the most resistant to emblematization. While their mangy bodies and grotesque sexuality have led critics to regard them as symbols of degraded humanity, they rarely elicit feelings of disapproval or even pity from Beckett's protagonists; more often, they inspire envy or fascination.[3] As Steven Connor notes of two scenes in *Molloy*, the canine encounter "arouses a powerful sense of *otherness*" that prompts Molloy and Moran "to suspend the fractious scepticism of their narratives and forget themselves in consoling reverie" (30).[4] Further, Beckett's humans and dogs are inextricably linked by an interspecies legacy that, Donna Haraway reminds us, "is not especially nice; it is full of waste, cruelty, indifference, ignorance, and loss, as well as of joy, invention, labor, intelligence, and play" (*Companion* 12). Perhaps counterintuitively, it is via the familiar and often darkly comic figure of the dog that Beckett expresses most forcefully the problem of animal alterity for humanist ethics.

Dogs' capacity to perforate the borders of the human is also evident in the work of Jewish philosopher Emmanuel Levinas, whose ethics of alterity shares a complex relationship with the humanist/antihumanist debate in which Beckett's work engages. By positing alterity as the basis for ethical subjectivity, Derrida notes, Levinas breaks with "a certain traditional humanism" that regards rationality and autonomy as essential attributes of the subject ("Eating" 279). His rejection of such criteria would seem to remove the obstacles that have barred animals from ethical subjectivity, yet Levinas maintains that the other who calls the subject into ethical relations can only be another human. Derrida thus dubs Levinasian ethics a "profound humanism" that excludes animals from moral consideration by drawing the boundaries of subjectivity at the borders of the human (279). A canine encounter, though, tempts Levinas to extend ethics beyond the species divide. In "The Name of a Dog, or Natural Rights," he describes a dog who wandered into the Nazi camp where he was imprisoned during World War II. Bobby, Levinas recalls, "would appear at morning assembly and was waiting for us as we returned, jumping up and down and barking in delight. For him, there was no doubt that we were men" (153). Bobby's welcome is so compelling that Levinas dubs him "the last Kantian in Nazi Germany" (153). Despite the ironic disavowal implicit in this statement, Levinas's attribution of something like subjectivity to Bobby indicates just how powerfully dogs confound humanist subject formation.

In what follows, I examine the destabilizing presence of dogs in Beckett's late-modernist fiction—especially *Watt* and *Molloy*—and Levinas's neohumanist philosophy in order to outline the ontological and ethical challenge posed by animal alterity in the aftermath of World War II. Beckett and Levinas both locate the dog in a paradoxical position within what Derrida deems the "sacrificial structure" of Western humanism, wherein the animal is excluded from subjectivity through discursive and literal sacrifice ("Eating" 278). The dog, as animal, belongs to a realm of abjection that defines through negation the humanist subject; yet, as Beckett and Levinas insinuate, dogs occupy a quasi-subjective status by virtue of their coevolutionary relationship with humans. As humans' longtime hunting and herding partners whose labor facilitated the rise of hunter/gatherer and agricultural societies, dogs are co-implicated in the subjugation and sacrifice of other animals, complicating the ethical quandary in which Western humanism finds itself vis-à-vis the animal. While the human's loss of species in Beckett's fiction evokes both the unspeakable horrors of World War II and the destructive and alienating forces of modernity, the canine encounter, as Beckett and (more reluctantly) Levinas indicate, precipitates a more radical, primary confrontation with the sacrificial logic of post-Enlightenment humanism.

In order to illuminate dogs' privileged role in Beckett's reconfiguration of the human/animal relationship, I first examine how the simultaneously subjugated and elevated status of the Beckettian dog complicates the problem of animal suffering for humanist ethics. I then turn to Levinas's essay on Bobby to demonstrate how humanist formulations of the subject persistently falter in the canine encounter. Finally, I link dogs' destabilizing power to their vital role in facilitating human violence against other animals, illustrating how Beckett and Levinas co-implicate humans and dogs in the crimes against animality epitomized by the modern slaughterhouse. The interconnected motifs of caninicity and slaughter in the Beckettian landscape thus signal dogs' special capacity to disrupt humanist configurations of the subject. Throughout, I reveal how Beckett's dogs, like Levinas's Bobby, mutely articulate the need for a posthumanist ethics that recuperates and respects the radical alterity subsumed under the category of "the animal."

A DOG'S LIFE

The persistence with which Beckett portrays animals in states of suffering makes it difficult to dismiss them as mere symbols of human futility or degradation. As Weller observes, one of the primary ways Beckett undermines the human/animal divide is by depicting animals experiencing suffering and "human beings expressing sympathy for that suffering" (although Beckett's refusal to efface alterity means that he remains skeptical as to "whether or not the attempt to alleviate the suffering of an animal is in fact an unambiguously ethical action"—a question to which I will return) (214). Belacqua in the early story "Dante and the Lobster" is troubled by the routine suffering of animals. He spots a downed horse with a man sitting on its head and acknowledges "that that is considered the right thing to do. But why?" (*More* 20). Later, he watches in horror as his aunt prepares to boil the eponymous lobster. Her insistence that lobsters "feel nothing" echoes the Cartesian view of animals as automata (22). For Descartes, "pain exists only in the understanding," so animals, though they may exhibit "the external movements which accompany this feeling in us," cannot experience "pain in the strict sense" because they lack reason ("To Mersenne" 148). Belacqua tries to reassure himself that "it's a quick death," but the narrator's retort—"It is not"—undercuts the Cartesian distinction between the human as rational animal and the animal as living machine (22). To the extent that Beckett represents animals as suffering beings, and that his characters' sympathy for their suffering indicates that it warrants ethical consideration, Beckett (like Derrida) appears to endorse Jeremy Bentham's oft-quoted formulation: "[T]he question is not, Can they *reason?* nor, Can they *talk?* but, Can they *suffer?*" (283n).[5]

Yet Beckett's blurring of the Cartesian divide neither negates alterity nor translates into a straightforward call to eliminate suffering in the name of animal rights or a utilitarian maximization of happiness. An autobiographical fragment from his late novella *Company* illustrates the danger of naïve attempts to assign rights or alleviate suffering. A boy "take[s] pity on a hedgehog out in the cold and put[s] it in an old hatbox with some worms," eventually reopening the box to discover the gruesome results of his "good deed" (*Nohow* 20): "The mush. The stench" (22).[6] Weller references this passage to show that, for Beckett, "the alterity of the animal means that any human intervention is liable to be catastrophic" (214–15). Yet as Belacqua's response to the downed horse suggests, animal suffering assumes multiple forms, complicating the questions of whether and how the human should respond. In the case of a non-domesticated animal like the hedgehog, intervention seems ill advised, especially when the animal's perceived distress is an anthropomorphic projection. By contrast, Beckett presents the suffering of equines as unjust when it results from their use as means to human ends. In *Malone Dies*, for example, Lambert rescues an old mule from slaughter, but only because he hopes to "screw" more labor out of him (*Three* 212). Equine suffering typically elicits genuine sympathy from Beckett's protagonists, such as when Molloy sees a man whipping a team of donkeys: "My eyes caught a donkey's eyes, they fell to his little feet, their brave fastidious tread" (26).[7]

Even among domesticated animals, suffering—and consequently its ethical import—is not a uniform phenomenon. While equines suffer as draft animals, Beckett's dogs suffer in their seemingly elevated status as humans' companions. The most obvious figures of canine suffering in Beckett's oeuvre are the famished dogs of *Watt*. While employed as a servant to the mysterious Mr Knott, Watt is instructed to give leftover food to the dog—a puzzling order because there is no dog to be found. So begins Watt's lengthy exposition of a convoluted system for uniting Mr Knott's leftovers with a dog hungry enough to ensure that "not an atom remained" (95). The resulting arrangement involves the employment of the five-generation Lynch family to maintain a "colony of famished dogs set up by Mr Knott in order that there should never be wanting a famished dog to eat his food on those days that he did not eat it himself" (100). The famished dog arrangement is typically regarded as a satire of pre-established harmony, Leibniz's attempt to reconcile Cartesian dualism with the apparent interaction of mind and body. Watt thus ponders "the manner in which this problem had been solved . . . in that far distant past, when Mr Knott set up his establishment" (93).[8] The absurd complexity of the system, moreover, mocks Descartes's method of making "enumerations so complete, and reviews so comprehensive, that I could be sure of leaving nothing out" (*Discourse* 120).

Beckett's emphasis on the suffering of the famished dogs reveals the ethical dimension of his satire of Cartesian rationalism. Even Watt, who dislikes dogs, is preoccupied with the canine participants in Mr Knott's arrangement: "But much more than with the Lynches, or with Mr Knott's remains, Watt's concern, while it lasted, was with the dog" (116). That he is most disturbed by their suffering is evident in his longing to know "which the sufferer, and what the sufferer, and what the suffering" (117). And suffer they do:

The dogs employed to eat Mr Knott's occasional remains were not long-lived, as a rule. This was very natural. For besides what the dog got to eat, every now and then, on Mr Knott's backdoorstep, it got so to speak nothing to eat. For if it had been given food other than the food that Mr Knott gave it, from time to time, then its appetite might have been spoilt, for the food that Mr Knott gave it. . . . Add to this that the dog was seldom off the chain, and so got no exercise worth mentioning. This was inevitable. For if the dog had been set free, to run about, as it pleased, then it would have eaten the horsedung . . . and all the other nasty things that abound, on the ground, and so ruined its appetite, perhaps for ever, or worse still would have run away, and never come back. (112)

That the famished dogs suffer from perpetual emaciation and confinement extends Beckett's critique of Enlightenment rationalism to the problem of animal suffering. Caught up in a Cartesian "mecanism [sic]" that rationalizes their condition as "natural" and "inevitable," the famished dogs offer a mute critique of the absurdity of a philosophical tradition that strips animals of feeling and agency in order to legitimize their exploitation (117).[9]

In Beckett's trilogy, the use of dogs to satisfy human desires is most visible in Teddy, the pet dog Molloy accidentally runs over with his bicycle. Teddy's death, rather than causing him pain, serves to "put [him] out of his misery" as his owner, Lousse, is taking him to be destroyed (*Three* 33). The dog is "old, blind, deaf, crippled with rheumatism and perpetually incontinent," yet the real misery from which Molloy unwittingly frees him is his degraded life as a woman's pet (33). As his name suggests, Teddy is little more than a comforting object, like the "woolly bear" Moran's son must "hug" in order to fall asleep (122). He belongs to that category of animals so disparaged by Deleuze and Guattari: "individuated animals, family pets, sentimental, Oedipal animals each with its own petty history" (240). Far from representing a radical alterity that dissolves human fantasies of identity and autonomy, Teddy merely "take[s] the place of a child" (47). Like Miss Dew's "so-called dog" in *Murphy*, he is an infantilized, neutered surrogate (98).[10] This logic of surrogacy enables Molloy to replace Teddy in turn, atoning for his misdeed by leading "a dog's life"—a phrase Beckett uses elsewhere to describe the situation of a henpecked man—while detained by the oppressively maternal Lousse (*More* 167). Lousse, whose name is a homophone for the singular form of "lice," buries Teddy with "ticks in his ears," confirming that his existence is delimited by parasitic human desires (37).

Lousse's smothering affection for dogs and men alike evokes Beckett's vexed relationship with his mother, May, whose well-documented fondness for dogs and donkeys no doubt informs their prominence in the Beckettian bestiary. Piecing together biographical accounts that indicate that Beckett ran over one of May's Kerry Blue terriers in 1926, Daniel Katz proposes that "Teddy's fatal accident is itself a re-elaboration of [this] traumatic event" (250).[11] Yet Beckett's critique of the profoundly humanist sentimentalization of the pet extends beyond his maternal characters.

A masculinized form of pet love is satirized in the story of Ernest Louit, told by the servant Arthur in *Watt*. Louit, a university student, embarks with his bull terrier O'Connor on a research expedition to County Clare. His pastoral vision of traversing the countryside with his faithful dog at his heels and sleeping "in the sweet-smelling hay . . . of the local barns" soon gives way to a harsh reality punctuated by his discovery of "the skeleton of a goat" in one of only three barns to be found (172). Starving and stranded in a bog, Louit is "reluctantly obliged . . . to hold O'Connor head downward in the morass, until his faithful heart . . . ceased to beat, and then roast him" (172). Man's best friend to the end, O'Connor makes the ultimate sacrifice for the human pursuit of knowledge represented by Louit's research findings, which "could not be of the smallest value to any person other than himself and, eventually, humanity" (173). O'Connor's sentimentalized fidelity, moreover, ironically allows Louit to ennoble the squeamishness that prevents him from skinning his beloved pet: "He took no credit for this, O'Connor in his place would have done the same for him" (173).

The paradoxically elevated and subordinated status of the dog as pet is also evident in Levinas's essay on Bobby. Just as canine companionship bolsters Lousse's maternal identity and Louit's pastoral fantasy, Bobby serves the (albeit worthier) purpose of affirming the humanity of the prisoners of Camp 1492. Bobby's welcoming behavior echoes that of the ultimate figure of canine fidelity: Argos, the ancient dog who "recognized Ulysses beneath his disguise" and, with his last ounce of strength, dropped his ears and thumped his tail in an unmistakably canine greeting (Levinas, "Name" 153). Bobby likewise recognizes the prisoners as "men" despite the fact that the Nazi guards have "stripped us of our human skin" (153). The central irony of Levinas's essay is that the dog emerges as the most human inhabitant of Camp 1492. The Nazi guards, though "called free," are brute enforcers of "Hitlerian violence," while the prisoners are "subhuman, a gang of apes" (153). Bobby, with his Kantian gesture, is able to do what the prisoners cannot: "deliver a message about our humanity" (153). In recognizing the prisoners' violently suppressed humanity, the dog seems poised to transcend his own animality.

Ultimately, though, Bobby's value for Levinas lies in his role as a vehicle for human transcendence. As Richard Nash observes, Levinas's account echoes "the sentimental logic of the pet—those special 'domesticated' animals who function to confer upon us a greater humanity by actions and articulations that simultaneously transcend their 'animal' status and accept the logic of domination and domestication in which such transcendence is recontained" (101). This paradoxical status of the pet is evident in the act of naming invoked by the essay's title: "The Name of a Dog." Bobby's name, though it seemingly elevates him by marking his individuality, also relegates him to the subordinate position he shares with Beckett's Teddy and O'Connor. In this essay, Levinas presents the act of naming sentimentally as something "one does with a cherished dog" (153). Elsewhere, though, he characterizes naming as "a violence and a negation

[that] denies the independence of a being: it belongs to me" ("Is Ontology" 9). Bobby's name, as I have argued elsewhere (Kendall 192–193), thus serves to neutralize the challenge he presents to humanist ethics by casting him in the familiar role of man's best friend: "[T]he dog will attest to the dignity of its person. This is what the friend of man means" (Levinas, "Name" 152). As we will see, though, Beckett insists (and Levinas intimates) that canine alterity is not so easily effaced, and its doggedness poses a grave threat to the intelligibility of humanist ethics.

THE FACE OF A DOG

Levinas famously dubbed his ethics a "humanism of the other man," marking both his affinity and dissatisfaction with Enlightenment humanism.[12] Levinasian ethics remains resolutely humanist in asserting the primacy of the human subject but breaks with a Cartesian or Kantian model premised on rationality. In *Totality and Infinity*, Levinas objects to the reduction of humans to mere "bearers of forces" like reason or free will (21). For Levinas, ethical subjectivity originates not in the self but in the encounter with the other, whose infinite alterity disrupts the egoistic being of the self. While the self seeks impulsively to "nullify separation" and possess the other as an object of knowledge, the face—Levinas's term for the inassimilable alterity of the other—prohibits this totalizing gesture by silently voicing the commandment, "Thou shalt not kill" (251). In Levinas's configuration, I emerge as a subject in my encounter with the other precisely because I become *subject to* the commandment issued by the face. My realization of the other-as-subject thus precedes and enables my own subjectivity. In this formulation, as Levinas readily notes, "Man is an unreasonable animal" in that he is compelled to suspend his self-interest for the sake of the other ("Paradox" 172).

Levinas's rejection of a subjectivity grounded in rational autonomy leads him to align his project partially with the antihumanism he associates with thinkers like Nietzsche, Heidegger, Lacan, and Lévi-Strauss: "Modern antihumanism, which denies the primacy that the human person, a free end in itself, has for the signification of being, is true over and above the reasons it gives itself" ("Substitution" 94). The antihumanist deconstruction of the a priori subject, far from bringing an end to ethical subjectivity, reveals (in spite of itself) that traditional humanism "is not sufficiently human"—particularly in light of the atrocities of World War II, which have "render[ed] tragicomic the concern for oneself and illusory the pretension of the rational animal to have a privileged place in the cosmos" ("Humanism" 127). Levinasian ethics, Peter Atterton observes, thus seems ideally suited "to accommodate the inclusion of the other animal, and thereby go beyond the very humanism—and human chauvinism—that has served as a philosophical justification for the mistreatment of animals for over two millennia" (61). What does the human encounter in the face of an animal if not an alterity even more radical than that of the other human? Something rather less compelling to Levinas, who explains:

> The Other is not other with a relative alterity as are, in a comparison, even ultimate species, which mutually exclude one another but still have their place within the community of a genus. The alterity of the Other does not depend on any quality that would distinguish him from me, for a distinction of this nature would precisely imply between us that community of genus which already nullifies alterity. (*Totality* 194)

Counterintuitively, Levinas proposes that animals cannot call humans into ethical relations because our evolutionary kinship negates the alterity of species difference. For Levinas, as for Kant, humans' ethical obligations to animals are indirect, "aris[ing] from the transference to animals of the idea of suffering" ("Paradox" 172). An animal cannot command of (or be commanded by) the other, "Thou shalt not kill."

Levinas's essay on Bobby is especially puzzling given his tendency to foreclose the possibility of animal alterity. Why not (forgive me) let sleeping dogs lie? The invocation of Bobby opens up questions that Levinas strenuously avoids throughout most of his oeuvre. When confronted with the question of the animal in a 1986 interview, he strains to affirm human exceptionalism while simultaneously implying a continuum of what I have elsewhere called "faciality" that problematizes the human/animal divide (Kendall 188). Here, Levinas admits, "I cannot say at what moment you have the right to be called 'face'" ("Paradox" 171). Moreover, he offers an astonishingly inclusive response to the question of whether humans have ethical obligations to other animals: "It is clear that, without considering animals as human beings, the ethical extends to all living beings" (172). In contemplating the extension of ethics to "all living beings" and thus threatening to muddle his entire philosophy, it appears that Levinas has Bobby in mind. When pressed to explain what differentiates the human face from the animal face, he replies, "One cannot entirely refuse the face of an animal. It is via the face that one understands, for example, a dog" (169). He quickly adds that "[t]he phenomenon of the face is not in its purest form in the dog" yet proceeds to undercut this qualification: "But it also has a face" (169).

While the face of a dog pushes Levinas to the brink of abandoning the human/animal distinction that underwrites his neohumanist ethics, Beckett uses the canine encounter as a point of departure for his more radical reconfiguration of the human and its relationship to animality. Like Watt, both Molloy and Moran are irresistibly drawn to dogs (though not necessarily fond of them). Moran takes perverse delight in teasing the neighbors' dog:

> They had an aberdeen called Zulu. People called it Zulu. Sometimes, when I was in a good humour, I called, Zulu! Little Zulu! and he would come and talk to me.... Crouching down I would stroke his ears, through the railings, and utter wheedling words. He did not realize he disgusted me. He reared up on his hind legs and pressed his chest against the bars. Then I could see his little black penis ending in a thin wisp of wetted hair. He felt insecure, his hams trembled, his little paws fumbled for purchase, one after the other. I too wobbled, squatting on my heels. With my

free hand I held on to the railings. Perhaps I disgusted him too. I found it hard to tear myself away from these vain thoughts. (*Three* 105)

This exchange seems initially to affirm the dog's function as a symbol of degraded humanity; in one of the earliest studies of the Beckettian dog, Philip Howard Solomon reads the implicit "comparison between man and dog" as offering an unflattering commentary on "the human condition" (85, 91). Yet while Moran's encounter with Zulu serves in part to blur the species boundary signified by the railings separating his yard from the Elsner sisters', it also underscores the alterity of the canine neighbor. The physical instability of human and dog recalls the calling into question of the self in the Levinasian encounter with the other, while Moran's musings testify to the dog's inassimilable alterity. His clarification that "people called it Zulu" alludes to the appropriative act of naming, and his observation of the dog's penis conjures the negated sexual agency of the pet.

Zulu's unknowability, however, does not prevent Moran from contemplating the dog's perspective; he speculates that Zulu "feels insecure" and wonders whether the dog reciprocates his disgust. His awareness of being looked at by Zulu parallels Derrida's realization in *The Animal That Therefore I Am* when he describes the experience of standing naked before a cat: "[I]t can look at me. It has its point of view regarding me. The point of view of the absolute other . . ." (11). Like Derrida, Moran sees himself *seen by* an animal and avoids both anthropomorphic projections that efface alterity and the anthropocentric refusal to acknowledge the animal's point of view. That Moran resists the impulse to appropriate the other is all the more significant given his tendency to define himself through possessions. Unlike Molloy, who intends but never manages "to draw up the inventory of my goods and possessions" (14), Moran peppers his narrative with references to "[m]y lamp," "my bees," "my house," "my grounds," etc.; he even adds his son to this inventory, first by naming young Jacques after himself and then—as if to retract the nod to individuality implicit in the act of naming—by referring to him almost invariably as "my son" (92–93).

As Moran's attraction to Zulu suggests, human/dog encounters in *Molloy* reveal the human's pitiable isolation within the subject position delineated by the humanist tradition. Molloy expresses frustration with this condition at the outset of his journey when he observes a "face to face" meeting between two men he calls A and C (9). After they part, Molloy continues to watch one of them—"A or C, I don't remember"—but, "in spite of my soul's leap out to him," sees him "only darkly" (11). The anonymity of this encounter, paired with Molloy's ineffectual desire to connect with the human other, stands in sharp contrast to A or C's subsequent interaction with a pomeranian who appears at his heels: "[T]he gentleman turned back, took the little creature in his arms, drew the cigar from his lips and buried his face in the orange fleece . . ." (12). This exchange portrays humans and dogs as always-already joined by an interspecies intimacy that permeates their encounters. Molloy thus wonders:

[W]hat prevented the dog from being one of those stray dogs that you pick up and take in your arms, from compassion or because you have long been straying with no other company than the endless roads, sands, shingle, bogs, and heather, than this nature answerable to another court, than at long intervals the fellow convict you long to stop, embrace, suck, suckle and whom you pass by, with hostile eyes, for fear of his familiarities? Until the day when, your endurance gone, in this world for you without arms, you catch up in yours the first mangy cur you meet, carry it the time needed for it to love you and you it, then throw it away. (12)

To some extent, this passage positions the stray dog, like the pet dog, as a disposable surrogate. Unable to embrace "the fellow convict," the wanderer grasps "the first mangy cur" to cross his path. Yet Molloy also expresses the loneliness peculiar to a being trapped within a "nature answerable to another court"—that is, human nature as circumscribed by the humanist tradition. Longing to transgress the borders of a subject position premised on the subjugation of embodiment and animality, he finds himself "up against [A or C], up against the dog, gasping" (12). Alarmed, A or C soon departs, leaving Molloy "alone, no . . . restored to myself, no, I never left myself" (13).

In contrast to Beckett's constrained and debilitated narrators, the dogs of *Molloy* are remarkably mobile, refusing to remain confined to their position in the humanist species hierarchy. An anonymous dog who strays into the grove where Moran has set up camp confirms just how thoroughly the latter is "exiled in his manhood" (169). Having suspended his search for Molloy, Moran wanders aimlessly around his camp for three days before this passing dog "relieve[s] the monotony" (153). Whereas Moran's search never progresses beyond the campsite, the dog exits the grove almost as soon as he has entered, "having simply as it were gone straight through" (153). Even Teddy outpaces Molloy, who is every bit as captive as Lousse's pet parrot as he "sweep[s], with the clipped wings of necessity," to his mother's house (27). Teddy, though similarly disabled, achieves Molloy's elusive objective: to "say my goodbyes, finish dying" (7). Molloy thus resents the dog, reasoning, "His death must have hurt him less than my fall me. And he at least was dead" (35). Teddy is buried "like a Carthusian monk, but with his collar and lead," his interment ironically signifying both spiritual ascension in death and degrading captivity in life (36). Ultimately, though, Molloy is the one who remains captive. He manages to escape from Lousse, but later falls into a ditch, where his narrative ends in resignation: "Molloy could stay, where he happened to be" (91).

The relative mobility of dogs makes them objects of fascination for Molloy and Moran, whose respective encounters with a flock of sheep driven by a shepherd and his dog offer a welcome respite from an all-too-human mode of being. Molloy experiences a rare moment of "tranquil assurance" (28), while the usually overbearing Moran finds himself "incapable of speech" (159). Observing the dog, Molloy wonders, "Did he take me for a black sheep entangled in the brambles and was he waiting for an order from his master to drag me out? I don't think so.

I don't smell like a sheep, I wish I smelt like a sheep, or a buck-goat" (28). Molloy seems eager to be "dragged out" of his human form and to encounter the canine other, not in the Levinasian realm of language, but on the dog's olfactory terms. While Molloy wants to smell like a sheep, Moran identifies with the dog in his longing to follow the shepherd: "I will serve you faithfully, just for a place to lie and a little food" (159). As with Zulu, he speculates about the dog's point of view without claiming unmediated access to it, noting that "there was no one to witness his contentment, if that is what it was" (160). Both encounters breed a powerful desire to transcend human form without negating canine alterity, pointing to dogs' special significance for Beckett's posthumanism.

FACING OTHER ANIMALS

The reverent awe Molloy and Moran exhibit in the presence of the human-dog-sheep assemblage, besides signaling the attraction of dogs for Beckett's human, ushers in Beckett's critique of the most potent instantiation of humanism's sacrificial structure—the modern slaughterhouse—and its devastating impact on humanity and animality alike. This critique emerges almost surreptitiously through ironic invocations of the British pastoral tradition, whose usual representative in Beckett's oeuvre is William Wordsworth. Molloy alludes to Wordsworth's notion of "emotion recollected in tranquillity [sic]" ("Preface" 611) when he notes, "It is in the tranquillity of decomposition that I remember the long confused emotion which was my life . . ." (*Three* 25). That Molloy awakens to the sight of the shepherd and his flock recalls a misreading of Wordsworth's *Immortality Ode* whereby "fields of sleep" ("Ode" l. 28) become "fields of sheep"—a "compositor's error" referenced in *Murphy* when Miss Dew tries vainly to feed lettuce to a "miserable-looking lot" of sheep (99). Moran's reverie likewise conjures "that most excellent man" (*Murphy* 100):

> What a pastoral land, my God. . . . The silence was absolute. Profound in any case. All things considered it was a solemn moment. The weather was divine. It was the close of day. . . . How I would love to dwell upon [the shepherd]. His dog loved him, his sheep did not fear him. (*Three* 158)

In the presence of animals, Moran ironically assumes the role of the Wordsworthian speaker, his reflections painting an idealized picture of rural life.

Yet Beckett's pastoral landscape, far from constituting a pristine retreat from the human world, is filled with signs of humanity's devastating presence. As a cultivated landscape, it conveys both the sublime and grotesque effects of humans' interactions with the nonhuman world. Thus, where Wordsworth's speaker finds "The anchor of my purest thoughts, the nurse, / The guide, the guardian of my heart, and soul / Of all my moral being" ("Lines" ll. 110–12), Molloy finds only "senseless, speechless, issueless misery" (*Three* 13). Here, animal presence, rather than signaling the peaceful coexistence of humans and nonhumans in a landscape where "every Beast keep[s] holiday," reveals the violent underside of the pastoral economy (Wordsworth, "Ode" l. 33). Molloy's encounter with the sheep leads him to wonder whether the flock is bound for pasture or slaughter, leaving him "with persisting doubts" about which "there is much to be said" (29). Moran interrupts his own Wordsworthian meditation with the disturbing thought that the sheep might perceive him as "the butcher come to make his choice" (159). Surrounded by animal death, Beckett's human cannot achieve the transcendence associated with the contemplation of nature in Romantic pastoralism.

Dogs' complicity in the violence of slaughter in *Molloy* brings us again to Levinas's essay on Bobby, which alludes to the sacrifice of other animals by opening with a verse from Exodus: "You shall be men consecrated to me; therefore you shall not eat any flesh that is torn by beasts in the field; you shall cast it to the dogs" ("Name" 151). Following this epigraph, his thoughts turn not to Bobby, but to the animals whom most humans encounter "at the family table, as you plunge your fork into your roast. . . . There is . . . enough there to make us want to limit, through various interdictions, the butchery that every day claims our 'consecrated' mouths!" (151). In these opening lines, it is animals destined for slaughter—not Bobby—who appear poised to make moral claims on Levinas. Unlike the named dog whose memory the essay preserves, these animals have become what Carol J. Adams calls "absent referents": beings who "enable the existence of meat" but who are "absent from the act of eating meat because they have been transformed into food" (51). They are likewise absent from Levinas's essay, effaced literally and figuratively as "roast" (Kendall 195).

By alluding to butchered animals and thus problematizing their material and rhetorical erasure, Levinas foregrounds the unpalatable matter of animal suffering at the start of his essay. While he upholds the primacy of the human with the modest proposal that we might merely "want to limit" ("Name" 151) the violence committed for the sake of our appetites, his reference to industrialized slaughter in the context of a Holocaust narrative intensifies what might otherwise be dismissed as a droll depiction of meat eating as a testament to humans' repressed animality. In this way, John Llewelyn argues, Levinas "all but proposes an analogy between the unspeakable human Holocaust and the unspoken animal one" (235). Levinas's obliqueness can be read in part as a response to Heidegger's infamous assertion that "[a]s for its essence, [the mechanized food industry] is the same thing as the manufacture of corpses in the gas chambers and the death camps"—a cursory comparison that Levinas elsewhere rejects as "beyond commentary" ("As If" 487). Yet as David Clark argues, the comparative subtlety of Levinas's rhetoric makes the analogy all the more powerful: "[T]he fact that the question of our obligations to animals is raised in such a maximally important context, indeed, as the opening move in the evocation of that context, puts to us that the thought of the human, no matter how profound . . . can never be wholly divorced from the thought of the animal" (171). By implicitly linking the institutionalized sacrifice of humans to that of other animals, without simply equating the two qua Heidegger, Levinas compels his reader to entertain thoughts that "make one lose one's appetite" for animal flesh ("Name" 151).

Levinas's analogy—like Molloy's and Moran's concerns about the fate of the flock—underscores the paradox of slaughter, which demonstrates powerfully both the violence that the human-as-subject permits itself to inflict on animals and the tenuousness of the humanity that serves as its justification. This paradox has only intensified, Derrida argues, with the "unprecedented transformation" of the human/animal relationship under the conditions of modernity (*Animal* 24). The most potent sign of this transformation is industrialized animal agriculture, the perverse cruelties of which Derrida also likens to genocide: "As if, for example, instead of throwing a people into ovens and gas chambers (let's say Nazi) doctors and geneticists had decided to organize the overproduction and overgeneration of Jews, gypsies, and homosexuals by means of artificial insemination, so that, being continually more numerous and better fed, they could be destined in always increasing numbers for the same hell . . ." (26). The dizzying magnitude of animal life and death in modernized farming prompts Molloy's exclamation: "Good God, what a land of breeders, you see quadrupeds everywhere" (*Three* 29). Their grim destination is confirmed by his observation that "slaughter-houses are not confined to towns, no, they are everywhere, the country is full of them" (29). So pervasive is the slaughterhouse that several of the trilogy's characters live near one. Molloy hears the "violent raucous tremulous bellowing . . . [of] shambles and cattle-markets" from his mother's room (22); Moran suspects his son of sneaking off to a nearby slaughterhouse to avoid church; and The Unnamable lives on "a quiet street near the shambles" (327).[13]

The unprecedented scale of slaughter in modernity—a result of increasingly efficient technologies for producing and processing animal bodies—generated equally unprecedented concerns about its implications for humanity. In his study of changes in slaughtering methods over a period that spans the first several decades of Beckett's and Levinas's lives (both were born in 1906), Jonathan Burt notes that debates over the fraught concept of humane slaughter typically "focused on the killing alone" rather than on broader animal welfare concerns (126). Molloy, too, fixates on the scene of animal death; he envisions the sheep "fall[ing], their skulls shattered, their thin legs crumpling, first to their knees, then over on their fleecy sides, under the pole-axe, though that is not the way they slaughter sheep, but with a knife, so that they bleed to death" (*Three* 29). The act of killing, imagined so vividly by Molloy, is precisely what interested a committee appointed by the British Admiralty in 1904 to evaluate contemporary methods of slaughter, including ritual Jewish slaughter, or *shechitah*. The committee concluded that *shechitah* "was not of 'equal humanity'" with methods employing a pole-axe to stun animals prior to killing them (Burt 127). The conflation of humanity and humanness in these findings prefigures the anti-Semitism of the animal welfare movement in 1930s Germany; in pursuit of the elusive goal of humane slaughter, the method of killing became a litmus test for humanity in both senses of the word. However, Molloy's blunt description of sheep "crumpling . . . under the pole-axe" or "bleed[ing] to death"—two methods deemed humane by their respective proponents—offers no assurance of a humane death.

For many, the key to making slaughter more humane lay in the development of increasingly sophisticated stunning tools, and technologies improving upon the pole-axe emerged in the 1920s. Electrical stunning in particular promised to "further the cause of humanity," as one of its developers boasted in 1929 (Müller 166). This method had the particularly attractive effect of silencing animals, according to a contributor to the *British Veterinary Journal*: "I have watched dozens of pigs being anaesthetised by the electro-lethaler in a most easy and perfect way. After each one was narcotized it was hoisted, stuck and bled without struggle or squeal; the slaughterhouse was thus made a place of peaceful quiet" (Hill 53). As this description indicates, the ethical impetus for humane slaughter became difficult to disentangle from the aesthetic. Burt thus notes that these efforts to make slaughter more humane disturbingly produced "slaughter at its most orderly and mechanistic. There are no sounds of pigs squealing in agony, nothing to indicate to a wider world, neighbors, or passersby the extent of the life-taking going on within the slaughterhouse" (131). The aestheticization of slaughter supports Derrida's observation "that men do all they can in order to dissimulate this cruelty or to hide it from themselves; in order to organize on a global scale the forgetting or misunderstanding of this violence" (*Animal* 26). In Beckett's trilogy, though, "the slaughter-house loom[s] larger and larger," signaling the inevitable failure of attempts to silence dying animals in the name of humanity (*Three* 212).

To some extent, Levinas's essay positions Bobby as a proxy for these silenced animals, and numerous commentators have read Bobby's Kantian gesture as an unheeded call to extend ethics to animals in general. Such readings overlook the decidedly unsentimental essence of Levinas's connection to Bobby signaled by the verse from Exodus. In citing a verse that compels humans to cast undesirable flesh "to the dogs," Levinas, like Beckett, exposes the violent underpinnings of the human/dog relationship. By underscoring how dogs facilitate and benefit from the sacrifice of nonhuman, non-*canine* animals, Beckett and Levinas indicate that dogs are best understood not as representatives of "the animal"—a homogenous category opposed to the human—but as what Haraway calls "[p]artners in the crime of human evolution" (*Companion* 5). The enterprising wolves who exploited "the calorie bonanzas provided by humans' waste dumps," Haraway explains, eventually became the domesticated companions whose labor facilitated the rise of hunter-gatherer and agricultural societies (29). Humans and dogs have shaped one another's biological and cultural histories precisely because each species enabled the other "to consume well" (Haraway, *When* 17). On an evolutionary scale, the shared appetite for meat engendered a partnership premised on the subjugation of other animals—a legacy that haunts the canine encounter in Beckett's fiction and Levinas's essay.

CONCLUSION

While Levinas ultimately attempts to assimilate Bobby's alterity by sentimentalizing him as "the friend of man," Beckett's dogs invariably exceed their roles as emblems of degradation, as surrogates for the other human, and as representatives of "the animal" ("Name" 152). Beckett's insistence on dogs' dual status as victims of the humanist disavowal of animality and as vital participants in systematized violence against other animals indicates that any ethical thinking about "the animal" must begin by interrogating that very category and acknowledging the heterogeneous multiplicity of life forms it purports to encompass. In this way, Beckett anticipates Derrida's critique not only of the *bêtise* whereby post-Enlightenment humanism condemns beings called animal to "a noncriminal putting to death" ("Eating" 278), but also of the residual humanism that inheres in much of the postmodern and poststructuralist thought with which Beckett's work is frequently aligned. It follows that any examination of the animal and its relationship to the human in Beckett's oeuvre must take into consideration how Beckett problematizes these terms by deconstructing the sacrificial logic that underwrites the death camps and the slaughterhouse alike.

At the same time, Beckett's dogs offer the human a kind of hope via the interruptive power of the canine encounter. In an oft-quoted passage, Molloy describes himself as confined to a "sealed jar to which I [owe] my being so well preserved," yet his need to shore up the self by shutting out exteriority competes with his persistent longing for connection—a longing both intensified and frustrated by the animal suffering that permeates the Beckettian landscape (*Three* 49). Even from within the jar, he hears "other things calling me and towards which too one after the other my soul was straining, wildly. I mean of course the fields . . . and the animals . . . and my hand on my knee and above all the other wayfarer, A or C, I don't remember, going resignedly home" (11). The sealed jar of the humanist subject position estranges Molloy from his environment, its animal inhabitants, his fellow human wayfarers, and even his own body, but occasionally "a wall [gives] way" as he strains toward exteriority (49). Dogs' ability to interrupt the endless cogitations of Beckett's narrators offers the human a way out of its egoistic being—one that requires a rethinking of the self/other relation that extends beyond the narrow category of the human. Thus, Beckett's apparently anethical stance toward animal suffering stems not from a reluctance to acknowledge the animal face, but from his cognizance of the immense but urgent task of learning, in Haraway's words, "how to see who [animals] are and hear what they are telling us, not in [the] bloodless abstraction" of sweeping pronouncements about "the animal," "but in one-on-one relationship, in otherness-in-connection" (*Companion* 45). Like Bobby, Beckett's dogs challenge the human to learn how to respond, not just to the human other in its relative alterity, but to animal others in their radical alterity and heterogeneity.

Notes

1. My use of gendered terminology throughout this essay is deliberate, for it is typically Beckett's male characters who find themselves unable to make sense of their species membership. Moreover, the post-Enlightenment subject under discussion is, I would argue, prototypically male.

2. For early studies that read Beckett's animals as emblems of degraded humanity, see Chambers and Solomon. Signs of a growing interest in animals within the field of Beckett studies are the Beckett and Animality conference held at the University of Reading in 2009 and an anthology based on its proceedings, *Samuel Beckett and Animality*, edited by Mary Bryden (2012).

3. The association of canine bodies with grotesque sexuality is visible in a number of texts. In *How It Is*, the narrator describes a dog "lower[ing] its snout to its black and pink penis too tired to lick" (30) and later remarks, "my spinal dog it licked my genitals" (85). At the beginning of *Mercier and Camier*, an awkward embrace between "our heroes" is rendered even more so by the presence of two dogs "copulating, with the utmost naturalness," a few feet away (9). Molloy describes his sexual relationship with Edith, a woman he meets "in a rubbish dump," in canine terms: "She bent over the couch, because of her rheumatism, and in I went from behind. . . . It seemed all right to me, for I had seen dogs, and I was astonished when she confided that you could go about it differently" (*Three* 56–57).

4. Connor attributes this response to "the presence of animals" more generally, as the scenes in question involve dogs and sheep (30). Below, I discuss the special significance of dogs in such multispecies assemblages.

5. See Derrida, *Animal* 27–29.

6. Biographer Anthony Cronin notes that this passage depicts "[o]ne of the traumas of [Beckett's] childhood" (21).

7. The expression of donkeys also proves compelling for Belacqua in *Dream of Fair to Middling Women*: "The appearance of domestic animals of all kinds he disliked, save the extraordinary countenance of the donkey seen full-face" (127). Beckett's mother, May, owned a number of donkeys, and at least one of these—Kisch, named by Beckett and his brother—was purchased from an abusive owner (Cronin 22).

8. See, for example, Ackerley and Gontarski 454, 630–31.

9. The breeding program outlined in Beckett's notebooks, in which Irish setters and Palestine retrievers are crossed to produce the optimal variety of famished dog found in the novel, further underscores the material ways in which human whims shape canine bodies by alluding to the world of dog breeding—a world with which Beckett no doubt came into contact via his mother, who owned and exhibited "a whole series of Kerry Blue terriers" (Beckett, qtd. in Knowlson and Knowlson 7). Regarding Mr Knott's breeding program, see Ackerley and Gontarski 146. Anna O'Meara de Vic Beamish, one of Beckett's neighbors while he was writing *Watt*, "used to breed Airedale terriers in a kennel in Cannes" (Beckett, qtd. in Knowlson and Knowlson 85) and had written two books inspired by her dogs in the 1930s (Knowlson 300).

10. When Murphy first meets Miss Dew, she is holding "a lead whereby her personality was extended to a Dachshund so low and so long that Murphy had no means of telling whether it was a dog or a bitch," indicating the literal and figurative neutering of the pet dog (98).

11. See also Knowlson 79–80. Cronin notes that Beckett "took care never to own an animal and take responsibility for its well-being or its love" (21). That Beckett viewed pet-keeping as a weighty responsibility indeed is indicated by the fact that he "contemplated suicide" following the death of one of his mother's Kerry Blues—the one killed in the accident, by Katz's account—and later grieved the death of another with whom he had taken many walks and who appears in *More Pricks Than Kicks* and *Krapp's Last Tape* (Cronin 248–49, 258). In the latter case, he regretted not being able to "be with her at the end, to try and make it perhaps a little easier," and had difficulty persuading his distraught mother "to take a reasonable view of what oneself could not take a reasonable view of" (qtd. in Knowlson 244–5).

12. This is a translation of the title of Levinas's 1972 book, *Humanisme de l'autre homme*, sometimes translated simply as "humanism of the other." As we will see, though, Levinas has in mind an exclusively human other.

13. See Beckett, *Three* 95, 97. In *Malone Dies*, too, the eponymous narrator tells the story of Lambert, "a connoisseur of mules" (212) with a "gift" for "sticking pigs" (201) and later imagines "the last stage of the horse" as it stands at the gates of the slaughterhouse (230). The Unnamable's location corresponds to that of a room Beckett rented near the cattle market in Camden Town, London, in 1932 (Knowlson 195). In *Murphy*, Celia rents a room in the same neighborhood "between Pentonville Prison and the Metropolitan Cattle Market" (63).

Works Cited

Ackerley, C.J., and S.E. Gontarski. *The Grove Companion to Samuel Beckett*. Grove, 2004.

Adams, Carol J. *The Sexual Politics of Meat: A Feminist-Vegetarian Critical Theory*. 10th anniversary ed. Continuum, 2000.

Atterton, Peter. "Ethical Cynicism." *Animal Philosophy: Essential Readings in Continental Thought*, edited by Matthew Calarco and Peter Atterton. Continuum, 2004, pp. 51–61.

Beckett, Samuel. *Dream of Fair to Middling Women*. Arcade, 1992.

———. *How It Is*. Trans. Samuel Beckett. Grove, 1964.

———. *Mercier and Camier*. Translated by Samuel Beckett. Grove, 1974.

———. *More Pricks Than Kicks*. Grove, 1972.

———. *Murphy*. Grove, 1957.

———. *Nohow On: Company, Ill Seen Ill Said, Westward Ho*. Grove, 1996.

———. *Three Novels: Molloy, Malone Dies, The Unnamable*. Translated by Patrick Bowles and Samuel Beckett. Grove, 1955.

———. *Watt*. Grove, 1970.

Begam, Richard. "Samuel Beckett and Antihumanism." *REAL: Yearbook of Research in English and American Literature*, vol. 13, 1997, pp. 299–312.

Bentham, Jeremy. *An Introduction to the Principles of Morals and Legislation*, edited by J.H. Burns and H.L.A. Hart. Oxford UP, 1996.

Boulter, Jonathan. *Beckett: A Guide for the Perplexed*. Continuum, 2008.

Burt, Jonathan. "Conflicts around Slaughter in Modernity." *Killing Animals*, edited by The Animal Studies Group. U of Illinois P, 2006, pp. 120–144.

Chambers, Ross. "The Artist as Performing Dog." *Comparative Literature*, vol. 23, no. 4, 1971, pp. 312–324.

Clark, David. "On Being 'The Last Kantian in Nazi Germany': Dwelling with Animals after Levinas." *Animal Acts: Configuring the Human in Western History*, edited by Jennifer Ham and Matthew Senior. Routledge, 1997.

Connor, Steven. "Beckett's Animals." *Journal of Beckett Studies*, vol. 8, 1992, pp. 29–44.

Cottingham, John, Robert Stoothoff, and Dugald Murdoch, editors. *The Philosophical Writings of Descartes*. 3 vols. Cambridge UP, 1985.

Cronin, Anthony. *Samuel Beckett: The Last Modernist*. Da Capo Press, 1997.

Deleuze, Gilles, and Félix Guattari. *A Thousand Plateaus: Capitalism and Schizophrenia*. Translated by Brian Massumi. U of Minnesota P, 1987.

Derrida, Jacques. *The Animal That Therefore I Am*. Translated by David Willis. Fordham UP, 2008.

———. "'Eating Well,' or the Calculation of the Subject." Translated by Peter Connor and Avital Ronell. *Points . . . Interviews, 1974–1994*. Edited by Elisabeth Weber. Stanford UP, 1995, pp. 255–287.

Descartes, René. *Discourse on the Method*. Translated by Robert Stoothoff. Cottingham, Stoothoff, and Murdoch, vol. 1, pp. 111–151.

———. "To Mersenne." 11 June 1640. Letter 86 of *Letters*. Translated by Anthony Kenny. Cottingham, Stoothoff, and Murdoch, vol 3, pp. 148.

Gill, Stephen, editor. *William Wordsworth: The Major Works*. Oxford UP, 2008.

Haraway, Donna. *The Companion Species Manifesto: Dogs, People, and Significant Otherness*. Prickly Paradigm Press, 2003.

———. *When Species Meet*. U of Minnesota P, 2008.

Hill, Leonard. "Electric Methods of Producing Humane Slaughter." *British Veterinary Journal*, vol. 91, 1935, pp. 51–57.

Katz, Daniel. "Beckett's Measures: Principles of Pleasure in *Molloy* and 'First Love.'" *Modern Fiction Studies*, vol. 49, no. 2, 2003, pp. 246–260.

Kendall, Karalyn. "The Face of a Dog: Levinasian Ethics and Human/Dog Co-evolution." *Queering the Non/Human*, edited by Noreen Giffney and Myra J. Hird. Ashgate, 2008, pp. 185–204.

Knowlson, James. *Damned to Fame: The Life of Samuel Beckett*. Simon & Schuster, 1996.

Knowlson, James, and Elizabeth Knowlson. *Beckett Remembering, Remembering Beckett: A Centenary Celebration*. Arcade, 2006.

Levinas, Emmanuel. "As If Consenting to Horror." Trans. Paula Wissing. *Critical Inquiry*, vol. 15, no. 2, 1989, pp. 485–488.

———. "Humanism and An-archy." *Collected Philosophical Papers*. Translated by Alphonso Lingis. Martinus Nijhoff, 1987, pp. 127–139.

———. "Is Ontology Fundamental?" Translated by Simon Critchley, Peter Atterton, and Graham Noctor. Peperzak, Critchley, and Bernasconi, pp. 1–10.

———. "The Name of a Dog, or Natural Rights." Translated by Seán Hand. *Difficult Freedom: Essays on Judaism*. Johns Hopkins UP, 1990, pp. 151–153.

———. "The Paradox of Morality: An Interview with Emmanuel Levinas." Translated by Andrew Benjamin and Tamra Wright. *The Provocation of Levinas: Rethinking the Other*, edited by Robert Bernasconi and David Wood. Routledge, 1988, pp. 168–180.

———. "Substitution." Translated by Alphonso Lingis, Robert Bernasconi, and Simon Critchley. Peperzak, Critchley, and Bernasconi, pp. 79–96.

———. *Totality and Infinity: An Essay on Exteriority*. Translated by Alphonso Lingis. Duquesne UP, 1969.

Llewelyn, John. "Am I Obsessed by Bobby? (Humanism of the Other Animal)." *Re-Reading Levinas*, edited by Robert Bernasconi and Simon Critchley. Indiana UP, 1991, pp. 234–245.

Müller, Max. "The Electric Stunning of Animals for Slaughter from the Humane Standpoint." *British Veterinary Journal*, vol. 85, 1929, pp. 164–166.

Nash, Richard. "Animal Nomenclature: Facing Other Animals." *Humans and Other Animals in Eighteenth-Century British Culture: Representation, Hybridity, Ethics*, edited by Frank Palmeri. Ashgate, 2006, pp. 101–118.

Peperzak, Adriaan T., Simon Critchley, and Robert Bernasconi, editors. *Emmanuel Levinas: Basic Philosophical Writings*. Indiana UP, 1996.

Puchner, Martin. "Performing the Open: Actors, Animals, Philosophers." *The Drama Review*, vol. 51, no. 1, 2007, pp. 21–32.

Sheehan, Paul. *Modernism, Narrative and Humanism.* Cambridge UP, 2004.

———. "Zoomorphism." Ackerley and Gontarski, pp. 662–663.

Solomon, Philip Howard. "Samuel Beckett's *Molloy*: A Dog's Life." *The French Review*, vol. 41, no. 1, 1967, pp. 84–91.

Weller, Shane. "Not Rightly Human: Beckett and Animality." *Samuel Beckett Today/Aujourd'hui*, vol. 19, 2008, pp. 211–221.

Wolfe, Cary. *Animal Rites: American Culture, the Discourse of Species, and Posthumanist Theory.* U of Chicago P, 2003.

———. *What Is Posthumanism?* U of Minnesota P, 2010.

Wordsworth, William. "Lines Written a Few Miles above Tintern Abbey." Gill, pp. 131–135.

———. "Ode ('There Was a Time')." Gill, pp. 297–302.

———. "Preface to *Lyrical Ballads* (1802)." Gill, pp. 595–615.

Yeoh, Gilbert. "Beckett's Persistent Humanism: Ethics and Epistemology in *Molloy*." *AUMLA: Journal of the Australasian Universities Language and Literature Association*, vol. 103, 2005, pp. 109–135.

KARALYN KENDALL-MORWICK is professor of English at Washburn University, where she teaches British and American literature, theory, and academic writing. Her research focuses on representations of animals and intersections of animality, race, and gender in literature and culture since 1900. Her book *Canis Modernis: Human/Dog Coevolution in Modernist Literature* examines how modernist representations of dogs challenge the autonomy of the human subject and the humanistic underpinnings of traditional literary forms.

III. Writing the Body: Disabled Ethics and Residual Laughter

11 A Defense of Wretchedness: *Molloy* and Humiliation

Rick de Villiers

In July 1946, *Les Temps modernes* published part of Beckett's short story, "Suite." Simone de Beauvoir had not understood, nor did she particularly care, that the piece was incomplete or that its author expected the concluding segment to appear in the review's next instalment. Naturally, Beckett was anguished by her refusal to let the story—later to be called "La Fin"—come to an end. In response, he wrote to her:

> You are giving me the chance to speak only to retract it before the words have had time to mean anything. You are immobilizing an existence at the very moment at which it is about to take its definitive form. There is something nightmarish about that. I find it hard to believe that matters of presentation can justify, in the eyes of the author of *L'Invitée*, such a mutilation.
>
> Your view is that the fragment which appeared in your last number is a finished piece. That is not my view. I see it as no more than a major premise.
>
> Do not be offended by this plain speaking. It is without rancour. It is simply that there exists a wretchedness [*une misère*] which must be defended to the very end, in one's own work and outside it. (*Letters 2* 42)

The situation was humiliating for reasons beyond the compromise of his artistic integrity. Beauvoir believed Beckett's attempt to submit further writing under the same title to be an act of deception, a ploy to secure publication in two consecutive issues and earn a greater fee than they had initially agreed upon. She also thought, as Knowlson points out (359), that the abounding scatology in the second part was unsuitable for the review.[1] Careful and deferential, Beckett's letter attests to an awareness of his awkward position: an *inconnu* on the French literary scene ("Suite" was his first work in French) who had now made a potentially damaging professional blunder. And yet he does not seek to redress the miscommunication or to save face, but instead pleads for the fictional character who has been "denied his rest."

The task of defending the "wretchedness" in his work was something Beckett had to face throughout his career. He refused, for instance, to capitulate to Houghton Mifflin's demands for major cuts to *Murphy*. He fought against the

Lord Chamberlain's insistence that *Endgame*'s infamous line, "The bastard! He doesn't exist!", be excised or replaced. And when *New World Writing* published a "horrible montage" from *Molloy* without indicating that the text was not continuous, he expressed his annoyance in a letter to Barney Rosset: "The excerpt is always unsatisfactory, but let it at least be continuous. I don't mind how short it is, or with how little beginning or end, but I refuse to be short-circuited like an ulcerous gut" (*Letters 2* 432).

These examples are not exhaustive, but they serve to reveal the opposing desires of the author and of the publishers (and censors). The two principal considerations that appear to compel editorial alterations are narrative cohesion and the moderation of obscenity. For Beckett, however, streamlining and sanitization were not processes distinct from each other. Given the anxious conclusion to "The End," the rest that Beckett felt his "creature" had been denied was not merely a question of narrative resolution. The rest also inhered in those debasing and indecent elements to which Beauvoir had objected. Bodily functions and dysfunctions—what the narrator of *How It Is* calls the "great categories of being" (9)—are part of what gives Beckett's work its "definitive form."

That famous reflection on Joyce's *Work in Progress*, "Here form *is* content, content *is* form" (*Disjecta* 27), has justifiably been applied to Beckett's own work: the words falter because the sense is faltering. Yet there was a time when Beckett was not Beckettian. This was before his realization that the "way [of his art] was in impoverishment, in lack of knowledge and in taking away, in subtracting rather than in adding" (qtd. in Knowlson 352), before the broken epiphany dramatized in *Krapp's Last Tape*. This was also the time before Beckett's widespread fame, before critical and public opinion marked him as an artist whose concern, both in form and content, was weakness. Beauvoir's decision falls within this period. And leaving aside questions of taste and personal disgruntlement, her failure to appreciate how essential infirmities and humiliations are to "Suite" may be explained as a failure to appreciate the Beckettian "agenda."

Today the opposite complication may be at play: the Beckettian agenda is perhaps too well appreciated. This is to say that critics have identified coherence where previous interpretations saw dehiscence or distinction. One example is the collective title often applied when speaking of *Molloy*, *Malone Dies*, and *The Unnamable*: the "Trilogy." Using this term goes against the author's expressed wishes; a sin committed quite often and, for the largest part, unwittingly. The third volume of letters, published in 2014, evinces Beckett's strong opposition to this handle by which to grab three separate bundles. Though he was pleased about John Calder's decision to publish the three works together, he could not propose a general title and was against Calder's suggestion, "Trinity": "It seems to me the three titles should be enough" (187). A month later, in a tone of greater desperation, he dismissed his publisher's next proposal: "Not 'Trilogy,' I beseech you, just the three titles and nothing else" (191). As the publication date of the "three in one" approached, Beckett expressed the same apprehension to Barbara

Bray about Calder's potential editorial choice: "Please God he doesn't call it a trilogy" (222).

The 1959 publication was titled *Three Novels* and not "Trilogy"—not, at least, until the Picador reprint of 1975 yoked the works together under the title, *The Beckett Trilogy*.[2] But to lay the blame solely at Calder's feet is to overlook that *Molloy*, *Malone Dies*, and *The Unnamable* are generally regarded as having more in common than just a single binding. Use of the term "trilogy" is pervasive in Beckett studies. V.S. Pritchett—one of *Three Novels*'s earliest reviewers—referred to the book as a "Trilogy" in the opening sentence of his review. Since then, critics as eminent as Hugh Kenner, Northrop Frye, and Harold Bloom have all applied it to these postwar novels. Even Christopher Ricks, who takes critics to task for curtailing titles, uses this substitutive word.[3] In the 2014 issue of *Samuel Beckett Today/Aujourd'hui* that "revisits" the three novels, five contributors have "Trilogy" in the titles of their respective articles.

This terse survey is not intended to point out lapses in critical practice. Rather, it is to indicate how the similarity of philosophical and aesthetic landscapes across Beckett's "three novels" has shaped its subsequent cartography. Ackerley and Gontarski argue that "'trilogy' or not, the three novels...form a cohesive and extended exploration of the imaginative consciousness" (586). This is undeniable. The question is where the cohesion begins and ends, and where the borders are to be drawn. Beckett himself saw *Molloy* as the "second last of the series begun with Murphy, if it can be said to be a series" (*Letters 2* 71), and the stories that became *Texts for Nothing* as the "afterbirth of *L'Innommable*" (300). This is not to suggest that critics have failed to explore the commonalities that extend from *Murphy* to *Texts for Nothing* or even beyond. But thinking of *Molloy*, *Malone Dies*, and *The Unnamable* as a trilogy or even as three works more intimately related than any other series of works in the Beckett canon—forgetting that three separate texts are collected not because of authorial design but because of publishing savvy—creates a problem not too dissimilar from the one identified in Beauvoir's "mutilation" of "Suite."

My concern here is not with an exclusionary effect, with the fact that the "series" Beckett conceived is amputated at both ends or that other products of the "siege in the room" (*Quatre Nouvelles*, *Mercier et Camier*, and *En Attendant Godot*) are—by dint of the definition of "trilogy"—not allowed to push this particular triangulation into a larger framework. My concern, rather, is with a surplus of correspondence that is created among these three works, with the possibility that this hyper-connection could lead to the *mobilization* of an existence beyond its definitive form. As early as 1929, Beckett warned that, for criticism, the "danger is in the neatness of identification" (*Dis* 19). But it is a danger that his works court through what appears to be their cohesive though amorphous quality. "The amoeba's neck is not easily broken" (*Letters 1* 383)," Beckett remarked about the prospect of cutting *Murphy*. If omission in Beckett is a violation that deprives characters of a necessary stasis, over-identification beyond the distinct borders of texts might amount to the same thing.

HUMILIATING ASSOCIATIONS AND EFFACEMENTS

An equivalent over-identification emerges in *Molloy*. The two principal characters, Molloy and Moran, share a strange resemblance. So uncanny is their likeness that *The Faber Companion to Samuel Beckett* lists twenty-one similarities between them. The correspondence goes deep enough for the editors to claim not just kinship but a kind of vanishing twin syndrome:

> It is not so much that Moran has become Molloy, or that the second half should precede the first, but that Molloy was always part of Moran, as were Gaber and Youdi, agents of a superego.... What the Moran section offers, and why it follows the Molloy section (and why the novel is called *Molloy*, not *Moran*), is a fiction written by Molloy of Molloy as Moran encountering Molloy. (Ackerley and Gontarski 378)

This reading may account for the abrupt change in perspective at the end of the novel where Moran is replaced as the first-person narrator; it may also suggest what Molloy's writing contains. But it perpetrates the same kind of permeability that use of the term "trilogy" allows, and fails to appreciate the novel's "definitive form" that realizes itself not only in parallels but also in differences.

It is telling that toward the end of the novel—the point at which Moran most closely shadows Molloy—Moran reflects on the divergence that may be found in ostensible similarities. Studying the dance of his bees, he remarks:

> I first concluded that each figure [of the dance] was reinforced by means of a hum peculiar to it. But I was forced to abandon this agreeable hypothesis. For I saw the same figure (at least what I called the same figure) accompanied by very different hums. So that I said, The purpose of the hum is not to emphasize the dance, but on the contrary to vary it. And the same figure exactly differs in meaning according to the hum that goes with it.... But there was to be considered not only the figure and the hum, but also the height at which the figure was executed. And I acquired the conviction that the selfsame figure, accompanied by the selfsame hum, did not mean at all the same thing at twelve feet from the ground as it did at six. (*Three Novels* 163-64)

Moran admits that he could be wrong, that the dance could be as pointless as the "dances of the people of the West." But he is content not to subject the phenomenon to his "cogitations" and refuses to conceive of the bees as creatures constituted by his understanding. He explains: "I would never do my bees the wrong I had done my God, to whom I had been taught to ascribe my angers, fears, desires, and even my body" (164). Where previously Moran is fastidious, authoritarian, and partial to the symmetries of accounting, he now resists the temptation to calibrate the world in familiar terms: "I could no longer be bothered with these wretched trifles which had once been my delight" (155). He does not achieve the ataraxy of Molloy, since his mind remains "avid...of the flimsiest analogy" (164). But he is ready to concede the unassimilable otherness of his bees and of God. Moran's comment on the latter relationship throws his newfound negative capability and former audacity into relief. Early in the narrative, his church-going is established as self-serving and self-centered, a ritual that helps to "buck [him] up" (90). The above statement declares this in its reversal of Genesis 1:26 ("Let us make man in our image"), but also undoes it: Moran now recognizes the "wrong" inherent in a subject-defined, Cartesian-inflected ("cogitations") interpretation of external reality.

The passage signals both Moran's metamorphosis and an ethical encouragement to resist the homogenization of alterity. The two things cannot be divorced, since it is at this point that Moran—sharing so many of Molloy's traumas and infirmities, "becoming rapidly unrecognizable" (164)—has the most lucid grasp of himself. As the different heights, hums, and figures of the bees remain beyond exact definition, so too does the exact relation between Molloy and Moran. Beckett brings Moran to the precipice of a humiliating effacement, blurring but not merging his being with Molloy's. This does not, however, preclude our *reading* Moran out of existence. In the *Faber Companion* gloss cited above, for instance, the character suffers a dispossession of self not only within the text proper but also from outside: having been stripped of health, possessions, and his familial relations, Moran is also stripped of the subjectivity which these losses ultimately constitute. Like *The Double*'s Yakov Petrovich Golyadkin, Moran faces erasure in the presence of his doppelganger. But where this erasure is operational in Dostoevsky's novel, it is only a suspended potentiality in Beckett's. The text offers an interpretive choice: to *inscribe* Moran within the consciousness of Molloy and thus to *unwrite* Moran, or to preserve Moran's otherness in following the ethical imperative implicit in the bee passage.

Conflicting responses to alterity are also explored in some of Beckett's other works. In *Company*, for instance, the narrator reflects on his past actions and their consequences. He remembers taking "pity on a hedgehog out in the cold," placing it in a hatbox, supplying it with worms, and feeling warmly triumphal about his humane efforts (18). He further recalls that the "glow" was replaced by "uneasiness" when doubts over his intervention started crowding in (18, 19); a debilitating guilt delays his return to the hatbox by weeks. When he eventually faces the scene of his charity he is met by a "mush" and "stench" that will plague his memory thereafter (19). Laura Salisbury sees the text as an "articulation of the ethical that refuses an ethics of knowledge or judgement which might turn otherness into an object of understanding for the self. It should be thought of as part of a historical moment that reads ethical anxiety and representational crisis as strikingly imbricated" (171). The difference between the bee passage in *Molloy* and the hedgehog passage in *Company* comes down to the difference between contemplative and instrumental reason. This is why Salisbury interprets the later text as an oblique and knotted question about post-Holocaust engagement. But *Molloy* is also a post-Holocaust text. And while it does not explore the problematic ethics of acting on behalf of another to the same extent, it does present the danger of absorbing individual narratives into larger ones.

Directly after pondering the otherness of his bees, Moran reflects on himself with uncertain certainty:

> And to tell the truth I not only knew who I was, but I had a sharper and clearer sense of my identity than ever before, in spite of its deep lesions and the wounds with which it was covered. And from this point of view I was less fortunate than my other acquaintances. I am sorry if this last phrase is not so happy as it might be. It deserved, who knows, to be without ambiguity. (164)

The passage is complex because it accommodates the anguish of self-knowledge and a tacit anxiety about its opposite. Moran regards his clear sense of identity as a source of misfortune, a painful awareness that does not afflict his "other acquaintances." In their turn, these blessed others would seem to be fading from selfhood. Whether this is due to a collective, swallowing identity (the very thing that menaces Moran in his proximity to Molloy) or to other factors is not known. What is of importance and what can be mapped, if only conditionally, is Moran's understanding of the self *as* self.

If the "[un]happy phrase" comprises the whole preceding sentence, its content and possible meanings can only be defined in terms of the first sentence where Moran's "point of view" finds expression. But taking him at his word for the time being, the last phrase ("my other acquaintances") betrays a peculiar element of his self-conception. No "acquaintance" is mentioned in this paragraph, so one cannot read the phrase as a differentiation between one particular acquaintance and other, unidentified ones. The word "other" appears to mark Moran himself, or a version of himself, as one among his familiars. In other words, his sense of identity is contingent on an apperceptive process in which subjectivity becomes objectified: a fault line surfaces between "I" and "me." Moran, then, becomes an object of his consciousness to the same extent that his acquaintances are objects of his consciousness. And while it may be that he has a clearer understanding of himself (than "ever before," but also than of his acquaintances), it results from within a splintered and self-estranged subjectivity.

In the same paragraph, we read: "it seemed to me I was now becoming rapidly unrecognizable"; "the face my hands felt was not my face anymore"; "this belly I did not know remained my belly" (164). This might appear fertile ground for reclaiming Beckett as a Cartesian dualist, but that would be to miss the point that Moran himself misses or can only grasp in ambiguous terms: just as his physical features have suffered a sea change, so too has his ego. Moran's subtle transition between reflection on the physical and reflection on the mental does, however, suggest his awareness of a metamorphic continuum. He does not separate his observations on body and mind with a dividing "but"; rather, he glissades between the two with "And."

It should already be clear that part of the "unhappiness" in the phrase "my other acquaintances" is its tentacular, uncontained ambiguity. To find possible explanations for Moran's idea that he is "less fortunate" than his "other acquaintances" demands that one consider the sentence in which his point of view is articulated and what, from that point of view, would make him less fortunate. Here, two possible meanings are kept in tension, which I will explore in some detail. On the one hand, Moran is less fortunate in that he has a clear sense of identity or, to state it inversely, his acquaintances are more fortunate in not having a clear sense of identity. On the other hand, he is less fortunate in that he has a clear sense of identity *in spite of* the injuries that attend his identity: that is, the lesions and wounds have not had the fortunate identity-obscuring effect they may have had on his acquaintances. Moran thus remains fully conscious of himself and—since there is a self-identifying subject to experience them—his sufferings.

The first meaning may seem an odd way of regarding self-knowledge: surely a clear sense of identity is a good thing? Good, perhaps; fortunate, no. Throughout his life, Beckett was drawn to authors who advocated a deprecated sense of self: certain pre-Socratics, numerous mystics, Thomas à Kempis, Jeremy Taylor, Blaise Pascal, Arnold Geulincx, Arthur Schopenhauer, Emil Cioran, and many others. In most of these cases, negative self-regard is rooted in an ontology of fallenness: the individual who truly knows himself also knows the true and eternal condition of humanity. For Bernard of Clairvaux, "Humility is a virtue by which a man has a low opinion of himself because he knows himself well" (30). Thomas à Kempis claimed that "He who knoweth himself well is vile in his own sight" (214). Jeremy Taylor considered humility to consist not in an external display of wretchedness, but "in hearty and real evil or mean opinion of thyself" (74). And Pascal believed that "Man's greatness lies in his capacity to recognize his wretchedness" (136).

That Beckett himself also regarded human existence as constituted by an ontological humiliation is borne out in many of his writings. In *Proust*, he reflects on the "sin of having been born" (67). In his reading of Windelband's *History of Philosophy*, he notes Anaximander's "doctrine that things must perish as an expiation for injustice" and that it "presents the first dim attempt to conceive the cosmic process as ethical necessity and the shadows of transitoriness [...] as retribution for sin" ("Philosophy" n.p.). A comparable idea finds expression in *Murphy* (43), this time through a reference to Bildad the Shuhite's mocking question, "How can he be clean that is born of a woman?" (Job 24:4). *Watt*'s "Addenda" include an enigmatic Latin phrase about being born "polluted" (233). In *Malone Dies*, Macmann feels, without knowing his "sin," that "living was not a sufficient atonement for it or that this atonement was in itself a sin, calling for more atonement, and so on, as if there could be anything but life, for the living" (233). In *The Unnamable*, the moment of existence is seen as coinciding with punishment: "I was given a pensum, at birth perhaps, as a punishment for having been born perhaps..." (304).

Since Geulincx is directly invoked in *Molloy*, his imperatives of self-inspection and self-disregard are most pertinent in the case of Moran's unhappy existence. It is well-known that the *Ethics* of the seventeenth-century philosopher had a major shaping influence on Beckett's creative output. In particular, Geulincx's "axiom of morals"—"*ubi nihil vales, ibi nihil velis*"—resonates throughout Beckett's work:

Wherein you have no power, therein neither should you will.... Note that this axiom includes both parts of humility...inspection and disregard. *Wherein you have no power*; we read in this the inspection of oneself...*Therein you should not will*; we read in this...disregard of oneself, or neglect of oneself across the whole human condition, and resigning ourselves into the power of His hand, in which we are, indeed, whether we like it or not.... Therefore, to will nothing concerning our condition, to leave the whole thing to Him in whose power it really is, this truly is to disregard oneself, this is to build virtue on the unshakable foundation of humility. (Geulincx 337)

In this regard, self-knowledge may well be seen as a source of misfortune. Inspection of oneself leads to a realization of powerlessness; disregard of oneself necessitates a resignation of will because of that powerlessness.

But if there is no potential to begin with, it is difficult to see how the will can come into play. *Molloy*'s single explicit reference to Geulincx suggests that, although there is some room for willful ignorance, the conditions of existence are not altered by what one chooses to believe or not to believe:

I who had loved the image of old Geulincx, dead young, who left me free, on the black boat of Ulysses, to crawl towards the East, along the deck. That is a great measure of freedom, for him who has not the pioneering spirit. And from the poop, poring upon the wave, a sadly rejoicing slave, I follow with my eyes the proud and futile wake. Which, as it bears me from no fatherland away, bears me onward to no shipwreck. (*Three Novels* 46)

The passage implies Geulincx's axiom of morals and, with its nautical metaphor, directly alludes to an image from the *Ethics* that illustrates the futility of our resistance to divine will: "Just as a ship carrying a passenger with all speed towards the west in no way prevents the passenger from walking towards the east, so the will of God, carrying all things, impelling all things with inexorable force, in no way prevents us from resisting his will" (317).

But in his conjunction of the *Ethics* and *Inferno* Canto 26, Molloy accepts neither Geulingian predestination nor Dantean ordination. And, as his sardonic tone suggests, neither does he glimpse anything more than momentary escape. Beckett's palimpsest of the transcendentally directed vessel and its cosmologically ill-fated counterpart creates a context in which all individual effort is rendered futile: both that of Geulincx's east-facing rebel and of the intrepid Ulysses who is damned by Dante for pride. Molloy sees himself as a slave—a being with no rights, no status, and no worth. But he also recognizes that these privations were never anything but privations.

Beckett's manipulation of *Inferno* Canto 26 in this final sentence quoted above significantly rewrites the fate of Dante's Ulysses, whose account of his voyage opens with reference to his family and concludes with a divinely-ordained tempest. What spurs on the Dantean Ulysses to forsake his familial duties and to tempt fate is a desire for enlightenment. Encouraging his followers, he says:

> Bethink you of the seed
> whence ye have sprung, for ye were not created
> to lead the life of stupid animals,
> but manliness and knowledge to pursue. (26.116-20)

But Molloy admits to having killed the "Aegean" (that is, Ulysses) in himself who craved "heat and light" (*Three Novels* 25).[4] He is of the same ilk as the Unnamable, who sees no common ground between himself and that other figure of humanist striving, Prometheus: "between me and that miscreant who mocked the gods, invented fire, denatured clay and domesticated the horse, in a word obliged humanity, I trust there is nothing in common" (297). Molloy's odyssey, then, has neither foundation (whether in the guise of privilege, destiny, or duty) nor a knowable *telos* (whether in the attainment of Ulysses' aims or in his destruction); his "calvary ... [has] no limits to its stations and no hope of crucifixion" (73). Humiliation, to twist T.S. Eliot's line, is endless.

Molloy's "sad rejoicing" thus emerges as an awareness of what Beckett called an "ontological indecency" (qtd. in Juliet 22). The sadness emanates from the state of powerless itself; the rejoicing is a payoff for recognizing this unchanging truth. The terms, though opposite, are not equal. If Molloy were a rejoicingly sad slave, he would be someone without worth who takes pleasure in his worthlessness, a masochist. But because his rejoicing is located in an epistemic certainty of humiliation, it remains in the shadow of ontological despair.

In this respect, Moran's "less fortunate" position seems to correspond. The ambiguity of his utterance, to consider another possible gray area, colors the very term "less fortunate." If Moran is less fortunate than his acquaintances because knowledge of his being leads to despair, he may at the same time be more fortunate in following the Delphic imperative to "know thyself," which, in its turn, occasions despair, and so on.

A comparable ouroboros of catastrophe and blessing emerges when Malone loses his stick and can contemplate its essence "shorn of all accidents" (201). A still more pertinent example of this ambivalence is found in his claim that "I would willingly attribute part of my shall I say misfortunes to this disordered sense were I not unfortunately rather inclined to look upon it as a blessing. Misfortunes, blessings, I have no time to pick my words, I am in a hurry to be done" (201).

The very last passage Beckett copied from Geulincx's *Ethics* centers on this Janus-faced kind of happiness: "A truly humble mind, having not only submitted to, but immersed itself in its Obligations ... *beyond concern* ... is capable of Happiness" (qtd. in Geulincx 353). Such happiness—such humility—is a sad rejoicing. It is born from "obligations" that necessitate the recognition of an abased condition as well as the practice of self-abasement; it entails, in Arsene's words to Watt, opening oneself up "to the long joys of being [oneself], like a basin to vomit" (33). The point is that such happiness (sad rejoicing or humility), dragged into the "eudemonistic slop" (*Three Novels* 50), cannot result in a sense of superiority. Unlike Socrates who is the wisest man because he appreciates his lack of wisdom, Moran cannot inflect his identity with any superlatives. Rather, he resembles Kierkegaard's Abraham, who is "great by reason of his power whose strength is impotence, great by reason of his wisdom whose secret is foolishness, great by reason of his hope whose form is madness, great by reason of the love which is hatred of oneself" (12).

There is, of course, a second possible meaning in Moran's point of view, which intimates that his acquaintances are relieved of identity through their suffering. The key words, here, are "in spite of": they suggest that Moran's heightened sense of self comes as a surprise in light of its "lesions and … wounds," that he would expect these afflictions to have an erosive rather than solidifying effect. Again, it is pointless to speculate about the unidentified others; one cannot claim that their pains and tortures have carried them mystically beyond themselves. But what Moran does disclose is a temporal marker: his identity is clearer than "ever before." The moment of self-realization coincides with the moment of greatest suffering. It is significant that these injuries are not physical though they are conceived in the language of bodily pain, which intimates that physical suffering may well occasion a deepened self-understanding. It is also significant that the injuries do not manifest only as part of Moran's new and self-estranged appearance; they belong to his identity itself and are part of its make-up. So another possible meaning is kept alive in the ambiguous point of view: Moran is surer of himself not *in spite* of the lesions and wounds but *because* of them. It is a causality suggestively glossed by The Unnamable: "[M]utilate, mutilate, and perhaps some day, fifteen generations hence, you'll succeed in beginning to look like yourself" (309).

That suffering provides access to a truer identity is a theory Beckett had propounded in *Proust*. Habit and boredom are condemned as enemies of reality because they instill a fallacious belief in the subject as self-consistent. The "suffering of being," on the other hand, "opens a window on the Real" (18, 19). Where habit seeks to create the semblance of continuity between splintered selves, suffering allows "perilous…dangerous, precarious, painful, mysterious and fertile [zones]" to come into focus (20). At such moments, the subject comes face to face with the division and deformity that result from its temporal existence:

> There is no escape from yesterday because yesterday has deformed us, or been deformed by us. The mood is of no importance. Deformation has taken place. Yesterday is not a milestone that has been passed, but a daystone on the beaten track of the years, and irremediably part of us, within us, heavy and dangerous. We are not merely more weary because of yesterday, we are other, no longer what we were before the calamity of yesterday. (11-12)

The suffering of being or, as Shane Weller astutely calls it, "the suffering of ever-less-than-being" (4), has both advantages and disadvantages. The ego undergoes a necessary loss of security when confronted with self-estrangement and "opposed by a phenomenon that it cannot reduce to the condition of a comfortable and familiar concept" (Beckett, *Proust* 21). This counts as an advantage since it makes self-knowledge possible. But the moment that the victim of time and habit becomes an "ex-victim" is also subject to flux. The self-realization brought about in the suffering of being disappears "with a wailing and gnashing of teeth. The mortal microcosm cannot forgive the relative immortality of the macrocosm" (21). Understood in terms of our earlier discussion, the "immortal macrocosm" may be seen as a condition unchanged and unchanging. The "mortal microcosm" is the individual's world of experience in which knowledge of the macrocosm is enabled by suffering but simultaneously deformed and distorted by time.

Moran shows some awareness of the interminable nature of this degradation:

> I forged my way through [the snow], towards what I would have called my ruin if I could have conceived what I had left to be ruined. Perhaps I have conceived it since, perhaps I have not done conceiving it, it takes time, one is bound to in time, I am bound to. But on the way home, a prey to the malignancy of man and nature and my own failing flesh, I could not conceive it. (*Three Novels* 160)

Ultimately, there is no Archimedean point from which Moran can fully know his being. Knowledge of one's being remains anchored in time and change. Here resides the tension between the vicissitudes of a cruel existence and the essential character of that existence. As with the purgatory Beckett identifies in Joyce's work, there is no culmination, no progress, and no absolute (*Dis* 30). There can be a groping "worstward," a *becoming* humiliated, but never a finally humiliated *being*.

Moran's self-assessment, then, is not willfully ambivalent but unavoidably so. The ambiguity of his reflection is a product of his powerlessness. He embodies Fernando Pessoa's beautiful formulation of the impossibility of complete self-knowledge: "We are two abysses—a well staring at the sky" (20). But that same ambiguity is also testament to a momentary humility in which Moran does not irritably reach after fact or reason even though realizing his insight "deserves" to be unambiguous. The passage represents an instance in which powerlessness is accepted and his own untranslatable hums are left untouched by instrumental reason.

"TEARS AND LAUGHTER": RESPONDING TO HUMILIATION

In *A Short History of Decay*, Emil Cioran writes that misery

> constitutes the texture of all that breathes; but its modalities have changed course; they have composed that series of irreducible appearances which lead each of us to believe he is the first to have suffered so. The pride of such uniqueness incites us to cherish our own pain and to endure it. In a world of sufferings, each of them is a solipsist in relation to all the rest. Misery's originality is due to the verbal quality which isolates it in the sum of words and sensations. (20)

Whether or not Beckett had read these words before writing *Molloy*, his novel nonetheless achieves something of their astuteness.[5]

What differentiates the two central characters in the end is not their suffering, hardly distinguishable in paraphrase, but their respective responses to suffering. If we briefly consider the concluding moments of the first part, it is clear that Molloy resists all stasis and comfort. At the nadir of his infirmity he finds it necessary to continue on a quest which is as much a search for his mother as it is an inexhaustible self-examination. Though an opportunity for capitulation presents itself in the forest, Molloy finds an "access of vigour" in his "weakness" (79), and this allows him to realize the Beckettian ethos of "going on" despite insurmountable obstacles. Molloy is aware that no net-gain is to be hoped for, that a change of location will not mean progress. Still he allows his imperatives to wrench him from situations where, "if all was not well, all was no worse than anywhere else" (80). Still he "submits" to this ineffable force though it leaves him in ever greater doubt.

By contrast, Moran's self-insight flickers without flaming into that "burning illogicality" (qtd. in Juliet 41) and stoic uncertainty that Beckett admired in St John of the Cross and other mystics. Like the self-centered sufferer described by Cioran, Moran's egotism returns to replace the apparent surrender of a moment before. Afflictions, fulfilling an earlier Freudian slip,[6] become affections; asceticism assumes the aspect of perverse delight. (This is far off from Simone Weil's understanding of affliction as a "state of extreme and total humiliation" [91] in which pride and self-reliance are utterly voided). Abandoning himself to the frailties of his flesh and the cruelty of the weather, he weds fresh destitution to former joys. His passion for enumeration sparks briefly in the ways his threadbare shirt can be worn; the umbrella/walking stick dilemma recalls his delight in linear logic, which trumps the primacy of bodily needs; and he prefers elemental exposure to facing a reminder of his son (or his son's raincoat) that would be brought about by building a real shelter (165-66). In short, there is a re-crystallization of preferences and prerogatives that causes the Geulingian axiom to gradually lose its grip on Moran. He goes too far in the direction of *despicio sui* so that he oversteps what may be taken as healthy self-disregard. "Humility," Geulincx warns, "does not require anyone positively to despise himself, to defame himself, scourge himself, or treat himself badly in some way or other" (29).

Even amid his suffering, Moran rediscovers a sense of superiority: "The thought of turning for help to the villages, to the peasants, would have displeased me, if it had occurred to me" (*Three Novels* 166). Leaving aside the difficulty that the writing is reflection—an act of "decomposition" (21)—the sentence above reveals Moran's contentedness in abjection at the time. The thought of seeking help does not even occur to him, and if it did he would not turn to "peasants." Moran has relapsed, more or less fully, into the microcosm where habit and prejudice solidify identity. Because the tensile connection between self-knowledge (a state of humiliation) and acceptance of what it implies (humility) loses its equipoise, Moran's understanding of himself as "less fortunate" vanishes. Contrasted with Molloy, he stands as a rejoicingly sad slave.

Juxtaposed, the respective conclusions of Parts I and II present a tale of two cries: the "publican's whinge" and the "pharisee's taratantara"—terms from Beckett's 1934 essay, "Humanistic Quietism" (*Dis* 68) apposite to *Molloy*. The essay's implicit reference to Luke 18:9-14 establishes oppositional attitudes of desperate humility and haughty certainty, of inner compunction and observable righteousness, of self-abasement and self-aggrandizement. It is telling that Moran, caught trespassing on another's land, resorts to an invented religious justification (a pilgrimage to the "Turdy Madonna") to account for his misdemeanor (167). The lie at once saves his skin and lets him feel superior to the "yokel" he has just duped. In his turn, the pharisee believes himself justified by the law, which is fulfilled in the advent of Christ and therefore no longer the means of redemption. Moran's "[h]umbly ask[ing] a favour" further extends the hypocrisy. He stands guilty of the "pretence of submissiveness," as La Rochefoucauld calls it—that "artifice by which pride debases itself in order to exalt itself; and though it can transform itself in a thousand ways, pride is never better disguised and more deceptive than when it is hidden behind the mask of humility" (73). Just as the pharisee's prayer is an affirmation of his superiority over others rather than an acknowledgement of his inferiority before God, Moran's manipulation is indicative of intellectual pride.

But the request, while ensuring that his brains are not knocked out, puts Moran in a position of indebtedness that undermines his cunning victory over the farmer. As evidenced in an earlier episode when an unidentified man asks him for a piece of bread, Moran regards dependency as "humiliating" (*Three Novels* 140). To tip the scales in his favor, he at once withdraws his request and reverses the dynamic by offering the farmer a florin. True to his retrospective resolve, Moran does not turn to a peasant for help. Moreover, he cements the achievement of his falsehood by keeping up appearances at all costs: "Above all nothing to eat," he declares (168), to show that he is not only a pilgrim but, like the pharisee, one who observes fasting. With satisfaction he reflects on his accomplishment: "Moran, wily as a serpent, there was never the like of old Moran" (168).

This resistance to acts of kindness recalls the attitude of the magnanimous man. Aristotle describes him in the *Nicomachean Ethics* as

> the sort of person to do good, but is ashamed to be a beneficiary himself, since doing good is characteristic of a superior, receiving it of an inferior. And he will repay benefits with interest, so that his original benefactor, in addition to being paid, will have become a debtor and a beneficiary. (70)

Moran's anxiety to avoid debts of kindness offers a caricature of the above. Conceived in Beckett's own terms, it pays into the "quantum of wantum" (*Murphy* 36), the closed circuit in which suffering and happiness remain in constant equilibrium. The idea occurs as early as *Murphy* but is more famously formulated in a speech of Pozzo's in *Waiting for Godot*: "The tears of the world are a constant quantity. For each one who begins to weep, somewhere else another stops. The same is true of the laugh" (*Complete Dramatic* 33). In *Rough for Theatre I*, however, an equilibrium of charity is threatened when B tucks A's leg snuggly without immediately asking a favor in return. Fearful to be indebted indefinitely, A demands to return the kindness: "you're not going to do me a service for nothing? [*Pause*] I mean unconditionally? [*Pause*] Good God!" (*Complete Dramatic* 231). It is in this vein—and with comparable pettiness or "smallness of soul"—that Moran wishes to avoid the humiliation of being done a kindness.

But Molloy, in keeping with a more consistent awareness of his weakness, seems more disposed to accept help. Toward the end of his narrative, he realizes that any further venturing will be rendered impossible without the support of "some kind person" (*Three Novels* 82). Not without irony or resignation, he remarks: "Well, I suppose you have to try everything once, succour included, to get a complete picture of the resources of their planet" (85). But there is an obvious instance where Molloy defies the "charitable gesture," which occurs during his detention for what appears to be indecent resting. Approached by a woman he takes to be a social worker, he is repulsed at the sight of her unappetizing alms. Running still deeper than his disgust with the "tottering pile of disparates" (19) is his abreaction to unsolicited aid:

> Let me tell you this, when social workers offer you, free, gratis and for nothing, something to hinder you from swooning, which with them is an obsession, it is useless to recoil, they will pursue you to the ends of the earth, the vomitory in their hands. The Salvation Army is no better. Against the charitable gesture there is no defence, that I know of. You sink your head, you put out your hands all trembling and twined together and you say, Thank you, thank you lady, thank you kind lady. To him who has nothing it is forbidden not to relish filth. (19-20)

The passage is significant in light of Beckett's own charitable endeavors following the war. Having volunteered as quartermaster and interpreter for the Irish Red Cross at the small Normandy town of Saint-Lô in 1945, he was witness to a scene of complete devastation. Memories from this time would later be reworked into the fabric of *Endgame*. Beckett's most immediate reaction to this experience was an enigmatic and vaguely philosophical report written for radio broadcast that never aired. The tone of "The Capital of Ruins" is sober: details of the destruction, hunger and squalor are presented factually rather than emotively. But there are notable instances in which Beckett moves from the journalistic to the moralistic:

> What was important was not our having penicillin when they had none, nor the unregarding munificence of the French Ministry of Reconstruction (as it was then called), but the occasional glimpse obtained, by us in them and, who knows, by them in us (for they are an imaginative people), of that smile at the human conditions as little to be extinguished by bombs as to be broadened by the elixirs of

Borroughes and Welcome,—the smile deriding, among other things, the having and the not having, the giving and the taking, the sickness and health. (*Complete Short Prose* 277)

Simon Critchley points out the proximity between this "smile" and *Watt*'s *risus purus* (109-11). For Critchley, it may be classed with the laughter in Beckett's work that so often attends and has unhappiness as its object. The smile, Critchley is careful to remark, is not the cause of unhappiness, but rather an indication of the human capacity for greatness in spite of wretchedness, of our ability to recognize our own folly. This Pascalian view, insightful as it is, too triumphantly posits the smile as a response to suffering and sickness. However, the smile (which may well be a grimace for its skeletal, unfeeling rigidity) also cuts across prosperity and good health. It does not only deride the moribund, but falls on all alike: it plagues him that gives and him that takes.

Something of this sentiment lies behind the concluding sentences of "The Capital of Ruins":

> But I think that to the end of its hospital days it will be called the Irish Hospital, and after that the huts, when they have been turned into dwellings, the Irish huts. I mention this possibility, in the hope that it will give general satisfaction. And having done so I may perhaps venture to mention another, more remote but perhaps of greater import in certain quarters, I mean the possibility that some of those who were in Saint-Lô will come home realising that they got at least as good as they gave, that they got indeed they could hardly give, a vision and sense of a time-honoured conception of humanity in ruins, and perhaps even an inkling of the terms in which our condition is to be thought again. These will have been in France. (278)

Given the pervasive accounts of Beckett's generosity and sensitivity to the needs of others, the passage should not read as an inveiglement against the Irish effort at Saint-Lô. What it does object to are the feelings of self-satisfaction that attend the charitable gesture.

This foreshadows something of the dilemma in *Company*'s hedgehog episode, but it also warns against the creation of a disparity or hierarchy between the haves and the have-nots. Where *Company* recognizes the danger in universally applying a provisional standard of the good, "The Capital of Ruins" intimates that neither fortune nor misfortune should obscure from view the fact of man's humiliated ontology, the smile that derides each station.

By the light of this short essay, Molloy's violent reaction to the social worker's offering symbolizes an effort to resist the stratification of giving and receiving. One should not forget that Molloy is placed within arm's length of the charitable gesture only because he represents a threat to normative conceptions of the good and the beautiful. His arrest and the subsequent treatment he receives, as he rightly reflects, are the result of his disconcerting presence in society, of an awful reminder of humanity in ruins:

What is certain is this, that I never rested in that way again, my feet obscenely resting on the earth, my arms on the handlebars and on my arms my head, rocking and abandoned. It is indeed a deplorable sight, a deplorable example, for the people, who so need to be encouraged, in their bitter toil, and to have before their eyes manifestations of strength only, of courage and of joy, without which they might collapse, at the end of the day, and roll on the ground. (*Three Novels* 20)

Molloy does not, cannot, like Moran, turn the tables on his benefactors. But the act of shattering the cup and saucer, deliberately and not accidentally, serves as a refusal—however small—to let a vacuous barrier rise up between the needy and the bountiful. To some extent, Molloy realizes Beckett's "dream," not only of an art, but of an existence "unresentful of its insuperable indigence and too proud for the farce of giving and receiving" (*Proust* 141).

"The End"—the eventual form taken by that story Beauvoir had so uncharitably rejected—also questions the good of goodwill. Pointing a finger at the narrator, who has resorted to begging on the street, a soapbox Marxist interrogates the passers-by: "Do you ever think? ... It never enters your head ... that your charity is a crime, an incentive to slavery, stultification and organized murder" (*Complete Short Prose* 94). The narrator, however, is unaffected by the display of pious rage. He believes that the orator must either be a religious fanatic or a fugitive madman; in any case, the discourse is "all Greek to [him]" (94). Not only do the terms of capitalism and communism mean nothing to him, but also the idea that charity can be the cause of degradation for those who receive it and a means of elevation for those who bestow it. Like Molloy, he refuses to participate in the vicious differentiation that goodwill might bring about—not obliviously, but because he recognizes that the act of giving is seldom unaccompanied by feelings of superiority. In giving no thanks to those who "stoop" to give him money, the narrator resists entering into an economy of moral debt and credit. Likewise, Molloy's shattering of the crockery disrupts a circular logic that fails to recognize that the human condition, no matter the particular material or moral station, is common to all, humiliating to all.

In the end, Molloy's is only one particular kind of reaction. Transforming the language of "The End" and admitting that "tears and laughter"—responses to humiliation and suffering—"are so much Gaelic to me" (32), he assumes a position of uncertainty that is characteristic of Beckett's aporetic art. By counterbalancing Molloy and Moran, the publican whinge and the pharisaic taratantara, Beckett does not suggest that all responses to suffering are equally ethical or valid. Rather, through the unresolved tensions and opposing perspectives of the novel he achieves an acknowledgement of differences and a defense of wretchedness—in his work and outside it.

Notes

1. For the publishing history of "Suite" and "The End," see Van Hulle 73-82.
2. For the publishing history, see McDonald 153-170.
3. See Ricks 112 and 116 on using the full title of "The Love Song of J. Alfred Prufrock."
4. Beckett on the conjunction of Geulincx and Dante: "I imagine a member of the crew who does not share the adventurous spirit of Ulysses and is at least at liberty to crawl homewards…along the brief deck" (*Letters 2* 458). For another discussion of Geulincx in *Molloy*, see Tucker 119-22.
5. In a 1956 letter, Beckett expresses his wish to reread *Précis de decomposition*, first published in 1949 (*Letters 2* 678).
6. "I was succumbing to other affections, that is not the word, intestinal for the most part" (*Three Novels* 160).

Works Cited

Ackerley, C.J. and S.E. Gontarski, editors. *The Faber Companion to Samuel Beckett*. Faber and Faber, 2006.

Aristotle. *Nicomachean Ethics*. Translated and edited by Roger Crisp. Cambridge UP, 2004.

Beckett, Samuel. *Company; Ill Seen Ill Said; Worstward Ho; Stirrings Still*. Edited by Dirk van Hulle. Faber and Faber, 2009.

———. *The Complete Dramatic Works*. Faber and Faber, 2006.

———. *The Complete Short Prose, 1929-1989*. Edited by S.E. Gontarski. Grove, 1995.

———. *Disjecta: Miscellaneous Writings and a Dramatic Fragment*. John Calder, 1983.

———. *How It Is*. Edited by Édouard Magessa O'Reilly. Faber and Faber, 2009.

———. *The Letters of Samuel Beckett, Volume 1: 1929-1940*. Edited by Martha Dow Fehsenfeld, et al. Cambridge UP, 2009.

———. *The Letters of Samuel Beckett, Volume 2: 1941-1956*. Edited by George Craig, et al. Cambridge UP, 2011.

———. *The Letters of Samuel Beckett, Volume 3: 1957-1965*. Edited by George Craig, et al. Cambridge UP, 2014.

———. *Murphy*. Grove, 1957.

———. ["Philosophy Notes"]. TCD MS 10967 Trinity College, Dublin Archives.

———. *Proust and "Three Dialogues with Georges Duthuit."* John Calder, 1965.

———. *Three Novels: Molloy, Malone Dies, The Unnamable*. Grove, 1994.

———. *Watt*. Edited by C.J. Ackerley. Faber and Faber, 2009.

Bernard of Clairvaux. *The Steps of Humility and Pride*. Translated by M. Ambrose Conway. Cistercian Publications, 1989.

Cioran, E.M. *A Short History of Decay*. Translated by Richard Howard. Penguin, 1975.

Critchley, Simon. *On Humour*. Routledge, 2002.

Dante. *The Divine Comedy of Dante Alighieri: The Italian Text with a Translation in English Blank Verse and Commentary, Volume 1: Inferno*. Translated by Courtney Langdon. Harvard UP, 1918.

Geulincx, Arnold. *Ethics: With Samuel Beckett's Notes*. Translated by Martin Wilson. Edited by Han van Ruler, Anthony Uhlmann, and Martin Wilson. Koninklijke Brill NV, 2006.

Juliet, Charles. *Conversations with Samuel Beckett and Bram van Velde*. Dalkey Archive P, 1995.

Kierkegaard, Søren. *Fear and Trembling* and *The Book on Adler*. Translated by Walter Lowrie. Everyman's Library, 1994.

Knowlson, James. *Damned to Fame: The Life of Samuel Beckett*. Simon and Schuster, 1996.

McDonald, Peter D. "Calder's Beckett." *Publishing Samuel Beckett*, edited by Mark Nixon. British Library, 2011, pp. 153-170.

Pascal, Blaise. *Pensées and Other Writings*. Translated by Honor Levi. Edited, introduced, and annotated by Anthony Levi. Oxford UP, 1995.

Pessoa, Fernando. *The Book of Disquiet*. Edited and translated by Richard Zenith. Penguin, 2011.

La Rochefoucauld, Francois (de). *Collected Maxims and Other Reflections*. Translated, annotated, and introduced by E.H. Blackmore, A.M. Blackmore, and Francine Giguère. Oxford UP, 2007.

Ricks, Christopher. *T.S. Eliot and Prejudice*. Faber and Faber, 1994.

Salisbury, Laura. *Samuel Beckett: Laughing Matters, Comic Timing*. Edinburgh UP, 2012.

Taylor, Jeremy. *Holy Living and Dying: With Prayers Containing the Whole Duty of a Christian, and the Parts of Devotion Fitted to All Occasions, and Furnished for All Necessities*. G. Bell and Sons, 1913.

Thomas á Kempis. *The Imitation of Christ*, translated William Benham. *The Harvard Classics: The Confessions of St Augustine* and *The Imitation of Christ by Thomas Á Kempis*. P.F. Collier and Son, 1909.

Tucker, David. *Samuel Beckett and Arnold Geulincx: Tracing "a Literary Fantasia."* Continuum, 2012.

Tucker, David, Mark Nixon, and Dirk van Hulle, editors. *Samuel Beckett Today / Aujourd'hui: Revisiting Molloy, Malone Meurt / Malone Dies and L'Innommable / The Unnamable*. Rodopi, 2014.

Van Hulle, Dirk. "Publishing 'The End': Beckett and *Les Temps modernes*." *Publishing Samuel Beckett*, edited by Mark Nixon. British Library, 2011, 73-82.

Weil, Simone. *An Anthology*. Edited and introduced by Siân Miles. Penguin, 2005.

Weller, Shane. *A Taste for Nothing: Beckett and Nihilism*. Legenda, 2005.

RICK DE VILLIERS is an associate professor in the Department of English at the University of the Free State, South Africa. His first book, *Eliot and Beckett's Low Modernism: Humility and Humiliation*, was published by Edinburgh University Press in 2021. He has written widely on modernism and contemporary South African fiction. His next book project, *Ctrl Z: Narratives of Undoing*, will look at the modes and motives behind literary recantation. For more, visit www.rickdevilliers.com.

12 Who Hobbles after the Subject: Parables of Writing in *The Third Policeman* and *Molloy*

Yael Levin

From peg legs to prosthetics, meniscus tears to arthritis, the experimental fiction of the twentieth-century is rife with slow men. The twentieth century evolution of the male protagonist from able to disabled is illustrated in Samuel Beckett's *Molloy* and Flann O'Brien's *The Third Policeman*. These fictional explorations of subjectivity resist the definitive coordinates of their Enlightenment antecedents and can be read as the metonymical expressions of the theoretical debate on the death of the subject. In "The End of Identity Politics," Lennard J. Davis conceptualizes "the dismodernist subject ... a new category based on the partial, incomplete subject whose realization is not autonomy and independence but dependency and interdependence. This is a very different notion from subjectivity [than that] organized around wounded identities; rather, *all* humans are seen as wounded.... The dismodernist subject is in fact disabled, only completed by technology and by interventions" (313). Such a rethinking of the subject is already in evidence in David Wills's *Prosthesis* where he writes that "the prosthetic body will not be an exception but the paradigm for the body itself" (137).

Davis's notion of the dismodernist subject is enlisted here in order to illuminate a conceptual offshoot of such a renegotiation of subjectivity that has received little attention. Rethinking the defining coordinates of the subject beyond autonomy and control demands that we make a respective shift in our understanding of the formation of creative agency. As will be demonstrated below, an Enlightenment ethos sees the creative act as a product of an autonomous mind housed in a "normate" body.[1] Davis's project of reconfiguring human agency is resistant to such formulations. He defines the dismodernist subject primarily through dependency and incompleteness. Drawn from disability studies, Davis's reformulation finds an interesting bioscientific correlate in Margrit Shildrick's "Re-imagining Embodiment: Prostheses, Supplements and Boundaries." Shildrick here approaches similar questions on the philosophical evolution of subjectivity from within the interpretative frame of somatechnics. She suggests that recent work in immunology, transplantation and genetics "may facilitate a new understanding of corporeal hybridity and a recognition that borders are permeable, and subject to startling changes" and a rethinking of "the whole nexus in terms of neither self/other nor intercorporeality, but rather of assemblages" (282).

Traditional explorations of physical impairment have figuratively signaled the breakdown of creative agency and the failure of artistic inspiration; an author struggles to conclude or promote the plot when his or her protagonist is resistant to forward movement. Such figurative treatments of disability perpetuate the Enlightenment model of creative agency wherein artistic expression is housed in the normate body and impairment spells an attending failure of expression. Beckett's *Molloy* and O'Brien's *The Third Policeman* repeatedly undermine such self-reflexive signposts. The manner in which they do so evinces two things about the authors' views on writing and text. First, the disabled subject is no longer a figure for blocked writing, but rather the site for the proliferation of language. Unmoored from the Enlightenment model of agency and control, writing is refashioned as an interminable project whose driving force is always outside the subject or in excess of subjectivity. Second, as the site for textual production, the protagonist's impairment functions as the figurative key to his maker's poetics. The method whereby Beckett and O'Brien stage their narrators' disability is illustrative not only of their views on writing, but also of the divide evident in their respective reflections on the craft. As such, the two authors may be seen as preserving the metaphorization of disability, a literary abuse that is challenged by a certain strand of disability studies scholarship. In *Narrative Prosthesis*, David Mitchell and Sharon Snyder formulate the objection to such stylized treatments of disability: "The study of disability must understand the impact of the experience of disability upon subjectivity *without simultaneously situating the internal and external body within a strict mirroring relationship to one another*" (58).

I will engage with the two novels' figurative treatments of impairment not in order to essentialize disability, but rather to show how such reconfigurations of the creative act necessarily attend any rethinking of subjectivity. Davis has suggested that a "solution to the postmodernist quandary presented by power, with its decentered, deracinated notion of action, along with the neorationalist denial of universals" entails "a temporary, contingent way of thinking about agency and change." *The Third Policeman* and *Molloy*, I argue, offer literary platforms for this kind of approach—an approach that registers a shift from the modern/disabled subject to the dismodern subject. Thus my readings are not limited to the specific case histories of protagonists or to the experiences of disability conveyed in the novels, but extend also to the conditions of possibility for dismodernism. Following Davis, mine is a project that is not exclusive to disability but rather pursues "a clear notion of expanding the protected class to the entire population; a commitment to removing barriers and creating access for all." Davis asks us to move "beyond the fixity of the body to a literally constructed body, which can then be reconstructed with all the above goals in mind" (314); I propose that O'Brien and Beckett have already begun this work.

Molloy seems, at first, to conform to traditional significations of the slow protagonist: the inability to write and move are drawn in parallel; Beckett's writing-wandering heroes appear to function as the quintessential markers of writer's block. This literary commonplace is nevertheless challenged by the repeated conflation of writing with passivity and paralysis. The Unnamable famously announces: "It is I who write, who cannot raise my hand from my knee" (*Three Novels* 301). *The Third Policeman* resists the collapsing of artistic and physical impairment in a very different manner. O'Brien's hero may have a prosthetic leg, yet he is anything but slow. Where movement in Beckett is belabored, forced, painful, and ineffectual, *The Third Policeman*'s disabled men suffer no such limitations. The prostheses encountered in the course of the novel signal movement and continuity. Beckett explores a writing that issues from inertia; O'Brien's vision of writing is an assemblage, a piecing together of multiple parts. His protagonist is as much a collation of bits and pieces as the de Selby Index he has written, which intrudes into his narrative in the form of discordant footnotes. Writing in the novel, in other words, follows a logic of prosthetic attachment.

The explorations of disability introduced in the two novels thus follow the figurative expressions of two distinct models of textual production. Where Gilles Deleuze's concept of Exhaustion is helpful in testing the ontological implications of a writing associated with stasis, Jacques Derrida's reflections on supplementarity allows for the unpacking of the metafictional significances of a prosthesis that spells perpetual movement. Though the two paradigms outlined here pertain to contradictory figurations of writing-the first issuing from paralysis and the second from movement, the first lodged in an accumulative verticality and the second a metonymical regression—both arise from an attempt to rethink writing beyond the coordinates of a unified, independent subjectivity and its symbolic expression in the normate body. Shildrick links the two thinkers through their negotiation of prostheses and the "potentially celebratory re-imagining of the multiple possibilities of corporeal extensiveness" (271). While she views Derrida as providing "a useful route out of humanist nostalgia," she concludes that Deleuze's notion of assemblage will provide "new opportunities to further explore our ongoing fascination with the nature of the body" wherein there is "no useful distinction" to be made between the human body as organic and technological assemblage (Shildrick 282). Such a distinction will be tested against the emerging relation between these newly envisioned subjects and the writing act.

If the two models of writing are suggestive of an essential difference, existing comparative analyses of O'Brien's and Beckett's works offer a method of reading the two authors together. Keith Hopper notes Anti-Cartesianism as the principle that sets the two writers against the modernist tradition and serves as "a springboard for an entirely new direction in Irish (and European) literature" (227). In keeping with Hopper's astute observation, I would suggest we further negotiate these authors' postmodernist poetics by tracing the very expression of the breakdown of Enlightenment subjectivity in the symbolic resonances of physical impairment. The disabled subjects explored in the two texts are significant in their insinuation of alternative models of textual production. By tracing the evolution of such writing subjects, we uncover a hitherto uncharted link between the authors' poetics and the manner in which they literally deconstruct their writer-narrators. That language exceeds subjectivity has been made clear by twentieth-century theories ranging from Saussure's linguistics to Lacan's psychoanalysis. *Molloy* and *The Third Policeman* bring this realization to bear on the ensuing displacement of the writing act. Our focus here will be this attempt to relocate, reshape, and rethink the writing subject.

SLOW MEN AND THE LITERARY TRADITION

Literature does not like its slow men. In her essay on artificial legs, Vanessa Warne quotes an amputee who issues a protest against the literary mistreatment of his unique social group. "Our station in literature is unhappy," he writes, noting that "the magnates of literature went out of their way to fling stones at the ideal wooden-legged man" (qtd. in Warne 362). Warne lends support to this view in stating that "Dickens's portraits of wooden-legged characters, most famously *Our Mutual Friend's* peg leg-wearing Silas Wegg, repeatedly associate prostheses with ignorance, intemperance, and greed" (32). Nicole Marotic has similarly argued that "a character presented as 'less' than able is not only a moral marker of social ill but is also a physical embodiment of cultural blunders" (179). Marotic traces Flannery O'Connor's suggestion that "a physical 'flaw' or 'defection' necessarily announce a corresponding moral 'defect'" (184) back to an Enlightenment cliché wherein "the 'nobility and 'gentlefolk' have a moral duty to remain healthy" (182). Mitchell and Snyder conclude that "Literature serves up disability as a repressed deviation from cultural imperatives of normativity, while disabled populations suffer the consequences of representational association with deviance and recalcitrant corporeal difference" (8).

If the social, economic, and moral implications of a semiotics of physical impairment are merciless, its metaliterary significances offer no compassion either. This is true, moreover, of any form of stunted movement, beyond its physically determined expressions. *The Divine Comedy* begins with its protagonist lost in a dark wood, his path blocked by the terrifying vision of a spotted leopard. The hero's inability to go forward functions literally as an obstacle to be overcome in the action, and figuratively as his soul's languishing in a state of sin. More pertinently for my reading is this scene's signaling of the paralyzing loss of poetic inspiration. It is not only the pilgrim but also the poet who cannot move forward. But where Dante will finally put foot before foot on his way to divine revelation, the heroes that follow centuries later lose their footing altogether and linger in these dark woods. The modern author, in turn, continues to be troubled by the blank pages that attend his characters' resistance to forward movement.

While this foundational text is important for mapping out the symbolic connection between forward movement and artistic inspiration, it does not provide an adequate introduction to the corresponding figurations of a physically disabled hero. A case in point, J.M. Coetzee's *Slow Man* offers a helpful presentation of the self-reflexive potential of such a character. The narrative begins with a traffic accident that results in the amputation of the protagonist's leg. The story, however, is more than an account of his rehabilitation and return to life; it is also a metafictional inquiry into what a writer might do with such a character. The protagonist's view on this is very clear. Turning to Elizabeth Costello, the (fictionalized) author supposedly writing his life story, he begs her to give him up. "I am not an amenable subject" (Coetzee 89), he protests. Costello agrees he could do better:

> "Think how well you started. What could be better calculated to engage one's attention than the incident on Magill Road, where young Wayne collided with you and sent you flying through the air *like a cat*. What a sad decline ever since! Slower and slower, till by now you are almost at a halt, trapped in a stuffy flat with a caretaker who could not care less about you." (100)

Costello's role in the story is reportedly to keep this "man with the bad leg" (89) on an appropriate narrative trajectory. "Most of the time," she tells him, "you won't notice I am here. Just a touch on the shoulder, now and then, left or right, to keep you on the path" (87).

Costello's words highlight the literal and figurative anxieties of a writer dealing with a disabled subject. A hero who comes to a halt interrupts narrative progression and brings his story to its premature end. Much like the start of *The Divine Comedy*, the threat of cessation here also doubles as the loss of creative inspiration; a character who cannot move forward in the story provides an apt figure for the writer blocked before a blank page.

At the outset of *The Third Policeman*, we encounter a hero-narrator who squares neatly with this paradigm. The narrator notes his reluctance to leave the house, as his wooden leg is "not very good for walking with" (12). Though this exposition appears to marry physical impairment—in this case, a prosthetic leg—with stunted movement, such a signification is soon undermined. M. Keith Booker remarks the challenging of the narrator's account of his limitation in the scene depicting the murder of Mathers where he exhibits both speed and agility.

The prosthesis similarly exceeds its traditional significance in the exploits of the army of one-legged men, the so-called "hoppy lads" (165) and their captain Finnucane. Much like the protagonist, these men are immune to the limitations dictated by their impairment and, in a "masterpiece of military technocratics" (164), come marching to his rescue. The "hoppy lads'" offensive against the police barracks points to the symbolic value of O'Brien's refigured prosthesis, which becomes the engine of an invading force, rather than a sign of physical incapacity.

Like bicycles, the road, and other inanimate objects become animate through the workings of the novel's atomic theory, the wooden leg functions as a live prosthesis that gradually takes over its host. In his cell at night, the protagonist notes a sensation wherein his leg is "spreading," "its woodenness" "slowly extending throughout my whole body, a dry timber poison killing me inch by inch." He senses that "soon my brain would be changed to wood completely and I would then be dead" (115). Rather than a figure for inertia, limitation, or a defect—be it moral, artistic or otherwise—the protagonist's prosthesis is a marker of his fragmentation, an incompleteness that is constantly in danger of being permeated and taken over. The prosthesis does not make him a complete subject so much as encroach on his freedom, rendering him dependent on this invading other.[2]

The anxiety associated with the experience of an artificially attached limb is powerfully illustrated in "The Cork Leg," one of the entries in a nineteenth-century compilation of Modern Street Ballads. The song describes the horrifying misadventures of a wealthy Dutch merchant who loses his leg as he turns away a destitute relation by literally kicking him out the door. The offender compensates himself for his injury by commissioning a "beautiful leg of cork" from a celebrated artist in Rotterdam. The limb, however, does not function quite as expected:

> He walked through squares, and past each shop,
> Of speed he went to the utmost top,
> Each step he took with a bound and a hop,
> And he found his leg he could not stop.
> Horror and fright were in his face,
> The neighbours thought he was running a race;
> He clung to a gas-post to stay his pace,
> But the leg wouldn't stop, but kept on the chace [sic]. ("Cork Leg" 154)

Though he repeatedly calls for help, throws himself to the ground and hangs onto lampposts and trees passed on the way, the battle with the demonic limb is finally lost:

> He walk'd of days and nights a score,
> Of Europe he had made the Tour,
> He died!—but though he was no more,
> The leg walked on the same as before. (154)

The narrator concludes the ballad with the following words:

> My tale I've told both plain and free,
> Of the rummest merchant that ever could be,
> Who never was buried, tho' dead we see,
> And I've been singing his L E G. (155)[3]

The ballad serendipitously anticipates O'Brien's tale of a dead man walking on and on in the circular infinity of his very own hell-dimension. In doing so, it once again highlights the fragmentation of the hero and the manner in which his incompleteness invites a powerful addendum that constantly threatens to invade its host. This shared plot design, I argue, is precisely what will allow us to map the thematic coordinates of the novel's metafictional significations.

In *Flann O'Brien: A Portrait of the Artist as a Young Post/Modernist*, Hopper argues that "Noman [Hopper's name for the unnamed protagonist]'s existential struggle is that of a metafictional character who wishes to transcend his condition—seeks the power (omnium) to create his own world where he shall reign as author-god" (102). Noman's difficulty, he continues, is that "he still sees himself as an author and not a character, a creator, and not a creation" (107). Hopper's diagnosis relies on the stable and mutually-exclusive coherence of the categories of author and character, subject of the creative act and its pawn or object. Such a reading is premised not only on the abiding existence of ontologically separate narrative levels or worlds, but also on the very concept of authorship as the activity of a singular subjectivity that is both independent and creative. The following analysis seeks to uncover a model of writing that eschews such definitions.

The ballad and the novel both describe an incomplete subject, one that lacks the coherence and control of a Cartesian *cogito*. At the same time, he is neither the object of another's act of creation nor the pawn of another's artistic agency. The disabled subject acts and is acted upon, is both the author and instrument of his adventures. The prosthesis is both other and an extension of himself, a focal point of liminality that allows him to live on, walk on into death. Read side-by-side with the ballad, then, we might see O'Brien's hero not as exhibiting the metaleptic confusion of a character who stubbornly adheres to the belief that he is author of the strange and inhospitable world in which he finds himself or a character who refuses to accept his ontological fictionality, but as a figure for textuality. To view the unfolding of his character as a parable of textual production rather than a parable of Being calls for a reinterpretation of Noman's adventure as the symbolic unfolding of a method of writing that exceeds subjectivity. In order to unpack such a network of figurations I will follow the protagonist's lead and turn to the aid of de Selby.

Noman's initial encounter with the philosopher's work is with an incomplete volume. "The book," he reports, "was a first edition of *Golden Hours* with the two last pages missing" (O'Brien 9). Much like this protagonist's physical lack, the ur-text around which his life evolves is incomplete. And much like the Rotterdam artist who fashions the artificial limb for the wealthy Dutch merchant, Noman's project is to complete de Selby's life work by writing the definitive Index "wherein the views of all known commentators on every aspect of the savant and his work [will be] collated," a book "useful ... and badly wanted," "containing much that was entirely new and proof that many opinions widely held about de Selby and his theories were misconceptions based on misreadings of his works" (14). The Index, then, is that prosthesis that the philosopher requires to live on past his death. Further contributing to the analogy, Noman's work can survive only by leeching onto the life force of his idol. As he announces at the start, should his name be remembered, "it would be remembered with de Selby's" (10).

This mapping of the different writing projects mentioned in the novel is in keeping with the narrator's stated scholarly commitments at the start. The novel unfolds, however, as the inverse of this textual scheme in that the main narrative is devoted not to the philosopher but rather to the narrator's adventures. The protagonist fleetingly references this more autobiographical writing when, staring at what appears to be Mather's ghost, he reflects that it was "hard to write of such a scene or to convey with known words the feelings which came knocking at my numbed mind" (24). It is this implicit writing project, those multiple scenes of confusion and stupefaction at the incidents of his daily life that form the novel's primary narrative. De Selby's philosophy, in turn, assumes the role of supplement, and provides the hermeneutic signposts with which both the protagonist and his readers might deal with his absurd encounters.

The two projects of writing, both the story of Noman's experiences as related in the novel and his commentary on de Selby, unfold side by side. Neither can exist in isolation. And yet, in keeping with the hierarchical structure that distinguishes the primary and secondary narratives, de Selby's contributions are gradually relegated to the margin. From their initial placement within the body of the text they are transformed into footnotes—a prosthesis attached to the story. And while these appear, at first, to honor the restraint and measure accorded to the supplement, they gradually proliferate to the point of hijacking entire pages of the narrator's story. As Hopper notes, "By chapter eight [...] a single footnote, spread over the space of four pages, threatens to spiral out of control, and overpower the point it initially set out to develop. The various commentators cited—with Noman acting as 'editor'—gradually begin to attack each other's reputations and the primary text begins to recede ..." (155). Joseph Brooker similarly finds that "a text ostensibly meant for secondary clarification has effectively displaced the primary narrative" (126). The prosthesis attached to the text thus takes on a life of its own and drags the story along with it, recalling the drama that unfolds in the ballad.

The mirroring of this unique method of textual production in the fragmentation and dependence of the novel's hero is once again emphasized when Joe, the narrator's soul, issues his threat of abandonment. Forced to attend the fragility of his being, Noman realizes that he is the sum of two corresponding deficiencies—incompleteness and dependence. The threat of the loss of his soul impels him to come to terms with "the complexities not only of my intermediate dependence and my catenal unintegrity but also my dangerous adjunctiveness and my embarrassing unisolation" (O'Brien 119). Articulating a combination of embarrassment and vulnerability, his insight appears to shuttle between the ontological threat of dissolution and the social impropriety of his apparent reliance. He is neither whole nor independent; he must continually attend and be attended by that which might complete him.

Such a model of "unintegrity" is similarly implicit in the desire that fuels Noman's life's work, his attempt to complete the lack first encountered in the missing pages of de Selby's book. Noman's Index is designed as the perfect addendum to the philosopher's *oeuvre*. By bringing together all the existing commentaries, interpretations, biographical notes, and other paratextual evidence linked with the philosopher's life and works, Noman hopes to explain away the gaps and contradictions detracting from the wholeness of the original. And much as Noman himself can never be complete, his commentary on de Selby's life and works proliferates with no end in sight. Remarking on this slippage, Booker writes that Hatchjaw, Bassett, and their fellow scholars not only "fail to reach conclusions but ... generate additional work by metacommentators (like Henderson, author of *Hatchjaw and Bassett*) whose work is similarly inconclusive" (53). Booker further associates this interminable process of textual production with "the many manifestations of similar phenomena of Nietzschean infinite regression to be found scattered throughout O'Brien's work" (53). While the implications noted here are epistemological, we might similarly attribute such regression to Noman's ontological reflections and their symbolic resonances in the perpetually generative nature of a text made to bring closure to an incomplete antecedent.

If the proliferation of textual production in *The Third Policeman* finds its symbolic expression in a prosthesis that sustains the *perpetuum mobile* of its host, such is not the case in Beckett's *Molloy*. Commenting on the distinctions evident in the treatment of physical impairment in the two Irish novels, Maciej Ruczaj notes that as opposed to Noman's agility, "Beckett's heroes are presented as really physically handicapped"; "their bodies," he adds, "are in a state of constant decomposition" (Ruczaj 97). Faced with the very challenge with which O'Brien tasks his own protagonist—the digging of his victim's grave—Molloy fails where his one-legged counterpart is successful. He muses that "my sick leg [...] was in a condition neither to dig, because it was rigid, nor alone to support me because it would have collapsed." His distress is so great, in fact, that he expresses regret that he is not one-legged, noting he "would have been happier, livelier, amputated at the groin" (*Three Novels* 35). The metafictional implications of such envy and the manner in which they allow us to distinguish the conceptualizations of writing in the two novels, are traced below.

Molloy opens with a picture of disability. Finding himself in his mother's room, the eponymous narrator wonders how he got there: "Perhaps in an ambulance, certainly a vehicle of some kind. I was helped. I'd never have got there alone" (7). Without external help, Molloy's movements pose something of a challenge. Describing how he set off to find his mother, he recounts how his progress was

> slow and painful at all times, was more so than ever, because of my short stiff leg, the same which I thought had long been as stiff as a leg could be, but damn the bit of it, for it was growing stiffer than ever, a thing I would not have thought possible and at the same time shorter every day, but above all because of the other leg, supple hitherto and now growing rapidly stiffer in turn but not yet shortening, unhappily. For when the two legs shorten at the same time, at and the same speed, then all is not lost, no. But when one shortens, and the other not, then you begin to be worried. (76–77)

Such disability, moreover, is quickly tied to a life of writing, conceived here as an obligation impressed upon him by a man "who comes every week" offering money and taking pages in return. In what first appears to be the recycling of a familiar literary topos, writing is as laborious for Molloy as is physical movement. His ability to produce text is drawn in parallel with his immobility. Bodily decay spells the death of inspiration. Not only has he "forgotten how to spell," he's also missing "half the words" (7). The trouble is compounded when he realizes that the character to which he devoted the first part of his narrative is escaping. Molloy muses: "To get up, to get down on the road, to set off hobbling in pursuit of him, to hail him, what could be easier? He hears my cries, turns, waits for me. I am up against him, up against the dog, gasping, between my crutches. ... What I need now is stories" (12–13). Molloy's metaleptic gesture here testifies to a curious commingling of his physical impairment and the inability to write. The writer in search of inspiration is recreated literally as a disabled subject chasing a story.

The self-same literary topos is in evidence in the second part of the narrative. Before setting on his journey to find Molloy, Moran is accosted by "an acute pain" in the knee (119) which worsens to the point of complete paralysis. His breakdown in a dark wood will not lead to divine inspiration but the decision to give up his quest for Molloy and return home. Here, too, we find that physical impairment and the writing are conflated: "That night I set out for home. I did not get far. But it was a start. It is the first step that counts. The second counts less. Each day saw me advance a little further. That last sentence is not clear, it does not say what I hoped it would" (165). The slippage here is subtle—but the belabored progress associated with physical impairment finds its expressive parallel in the writing itself. The difficulty in negotiating forward momentum occurs on a double axis—his legs and his language are equally treacherous: both betray him. The imagery of snow that follows amplifies this duality. Moran reflects that given his extreme physical decline, anyone else "would have lain down in the snow, firmly resolved never to rise again" (165). The snow here doubles as physical obstacle and blank page, a difficulty to both writer and traveler. And both are victorious. As he reports. "I vanquished it, grinding my teeth with joy" (165).

Against this model of progression and triumph wherein conquering one's impairments and putting pen to paper are alike symbols of the successful articulation of one's agency and control, testament to a coherent and independent identity, the novel offers a contradictory model of writing. While the Molloy who hobbles after the character starring in his narrative might be likened to Noman's pursuit of de Selby's various truths, Beckett also offers a figure of the writer who, "perched higher than the road's highest point and flattened what is more against a rock" (10) invokes Dante's Belacqua. The correspondence between the figure of the sloth and the physical decay described in the narratives of both Molloy and Moran is no longer suggestive of impairment as a limitation to be overcome, but as the very condition of textual production. The Belacqua we encounter in Dante's *Purgatorio* is associated with indolence, laziness, procrastination. But he is also a figure for the poet. Writing that issues forth from sloth cannot follow the model of an endlessly proliferating addendum after which the writer is dragged along in a circular chase.

The slippage of emphasis from movement in *The Third Policeman* to that of immobility in *Molloy*—a key distinction, as we have noted, in the treatment of physical impairment—signals a parallel shift in the conceptualization of writing.

Here, writing is no longer progressive; it no longer assumes the form of an encounter between the disabled subject and the prosthetic supplements that draw him forward in a futile yet ongoing effort towards completion or normalcy. The writing explored here is stationary; it is an accumulative writing that proceeds vertically rather than horizontally. Stretched in complete immobility on a rock, Molloy lists "the cows, the sky, the sea, the mountains," A, C, the rock, and himself—all of which, he claims, arise "from one and the same weariness, on and on heaping up and up, until there is no room, no light, for any more" (14). Such a model of composition recalls Joyce's rubbish heap more than it does O'Brien's models of atomic theory or infinite regression. However, rather than follow Joyce in viewing this as an alternative method of textual production, an alchemy of sorts whereby, as Barbara DiBernard writes, the garbage heap "is transformed into art" (16), Beckett utilizes such a method of writing to stage a return to the blank page.

The Enlightenment model of writing traced earlier—wherein the writer vanquishes that self-same image of the white page—finds its accelerated and transgressive subversion in *Molloy*'s motif of writing as destruction. Composition is likened to "a firm hand weaving inexorably back and forth and devouring my page with the indifference of a shuttle" (*Three Novels* 132–33). This writing method is the product of the suspicion "that you would do better, at least no worse, to obliterate texts than to blacken margins, to fill in the holes of words till all is blank and flat and the whole ghastly business looks like what it is, senseless, speechless, issueless misery" (13). Once again, the insistence on obliterating and devouring pages mirrors the physical decay encountered throughout the novel. Much like the writing described above, the body becomes the site of an accumulation of ailments, pains, and weaknesses. The motifs of writing and disability are brought together in a mutual exploration of a loss of agency whose manifold articulations spell destruction.

A fitting emblem for this alternative trajectory of textual production is offered in the novel's most striking subversion of Romantic poetics. "It is in the tranquillity of decomposition," Molloy notes, "that I remember the long confused emotion which was my life, and that I judge it, as it is said that God will judge me, and with no less impertinence. To decompose is to live too, I know, I know, don't torment me, but one sometimes forgets" (25). The figure of decomposition conflates the physical and the metafictional in mutual ruin. In a reversal of the Enlightenment principles of improvement and progress, life and composition are transgressively associated with death and decay. And once again, as we saw in our reading of *The Third Policeman*, such textual production is not one of agency but of passivity. One is involved in one's physical decay as one writes—but this is not due to a Cartesian subject exerting agency. One falls into writing much as one falls ill. Molloy finds himself before a blank page at the end of a journey to find his mother; Moran similarly ends his narrative before a blank page in order to write a report. The writing act is not the expression of creative independence and control; it is an externally enforced imposition. As Moran repeatedly reminds us, "All is tedious in this relation that is forced upon me" (131). Youdi requires him to write his report; the unnamed agents initially hounding Molloy enforce his work.

We have so far attended to impairment and physical decay as markers of a method of textual production that exceeds the cohesive, independent subjectivity we associate with the Cartesian *cogito*. In *The Birth of the Clinic,* Foucault offers an alternative interpretation in the claim that medical monitoring, specifically clinical negotiations of death and disease, serves as the articulation of individuality. "Death," Foucault writes, "is the great analyst that shows the connexions by unfolding them, and bursts open the wonders of genesis in the rigour of decomposition" (*The Birth* 144). Such a philosophical treatment of disease challenges the distinction between agency and illness, suggesting that from the nineteenth century onwards, the broken or diseased patient assumes the privilege of subjectivity. Foucault writes: "it is in that perception of death that the individual finds himself, escaping from a monotonous, average life; in the slow, half-subterranean, but already visible approach of death, the dull, common life becomes an individuality at last; a black border isolates it and gives it the style of its own truth" (171). Foucault's analysis might be seen as the literalization of Hegel's claim that "The life of the mind begins with death" (qtd. in Blanchot 252). As Blanchot explains: "when death becomes power, then man begins, and this beginning rules that, in order for there to be a world, in order for there to be beings, being must lack" (Blanchot 252).

To reframe the matter of impairment as identity marker allows us to return to the protagonists' descriptions of their respective physical afflictions and their correspondences with the motif of writing. Molloy's and Moran's obsessive narrations of their physical decline and its minutia of expressions might by seen as an attempt to combat the fluidity of their respective identities and to anchor their individuality by carefully attending to their unique physicality. The narrative pertaining to Noman's impairments—from the description of his accident to the odd sensations linked to his prosthesis—might be seen as a similar effort to chart an individuality to protect it from the loss of memory and identity. Though the writing acts might be devoted to or imposed by others (the de Selby Index and Molloy's and Moran's commissioned writing tasks, for instance), these unique compositions appear transgressively personal.

Foucault's paradigm nevertheless falls short in its application to the two novels when the transgressively personal is repeatedly recuperated with the impersonal; the unique signatures of the protagonists' impairments are mirrored by the characters they encounter. The prosthesis that defines O'Brien's protagonist is constantly echoed in a host of other characters from Martin Finnucane to his band of hoppy lads. This repetition functions as one of the novel's greatest jokes, perhaps most rewarding in the scene where the man building the gallows on which Noman is to hang accidentally drops a hammer on his foot and is insensible to the pain, showing himself to be an additional entry in this ever-expanding group.[4] Similarly, Moran's narrative of decline echoes the experience related in Molloy's account. Aspects of the weaknesses that are so integral to the two characters' identities are then refracted in various others encountered along the way, not least of which is Molloy's "true love." Extending beyond the borders of gender, she too "move[s] with short stiff steps, leaning on an ebony stick" (*Three Novels* 57). Rather than set them apart, the impairments of all three protagonists further establish the fluidity of their identity.[5]

The repetition traced here also plays out in the novels' circular designs. At the end of *The Third Policeman*, O'Brien's protagonist unknowingly falls back onto the very path from which he embarked. Similarly, Moran's narrative opens and ends in one and the same scene: "It is midnight. The rain is beating on the windows" (92). Booker argues "that so much of the text at the end of *The Third Policeman* is repeated verbatim from earlier in the book serves to signal not only the futility of the narrator's efforts to break out of his confined condition but also to indicate the inability of the writer to produce anything genuinely new" (15). Molloy appears to extend the truth of this observation in his own comment about writing: "And truly it little matters what I say, this or that or any other thing. Saying is inventing. Wrong, very rightly wrong. You invent nothing, you think you are inventing, you think you are escaping, and all you do is stammer out your lesson, the remnants of a pensum one day got by heart and long forgotten" (32). In this recurrence of the self-same to the exclusion of difference we find that once again, textual production and physical impairment are drawn in parallel. Much as the idea of a unique physical marker is unmasked as illusory in its ability to separate the self from the other, the possibility of an original contribution to letters is unmasked as a hoax. Everything has been said already.

That the writer cannot harness his unique identity and his creative agency to say anything new may be attributed to the novel's staging of the demise of a particular conceptualization of writing—one tied to the Enlightenment subject. We have already seen that both novels demonstrate the manner in which text is generated outside the defining coordinates of such an entity. *The Third Policeman* and *Molloy* offer disabled subjects; the models of textual production explored in the two novels overthrow a cohesive, independent creative agency. The representation of disability does not mark the protagonists as unique, but as dependent, subject-object hybrids in the process of becoming. The signifying key in O'Brien's parable of writing, Noman's prosthesis serves as a model of textual production that may be likened to the Derridean Supplement. Like a prosthesis complementing the living body that hosts it, the supplement is artifice—it "adds itself, it is a surplus" (*Of Grammatology* 144) that is "*exterior*, outside of the positivity to which it is super-added, alien to that which, in order to be replaced by it, must be other than it" (145). And much like that demonic limb we encountered in the ballad, that "dangerous supplement destroys very quickly the forces that Nature has slowly constituted and accumulated. In 'out-distancing' natural experience, it runs non-stop [*brûle les étapes*— literally "burns the halting-points"] and consumes energy without possibility of recovery ... it bypasses the presence of the thing and the duration of being" (151). Those various additions—the run-on commentaries on de Selby and the endless texts they generate—form the new as an accidental by-product of textual accumulation and slippage. Writing in *The Third Poliecman* occurs at the margin; it is not the product of a creative agent but slippage that occurs in the constant tension between the broken subject and the prosthesis that propels him forward.

Beckett's model of writing similarly transgresses traditional models of subjectivity. The key to this transgression, however, differs from O'Brien's, and might be seen to follow the etiology of the protagonists' impairments. Noman's disability is the result of a past accident; Moran and Molloy fall prey to a host of symptoms that gradually accumulate over time. The accidental in the first novel thus gives way to accumulation in the second. Deleuze and Guattari explain that "Molloy and Moran no longer designate persons, but singularities flocking from all sides, evanescent agents of production. This is free disjunction; the differential positions persist in their entirety, they even take on a free quality, but they are all inhabited by a faceless and transpositional subject" (77). Audronė Žukauskaitė sums up the method whereby Deleuze and Guattari stage the "philosophy of life" or "the philosophy of the impersonal": "a condition in which all living beings and all modes of existence can coexist on the same plane of immanence" (63). Deleuze defines this Beckettian strategy as "exhaustion," the combination of a "set of variables of a situation" without "preference," "organization in relation to a goal" or "signification" (*Essays* 153) that he believes to be copresent with "a fantastic decomposition of the self" (*Essays* 154). The emphasis on physical lassitude in Deleuze's analysis pays homage to what he sees as "Beckett's great contribution to logic," his having shown "that exhaustion (exhaustivity) does not occur without a certain physiological exhaustion" (154). The physical toll and the virtual cataloging of permutations are co-present—one does not occur without the other.

Where *The Third Policeman* plays with both its protagonist and its readers by offering an ever-expanding array of one-legged characters—a spilling over of the very figure that has allowed us to trace the novel's poetics, *Molloy* follows the law of permutations to stage a practical joke that hinges on its own figurative key. A perfect complement to the narrative of physical decay and the various aches and pains associated with the two protagonists' legs, Molloy's final statement is striking in its implied retraction of the narrative that precedes it: "The fact is and I deplore it, but it is too late now to do anything about it, that I have laid too much stress on my legs, throughout these wanderings, to the detriment of the rest. For I was no ordinary cripple, far from it, and there were days when my legs were the best part of me, with the exception of the brain capable of forming such a judgement" (*Three Novels* 82). Molloy's and Moran's legs betray them. And they do not.

O'Brien's and Beckett's protagonists are "no ordinary cripple[s]." The authors' treatments of disability figuratively explore a writing generated outside the coordinates of the liberal-humanist subject. As models of writing, both supplementarity and accumulation transgress the convention of creative agency. Anthony Uhlmann describes such a shift as that which occurs between "a notion that art needs to be understood through recognition of the individual intuition of the artist, an intuition which often cannot be contained or expressed by language, to a notion that discourse is anonymous, belonging to groups rather than individuals, and which, in passing through individuals, animates them, playing them like marionettes" (*Philosophical Image* 111–12). *The Third Policeman* and *Molloy* offer an alternative to the method of textual production whose decline is already noted in the agonies of interrupted inspiration in Romanticism.[6] Here, the writer no longer controls the generation of text, but participates in it. The text happens to the writer; he suffers its production much as he does his physical impairments. Innovation and change are no longer the products of an independent and cohesive subject who masters expression and willingly creates. The new occurs, but it does so without intent, without design. It happens in that liminal space between the dismodernist subject and those texts that are constantly invading and attending on him. Moran's thoughts on Sisyphus are instructive in fleshing out the manner in which aberrations might occur in the "nothing new" (*Murphy* 1) of a universe of endless repetition. He notes: "it would not surprise me if I deviated, in the pages to follow, from the true and exact succession of events. But I do not think even Sisyphus is required to scratch himself, or to groan, or to rejoice, as the fashion is now, always at the same appointed places" (*Three Novels* 133).

Notes

1. Rosemarie Garland Thomson coins the term "normate" in *Extraordinary Bodies*. The neologism "names the veiled subject position of cultural self, the figure outlined by the array of deviant others whose marked bodies shore up the normate's boundaries" (8).

2. Note a corresponding shift in the bioscientific language that describes the migration of donor cells within the transplanted subject's body. Shildrick traces the manner in which the process is no longer dominated by "metaphors of alien intrusion or invasion—which fit with conventional immunological discourse" but rather by "that of productive migration" (280). Pertinent to my paper is her suggestion that "Like every other authoritative discourse, bioscience invests in strategies of representation that finesse the evidence to fit a particular structure, but perhaps what is happening is a *subtle shift in the imaginary itself*" (280; italics added).

3. Hans Christian Andersen's "The Red Shoes" depicts a more widely known version of the story. Here the ill-fate is that of a spoilt girl whose new red shoes will not allow her to stop dancing. The story was first published in 1845.

4. Maciej Ruczaj notes this coincidence as a marker of the protagonist's moral weakness:

> the theme of the left leg surfaces several times with possible ethical undertones, most prominently when Noman meets "the killer and the robber" Martin Finnucane, a character that fills him with fear and disgust but in reality is simply a mirror of his own self. This coequality is signalled in the text by the ultimate revelation that the robber also has a left leg made of wood. "Funny coincidence," Noman thinks, but it is not. ("Infernal Poetics" 98)

5. Anthony Uhlmann unpacks the symbolic significance of Moran's metamorphosis, in a passage which is particularly relevant to my understanding of the correspondence between disability and subjectivity. He writes:

Moran changes physically, and the physical changes ... produce corresponding affects in his mental state. The degeneration of the mind and body run parallel, and together they constitute a molecular metamorphosis which ends in prising Moran from his comfortable existence within the molar institutions. He was religious, a disciplinarian father, a good worker understanding both his station and his duty, with a well-kept house in a respectable community in which he was readily accepted; he ends with no belief in God (against whom he blasphemes), no interest in his son (whom he is about to abandon), unemployed and without interest in further work, allowing his house and property to run down, largely outside the community, on the verge of vagabondage. (*Poststructuralism* 68)

6. On the correspondences between Romantic and Modernist conceptions of interrupted inspiration, see Lawley as well as Levin.

Works Cited

Beckett, Samuel. *Three Novels: Molloy, Malone Dies, The Unnamable*. Translated by Patrick Bowles. Grove, 1958.

———. *Murphy*. Grove, 1957.

Blanchot, Maurice. *The Space of Literature*. Translated by Ann Smock. U of Nebraska P, 1982.

Booker, M. Keith. *Flann O'Brien, Bakhtin and Menippean Satire*. Syracuse UP, 1995.

Brooker, Joseph. "'That Carrousel Inside and Outside My Head': Flann O'Brien and *Pale Fire*." *The Review of Contemporary Fiction*, vol. 31, no. 3, 2011, pp. 120–134.

"Cork Leg." *Modern Street Ballads*. Edited by John Ashton. Chatto & Windus, 1888, pp. 153–55.

Coetzee, J.M. *Slow Man*. Penguin, 2005.

Davis, Lennard J. "The End of Identity Politics." *The Disability Studies Reader*, edited by Lennard J. Davis. Routledge, 2010, pp. 301–315.

Deleuze, Gilles. *Essays Critical and Clinical*. Translated by Baniel W. Smith and Michael A Greco. Verso, 1998.

Deleuze, Gilles, and Guattari Felix. *Anti Oedipus: Capitalism and Schizophrenia*. Translated by Robert Hurley, Mark Seem, and Helen R. Lane. U of Minnesota P, 1983.

Derrida, Jacques. *Of Grammatology*. Translated by Gayatri Chakravorty Spivak. Johns Hopkins UP, 1997.

Di Bernard, Barbara. *Alchemy and Finnegans Wake*. State U of New York P, 1980.

Foucault, Michel. *The Birth of the Clinic: An Archaeology of Medical Perception*. Translated by A.M. Sheridan. Routledge, 2003.

Hopper, Keith. *Flann O'Brien: A Portrait of the Artist as a Young Post-Modernist*. Cork UP, 2011.

Lawley, Paul. "Failure and Tradition: Coleridge / Beckett." *'All Sturm And No Drang': Beckett And Romanticism: Beckett At Reading 2006*, edited by Mark Nixon and Dirk van Hulle. Brill Academic, 2007, pp. 31–46.

Levin, Yael. "The Interruption of Writing in *Molloy*: Sunday Visits from Porlock." *Partial Answers*, vol. 14, no. 2, 2016, pp. 255–273.

Markotic, Nicole. "Re/Presenting Disability and Illness: Foucault and Two 20th Century Fictions." *Disability Studies Quarterly*, vol. 23, no. 2, 2003, pp. 178–192.

Mitchell, David T., and Sharon L. Snyder. *Narrative Prosthesis: Disability and the Dependencies of Discourse*. U of Michigan P, 2014.

O'Brien, Flann. *The Third Policeman*. Dalkey Archive P, 2006.

Ruczaj, Maciej. "Infernal Poetics/Infernal Ethics: 'The Third Policeman' Between Medieval and (Post)Modern Netherworlds." *Review of Contemporary Fiction*, vol. 31, no. 3, 2011, pp. 91–105.

Shildrick, Margrit. "Re-imagining Embodiment: Prostheses, Supplements and Boundaries." *Someatechnics*, vol. 3, no. 2, 2013, pp. 270–286.

Thomson, Rosemarie Garland. *Extraordinary Bodies: Figuring Physical Disability in American Culture and Literature*. Columbia UP, 1997.

Uhlmann, Anthony. *Beckett and Poststructuralism*. Cambridge UP, 1999.

———. *Samuel Beckett and the Philosophical Image*. Cambridge UP, 2006.

Warne, Vanesse. "Artificial Leg" *Victorian Review*, vol. 34, no. 1, 2008, pp. 29–33.

Wills, David. *Prosthesis*. Stanford UP, 1995.

Žukauskaitė, Audronė. "The Philosophy of the Impersonal" *Deleuze and Beckett*. Eds. S.E. Wilmer and Audronė Žukauskaitė. London: Palgrave Macmillan, 2015.

YAEL LEVIN is associate professor of English and associate provost for academic affairs at the Rothberg International School at the Hebrew University of Jerusalem. She is author of *Tracing the Aesthetic Principle in Conrad's Novels* (Palgrave Macmillan, 2008) and *Joseph Conrad: Slow Modernism* (Oxford UP, 2020). Her work on modernism, disability and attention studies has appeared in journals and volumes including *The Conradian*, *Conradiana*, *Partial Answers*, *Twentieth-Century Literature* and *Journal of Beckett Studies*.

13   " 'Tis my muse will have it so": Four Dimensions of Scatology in *Molloy*

Andrew G. Christensen

> The night will come when the Academy of Science itself will not disdain to plunge its gaze into the sewers of the world.
> —Max Ernst, *A Little Girl Dreams of Taking the Veil* (7)

We see an undeniable asymmetry when we look at the culture-producing properties of biological imperatives. Diet and eating account for an enormous proportion of what we refer to collectively as "culture," occupying a central or foundational position in most social events, celebrations, holidays, and rituals. At the other end, we find nearly the opposite situation—the "afterlife" of food is more often than not seen as antithetical to culture. While eating is made a focus of social life, excrement is pushed as far into the margins as possible. The scatological works of artists and writers (and, I would add, psychoanalysts) are an intellectual corrective—sometimes subversive, often humorous—to this asymmetry.

For example, Luis Buñuel draws attention to this lopsided aspect of society in a sequence from his *Phantoms of Liberty*. Guests arrive at an upper-middle-class home for what appears to be a dinner party but are then seated around the table on toilets (after dropping their pants, of course). The guests smoke, read newspapers, and discuss current events (including how much human waste the world can expect in the future if population projections are accurate), and a child is told to watch her language when she mentions that she is hungry. One guest then excuses himself and goes to a small closet down the hall to eat and drink, making sure to lock the door.

Historically, a similar imbalance can be seen in the world of letters. In addition to outright censorship, there was very little critical and theoretical acknowledgement of or commentary on scatology, considering the great amount of it in literature. Ever since Bakhtin's work came to prominence—and especially since "the body" became a popular focus in literary studies—there has been a steady countermeasure to this. More recently, we have since seen a wealth of criticism focused on excrement in literature—perhaps, some might argue, a surfeit, for the power of scatological writing rests precisely in the marginality of excrement. But the margin still holds—the sewers are in no danger of running over. As much of this recent criticism points out, the uses of scatology in literature are many but include (ultra-) realist detail, grotesque humor, shock value, a means of satire, and more rarely, a stimulus, however base, to higher thought.

In *Molloy*, Samuel Beckett employs scatology to all of these purposes in ways that, far from being gratuitous, are integral to the larger themes of the novel. This article considers primarily Beckett's use of scatology for the purposes of satire and philosophical speculation as applied to the topics of language, creativity, religion, and the human condition. My examination of *Molloy* implicitly presents the novel as both satirical and constructive. By bringing together a wide range of historical precedents, I show that, while the novel is in its own way exemplary of modernism/postmodernism, it also belongs to a long tradition of scatological writing. All of this is not to downplay the humor in Beckett's scatological humor. That it is funny is taken as granted—I want to consider why and how it is funny.

EXCREMENT AND LANGUAGE

In one of the funniest scenes in the novel, a policeman asks Molloy for his "papers," and Molloy presents, right under the policeman's nose, the only papers he has: "bits of newspaper. To wipe myself with, you understand, when I have a stool" (26). Molloy's literal connection of words and excrement is rich with symbolic significance, and the scene is a crystallization of one of the novels primary themes: "that all language was an excess of language" (159). Language is frequently an excess production, just as excrement is that which the body cannot use.[1] Yet with the metaphor of excrement comes also the ambiguity—language in the novel is both excessive and deficient: "I always say either too much or too little, which is a terrible thing for a man with a passion for the truth like mine" (45). And just as Molloy confuses east and west and inverts the poles, the novel's loose interrogation of language drifts between coordinates of excess and deficiency as well as speaking and writing.

Various excesses of language are embedded in the text, from pleonasms—"free, gratis, and for nothing" (30), "in a word I struck camp" (208)—to nonsensical hyperbole—"I fell, literally boneless" (73). Both Molloy and Moran are particularly concerned about verb tenses—"this should all be re-written in the pluperfect" (20), "it's the mythological present" (34), "a simple prophetic present" (149), "at the same time it is over and it goes on, and is there any tense for that?" (47). This fascination with grammar also accords with the question of the excess or deficiency of language, for grammar is by nature descriptive (not prescriptive, as many people assume), but it aims for a minimum of description. But leaving the pragmatic minimum and the desire for mathematical elegance aside, could we not have an expanded grammar as well? Is not there, after all, a "prophetic present" tense?

The topic of grammar also raises questions in the opposite direction—how much grammatical structure, really, is necessary? English has no future tense and no longer has nominal case inflection; Russian has no present perfect and no definite article; Bulgarian has no infinitive; Chinese, unlike most European languages, has no gender, and European languages, unlike Chinese, do not have tones.[2] Is there a minimum of grammar? Or vocabulary?

Beckett was interested in linguistic minimalism throughout his career, most prominently demonstrated in *Act Without Words I* and *II* (1956) and *Film* (1965). In his essay on Dante, Bruno, Vico, and Joyce, he writes that "in its first dumb form, language was gesture. If a man wanted to say 'sea,' he pointed to the sea" (24). Molloy in particular has problems communicating[3]—"this trouble I had in understanding not only what others said to me, but also what I said to them"—and reverts to gesture and physical contact in communicating with his mother, "by knocking on her skull. One knock meant yes, two no, three I don't know, four money, five goodbye" (22). Later, when he has a communication problem with the charcoal burner, he responds in a the same way, but more violently, "deal[ing] him a good dint on the skull" (113). Communication may be implicated in Moran's murderous encounter as well, as, after killing his man in a similar manner, Moran finds an "ear" on the ground. We may also have an allegory of language and speech in the famous "sucking stone" sequence, where the stones, going in and out of the mouth, could stand for words, which Molloy agonizes over putting into proper sequence. Such an allegory also fits into the "language as excess" theme: "deep down it was all the same to me whether I sucked a different stone each time or always the same stone, until the end of time. For they all tasted exactly the same." His solution: "throw away all the stones but one" (100). We are back, then, to a minimum—he needs only one rock, just as he needs only one unambiguous word with his mother: "that she should confuse yes, no, I don't know and goodbye, was all the same to me, I confused them myself. But that she should associate the four knocks with anything but money was something to be avoided at all costs" (22).

The theme of minimal language or, rather, communication, is extended beyond human language—first, in the parrot, whose "language" is offensively scatological—"*putain de merde!*" (49; "Holy Shit!") and then in the bees.[4] The two cases present an interesting contrast, as the parrot uses words but does not communicate and does not "understand" what it says, while the bees communicate without using words. Both scenarios are present in *Molloy*: "the words I uttered myself, and which must nearly always have gone with an effort of the intelligence, were often to me as the buzzing of an insect" (67), with the added ironic reversal here that the "buzzing" of the bees conveys meaning in the end, whereas words do not.

Moran's description of the man he ends up killing explicitly links speech with excrement: he had "a thin red mouth that looked as if it was raw from trying to shit its tongue" (206). The same connection is implied by the pun in "*oratio recta*" (119), and the link between the mouth and anus is made several times, as when Moran asks his son if he knows "which mouth" to put the thermometer in (161) and in Molloy's (mock) poetic/rhetorical question: "We underestimate this little hole, it seems to me, we call it the arse-hole and affect to despise it. But is it not rather the true portal of our being and the celebrated mouth no more than the kitchen-door" (197–198).

In considering the ways in which Beckett links excrement with the written word and with literature in particular, let us return to the scene with the policeman and the "papers." Molloy, like Leopold Bloom before him, is employing the printed page in a utilitarian function which has a long history. Sir William Cornwallis, essayist and friend of Ben Jonson, writes:

> Pamphlets and lying Stories, and News, and two penny Poets I would knowe them, but beware of beeing familiar with them, for they lie in my privy, and when I come thither, and have occasion to imploy it, I read them, halfe a side at once is my ordinary, which when I have read, I use in that kind, that waste paper is most subject to, but to cleanlier profit. (Qtd. in Schmigdall 80)

In the case of Bloom and Cornwallis, their act is not strictly practical, but also an insult to the written material. This may be the case with Molloy as well. We learn later that in the winter he wraps himself in newspaper, specifically the *Times Literary Supplement* because of its "toughness and impermeability. Even farts made no impression on it" (39). After writing that he will not write details of the murder, Moran states that he does not "intend to give way to literature" (207). He has a sense for the literary, but will not indulge it. In addition to murder, he considers the scatological a literary category: "I was succumbing to other affections, that is not the word, intestinal for the most part. I would have described them once, not now, I am sorry, it would have been worth reading" (228). This, of course, is pure irony, given the abundance of "intestinal" description in his report. But it highlights the fact that he is aware of it and that he considers it "worth reading," as does Molloy: "are not these significant facts" (108), the lack of question mark leaving no doubt as to his answer.

In his *History of Shit*, Dominique Laporte writes:

> no doubt beautiful language has more than a little to do with shit, and style itself grows more precious the more exquisitely motivated by waste. Proof of this lies in the pedantry of the countless anonymous poems found even in today's latrines, or in the obscene syntactic contortions of those marginal literatures that elevate the excremental to a form of art. (10)

Laporte's language becomes ambivalent in this passage, which is to be expected, as ambivalence is perhaps the most constant quality of scatological writing. But Beckett stands in a long line of literary luminaries who did not hesitate to wax scatological, including Joyce, Kafka, Mann, Thoreau, Carlyle, Coleridge, Blake, Swift, Pope, Jonson, Shakespeare, Rabelais, and Chaucer, to name just a few. Joyce's Shem writes not only *about* but *with* excrement, as does the poet Sherman Krebbs in Vonnegut's *Cat's Cradle*.

The use of excrement as a medium has become almost commonplace in painting and sculpture these days, but it was in practice even in Apollinaire's day: "I am not in awe of art and I have no prejudice against any materials used by painters.

Mosaicists paint in marble or coloured wood. We have heard of an Italian painter who painted in shit; in the French Revolution someone painted with blood" (56). Shortly after Apollinaire wrote this, the Dadaists proclaimed that "*Kunst ist Scheisse*" and Duchamp hung his urinal, and not long after Beckett wrote *Molloy*, the Italian artist Piero Manzoni produced "Merda d'artista"—ninety cans, each containing thirty grams of shit, each of which he sold for the price of thirty grams of gold. Compared to such extremes, the scatology in *Molloy* might even seem minimal, a realization which could echo Molloy's: "After all it's not excessive. . . . Damn it, I hardly fart at all, I should never have mentioned it" (39).

The topic of writing pervades the novel on a number of levels. The book's two sections are ostensibly reports written by Molloy and Moran, both of whom claim to be under orders and not pleased about it: "All is tedious, in this relation that is forced upon me" (180). Moran calls his writing "paltry scrivening" (80) and often bitterly retorts "he'll get his report." Molloy remarks that "you would do better, at least no worse, to obliterate texts than to blacken margins, to fill the holes of words till all is blank and flat and the whole ghastly business looks like what it is, senseless, speechless, issueless misery" (16). There is ample nihilism or at least darkness here, enough to cover writer as well as reader. Literary critics are perhaps especially implicated—they who "blacken margins" with their notes.

Moran makes the etymological connection, through *textus*, of writing and weaving, which, accompanied by the image of the shuttle taken from Job, makes visual and kinetic connections as well: "weaving inexorably back and forth and devouring my page" (182). Keeping the *weaving* metaphor in mind, Moran does, in the end, obliterate his text(iles) with excrement: "my drawers . . . had rotted, from constant contact with my incontinences" (234). Another kinetic/visual image of writing/reading appears in one of Molloy's many passages on the moon, which moves from left to right across his room—"its tranquil course was written on the walls." Again, he is quick to equate the moon and its left-right motion with the Bakhtinian "downward motion": "it must be her arse she shows us always" (52). The sucking stone sequence, which we have previously equated with speech, also contains a similar image that corresponds to writing/reading—due to unequal distribution of stones in his pockets, Molloy is "dragged to the right hand and the left, backwards and forwards" (100).

We have noted Moran's contempt for literature, but, characteristically, he contradicts himself on this. In places he shows a clear concern for the literary, perhaps most intriguingly in the opening and closing lines of his section, which opens much more like a novel or story than a "report." The closing lines repeat the opening lines and then negate them—it is Moran's confession that he does, indeed, "give way to literature" (207).

Toward the end of Moran's narrative, he gives the tongue-in-cheek observation: "sometimes you would think I was writing for the public" (232). This exemplifies another way in which the text is loaded on multiple levels with a (hyper) consciousness of writing. Some of Moran's musings on writing and literature, if read polyphonically, seem to include Beckett's voice as well: "in writing these lines I know in what danger I am of offending him whose favour I know I should court, now more than ever" (181). For Moran, "him" implies Youdi. For Beckett, the reader—in which case, we have an instance of the mock *apologia pro sua stercus*[5] which often accompanies scatological writing. Swift was a master of this:

> I hope the gentle Reader will excuse me for dwelling on these and the like Particulars, which however insignificant they may appear to grovelling vulgar Minds, yet will certainly help a Philosopher to enlarge his Thoughts and Imagination, and apply them to the Benefit of public as well as private Life. ... (89)

Molloy offers a similar apology in his section: "I apologize for having to revert to this lewd orifice, 'tis my muse will have it so" (107). In linking excrement and creativity, he has invoked another age-old scatological tradition and an association deeply rooted in the psyche.

EXCREMENT AND CREATIVITY

In one of his many scatological vignettes, Gulliver notes that "Men are never so Serious, Thoughtful, and Intent, as when they are at Stool" (Swift 178). Swift was the most extensively and consistently scatological writer of his day, but he was by no means the only one. Raymond Stephanson notes that "within the collective imagination of late seventeenth- and eighteenth-century writers and readers, male brains could be made analogous to the body's nether regions in various fashion: as wombs issuing book-children (or deformed offspring), as male genitalia, and as aresholes shitting words and paper" (113). He cites such a verse from Edward Ward:

> My Tail Prophetick Poems should excrete;
> I'd Rise Arse upwards e'ery Day by-time;
> On Boghouse Walls I'd digitize my Wit,
> And shitten luck should wait upon my Rhimes. (Qtd. in Stephanson114)

Ward and Swift use scatology in their writings most often, though not always, for satirical purposes. Yet the connection between excrement and artistic production, creativity, and generation is certainly not limited to satire. Nor is it much constrained by time and place. In the European tradition, certain centuries could be said to be more scatological than others, but the association of excrement and creativity/production seems to be universal.

Excrement plays a large role in mythologies the world over, often specifically in creation myths (the number increases dramatically if we read "dirt" or "clay" as excrement, which the myths themselves often do).[6] Dung has neutral or negative associations in the Hebrew Bible (more on this in the next section), and the creation myth found in Genesis probably does not belong to this class (unless we read the "dust" of the second, or Jahwist, version of the Creation as excrement). Beckett makes up for this, though, through the first of Moran's theological questions: "What value is to be attached to the theory that Eve sprang, not from Adam's rib, but from a tumour in the fat of his leg (arse?)?" (228).

Beckett also alludes to the psychoanalytic dimension of scatology in the novel. Freud speaks of "a universal conviction among children, who long retain the cloaca theory, that babies are born from the bowel like a piece of faeces" (125). Molloy holds this theory—"to speak ... of her who brought me into the world, through the hole in her arse if my memory is correct" (20)—and frequently associates his mother with excrement, calling her the "Countess Caca," and noting that he "piss[es] and shit[s] in her pot" (8). There are numerous references to Freud in the text, both explicit and oblique, and Beckett may allude to Freud's theory in the second section when Moran invokes the image of the labyrinth (144).

The labyrinth is undoubtedly among the most polysemous of symbols but is often associated with both the brain (as Moran seems to do) and the bowels. Many artists around the Surrealist movement, steeped in Freud and in mythology, were fond of both associations. Freud makes the latter connection: "I cannot resist pointing out how often light is thrown by the interpretation of dreams on mythological themes in particular. Thus, for instance, the legend of the labyrinth can be recognized as a representation of anal birth: the twisting paths are the bowels and Ariadne's thread is the umbilical cord" (31). Jung extends Freud's theory somewhat, noting that children create a "theory of propagation" with defecation (211). He recounts the story of a young patient who would spend inordinate amounts of time on the toilet. When her father asked what she was "doing" in there, she replied, "a little wagon and two ponies" (212).

In another association of creativity and scatology, Molloy sums up human society as "so many citizens, dreaming and farting" (14). Kant would surely have appreciated the image. Satirizing priests, and paraphrasing Hudibras, he wrote: "whenever a hypochondriacal wind blows in the guts, it is a question of which direction it takes: if it goes downwards, it comes out a fart; but if it goes upwards, it is an apparition or sacred inspiration" (qtd. in Fenves 97). But there may be Freudian allusions here as well. Molloy makes the observation as a man, A or C (he is not sure), is approaching. He is smoking a cigar (a detail perhaps too obvious). But also he is followed by a Pomeranian—a detail which has possible connections to Freud and psychoanalysis. Pomeranians, or "Spitz dogs," play a significant role in Freud's analysis of the Wolf Man, and Wilhelm Fleis, Freud's friend and collaborator, came from the region of Pomerania. Yet another source for the dog is the fact that Beckett's mother had a Pomeranian (Baire 337). This may be the most likely explanation, but it is still, in its way, a Freudian one.

EXCREMENT AND RELIGION

The perennial intermingling of scatology and religion is so extensive that cataloging it could fill volumes. The conjoining of excrement and divinity may bring about cognitive dissonance in some, or even most, but for many throughout history it has been a harmony that leaps immediately to mind, though to various ends. On the one hand, the persistence of scatology in religious traditions comes as no surprise, given the ancient roles played by excrement in mythology and the creative/generative association in the psyche. Bakhtin stresses that the image of defecation is "linked to the generating force and to fertility" (175). On the other hand, the ultimate "baseness" of shit makes it an unsurpassed tool for satire, of which religion is so often a target. Either way—by elevating base materiality through myth, psychology, alchemy (urine and excrement were common materials for medieval alchemists), or art, or by bringing down religion and theology by the same means—low and high are joined to come full-circle. Beckett's scatology in *Molloy* travels in both directions.

Moran, perhaps because he has absolutely no sense of shame regarding the lower bodily stratum, does not include it in his list of questions, but defecation has long posed theological conundrums. Jacob Grimm came across a troubling intersection of scatology and theology in his work on historical linguistics. If God speaks a language, he must have teeth, and since teeth were designed not for speaking but eating, then God must eat, and if God eats. ... Grimm thought it best not to carry his thought to its blasphemous yet logical conclusion (recounted in Staal). In *The Unbearable Lightness of Being*, Milan Kundera writes that he came upon the same problem as a child and concludes: "Either/or: either man was created in God's image—and God has intestines!—or God lacks intestines and man is not like Him." It is a debate, he notes, that has gone on since the Early Church: "the great Gnostic master Valentinus resolved the damnable dilemma by claiming that Jesus 'ate and drank, but did not defecate'" (245–246).

A related issue (we might call it the inverse) comes up in Moran's anxieties about communion. His concern is whether or not the Eucharist would "produce the same effect, taken on top of beer, however light" (132). Moran's religion is regimental—"I who never missed mass" (129)—which fits his portrayal at the beginning of his narrative as an authoritarian figure. He claims to despise superficial religiosity, as we see in his response to Gaber's dress: "this gross external observance, while the soul exults in its rags, has always appeared to me an abomination" (127), but he clearly has a literalist, material interpretation of the Eucharist: "The host, it is only fair to say, was lying heavy on my stomach. And as I made my way home I felt like one who, having swallowed a pain-killer, is first astonished, then indignant, on obtaining no relief" (139).

The physical nature of the Eucharist and its fate in the digestive system was, in fact, a topic of fierce debate going back at least to the tenth century. Those who believed that the body of Christ was digested came to be known as *stercoranists*, and the doctrine became a point of heated contention especially after the Reformation. Milton finds the idea particularly repulsive:

> The Mass brings down Christ's holy body from its supreme exaltation at the right hand of God. It drags it back to the earth, though it has suffered every pain and hardship already, to a state of humiliation even more wretched and degrading than before: to be broken once more and crushed to the ground, even by the fangs of

brutes. Then, when it has been driven through all the stomach's filthy channels, it shoots it out—one shudders even to mention it—into the latrine. (1290)

The name of the priest who "dispatches" Moran is significant here, as it was Ambrose who first declared unequivocally that the Eucharist is not a symbol, that the bread and wine *literally* become the flesh and blood of Christ (Cummings 66–70; Ramsey 51). He also emphasized that it was the Eucharistic words which brought about this physical transformation—a doctrine that Beckett parodies as "the magic words" (139).

Christianity and theism in general are the target of satire in *Molloy*, but Catholicism is singled out for particular ridicule, as we see in the case of the Eucharist. Another particularly funny (or offensive, depending on the reader) instance is the treatment in the text of the Virgin Mary. The geography that Moran travels is like Bakhtin's material bodily lower stratum mapped onto the landscape: "Condom on the Baise," "Hole,"[7] "Turdy." Beckett then makes the leap to scatological religious satire when Moran tells the farmer that he is on a pilgrimage to the "Turdy Madonna" (237).[8] This need not necessarily be read as degrading. For Bakhtin, after all, excrement is "gay matter." On another level, what we have in the Turdy Madonna is Molloy's Oedipal/scatological associations with his mother transferred onto the mother of God. Martin Luther, notorious for his scatological discourse, did not always associate excrement with evil—he claimed to have been visited by the Holy Spirit for the first time while on the toilet. Most often, however, he reserves his scatological language for attacking his adversaries, primarily the Devil and the Pope.[9] One of his imaginary dialogues with the Pope runs:

> POPE: Silence, you heretic! What comes out of your mouth must be kept!
> LUTHER: I hear it—which mouth do you mean? The one from which the farts come? (You can keep that yourself!) Or the one into which the good Corsican wine flows? (Let a dog shit into that!)
> POPE: Oh, you abominable Luther; should you talk to the pope like this?"
> LUTHER: Shame on you too, you blasphemous, desperate rogues and crude asses.... You are a crude ass, you ass-pope, and an ass you will remain. (281)

That excrement is such an effective satirical tool against the Church is in large part due to the centuries of effort on the Church's part to link human waste with sin, punishment, Hell, and the Devil. In the Old Testament, "dung" is mentioned most often in pragmatic contexts—sanitary prohibitions and recommendations, use as fertilizer and fuel, etc.—though there are also some punitive associations, such as in Job. The New Testament does not mention dung much at all, but when it does, it is for a symbol of what is low and worthless. Beginning with the early Church Fathers, however, there is an aggressive campaign to link anything deemed vile with excrement, and for many, this meant nearly everything outside of Heaven. A dictum attributed to Augustine (and often quoted by Freud) says that man is *inter faeces et urinam nascimur*, and Bernard of Clairvaux writes that "man is nothing but stinking sperm, a sack of excrement and food for worms" (qtd. in Camporesi 78).

The literature behind the scatological figuration of Hell is enormous, but we need look no further than Dante, in whose eighth circle flatterers are condemned to live in a river of shit, and farting devils are to be found all around. Or, for a more recent version, consider the sermon that frightens Stephen Dedalus into servility in *A Portrait of the Artist as a Young Man*. The heightened emotive content of excrement, then, is the Church's own doing, and it is no surprise to see it thrown back in its own face so often. Chaucer was a master of such satire. In the *Summoner's Tale*, he first ridicules mendicant friars by having a sick man, instead of giving alms, deliver a fart into a friar's hand; then scholastic logic by having the friars work out how to divide the fart evenly among them; and lastly the Godhead itself in the solution, which equates the Holy Spirit with flatulence. Bakhtin observes that "not a single saying of the Old and New Testaments was left unchallenged as long as it could provide some hint of equivocal suggestion that could be travestied and transposed into the language of the material bodily lower stratum" (86).

Scatological satire of the church came from both within and without, and Beckett's, like Joyce's, is definitely from without. Molloy is anti-theistic from the beginning, noting that anthropology interests him in "its relentless definition of man, as though he were no better than God" (52). Moran's faith, as we have noted, is rather hollow from the beginning, but he comes to reject it completely in the course of his narrative: "as for God, he is beginning to disgust me" (144); "there are men and there are things, to hell with animals. And with God" (227); "Our Father who art no more in heaven than on earth or in hell, I neither want nor desire that thy name be hallowed" (229). Beckett does employ scatological humor in his jibes at religion; the "Turdy Madonna" is the most acute example, but there is also Molloy's interjection of "Jesus-Christ" when he has his finger in his rectum (107). Moran's comment, "the seat of my breeches, before it too decomposed, sawed my crack from Dan to Beersheba" (243) again overlays the lower bodily stratum on geography, in this case the geography of the Holy Land. And another juxtaposition: "I was not going to expose myself to thunderbolts which might be fatal, simply because my son had the gripes. ... It was not for nothing I had studied the old testament. Have you shat, my child, I said gently" (162). But the scatology in Molloy goes beyond bringing down religion and dragging it through the filth.

EXCREMENT AND THE HUMAN CONDITION

Let us return one last time to the scene with the policeman and the papers. The policeman asks for Molloy's identification, and what he gets is an identification of sorts—of a living human. Or at least a living animal. We have here an entry into the existential nature of scatological writing, for excrement is the great leveler, both among humans and of humans—recall Molloy's description of the blind alley "littered with miscellaneous rubbish and with excrements, of dogs and masters" (81). Are we more than "eating and shitting machines"? Such is the simplistic caricature of many a biologically informed examination of man. It suggests that much of the sentiment behind the taboo, shame, disgust, and evasion of excrement is rooted in a certain existential anxiety or an unwillingness to confront questions of human identity, man's place in nature, and the nature of the world. Kundera summarizes this nicely:

> The fact that until recently the word "shit" appeared in print as s--- has nothing to do with moral considerations. You can't claim shit is immoral, after all! The objection to shit is a metaphysical one. The daily defecation session is daily proof of the unacceptability of Creation. Either/or: either shit is acceptable (in which case don't lock yourself in the bathroom!) or we are created in an unacceptable manner. (248)

Many have theorized that, to the human psyche, civilization itself is built on the principle of managing human waste. Freud is the obvious authority on this idea, but perhaps Joyce expresses it best in *Ulysses*:

> —What was their civilisation? Vast, I allow: but vile. Cloacae: sewers. The Jews in the wilderness and on the mountaintop said: *It is meet to be here. Let us build an altar to Jehova*. The Roman, like the Englishman who follows in his footsteps, brought to every new shore on which he set his foot (on our shore he never set it) only his cloacal obsession. He gazed about him in his toga and said: *It is meet to be here. Let us construct a watercloset*. (126)

To the civilized mind, excrement represents disorder, chaos, and is a pungent daily reminder that although technology allows us some degree of self-determination regarding man's place in nature, we have no say over nature's place in us. William G. Plank, drawing on the dramaturgical sociology of Erving Goffman, writes that "scatological humor removes the props by which the self attempts to create and control its image: clothing, privacy, secrecy, composition of the face, and self-control. There is a general debasement of the human individual and at the same time an exaltation of the basic organic existence of the self" (n.p.).

Plank also makes a passing suggestion that the "psycho-social bases of scatological humor" can be related to Sartre's concepts of the *en-soi*, or being-in-itself, and *pour-soi*, or being-for-itself. Beckett and Sartre had a collegial but distant relationship; in her biography, Dierdre Bair writes that Beckett "studied Sartre from afar" (352). There are many points of similarity between the two, however. The meditations on objects in *Molloy*, for example, are reminiscent of Sartre's discussion of the *en-soi*—the class of things (rocks, plants, artifacts) that are not conscious of their own existence. Molloy, who spends a lot of time handling and looking at objects, such as the unidentifiable knife-holder, philosophizes that "to restore silence is the role of objects" (16). Moran, complementing the idea, praises those who can "be silent and listen" and who can "detect, beyond the fatuous clamour, the silence of which the universe is made" (166).

Beckett was not a self-identified "existentialist," but the term is apt for many of his works. It almost goes without saying that *Molloy* is pervaded by issues of identity, existence, and essence, and the pervasive excrement has a significant relation to this existentialist key, just as it did to existentialism proper. A French journal once commented that people should stop using the term "existentialism" and call it "excrementalism," and Raymond Las Vergnas, lector of the universities of Paris, wrote that Sartre's work was like "pathways deep in shit on which it is best to venture equipped with stilts" (Lévy 34). Sartre was constantly accused of coprophilia but defends himself eloquently:

> the reason why we must speak of even the most humble functions of the body is that we must not pretend to have forgotten that the spirit descends into the body, or in other words the psychological into the physiological. ... I don't speak about these things for my amusement but because in my view a writer ought to grasp man whole. (258)

Bakhtin writes that "dung is a link between body and earth (the laughter that unites them), [and] urine is a link between body and sea" (335). Similarly (to improve on Plank's idea), we might conceive of excrement as *mediating* between the *en-soi* and *pour-soi*. Given its position—central, fundamental, mediatory—it is all but inevitable that excrement will figure in existential discourse or discussion of the human condition. And, given the persistent ambiguity of excrement, the tone of such discourse can vary, ranging from pessimism to optimism, denial to acceptance. We have already seen the Christian version of this—*inter faeces et urinam*. In one of his darker moods, Martin Luther remarks, "I am like ripe shit, and the world is a gigantic ass-hole. We probably will let go of each other soon" (qtd. in Erikson 206). The sentiment is echoed by Moran—"this image hardly fitted my situation, which was rather that of the turd waiting for the flush" (223)—as well as Molloy—"fate had earmarked me for less compassionate sewers" (23).

Ultimately, scatological art makes us face excrement, and in facing excrement we face a dilemma: we find it disgusting, yet we produce it—we are the source of our own disgust. What are we to do? One option is to laugh. Molloy's presentation of his used toilet paper as identification and his observation of human and dog excrement intermixed remind us of our natural condition. But, as Father Ambrose points out, there is another condition which defines man—the ability to laugh. We could do worse than to bring the two together.

Notes

1. Jeanne-Sarah de Larquier makes the astute observation that Beckett also implicitly compares writing to masturbation in his euphemism "twixt finger and thumb," which is where one would expect to find a pen (de Larquier 53).

2. A possible exception is Norwegian, whose pitch accent could be considered as a form of tone.

3. Moran does as well and makes several remarks to this effect. One interesting suggestion is when he claims that he had "lived like a Hottentot" (166). Moran presumably means that he lived in poverty, but Beckett likely had an added meaning in mind, given that the most common etymology for the term is that it derives from a Dutch word meaning "stutter, stammer," applied to the Khoekhoe people because of their language, which, with its clicks, sounded strange to the colonial invaders. This linguistic chauvinism is a common phenomenon in world languages: the word *barbarian* (and *berber*, whence it comes) may also have the same etymology in Greek ("blather, stammer"), and the Slavic word for German, *němec*, means "mute"; the *Slavs*, conversely, are the "people who have language"— *Slav* comes from *slovo*, "word."

4. The precise nature of communication in bees was discovered in 1945 by the Austrian ethologist Karl von Frisch, whose work Beckett seems to have been somewhat familiar with, as many of the details of Moran's "discovery" match that of von Frisch. Other details seem to be of Beckett's own imagining.

5. I take the phrase from Kelly Anspaugh, who notes that even John C. Bourke found it necessary to include such an apology in his *Scatologic Rites of All Nations* (1891), an early ethnological examination of excrement and culture that had interested Sigmund Freud in 1913. Bourke's *apologia* is, of course, meant to be taken as sincere, unlike the usual literary versions, though many, including Stephen Greenblatt, speculate as to the sincerity of his protests of disgust (Anspaugh 2–3). Another classic example of the mock apology is found in Chaucer's Prologue to the *Miller's Tale*, where he says that as a truthful recorder of events, he "moot reherce" the material and recommends the squeamish reader to "Turne over the leef and chese another tale" (3174, 3177).

6. Bourke catalogs several such myths in his aforementioned work (266–72). See also Lévi-Strauss (86–107, 118–177).

7. In fact, Rabelais mentions "St. Patrick's Hole," which according to Irish legend was a gateway to Hell, and other similar "Holes" in the geography of Europe, which, Bakhtin notes, had "indecent overtones" already in the Middle Ages (377).

8. Precisely this juxtaposition became the source of a highly publicized controversy in 1999, when the Brooklyn Museum of Art exhibited a painting by British artist Chris Ofili called *The Holy Virgin Mary*, a portrait of Mary which included cutouts of pornographic images and pieces of elephant dung affixed to the canvas. Outraged Mayor Rudy Giuliani withheld city government funding and attempted to have the museum evicted from the building which it leases from the city until a court order from a US District Court judge ruled in favor of the museum, and all legal actions were dropped. Ten years earlier, a similar scandal surrounded Andres Serrano's *Piss Christ*, a photograph of a plastic crucifix submerged in urine.

9. In one such dispute, Thomas More lashed back at Luther and did not hesitant to answer in kind: "But meanwhile, for as long as your reverend paternity will be determined to tell these shameless lies, others will be permitted, on behalf of his English majesty, to throw back into your paternity's shitty mouth, truly the shit-pool of all shit, all the muck and shit which your damnable rottenness has vomited up...." This, of course, was followed with an *apologia*: "In your sense of fairness, honest reader, you will forgive me that the utterly filthy words of this scoundrel have forced me to answer such things, for which I should have begged your leave. Now I consider truer than truth that saying: 'He who touches pitch will be wholly defiled by it' (Sirach 13:1). For I am ashamed even of this necessity, that while I clean out the fellow's shit-filled mouth I see my own fingers covered with shit" (311).

Works Cited

Anspaugh, Kelly. "Powers of Ordure: James Joyce and the Excremental Vision(s)." *Mosaic*, vol. 27, no. 1, 1994, pp. 73–101.

Apollinaire, Guillaume. *The Cubist Painters*. Broadwater House, 2000.

Bair, Deirdre. *Samuel Beckett: A Biography*. Harcourt Brace, 1978.

Bakhtin, Mikhail. *Rabelais and His World*. Indiana UP, 1994.

Beckett, Samuel. "Dante ... Bruno. Vico . . Joyce." *Disjecta: Miscellaneous Writings and a Dramatic Fragment*. Edited by Ruby Cohn. Grove Press, 1984.

———. *Molloy*. Grove, 1994.

Bourke, John C. *Scatologic Rites of All Nations: A Dissertation Upon the Employment of Excrementilious Remedial Agents in Religion, Therapeutics, Divination, Witchcraft, Love-Philters, Etc., in All Parts of the Globe*. W.H. Lowdermilk & Co., 1891.

Camporesi, Piero, and Tania Croft-Murray. *The Incorruptible Flesh: Bodily Mutation and Mortification in Religion and Folklore*. Cambridge UP, 1988.

Chaucer, Geoffrey. *The Miller's Tale*. *The Riverside Chaucer*. Edited by Larry Benson. Houghton Mifflin, 1987.

Cummings, Owen F. *Eucharistic Doctors: A Theological History*. Paulist Press, 2005.

De Larquier, Jeanne-Sarah. "Beckett's *Molloy*: Inscribing Molloy in a Metalanguage Story." *French Forum*, vol. 29, no. 3, 2004, pp. 43–55.

Erikson, Erik H. *Young Man Luther: A Study in Psychoanalysis and History*. Norton, 1958.

Ernst, Max. *A Little Girl Dreams of Taking the Veil*. Translated by Dorothea Tanning. G. Braziller, 1982.

Fenves, Peter David. *Late Kant: Towards Another Law of the Earth*. Routledge, 2003.

Freud, Sigmund. *New Introductory Lectures on Psycho-Analysis*. Standard Edition. Edited and translated by James Strachey. Norton, 1989.

Joyce, James. *A Portrait of the Artist as a Young Man*. Dover, 1994.

———. *Ulysses*. Edited by Jeri Johnson. Oxford UP, 2008.

Jung, C.G. *Psychology of the Unconscious: A Study of the Transformations and Symbolisms of the Libido*. Translated by Beatrice M. Hinkle. Moffat, Yard and Co., 1916.

Kundera, Milan. *The Unbearable Lightness of Being*. Translated by Michael Henry Heim. Harper, 1999.

Laporte, Dominique. *History of Shit*. MIT Press, 2000.

Lévi-Strauss, Claude. *The Jealous Potter*. Translated by Benedicte Chorier. U of Chicago P, 1988.

Lévy, Bernard Henri. *Sartre: The Philosopher of the Twentieth Century*. Translated by Andrew Brown. Polity Press, 2004.

Luther, Martin. *Against the Roman Papacy, An Institution of the Devil*. Translated by Eric W. Gritsch. *Luther's Works: Church and Ministry III Volume 41*. Edited by Helmut Lehmann. Fortress Press, 1966.

Milton, John. *Complete Poetry and Essential Prose*. Edited by William Kerrigan, John Peter Rumrich, and Stephen M. Fallon. Modern Library, 2007.

More, Thomas. *The Complete Works of St. Thomas More*. Yale UP, 1963.

Plank, William G. "The Psycho-Social Bases of Scatological Humor: The Unmasking of the Self." N.d. n.pag. www.msubillings.edu/CSAFaculty/Plank/humor.htm. Accessed 25 Apr. 2009.

Ramsey, Boniface. *Ambrose*. Routledge, 1997.

Sartre, Jean-Paul. *The Writings of Jean-Paul Sartre, Vol 1*. Edited by Richard C. McCleary, Michel Contat, and Michel Rybalka. Translated by Richard C. McCleary. Northwestern UP, 1974.

Schmidgall, Gary. *Shakespeare and the Poet's Life*. UP of Kentucky, 1990.

Staal, Frits. "Noam Chomsky between the Human and Natural Sciences." *Janus Head* Special Issue, 2001, pp. 25–56 www.janushead.org/gwu-2001/staal.cfm.

Stephanson, Raymond. *The Yard of Wit: Male Creativity and Sexuality, 1650–1750*. U of Pennsylvania P, 2004.

Swift, Jonathan. *Gulliver's Travels*. Edited by Robert DeMaria. Penguin 2003.

ANDREW G. CHRISTENSEN received his BA in history of art and architecture from the University of Cambridge and his PhD in English from Boston University. His work has appeared in *Word & Image*, *James Joyce Quarterly*, *Journal of Modern Literature*, *The Explicator*, and *Utopian Studies*.

14 "Strange laughter": Post-Gothic Questions of Laughter and the Human in Samuel Beckett's Work

Hannah Simpson

The laughter of Samuel Beckett's characters is frequently strange and unsettling. Laughter in realistic literature tends to be prompted by some recognizable source, and often provokes the reader or audience to laugh as well. By contrast, it is often difficult to pin down the source of the Beckettian character's laughter or to join in with it. Readers or spectators who do laugh in response to Beckett's work often feel uncomfortable with their own laughter, "shocked" by its apparent "impropriety," as Wolfgang Iser notes (140). Reading the unfamiliar laugh represented in and provoked by Beckett's work in conjunction with influential laughter theory helps us understand why this occurs and what some of its implications are.

Laughter theory frequently begins by defining laughter as a uniquely human trait, and goes on to narrowly define when, why, and how human beings are expected to laugh. We have "conventional expectations" of laughter, laughter having become "an institutionalized pattern of social behaviour" (Iser 160). Gothic literature in particular has exploited our consequent ingrained narrow sense of what constitutes human laughter: the laughing Gothic figure indulges in an activity we have been trained to recognize as human, yet does so incorrectly, producing seemingly non-human laughter.

Beckett follows conceptually as well as temporally this Gothic precedent. His characters laugh inappropriately, unpredictably, and often inexplicably, and because their laughter is not familiarly human according to our ingrained concepts, it makes these otherwise human characters appear unsettlingly non-human. Consequently, readers or spectators often become self-conscious about their own inappropriate laughter, provoking a disconcerting identification with the being who laughs in an apparently non-human manner. The uncertainty generated by Beckett's works has an antecedent in the uncertainties that arise in response to Gothic narratives.

Gothic and Beckettian texts exploit our narrow sense of human laughter both to render certain figures more unsettling and to question the boundaries of our definition of the human. Whereas certain critics have read Beckettian laughter as redemptive of the miserable human condition, Beckettian laughter in fact gestures toward a simultaneously human-and-non-human condition, with complicating implications for the link between laughter and mortality, following the Gothic precedent. "Laughter is peculiar to man," Father Ambrose states in *Molloy* (96), invoking the popular idea that laughter is a uniquely human phenomenon, but "peculiar" has multiple implications in relation to laughter. Rather than laughter belonging exclusively to the human being, Beckett's work encourages us to recognize how "peculiar" or unfamiliar laughter can equally belong to the human, in an expanded understanding of the human that includes more inappropriate and unfamiliar elements than much theorizing on laughter would allow. Moreover, the reader's or spectator's self-recognition in the encounter with the non-human being recurs in both Gothic and Beckettian texts through this dark, uncanny laughter.

Below I survey laughter theory selectively and briefly, in order to ground my claim that the modern Western audience has been trained to recognize laughter as something uniquely human and narrowly defined: a predictable response to specific stimuli that cause a foreseeable, appropriate loss of physical and/or mental control. Against this backdrop, similarities emerge between the Gothic and Beckettian texts concerning the rendering of some figures as less than human through inappropriate or unpredictable laughter. Such instances appear across both waves of Gothic fiction,[1] from *The Monk* (1796) to *Dracula* (1897), and in a number of Beckett's texts from the 1950s: *Waiting for Godot* (1952), the Trilogy (1951–3), *Watt* (1953), *Texts for Nothing* (1954) and *Endgame* (1957).

LAUGHTER THEORY: HUMAN CONTROL

Although there is variation between theories of laughter across the centuries, such theorizing is united by two elements: the recurrent emphasis on laughter as a uniquely human act, and on laughter as constituted by a predictable loss of control. The question of when and how far human individuals can retain physical and mental control over themselves becomes key to most laughter theorists' idea of when and why individuals laugh, and to the very identification of the human being.

Helmuth Plessner explicitly links questions of physical and mental control to both the provocation of laughter and the definition of the human being. He argues that humans occupy a unique "eccentric position" (32) in relation to their bodies: the desire to maintain a distinction between the mind and the body, with the mind operating "mastery" (34) over the body. Only humans, Plessner argues, envision this mind-body hierarchy. He therefore defines laughter as one of the "universally human" traits (11), because it reveals both this desire for such a hierarchy and its illusory nature. When we laugh, the mind's "dominant relation to the body is disrupted" (117). The body is "uncontrolled," and "acts, as it were, autonomously" (31). Laughter reveals the human mind's lack of any permanent or reliable control over the body. Consequently, Plessner qualifies laughter as something definitively human: it demonstrates both the human being's desire to retain mental mastery over the body and the human body's essentially unruly nature, its ability to break free and act "autonomously" from the mind. The "creature without the possibility of laughing" is "not human," he argues (7), since humans cannot retain permanent control over their bodies.

The incongruity theory of laughter takes Plessner's model and explores precisely when and why we can expect the human being to succumb to the loss of mental control that leads to the loss of physical control and laughter. Incongruity theorists argue that when the mind meets with an incomprehensible incongruity that it cannot process, it surrenders control. Iser summarizes, "We normally laugh when our emotive or cognitive faculties have been overtaxed by a situation they can no longer cope with. The disorientated body takes over the response from it" (160), laughter being "a crisis response by the body when the cognitive or emotive faculties prove incapable of mastering a situation" (143). Elliott Oring similarly notes that it is the "tension between incongruous domains" or "a violation of logic, sense, reality or practicable action" (14) that occasions the mind's loss of control and consequently stimulates laughter. Crucially, Marjorie Grene adds that the incongruities that produce laughter are only those that appear "not in such a way that harms us" (qtd. in Plessner xii).

Superiority theory likewise focuses on the relation between the loss of mental and of physical control as the catalyst to laughter, but formulates the operation of this catalyst differently. According to the superiority theory, the instinctive human response is to laugh at another's suffering or inferiority because it is not one's own, and so provokes "the idea of one's *own* superiority" (151), as Charles Baudelaire puts it in "On the Essence of Laughter" (1855). Resultant laughter is read as an expression of delight in this sense of "suddaine Glory arising from suddaine Conception of some Eminency in ourselves, by Comparison with the Infirmityes of others," Hobbes summarizes (qtd. in Critchley 2). Crucially, this laughter is permitted only by a precise relation of mental and physical control postulated by superiority theorists. Following Plato's statement in *Philebus* that we laugh at the suffering of another only when we think them not sufficiently powerful to strike us in retaliation, Marcel Gutwirth observes, "In laughter, the body is defenceless" and consequently humans can surrender to "that physical vulnerability" only when they feel "mental security, the sense of confidence that allows the organism to let down its guard so entirely" (11). Hence we laugh when someone falls over, according to the superiority theorists, because *we* have not fallen over and are hence superior, and because the person on the ground is in no position to retaliate against us.

In distinction to the more complete losses of physical and mental control postulated by Plessner and the incongruity theorists, the superiority theory imagines a qualified loss of physical control alone, humans being so constituted that they cannot find delight in a frighteningly total loss of control. Again, laughter is described by most superiority theorists as "a human phenomenon," "one of the most widespread—indeed, universal—responses of human beings" (Heyd 285), but the boundaries of what constitutes laughter remain narrowly drawn. Laughter otherwise stimulated falls outside the remit of the human within this context.

Finally, the relief theory characterizes laughter as "a release of pent-up nervous energy" (Critchley 2). In "The Physiology of Laughter" (1860), Herbert Spencer theorizes an unconscious, involuntary relationship between the mind and the body: "Nervous excitation always tends to beget muscular action" (395). Thus laughter is "caused by the gush of agreeable feeling that follows the cessation of mental strain" (399): the cessation of mental strain produces an excess of emotion that must be physically discharged, a loss of mental control provoking a loss of physical control. In *Jokes and their Relationship to the Unconscious* (1905) and "Humour" (1927), Sigmund Freud transforms Spencer's theory into a model of how the individual escapes the pressure of social repression. According to Freud, humor is "liberating" (162) in that it allows us to temporarily overcome the constraints that prevent us from expressing aggressive or obscene ideas not usually permitted social expression; the consequent laughter signals the release of the energy usually employed to repress such ideas. Here again, laughter signals a surrendering of control, the release of mental energy via the uncontrolled physical convulsion that we recognize as laughter. The human being, according to the relief theory, cannot lose mental control without losing physical control.

This overview of laughter theory reveals how each definition of laughter, coupled with the recurrent emphasis on laughter as a human act, places strict boundaries on precisely what loss or retention of control we recognize as human. Human beings, according to these theorists, lose control and laugh predictably and appropriately, only at certain stimuli and under certain circumstances. The theorized predictable nature of laughter, then, assumes that laughter that is recognizably "human" is also necessarily "convivial" (Gutwirth 13). To retain mental control where we would expect its loss, or to lose physical control with no apparent reason, may strike us as so unfamiliar as to be non-human.

We find frightening the idea of another creature unexpectedly losing control in our presence. If beings around us retain a control over themselves that we recognize and share, we can predict how they are going to act, and this is reassuring. When the beings around us do lose control, we again want this loss of control to be predictable: we want to know when and why it will happen and what form it will take, so that we are prepared to react accordingly. Hence, we are unsettled or even frightened by the being who laughs inappropriately. We may become so unsettled by beings whose actions we cannot predict or understand that we start to see them as non-human. We are unlikely to accept that such an incomprehensible being is human in the same sense that we understand ourselves to be. Unexpected, inappropriate, unpredictable laughter, then, is unsettling because an activity we have been taught to think of as uniquely human is performed in a way that seems non-human to us.

LAUGHTER AT SUFFERING

Armed with a fuller understanding of why we are inclined to identify inappropriate or unpredictable laughter as non-human, we can more productively explore the effect of inappropriate or unpredictable laughter in the Gothic and the Beckettian text. John Paul Riquelme observes the recurrent interest throughout much Gothic fiction "concerning the limits of the human (…) about what it means to be a human as a species by contrast with the subhuman" ("Gothic" 6). Unexpected laughter is a crucial means by which both Gothic and Beckettian texts render certain figures simultaneously human and non-human, a disconcerting contradiction that troubles us both cognitively and affectively as we try to comprehend it and its implications.

It is common in the Gothic text to find laughter explicitly identified as non-human. In Bram Stoker's *Dracula* (1897), for instance, the laughter of the vampiric women directly signals their non-human nature, their laughter being explicitly dissociated from the human body, "hard as though the sound could never have come through the softness of human lips" (45). The next time the vampiric women laugh, Stoker describes it as a "soulless laughter" (46). Western theology understands the soul to be unique to the human being, likewise laughter theory also sees laughter as a uniquely human activity, yet in Stoker's text the human activity of laughter is conversely linked to a non-human nature. Stoker draws the troubling association still more tightly when he describes the women's laughter as explicitly demonic, signaling "the pleasure of fiends" (46) rather than the human. This association is a common one in Gothic texts. Melmoth in Charles Maturin's *Melmoth the Wanderer* (1820) utters a "demoniac laugh" (39). The "loud and fiendish laughter" of Victor Frankenstein's monster disgusts him in Mary Shelley's *Frankenstein* (1818); his description of his feeling "as if all hell surrounded me with mockery and laughter" (169) replicates Stoker's disconcerting association of the human act of laughter with an explicitly non-human subject. It is unsettling to find the explicit rendering of laughter—an act we are accustomed to identify as uniquely human—as something non-human, even expressly denoted as demoniac. The manner in which a monster's laughter increases its dramatic impact proves a notably effective and consequently oft-repeated technique within the Gothic novel, one whose contradictory character has implications for the reader's or spectator's view of their own professed humanity.

It is not only such explicit description that pushes the reader to recognize laughter in the Gothic text as frequently non-human, however. Often, it is the laughter's unexpected provocation that renders it suspect. We noted concerning laughter theory that the boundaries drawn around what should naturally provoke laughter in the human being, and the assumption that human beings share predictable physical and mental responses to certain phenomena, are key recurrent elements of the definition of laughter. The Gothic figure, by contrast, frequently laughs at unexpected provocations. Stoker's vampiric women laugh at the pitiful movements of the doomed human child in Count Dracula's bag (47), at the anticipation of Jonathan's destruction at their hands, and at his subsequent rage and terror (58). Few human beings could fathom laughing at the injured child's fate; given the anthropological imperatives against infanticide and cannibalism, such a response would contravene the anthropological perspective on what it means to be human.

Moreover, the unpredictable nature of the vampire's laugh heightens this sense of distinction between human and vampire. The individual who did laugh would be labeled "monstrous" or "inhuman" by others; modern Western society is trained to interpret unpredictable or inappropriate laughter as signaling a lack of recognizably human traits, a fact that Stoker here exploits. Even in earlier Gothic texts that stand as pre-anthropological in relation to the rise of anthropology in the wake of evolutionary theory, laughter provoked by an inappropriate source heightens the reader's sense of the laugher's non-human status. In *Melmoth the Wanderer*, Melmoth's laughter at the sight of the dead lovers' bodies is described by Stanton as "an outrage on humanity" (31); Melmoth's reaction is set in explicit contrast to the conventional understanding of what predictably or appropriately might provoke human laughter. Thomas de Quincey's protagonist in *Confessions of an English Opium-Eater* (1821) similarly apologizes for his own "very reprehensible" laughter "in the midst of my own misery" (39). Inappropriate laughter renders him, by his own admission, "guilty" of an "indecent practice," and of "infirm nature" (39), monstrous. In John Polidori's *The Vampyre* (1819), Lord Ruthven's "loud laugh" is provoked by and mingles with "the dreadful shrieks" (47) of the woman he attacks, and such unexpected laughter, with which the reader is not likely to join, heightens appreciably the unsettling nature of the scene. The being who laughs at what we do not, who laughs at what does not usually provoke human laughter, appears less-than-human to the self-identified human being.

Beckett's characters also frequently laugh unexpectedly or inappropriately, and such laughter likewise makes them appear disconcertingly less-than-human. The Beckettian text rarely labels laughter as non-human as explicitly as the Gothic text does, but the source of the laughter renders such laughter disconcertingly unexpected. Like the vampires laughing at the frightened child and Melmoth laughing at the dead lovers, the Beckettian character laughs at suffering, albeit on a frequently less melodramatic scale: the pitiful, the painful, the inadequate. Two of the best-known references to laughter in Beckett's work emphasize this. In *Watt*, Arsene summarizes the prevalence of laughter at "that which is not good," "that which is not true" and "that which is unhappy" (40). Similarly, in a direct response to Arsene, Nell in *Endgame* declares that though one shouldn't "laugh at these things," nevertheless "[n]othing is funnier than unhappiness, I grant you that. (...) Yes, yes, it's the most comical thing in the world" (101).

Other Beckettian texts are replete with instances of characters laughing at the sight or thought of suffering. When Clov laughs at the story of the starving beggar and his son in *Endgame*, he and Hamm assume that it must have been one of the pitiful elements of the story that made him do so:

CLOV: A job as a gardener!
HAMM: Is that what tickles you?
CLOV: It must be that.
HAMM: It wouldn't be the bread?
CLOV: Or the brat.
(*Pause.*)
HAMM: The whole thing is comical, I grant you that. (121)

The man driven to beg for a job, the pitiful request for bread, the starving child, or the whole sad mess: one of these has provoked Clov's laughter. Lousse in *Molloy* laughs at her dog's graveside (32). The "Israelite" in *Malone Dies* laughs when faced with Malone's "wetted trousers and the little pool of urine at my feet" (211). The narrator of *The Unnamable* records "a great cackle of laughter, at the sight of his terror and distress[.] To see him flooded with light, and then suddenly plunged back into darkness, must strike them as irresistibly funny" (349). In *Waiting for Godot*, we find Pozzo "*in raptures*" at the discrepancy between Lucky's miserable state and Estragon calling him "Mister" (28). Later, Estragon is "*convulsed with merriment*" (35) at Pozzo's tears. Mr de Baker laughs at Mr Nackybal's mute, humiliated ignorance in *Watt* (164). Beckett's characters frequently laugh as inappropriately as the non-human, monstrous Gothic figures.

Although they often laugh at their own suffering, rather than at suffering they have inflicted on another, Beckettian figures' inappropriate laughter at suffering elicits the same set of anxieties provoked by the Gothic figure's laughter at the terrifying or the horrific. We have not been taught to recognize the unhappy or the pitiful as a legitimate source of humor, and consequently such laughter is disconcertingly unexpected, unfamiliar to the point of appearing non-human. Like Lord Ruthven's "mockery of a laugh" (46) at the woman's shrieks in Polidori's *The Vampyre*, laughter provoked by misery is referred to in the Beckettian text as not really laughter. Moran in *Molloy*, for example, finishes his description of his laughter at the thought of his future punishment at Youdi's hand with the comment, "Strange laughter truly, and no doubt misnamed" (156). Similarly, in describing the "*risus puris*" in *Watt*, Arsene notes that "the bitter, the hollow and the mirthless" laughs are "strictly speaking not laughs, but modes of ululation" (40). As the Gothic monsters' laughter at pain and death emphasizes their non-human status, so too the Beckettian figure who laughs at suffering does not strike us as human. To laugh at suffering is explicitly coded in the Gothic text as not really human, and in the Beckettian text as not really laughter; neither form of laughter signals human status.

The superiority theory, however, may offer a lens through which the Gothic and Beckettian laughter at suffering can be read as predictable, recognizable, and human. According to the superiority theory, to laugh at another's suffering is to revel in the sense of one's own superior position, and without fear of the weaker being's retaliation. Thus Stoker's vampires can laugh at the injured child and Ruthven at his female victim, not being subject to their suffering and fearing no potential retaliation on their part. Within Beckett's work, the watchers in *The Unnamable* who laugh at Worm are not subject to the same painful experiences that he is, and have no reason to fear any potential retaliation on his part. The irresistible loss of physical control signaled by their laughter is permitted by their mental sense of control, and their indulgence in it can be read as predictable and the recognizably human in the context of the superiority theory. Similarly, Pozzo can laugh at Lucky and the "Israelite" at Molloy, not suffering as they do and anticipating no retaliation. In the context of the superiority theory, to laugh at the unhappy is in these instances an understandable and predictable human response.

However, Beckett extends the Gothic idea of non-human laughter provoked by suffering by having his characters laugh at their own as well as others' suffering. In doing so, they negate the potential of the superiority theory to explain such laughter as predictable, recognizable, human. We noted, for example, that Moran in *Molloy* laughs "at the thought of the punishments Youdi might inflict on me" (156). In *Endgame*, Hamm laughs at the thought that he "wasn't much longer for this world" (118), a laugh provoked both by the thought of his own demise, and the pitiful fact that he still endures his miserable existence. Hamm and Nagg laugh at Hamm's conspicuous lack of any "honour" (116), a personal failing on Hamm's part and the source of further suffering on Nagg's, for instance when Hamm refuses him the promised sugar-plum. Moreover, Clov's laughter at Hamm's story is complicated by the suggestion that Hamm could be retelling the story of how Clov came to live with him: is Clov laughing at his and his father's own past suffering? Similarly, when Lousse in *Molloy* laughs at her dog's graveside, she might well be laughing at her own grief rather than, or as well as, at the dog's death.

Characters laughing at their own misery complicates the application of the superiority theory in two ways. Firstly, to laugh at oneself involves considering oneself simultaneously superior and inferior; secondly, one can always fear retaliation from oneself, the self being perfectly capable of punishing the self. The Beckettian individuals who laugh at their own suffering confound the possibility of reading laughter at the unhappy as a recognizable, comprehensible human response.

LAUGHTER AS FRIGHTENING LOSS OF CONTROL

We noted above that inappropriate or unpredictable laughter unsettles us to point of pushing us to see the laugher as less-than-human because we take comfort in the sense of a shared, predictable control over our minds and bodies. We feel vulnerable when confronted with beings whose loss of control is unexpected since we are unable to predict their actions, or even to identify them as "human like us." Beyond laughter explicitly labeled as non-human, Gothic texts frequently use unexpected or inappropriate laughter to signal a protagonist's unsettlingly complete loss of control when confronted by horror. Of course, for the mind to be able to retain control when confronted with such inexplicable incongruities or violations of logic and reality as the Gothic protagonist faces would be to exhibit a distinctly non-human degree of control. Consequently, certain losses of physical control that result from a loss of mental control when facing incomprehensible Gothic phenomenon can mark an individual as recognizably human. However, this is crucially only if the loss of physical control takes certain forms—and laughter is notably not one of these forms.

We have already noted Grene's assertion that the human being laughs at the inexplicable only if it does not appear to exist "in such a way that will harm us" (qtd. in Plessner xii). The individual who laughs when faced with the Gothic phenomenon violates this expectation. An appropriate human manifestation of a loss of physical control following a loss of mental control may be weeping, trembling, or fainting in a Gothic text. For example, the narrator faints and weeps at the sight of his punishment in Edgar Allan Poe's "The Pit and the Pendulum" (1842) (215, 221, 226); Victor Frankenstein trembles at the memory of his grave-robbing; Mina faints as Dr. Van Helsing spells out to her the consequences of Count Dracula's bite and his immortal condition (Stoker 334). These losses of physical control occasioned by the loss of mental control mark Poe's victim, Victor, and Mina as recognizably human, since only a non-human being could retain mental control faced with such overwhelming terrors.

By contrast, to laugh before a threatening, incomprehensible phenomenon appears a distinctly non-human reaction, and consequently signals a disconcerting rather than familiar degree of lost control. When Victor Frankenstein laughs hysterically at the impression that his monster is about to enter the room where he and Clerval sit, his laughter is described in terms that emphasize his unsettling loss of control, being "unrestrained," "unusual" and of a "wildness" that "frightened and astonished" his friend (Shelley 61). Victor's laughter is unfamiliar in form and unexpected in provocation; when Clerval begs him, "Do not laugh in that manner" (61), he implies *in that unfamiliar, unruly, non-human manner*. In *Melmoth the Wanderer*, the "wildest paroxysms" of laughter signal the captives' descent into utter madness, the extinction of "all humanity" (57) that Melmoth warns Stanton will soon occur within him. Stanton's attempt to laugh like the other captives will act as "an invocation to the demon of insanity to come and take full possession of you" (57), Melmoth predicts. Inappropriate laughter is here coded in terms of demonic possession, highlighting the non-human state that such laughter not only signals but also causes. In Poe's "The Fall of the House of Usher" (1839), Roderick Usher's hysterical laughter "appal[s]" his friend. The "unrestrained," "mad hilarity" (104) he demonstrates at the thought of Madeline breaking out of her tomb is closely aligned with the idea that Roderick is "giving up his soul" (104) over the course of the narrative. Roderick must inevitably fall with the house rather than escape with the narrator, having surrendered his human existence. In each of these cases, laughter is unsettling because the form and the degree of control lost—rather than the reason that control is lost—are unfamiliar to our received ideas of human laughter.

Similarly, Beckett frequently heightens the discomfort caused by his characters' unsettlingly unexpected laughter by emphasizing the degree of lost control that such laughter entails. Clov "*bursts out laughing*" (123) at the story of the starving beggar, his body apparently unable to contain his laughter. Similarly, the laughter of the watchers in *The Unnamable* comes "irresistibly" (349). Estragon's being "*convulsed*" by his laughter at Pozzo's tears (35) replicates the language of convulsion and contortion that many of the theorists we have discussed use to mark the loss of physical control that occasions laughter. So too does the Israelite's "fit of laughter" (211) at Malone's wet trousers. Moran's laughter at his anticipated punishment entails such a loss of physical control that he has to "lean against a tree" to "keep me from falling" (156).[2] Laughter in these all cases is provoked by an unexpected source, constitutes an unexpected form of the loss of physical control, and signals a degree of lost control that is unexpectedly and consequently unsettlingly extreme.

LAUGHTER PROVOKED BY GOTHIC AND BECKETTIAN TEXTS

We have thus far restricted our examination to laughter presented *in* the Gothic and Beckettian text. As we turn to consider how these texts not only exploit our narrow ideas of human laughter to affective ends, but also trouble those definitional boundaries, the laughter provoked *by* the texts reveals itself as crucial. If the Gothic and the Beckettian text exploit our ingrained sense of inappropriate and unpredictable laughter to render certain figures unsettlingly less-than-human, what is the effect when the readers or spectators themselves are driven by these texts to laugh in inappropriate or unpredictable ways?

While figures laugh within the Gothic text, we do not usually expect the reader of the Gothic text to laugh. This is a mode, after all, populated with terror, rape, enforced confinement, mental collapse, murder: to laugh at such things would be to laugh as inappropriately as the monstrous antagonists themselves do.[3] Yet there are instances when the Gothic text may make us laugh. André Breton, for example, included Poe and de Quincey in his seminal *Anthologie de l'humour noir* (1940), which uses the incongruity theory described in the first section of this paper to explain how the Gothic work can become a source of dark humor. Breton declares that de Quincey is a "humorist" (81), invoking the "wilful extravagance" and the "levity" of his works despite their "pathetic," "cruel" and "shocking" ideas and images (86). The similarly contradictory nature of Poe's work, Breton continues, makes it "generate humour" (116), black humor rendered from the recurrent juxtaposition of the individual's capacity for greatness and the more "shadowy" existence, the "human inconsistencies" and "morbid states" (116) that recur within his tales. According to Breton, the reader is in fact likely to laugh at the "agonies" (62), "intense suffering" (63), "phantoms" (67), "cancerous kisses" (73), "unutterable monsters" (74), and visions of being buried alive in *Confessions* and at the threat of death and of the undead in Poe's work.

Breton's recognition of the role played by the "extravagance" of the Gothic mode leads us also to the manner in which the "Gothic excess" (Botting 2) of style and narrative event provoke the reader's laughter. Riquelme has suggested that when the modern reader, skeptical of or jaded by such melodrama, laughs at the Gothic's "exaggerated forms" ("Gothic" 5), we might also assume that such moments were also intended to elicit similar laughter from the contemporary reader: "Read belatedly, the narratives can sometimes cause laughter because of their exaggerations, the self-parodic character of which could not have escaped their authors" ("Gothic" 1). Botting observes that the Gothic's "overabundance of imaginative frenzy" (3) often "provoke[s] ambivalent emotions" (2): one of these emotions might well be a deliberately induced incredulity that results in laughter. If we laugh at Stoker's description of Renfield guzzling down his flies, spiders, and birds, or when Frankenstein cries histrionically to the "[w]andering spirits, if indeed ye wander, and do not rest in your narrow beds" (89), such ostensibly inappropriate laughter might well have been deliberately induced by the text, Riquelme suggests. Breton's citing of the Gothic mode's black humor and Riquelme's sense of the possibility of Gothic self-parody both point us toward the Gothic text's pushing the reader to laugh at unexpected moments in unexpected ways. As readers of the Gothic text, we find ourselves laughing as inappropriately or as improperly as the monstrously laughing figures we find in their narratives. Having witnessed the laughter of the monsters in the Gothic texts, such inappropriate laughter coming from ourselves offers the disconcerting possibility of self-identification with the non-human laughers.

The Beckettian text also pushes the reader to laugh in a manner we identify as inappropriate, both because of its source and because of its non-accordance with the laughter of others. Laughter theorists frequently emphasize the significance that the individual in society accords to simultaneous laughter, individuals laughing in unison at the same phenomenon. From this shared, contagious laughter we construct a sense of a shared human community. Oring observes that to laugh together "implies a community, a fellowship of laughers with whom the humour is shared" (56), and W.W. Pilcher likewise notes the power of laughter to maintain "group solidarity" by imposing and reflecting "a stable system of social behaviour" (qtd. in Gutwirth 42). Beings who laugh at what we laugh at react like us, think like us, are like us; we are safe in their company, able to predict their behavior, made vulnerable by the loss of mental and physical control at the same time as they are. Gutwirth goes so far as to assert that the fact that the "infectious" (12) and "convivial" (13) aspects of laughter make it "when all is said and done, human" (13). We recognize the being that reacts to the same phenomena in the same way that we do to be human in the same way we believe ourselves to be human.

Iser argues, however, that laughter in Beckett's theater "has lost its contagious nature," and is "apparently robbed of its contagious qualities" (159). Spectators of Beckett's drama, he observes, often find themselves laughing alone at an apparently inappropriate or unexpected moment. Iser focuses on how *Waiting for Godot* and *Endgame* stifle the audience's laughter by making their own faith in language, their "compulsion to understand" (180) into the comic butt; we resist the experience of suddenly regarding "our interpretations and guiding norms as nonsense" (163).

More relevant to our exploration is the effect he traces in the reaction of the audience member who does laugh inappropriately, in isolation, without the rest of the audience joining in. The spectator is "deprived of a collective confirmation" at such moments, Iser observes, stripped of the "communal laugh by means of which the audience confirm one another's reactions" (40). The spectator's laughter in this context seems "somehow inappropriate" (159), making the spectator "conscious of his own loss of control" (160). Rather than laughter acting as "confirmation" (140) of the shared humanity of the audience members, the spectators who laugh alone seem to exhibit the same "impropriety" (140), the same unexpected loss of control and the same improperly-human action that the seemingly less-than-human characters onstage demonstrate. Spectators provoked by Beckett's drama to laugh in isolation are driven to question either their own humanity or the narrow boundaries we have placed on our attitudes towards the human that are bound up with laughter.

FORCED LAUGHTER AND MORTALITY

When we think of how the Gothic or Beckettian text might trouble as well as exploit our ingrained sense of what the human is based on our understanding of laughter, it is worth noting one form of laughter that renders the Beckettian figure seemingly recognizably human. This is the forced or conscious laugh, which can frequently be understood as a self-protective gesture. Gutwirth testifies to the human experience of using laughter as a defense mechanism, the "creation of a comic perspective from which to maintain one's distance" from "the dubious, the threatening, the unspeakable" (123–124, 125). Freud likewise observes the potential for laughter as a mechanism "by means of which a person refuses to suffer," adopted "in order to ward off suffering" ("Humour" 163, 164). Fry describes sufferers of cataplexy (muscle weakness and/or loss of consciousness triggered by a range of emotional responses, including laughter) using a similar technique: "If the humor-cataplexy link is more specific and the weakness appears only with the stimulus of a deep belly-laugh, this reaction has sometimes been prevented by the hasty substitution of a high, twittering laugh" (80). This substitute laugh may "govern, by its artificiality, the intensity" (80) of the emotion experienced.

Similarly, certain instances of forced laughter in Beckett's work offer the possibility of reading such laughter as the attempt to control more negative emotions, to distance oneself from "possibly dangerous involvements" (Fry 81) with the chaos or despair of the individual's existence. Clov's repeated "*brief laugh*" (92) that opens *Endgame* might be interpreted as this kind of laugh, as he observes the bleak landscape outside the house and Nagg and Nell's miserable state in their bins. So too could his laughter at Hamm's suggestion that the two of them are beginning to "mean something" (108). The reader or audience member can empathize with Beckettian individuals whose forced laughter is a self-protective attempt to distance themselves from the misery of their existence. Such empathy with the experience of pain and the attempt to avoid or overcome pain is different from other forms of laughter in the Gothic or Beckettian text discussed above.

Thus, these beings seem more immediately human because self-identified human readers or spectators can recognize their own reaction in them in a manner that does not cause discomfort. Notably, the forced laugh is one that seems distinctly wrong, unnatural or non-human according to the strict definitions imposed by the theorists reviewed above. Yet it is this form of theoretically non-human laughter, alone among all the other instances of laughter we have examined, that makes the Beckettian figure seem more recognizably, identifiably human.

Like the inappropriate laughter provoked in the reader or spectator, the humanizing effect of this ostensibly unnatural forced laughter enables a recognition that the Gothic and the Beckettian texts involve or trigger a re-imagining of the human. Riquelme has identified this (although not specifically via the presentation of laughter) as a recurrent feature in Gothic fiction, arguing that the most interesting Gothic texts do not merely reinforce our sense of "the limits of the human" ("Gothic" 6), but also encourage new ways of thinking about "what it means to be human" ("Gothic" 3) by "challeng[ing] prevailing notions of the human" ("Modernist Gothic" 21) and troubling the traditional hierarchies that designate some modes of behavior "more fully human than others" ("Modernist Gothic" 33).

Dracula offers a memorable instance of such an impulse in the context of laughter. We have already noted how the unexpected, inappropriate nature of the vampires' laughter plays a crucial role in rendering them so unsettlingly non-human. However, elsewhere in the text, unpredictable and conventionally inappropriate laughter is reinstated as befitting and indeed constitutive of the human condition. Van Helsing laughs hysterically following Lucy's funeral, in a manner that initially appears to John Seward—and most likely to the reader as well—as utterly inappropriate and inhuman. However, Van Helsing's subsequent explanation of his laughter positions it as a fundamentally human response; indeed, a redemptively human response, one that both signals and conserves the humanity of the laugher:

> Oh, friend John, it is a strange world, a sad world, a world full of miseries, and woes, and troubles; and yet when King Laugh come he make them all dance to the tune he play. (…) And believe me, friend John, that he is good to come, and kind. (…) King Laugh he come like the sunshine, and he ease off the strain again; and we bear to go on with our labour, what it may be. (Stoker 186–7)

Against our learned idea of human laughter as almost clinically predictable, Van Helsing posits that "true laughter" is always unpredictable and often inappropriate, and "chooses no time of suitability (…) the laugh he come just the same" (186). Unruly, unpredictable, or inexplicable laughter may be as human a laughter as any other, Van Helsing asserts. Against the strain of an often miserable human existence, unruly laughter might be welcomed as a redemptive human response rather than condemned as something unsettlingly non-human in the doctor's mind. Here, the Gothic text plays on our ingrained sense of what in laughter is recognizably human in a way that troubles our sense of what it might mean to be human and what counts as acceptable human behavior, rather than simply to signal the unsettlingly non-human figure.

Our analysis of how the Beckettian laugh functions as a self-defensive gesture against life's suffering bears a significant resemblance to Van Helsing's vaunting of inappropriate, unpredictable laughter as not merely a human act, but an act that allegedly redeems and protects one's very humanity. Some critics who emphasize the alignment of laughter and misery in Beckett's texts similarly read laughter as redemptive of human existence and our mortal condition. However, they do so to an extent that may not be supported by the texts themselves. When Arsene describes the *risus puris* as "the laugh of laughs" (40), or "the beholding, the saluting of the highest joke" (40), it has led some readers to interpret that "highest joke" as death itself, being "the joke of mortality" as Gutwirth argues (185). If mortality is "the highest joke," and if we can laugh at this joke, we discover a method of both accepting and withstanding the human condition, "a way of facing up to this unhappiness and of acknowledging the inevitable futility of the 'human condition,'" as Salisbury summarizes (4). Shane Weller, for example, asserts that laughter acts in the Beckettian text as a positively-inflected "mode of knowing (…) of being certain, if only of our own finitude" (23), a consolatory acknowledgment of the mortal state that consequently offers "resistance to nihilism" (23). Similarly, Critchley reads laughter's "acknowledgement of finitude" as a "powerful" healing recognition (187). While not going so far as to invoke question of mortality and finitude, Iser also presumes laughter is a source of "relief" (180, 181), rendering "the human condition both experienceable and palatable" (181). Being "able to laugh in spite of it all" (163–4), he asserts, might signal a liberation, a triumph of sorts, whereas the Beckettian spectator's inability or refusal to laugh indicates "that they cannot cope" with "the human condition" (163).[4]

Such determined optimism ignores the more unsettling lived experience of Beckettian laughter. The laughter that renders the Beckettian character recognizably human is, we have seen, a rare occurrence, and even then it is an unwarranted leap to go from reading such laughter as humanizing to reading it as redemptive of the human condition. Even when Beckettian laughter does suggest the human rather than the non-human, to be rendered recognizably human is not necessarily to be redeemed. Beckettian laughter provokes revulsion, fear, or at best pity or empathy, rather than any sense of liberating, healing redemption. More significantly, the more common "strange laughter" usually evokes suspicion, discomfort, or even fear. Although some forms of Beckettian laughter can be understood as humanizing, they stop short of the redemption that Van Helsing declares in Stoker's Gothic text or Critchley and Weller declare of Beckett's work.

Weller's and Critchley's similar views of the Beckettian laugh as redemptive do, however, point us helpfully in the direction of the frequent association of laughter and death in the Beckettian texts under discussion. The narrator of *The Unnamable* imagines that his eventual death will be in laughter: "I'll laugh, that's how it will end" (401). In *Texts for Nothing,* the narrator of text V reminds himself, "If only I could laugh, all would vanish, all what, who knows, all, me" (22), and in text XII laughter is qualified as the domain of the "non-exister" (50). In *Endgame*, Nagg remembers that Nell's laughter nearly killed them on their boating expedition: "It always made you laugh. (*Pause*.) The first time I thought you'd die. (...) You were in such fits that we capsized" (102). Estragon, laughing at Pozzo's tears in *Waiting for Godot*, declares "He'll be the death of me!" (35). Lousse in *Molloy*, we recall, laughs beside her dog's grave. Hamm and Clov's acknowledgment in *Endgame* that they no longer laugh is linked with their inability to end their miserable existence. This association is heightened by the double meaning of the word "corpsed," onstage laughter elided with the dead body. Beckett includes a similarly loaded wordplay in *Texts for Nothing*, when the narrator of text VI links the "danger of mirth" with his determination to be "grave" (28). As with "corpsed," the association of the dead body in the double meaning of "grave" renders it evident that the "danger of mirth"—or indeed the "promise of mirth" in *The Unnamable* and *Endgame*—is death.

Baudelaire's writing on laughter offers a Gothic perspective on the connection between laughter, death, and the recurrent sense of the simultaneously human-and-non-human that is more appropriate to the reader's unsettling experience of Beckettian laughter than Weller's and Critchley's interpretations. Baudelaire links laughter to death by way of the Biblical Fall, which, he speculates, made laughter as well as death part of the human condition. "Human laughter is intimately linked with the accident of the ancient Fall" (49), he asserts, and when "knowledge comes (...) laughter will come too" (151). The human being's laughter, thus connected with the postlapsarian condition, becomes the signal of the need for redemption, rather than the achievement of redemption that Critchley and Weller theorize. Beings that laugh are, according to Baudelaire's model, distinctly human, prey to pain and death. The divine do not laugh, and the prelapsarian, immortal being in Paradise did not laugh, he declares.

"[F]initude inheres in the human condition" (122), Gutwirth asserts, and Baudelaire posits both the Biblical knowledge that leads to finitude and the knowledge of this finitude as an essential basis for laughter. This association accords closely with the recurrent connection between laughter and death in Beckett's work, offering the opportunity to interpret laughter as a potentially unsettling reminder of mortality rather than a redemptive acceptance of it or a complete negation of humanity itself. However, alongside the human, Baudelaire also reads the non-human, the "Satanic" (150), and "monstrous" (151), in laughter. While it is the action of the fallen and hence mortal human being, laughter also signals the "diabolic" (154), recalling how Gothic laughter is "soulless," "fiendish" and "demoniac" in *Dracula*, *Frankenstein*, and *Melmoth the Wanderer* respectively.

Baudelaire's model of how laughter might signal the inextricable mix of the human and the Satanic, the human and the non-human, accords closely to our experience of Beckettian laughter, which renders the laughing figure alternately—or sometimes simultaneously—human and non-human, mortal and immortal. Following his Gothic predecessors, Beckett's association of laughter with death muddies the idea of the human condition rather than crystallizing and redeeming it. Their laughter may remind us of their mortal state, but the reminder is a promise that frequently remains unfulfilled. Hamm and Clov cannot end their miserable existence; Didi and Gogo fail to hang themselves; Molloy, Moran, and the Unnamable must "go on" (407) and on and on.[5] Their laughter reminds us of a human mortality that the texts do not enact; they live an undead and undying existence comparable to the Gothic creature, the vampire, ghost, or zombie, in short all those who are not quite living yet not quite dead. Beckettian laughter complicates the way we define the nature and limits of the human. The laughing Beckettian subject offers gradations of the human rather than a strict binary division between the human and the non-human. His characters fall somewhere between the two poles: not fully non-human, yet not human as defined by our usual recognitions and identifications.

CONCLUSION

While laughter theorists have repeatedly claimed that laughter is a uniquely human phenomenon, their theorizing marks out a narrow range of laughter that we define as recognizably "human." Both the Gothic and the Beckettian text exploit this ingrained attitude. In Gothic texts, inappropriate laughter repeatedly signals the non-human, the monstrous. Gothic (and subsequently Beckettian) texts include laughter that the modern Western reader or spectator is conditioned to identify as inappropriate and unpredictable to render their characters unsettlingly non-human—unsettling not only because of their monstrous status and behavior, but also because they engage in the laughter that much theory claims as a uniquely human activity. *Dracula* offers a reworking of this idea: Van Helsing proposes that unpredictable, inappropriate laughter may be as proper to the human being as the predictable, appropriate laugh.

The dark laughter of Gothic texts throw light on the related effects and implications of the "strange laughter" in Beckett's texts, but Beckettian laughter extends and complicates the implications of Gothic laughter. The Beckettian laugher is frequently both monstrous and human, replicating Baudelaire's idea of laughter as simultaneously human and Satanic. It is thus disconcerting in two ways.

Firstly, it signals the melding of what we might have considered to be a clear binary, the human and the non-human or monstrous. In the absence of a stark contrast between the two qualities, we are left with the question of what the relationship between the human and the non-human has become in Beckett's texts. We are presented with a co-existence of opposites that seems to establish a new kind of identity. This new idea of the human resists traditional definition; it breaks free of the concepts previously expected or accepted. Yet imposing too rosy an interpretation on this new identity disregards the distinctly disconcerting effect of the laughing Beckettian creature. The similarities between the half-human laughter in the Gothic and the Beckettian text warn us against placing any too determinedly optimistic framework of interpretation onto Beckettian laughter. There is something comforting, certainly, in the idea that even when laughter, the thing theorized as making us uniquely human, is distorted or corrupted, the individual does not become entirely monstrous, unrecognizable to the point of being clearly non-human. However, emphasizing inclusivity ignores the unsettling experience of confronting the laughing Beckettian being.

Secondly, Beckettian laughter disconcerts by triggering the reader's or spectator's laughter at unexpected or inappropriate moments. Such moments elicit an unsettling self-recognition by the reader or spectator concerning the similarly inappropriate laughter of the human-non-human Beckettian being. Readers and spectators laugh inappropriately in response to these texts, and such unexpected, inappropriate laughter challenges any complacent idea they might have of themselves as human. Much as we might still wish to, we cannot distance ourselves from these not-quite-human, not-quite-non-human laughers. "Strange laughter," both presented in and provoked by the texts, complicates and potentially extends our ideas of what constitutes the human laugh, and therefore the human. Neither unambiguously human nor absolutely non-human, the laughing Beckettian subject is "strange" and estranging—above all disconcerting because it troubles our ideas of human identity and of our own identities.

Notes

1. In "Gothic," Riquelme identifies a distinction between "'first-wave Gothic novels" (6) published between 1764 and 1825, and a second wave beginning in 1860. He cites "the cataclysm of the French Revolution" (9) as a significant turning-point between the two waves.

2. In fact, Moran's laughter at the prospect of his punishment is rendered even more unsettlingly non-human by the unfamiliar manner in which he loses control, as well as his unfamiliar reason for doing so. Although he loses control of his body, his facial features remain "composed in their wonted sadness and calm" (156). How does one laugh so hard while retaining control of one's facial features? We are frightened not only by the being who loses control but the being who retains control in ways we cannot predict or understand.

3. While affect is central to the Gothic, and the fear elicited by the Gothic novel is often thrilling and thus enjoyable, it is a great step from "illicitly enjoyable thrill" to "wholehearted laughter" when faced with the cited scenes.

4. Iser does ask, "But are we really able to free ourselves from unhappiness by facing up to it?" (164). However, this is not a question he explores in any real depth in the cited text.

5. Malone, one of the rare Beckettian characters of whose death we can be reasonably assured, notably fails to laugh throughout the narrative.

Works Cited

Baudelaire, Charles. "On the Essence of Laughter and, in General, On the Comic in the Plastic Arts." *The Painter of Modern Life and Other Essays*. Translated by Jonathan Mayne. Phaidon, 1969, pp. 147–165.

Beckett, Samuel. *Endgame. The Complete Dramatic Works*. Faber and Faber, 2006, pp. 89–134.

———. *Texts for Nothing and Other Shorter Prose, 1950–1976*. Edited by Mark Nixon. Faber and Faber, 2010.

———. *Three Novels: Molloy, Malone Dies, The Unnamable*. Grove Press, 2009.

———. *Waiting for Godot. The Complete Dramatic Works*. Faber and Faber, 2006, pp. 7–88.

———. *Watt*. Faber and Faber, 2009.

Breton, André. *Anthology of Black Humour*. Translated by Mark Polizzotti. Telegram, 2009.

Botting, Fred. *Gothic*. Routledge, 1996.

Critchley, Simon. *On Humour*. Routledge, 2002.

———. *Very Little ... Almost Nothing: Death, Philosophy, Literature*. Routledge, 2004.

De Quincey, Thomas. *Confessions of an English Opium-Eater, and Other Writings*. Edited by Grevel Lindop. Oxford UP, 1985.

Freud, Sigmund. "Humour." *The Future of an Illusion, Civilization and its Discontents, and Other Works*. Vol. 21. Translated by James Strachey. The Hogarth Press, 1961, pp. 156–166.

———. *Jokes and their Relationship to the Unconscious*. Edited by Joyce Crick. W.W. Norton, 2003.

Fry, William F. Jr. *Sweet Madness: A Study of Humor*. Pacific Books, 1963.

Gutwirth, Marcel. *Laughing Matter: An Essay on the Comic*. Cornell UP, 1993.

Heyd, David. "The Place of Laughter in Hobbes's Theory of Emotions." *Journal of the History of Ideas*, vol. 43, no. 2, 1982, pp. 285–295.

Iser, Wolfgang. "The Art of Failure: The Stifled Laughter in Beckett's Theatre." *Theories of Reading, Looking and Listening*, edited by Harry R. Garvin. Bucknell UP, 1981, pp. 139–81.

Maturin, Charles. *Melmoth the Wanderer: A Tale*. Edited by Douglas Grant. Oxford UP, 1972.

Oring, Elliott. *Engaging Humor*. U of Illinois P 2003.

Plessner, Helmuth. *Laughing and Crying: A Study of the Limits of Human Behavior*. Translated by James Spencer Churchill and Marjorie Grene. Northwestern UP, 1970.

Poe, Edgar Allan. *The Fall of the House of Usher and Other Writings*. Penguin, 2003.

Polidori, John. *The Vampyre*. Woodstock Books, 1990.

Riquelme, John Paul. "Gothic." *A Companion to the English Novel*, edited by Stephen Arata, J. Paul Hunter, and Jennifer Wicke. Blackwell, 2015.

———. "Modernist Gothic." *The Cambridge Companion to the Modernist Gothic*. Edited by Jerrold E. Hogle. Cambridge UP, 2014, pp. 20–36.

Salisbury, Laura. *Samuel Beckett: Laughing Matters, Comic Timing*. Edinburgh UP, 2012.

Shelley, Mary. *Frankenstein; or, The Modern Prometheus*. Edited by Johanna M. Smith. St. Martin's Press, 1992.

Spencer, Herbert. "The Physiology of Laughter." *Macmillan's Magazine*, vol. 1, 1860, pp. 395–402. https://doi.org/10.1037/12203-004. Accessed 25 Apr. 2015.

Stoker, Bram. *Dracula*. Penguin Books, 2003.

Weller, Shane. *A Taste for the Negative: Beckett and Nihilism*. Legenda, 2005.

HANNAH SIMPSON is a lecturer in drama and performance at the University of Edinburgh. She is the author of *Samuel Beckett and the Theatre of the Witness: Pain in Postwar Francophone Drama* (Oxford UP, 2022) and *Samuel Beckett and Disability Performance* (Palgrave Macmillan, 2022). She has edited special issues for *Twentieth Century Literature, Medical Humanities* and the *Journal of War and Culture Studies*, and is co-editor of the Palgrave book series Studies in Theatre and Disability.

15 The Illusionless: Adorno and the Afterlife of Laughter in *How It Is*

Michelle Rada

> Now in what does this humorous attitude consist, by means of which one refuses to undergo suffering, asseverates the invincibility of one's ego against the real world and victoriously upholds the pleasure-principle, yet all without quitting the ground of mental sanity, as happens when other means to the same end are adopted? Surely it seems impossible to reconcile the two achievements.
>
> —Freud, "Humour"

> He who has laughter on his side has no need of proof.
>
> —Adorno, *Minima Moralia*

LAUGHTER IN REGRESS

In Samuel Beckett's *How It Is*, the experience of laughter shifts between pure sadism and infantile babbling. Humor is uncertain even at its most explicit moments, making for an ambivalent and anxiety-driven reading experience. *How It Is* marks a transformative shift in Beckett's work, coming about in the wake of the first trilogy and its afterbirth, *Texts for Nothing*. Nearly imperceptible, the comedic event of *How It Is* faintly reengages some of Beckett's earlier humorous topoi, such as the clown figure, while also breaking with these elements through a narrative that contradicts the possibility of laughter as soon as it is posed. The situation of *How It Is* is an ambivalent one: while it presents torture scenarios and provides a torturous reading experience, the subject of the story is infantile and oblivious in an almost comical way. The speaking subject, while enduring terrible pain, is disposed to playful antics and senseless, childlike muttering.

In Theodor Adorno's readings of Beckett, humor is crucial because of its self-reflexive effect, which facilitates the advent of reconciliation and hope. Working mostly on *Endgame*, *The Unnamable*, and *Waiting for Godot*, Adorno reads the Beckettian subject as one who parodies its own impossibility, producing laughter out of a lack thereof. In Beckett's late works, subjectivity emerges in the aftermath of the situation Adorno identifies. Such a distinction points to *How It Is* as a decisive work, marking an aesthetic and philosophical shift in Beckett's approach to the possibility of humor, the encounter with alterity, the subjectivity of the subject, and the production of meaning. In "Trying to Understand *Endgame*," Adorno writes: "Meaning nothing becomes the only meaning. The deadliest fear of the characters in the drama, if not of the parodied drama, is the fear, disguised as humor, that they might mean something" (261). Humor here is a disguise donned by the clownish characters on stage, a concealment of the damaged condition in which they exist. In the aftermath of the already post-apocalyptic scenarios of *Endgame* and *The Unnamable*, *How It Is* comes about as both a regenerative and disintegrative work. The possibility of meaning something—even of meaning via meaninglessness—is reduced, stripped down to its minimal capacity in a voice that emerges as a mere murmur, in laughter as a feeble choke.

For Adorno, the event of laughter in Beckett's work is a moment of self-reflexive realization for the audience. It is the noisy acknowledgement of their own reified, corpselike voices echoing in a room: "An artwork is, as Beckett wrote, *a desecration of silence*" (*Aesthetic Theory* 134). But once silence has been ruined and the echoes of laughter subside, one may ask what remains. What feebly clings to the air once laughter dissolves? What takes place in a work like *How It Is* can be read as an aftermath of laughter, the soft murmur that remains in a ceaseless slope towards silence—a silence that can never be fully redeemed from its desecration. In *A Taste for the Negative*, Shane Weller identifies *How It Is* as the marker of a shift in Beckett's work, in which the reduced existence of the other in *The Unnamable* and *Texts for Nothing* is given rather as an overstated self-presence. Weller writes: "With the absolute reduction of all alterity, with the complete identification of dictated and dictating being, the 'comfort' provided by all those disintegratively projected others may have been lost" (167).

The subject who speaks in *How It Is* comes about in the aftermath of parody, in which interpersonal relations, like those found in *Endgame*, are reduced to a game of mirror images. Here, laughter itself retains no definite point of origin or end. The subject is born in its own wake, retaining no sense of a past or childhood, thus lacking the possibility for the very regression with which Adorno characterizes Beckett's humor. For example, the subject says: "that childhood said to have been mine the difficulty of believing in it the feeling rather of having been born octogenarian at the age when one dies in the dark the mud" (*HII* 60). Born at the moment of its own decline, the subject of *How It Is* can be seen in the wake of Adorno's Beckettian laughter, a muddied site in which birth already comes too late, and what's left of the other is a maddening murmur.

Anticipating his inquiry into the source and purpose of laughter within a work, Adorno distinguishes between types of laughter. In *Dialectic of Enlightenment*, Adorno and Horkheimer identify laughter with the numbing effects of the culture industry: "There is laughter because there is nothing to laugh about.

Laughter, whether reconciled or terrible, always accompanies the moment when a fear is ended" (112). Referred to bluntly as "wrong laughter," this collective sitcom-like laughter produces a form of release from fear that "echoes the inescapability of power" (112). A concealed form of violence, the comic element is here intimately linked to sadism. Parody becomes a terrorizing force that excludes and humiliates difference, while rendering impossible any type of criticism from the outside. Adorno and Horkheimer note that "In the wrong society laughter is a sickness infecting happiness and drawing it into society's worthless totality. Laughter about something is always laughter at it. . . . The collective of those who laugh parodies humanity" (112). Pleasure and play here lose their reconciliatory potential. Instead they are posited as collective performances put on to strengthen a totalitarian industry. As soon as an artwork partakes in this form of "wrong" pleasure, it loses its role as art and is transformed into entertainment or advertisement.

But laughter isn't always so wrong. Adorno makes room for a second category, in which humor isn't synonymous with reification. Rather, it is a powerful force against alienation, a rupture with the culture industry instead of its imposition: "Reconciled laughter resounds with the echo of the escape from power" (112). In another passage from *Dialectic of Enlightenment*, this laughter is described as an event in which "blind nature becomes aware of itself as such and thus abjures its destructive violence" (60). Critical self-awareness—a circular insight into the subject's own claustrophobic entrapment within a damaged world—is a necessary effect of the parodic element Adorno finds in Beckett. In "Funnier Than Unhappiness: Adorno and the Art of Laughter," Shea Coulson notes that Adorno's "apparent mirthlessness is actually disdain for an uncritical use of laughter that simply concretizes social repression. Laughter, for Adorno, should act violently against reified structures and unhinge the subject from reification" (143). Coulson's title, taken from Nell's line in *Endgame*, points to the necessary doubleness of reconciled laughter: it reveals the radical unhappiness of the subject who cries out in pleasure (Beckett, *Endgame* 18). What Adorno identifies in *Endgame* is a doubly conscious mode of this kind of parody: a parody of parody, laughter that is always already an echo of itself. The only discernible change in the repetition or echo of laughter is its gradual lessening, an ever-approaching silence: "Yes, yes, it's the most comical thing in the world. And we laugh, we laugh, with a will, in the beginning. But it's always the same thing. Yes, it's like the funny story we have heard too often, we still find it funny, but we don't laugh any more" (19). Nell's comment here tellingly describes the experience of the spectators: laughter dissolves with the constant repetition of the familiar, of the same joke being told over and again. The ceaseless flow of words eventually turns into their saying nothing, doing nothing, going nowhere, yet somehow going on and on.

Adorno distinguishes between the laughter of the on-stage characters in Beckett's plays and that of the spectators. In *Aesthetic Theory*, he claims that "plays like *Godot* and *Endgame*—in the scene in which the protagonists decide to laugh—are more the tragic presentation of comedy's fate than they are comic; in the actor's forced laughter, the spectator's mirth vanishes" (340). The difference drawn here between the action taking place on stage and the spectator's reaction complicates an account of the comic in Beckett's novels, even more so in a generically ambiguous text like *How It Is*. Reading *How It Is* is an odd experience. The relation between the two, actor and spectator, becomes that of a reader who silently takes in the words dictated by an unnamable voice to an unnamed narrator attempting to reproduce them. Consider, for example, this early passage: "memories I say them as I hear them murmur them in the mud / in me that were without when the panting stops scraps of an ancient voice in me not mine / my life last version ill-said ill-heard ill-recaptured ill-murmured in the mud" (*HII* 3). The narrator's experience is reproduced in the reading of *How It Is*, a text that situates its reader as a second-order listener to the doubly distant voice, a listener whose suspicion that there may be someone else around also listening is always brought back to "the same" solitude (3). Adorno's claim that the protagonists' "forced laughter" evokes the critical dissolution of pleasure in the spectator is contingent upon the forced nature of the spectacle. Such a nonsensical circus-like production acknowledges itself as farce:

> If Beckett's plays, as crepuscularly grey as after sunset and the end of the world, want to exorcise circus colors, they yet remain true to them in that the plays are indeed performed on stage and it is well known how much their antiheros were inspired by clowns and slapstick cinema. Despite their *austerity* they in no way fully renounce costumes and sets. (*Aesthetic* 81)

But in a prose work like *How It Is*, the possibility for laughter lies solely in the reader, whose own experience is a disorienting one. Not only is genre indiscernible, but voices are dislocated, and the slapstick element usually present in Beckett's works is absent. If for Adorno "[h]earing oneself talking is like watching a Beckett play," then reading *How It Is* is like listening to a feeble murmur emanating from nowhere in particular ("Notes on *Endgame*" 162). The question of telling laughter and weeping apart is no longer necessary, since both are conflated and lost in disorienting blocks of text drained of syntax and in voices drained of even the mere performance of subjectivity.

As in Adorno's claim that "[h]earing oneself talking is like watching a Beckett play," *How It Is* proposes a subject that remains both alone and othered before its own voice. In *How It Is*, words revolve around the possibility of another's presence (Pim), which is often conflated with a mirror image of the self. The text presents a semi-subject listening to a voice in the dark, a voice that narrates its own memories and dictates its own words to itself. It is a voice much like one's own, hearing oneself talking. This scenario is perhaps an intensified version of the post-apocalyptic one Adorno finds present in *Endgame* and *The Unnamable*, in which the last human being can only laugh at the impossibility of laughter. The comic element is present here insofar as it is absent, an absence that parodies itself interminably. Adorno writes in the Notes: "The humour of the last human being: that is the humour that can no longer count on any laughing. B[eckett] has recovered for humour what otherwise only applies to the categories of the Arts with a capital A—which he tacitly liquidates: the resignation of communication" ("Notes on *Endgame*" 168). The humor of the last human being is the humor of the subtracted subject, a subject ironically—perhaps in a horrifyingly comic way—searching for the other, for the possibility of an encounter. Laughter is reduced to the one, to an inward turning subject. Laughter and speech become symptoms of subjectivity in regress, replacing silence with desperate, childlike babbling.

Regression takes on a force of its own in Beckett's work, in which moving backwards, lessening, and worsening are intimately tied to temporality. The subtracted subject is less than "the last human being," as reduction takes place *within* the subject as well. Beckett's decrepit, aging characters are surprisingly childlike, crawling around in womblike cylinders or puddles of mud with names like Bom, Bim, and Pim. Progress and regress are indiscernible in *How It Is*, the "octogenarian" narrator inhabiting the claustrophobic space of Adorno's "ontogenetic" Beckettian subject. This subject is at once senile and underdeveloped, as Adorno explains:

> Thus the sequence of situations in Beckett, which flows on without opposition from the individuals, ends in the stubborn bodies to which they regress. Judged in terms of this unity, the schizoid situations are comical, like hallucinations. Hence the clowning which one sees immediately in the behavior and the constellation of Beckett's figures. Psychoanalysis explains the clown's humor as a regression to an extremely early ontogenetic stage, and Beckett's drama of regression descends to that level. But the laughter it arouses ought to suffocate the ones who laugh. ("Trying" 257)

The narrator of *How It Is*, whose name oscillates between clownish one-syllable utterances, undergoes a process of regress in which death and birth are conflated. Through a "divine forgetting" (*HII* 68), the speaker is fixed in a childlike state. Memories are not his own and, as if the narrator had not yet acquired an adult language, words and phrases repeat themselves over and over again. Adorno cites Freud's psychoanalytic conception of humor as a regressive defense mechanism. In *Jokes and Their Relation to the Unconscious*, Freud notes that repetition of the familiar is particularly pleasurable to children who are "learning to make use of words," who find humor in "repetition from what is similar, a rediscovery of what is familiar, similarity of sound" (128). After childhood, the purpose of humor becomes a regression to that previous state: "For the euphoria which we endeavor to reach by these means is nothing other than . . . the mood of our childhood, when we were ignorant of the comic, when we were incapable of jokes and when we had no need of humour to make us feel happy in our life" (Freud, *Jokes* 236). In this sense, Adorno's conception of Beckett's staged humor of regression in *Endgame* is embodied by *How It Is*, in which the octogenarian indeed regresses into the ontogenetic, erasing a damaged adult life and crawling his way back into a world in which there is no need of humor.

Regression for Freud is intimately linked to the pleasurable effects of the absurd, or what he terms "comic nonsense" (*Jokes* 194). Under the category of nonsense, Freud includes parody, where the "old pleasure" of the absurd is turned into its own purposeful end: "the nonsense in a joke is an end in itself, since the intention of recovering the old pleasure in nonsense is among the joke-work's motives. There are other ways of recovering the nonsense and of deriving pleasure from it: caricature, exaggeration, parody and travesty make use of them and so create 'comic nonsense'" (176). In "Notes on *Endgame*," Adorno thinks of parody as the form a work takes when its own genre or formal preconditions are no longer possible. Parody is a mode of regression through which form becomes self-conscious and degrades itself: "Parody of drama = drama in the age of its impossibility . . . it turns into slackening: less and less talkative protagonists, complete regression" (164). Parody as comic nonsense is associated with the "slackening" of speech, in which "complete regression" takes place through a gradual reduction of the *capacity* for language. Thus, characters on stage speak less, and written ones are given a limited availability or stock of words and syntactical arrangements. In another note, Adorno writes of "literature in the age of the impossibility of humour," in which humor has become a residue of itself: "What has become of humour. Residual humour. —Humour as regression (clown)" (158). In this passage, humor takes place as the acknowledgment of its own end. *How It Is* participates in humor by depicting its own decay or afterlife as a desperate beginning, an irrecoverable childhood forced to live itself out. Freud explains:

> the jest made in humour is not the essential thing; it has only the value of a proof. The principal thing is the intention which humour fulfills, whether it concerns the subject's self or other people. Its meaning is: 'Look here! This is all that this seemingly dangerous world amounts to. Child's play—the very thing to jest about!'" ("Humour" 5)

Child's play—what the regressive Freudian joke entails—is an escape from the damaged world of adulthood. Any liberation one experiences is merely a temporary escape from a less-than-enchanted reality that lies outside. Freud describes this narcissistic, potentially sadomasochistic aspect of humor:

> Obviously, what is fine about [humour] is the triumph of narcissism, the ego's victorious assertion of its own invulnerability. It refuses to be hurt by the arrows of reality or to be compelled to suffer. It insists that it is impervious to wounds dealt by the outside world, in fact, that these are merely occasions for affording it pleasure. This last trait is a fundamental characteristic of humour. ("Humour" 2)

The subject here transforms the wounds inflicted on it by society into an occasion for pleasure, consciously taking on the role of the reified spectator, whose pleasure and pain are simply interchangeable mandates from society. But Freud goes on to account for the possibility of transgression, in which the subject breaks from its passive resignation by using humor to criticize and parody the circumstances that are the cause of its painful laughter. He explains: "Humour is not resigned;

it is rebellious. It signifies the triumph not only of the ego, but also of the pleasure-principle, which is strong enough to assert itself here in the face of the adverse real circumstances" ("Humour" 3).

This reformulation of humor as self-conscious critique becomes useful when thinking of the way Adorno interprets Beckett's comedy of regression. Erica Weitzman writes of Adorno's twofold analysis of humor in art, in which ironically "only fun in art protects art against fun" (196). The emphasis on "fun" here points to the inherently childish or regressive aspect of a certain aesthetic (or anti-aesthetic) practice. As in Freud's claim, Weitzman notes that by participating in fun, "the unseriousness of art risks getting sucked into a whirlpool of narcissistic pleasure that, for Adorno, similarly compromises the very purpose and grounds of art" (191). Yet while Adorno relegates fun to the culture industry, he believes that art must somehow incorporate fun in order to critique and attain freedom from it. He writes: "If art must preserve an absolute freedom of form in order to maintain itself as art, 'fun'—as well as play, pleasure, and affects of all kinds—must, however paradoxically, be allowed to be included in its repertoire" (200).

Even within torturous verbiage, the narrator of *How It Is* manages to lighten (or at least contrast) his notably decrepit existence by introducing the clown figure, a horrifying yet comic visage of childhood. For Adorno, the clown is a being subjected to the sadistic laughter of others, a laughter that regurgitates familiar language as nonsense, and thus embodies its very decay. The naming of the Pim and Bom figures in *How It Is* forces upon them the clown masks, whereupon the repetition of the familiar *ad nauseam* begins: "it must have appealed to him it's understandable finished by appealing to him he was calling him by it himself in the end long before Pim Pim ad nauseam I Pim I always say when a man's name is Pim he hasn't the right" (51). Already stripped of his rights and referring to himself in the alienating third person, the nauseating meaninglessness of repetition arrives when Pim discovers he is not the only Pim. In fact, Pim may be a mirror image without any definite point of origin: "when this has sunk in I let him know that I too Pim my name Pim there he has more difficulty a moment of confusion irritation it's understandable it's a noble name then it calms down" (51). Pim goes from "he" to "it" in this passage, him/itself embodying the "objective decay" of language that Adorno identifies with the Beckettian clown, whose words dissolve into the irritating sound of a broken tape recorder ("Trying" 262). Adorno writes:

> Instead of trying to liquidate the discursive element in language through pure sound, Beckett transforms it into an instrument of its own absurdity, following the ritual of the clown, whose babbling becomes nonsense by being presented as sense. The objective decay of language, that bilge of self-alienation, at once stereotyped and defective, which human beings' words and sentences have swollen up into within their own mouths, penetrates the aesthetic arcanum. ("Trying" 262)

Adorno distinguishes Beckett's repetition of the familiar into nonsense from the phonetic mechanics of *Finnegans Wake*, in which nonsensical sound is transformed into sense and given elevated symbolic meaning. While in the *Wake* there is a potentiality for meaning within any sound or neologism, in *How It Is*, all potential subjects are reduced to objects, to two-dimensional Pims and Boms that can no longer hold on to any sense of linguistic purpose, much less their own names. Language in this case is always already a joke, a parody of its own impossibility. Language and the semi-subjects that utter it are clowned, are jokes in Adorno's sense, which "like colors, have had the marrow sucked out of them" (258). The humor and plentiful gloom in Beckett serve the same function, that of regurgitated language that recycles itself into nonsense. Clowns and corpses are found on the same stage: the torturer is the very clown that arouses sadistic laughter. All language is in regress, unable to cling onto meaning and left crawling in the mud of its own decay.

Adorno sees Beckett's regressive style as allowing for humor and play to become available to art, in their self-conscious presentation. The reduced subject of regression in these works parodies an exalted existential subject. In works like *Endgame*, the subject's reduction to its minimum capacity emphasizes its historical limitations and the staged nature of any and all its actions. Laughter as it occurs here is linked to suffering, a relation necessary for the work's critical potential. Adorno situates this ironic attachment in the figure of the clown, who in Beckett takes on the hauntingly monstrous state of being at once "childish and bloody." He elaborates: "The negativity of the subject as the true form of objectivity can only be presented in radically subjective form, not by recourse to a purportedly higher reality. The grimacing clowns, childish and bloody, into which Beckett's subject is decomposed, are that subject's historical truth; social realism is, by comparison, simply childish" (*Aesthetic* 250). Adorno is not satisfied with the "childish" antics of social realism. According to Adorno, childhood itself needs to be "decomposed" within the artwork as a time that is impossible to recover, through which it becomes distorted into the horrifying mask of a clown subjected to the audience's hollow laughter.

BOREDOM, PLEASURE, AND THE TORTURES OF ALTERITY

In her recent study of laughter and comedy in Beckett, *Samuel Beckett: Laughing Matters, Comic Timing*, Laura Salisbury claims that an element of "comic aggression" is not entirely dissolved in his late works—despite the fact that aggression itself becomes much more prevalent in these texts (51). This specific type of comedy is for Salisbury attached to a meticulous or scholarly form of humor in Beckett. It begins to wane in the late works but can still be identified in the "perfected chain of being tormentor and tormented" in a text like *How It Is* (48). Salisbury writes: "Even the most sadistic of those later works, the horror stories of *How It Is* and *What Where*, are able to squeeze a little humour from the cruelly rational and mathematically perfected reversibility of their systems of torturers and tortured" (51). For Salisbury, the central conflict of these late works is the uncertainty of their production of affect. In them, "it becomes increasingly uncertain where or at whom such laughing violence is aimed" (51). The experience of affective uncertainty is at the center of Adorno's monstrous clown figure, who arouses laughter and horror simultaneously. The reader or spectator is put in a state of infantile regression that is paradoxically paired with the revelation of a damaged adult life. This pairing is, for Salisbury, attached to an ethical question in the late works, which appears alongside an "indefatigable interrogation of the comic," both as the "products and producers of uncertainty" (150).

Such critical uncertainty manifests itself in *How It Is* through the narrator's confusion about the other's affective responses. Once, after being tortured, Pim replies by singing rather than crying: "the day when clawed in the armpit instead of crying he sings his song" (*HII* 54). The song turns out to be pleasurable for the narrator, which ironically he can only listen to by inflicting torture on the other: "that's not all he stops nails in armpit he resumes cheers done it armpit song and this music as sure as if I pressed a button I can indulge in it any time henceforward" (55). But eventually it becomes entirely uncertain for the narrator what the sound being emitted is, whether song or cry or even a type of convulsive laughter: "not a movement apart from the lips and thereabouts the lower face to sing cry and convulsive now and again" (56).

This doubt about the meaning of the other's response is repeated for the reader, whose own uncertainty about how to react to the text becomes definitive of the reading experience. Crucially, Salisbury claims that doubting the possibility of humor further affirms its presence: "If a text persists in asking whether any laughter or anything comic obtains, the answer need not necessarily be 'no', and, in fact, probably isn't absolutely 'no', if the question remains as one that is posed at all" (149–50). The "atrophied comedy" of the late prose is marked by a definitive uncertainty, which both affirms and questions the status of the comic and the possibility of laughter; as such, laughter is displayed rather as boredom or an affective short-circuit in the reading experience (Salisbury 183, 194). Boredom and anxiety arise out of the inability to decide on or securely feel anything in response to the text. This insecurity results in a similar set of ambiguous reactions as those the narrator of *How It Is* identifies in his tortured other, who sings and cries and spastically laughs all at once.

A passage from *How It Is* attempts to distinguish between weeping and happiness, failing to discern either, except for the certainty that both are somehow lacking: "a little cheerful the less you're there the more you're cheerful when you're there less tears a little less when you're there words lacking all lacking less tears for lack of words lack of food even birth it's lacking all that makes you cheerful it must be that all that a little more cheerful" (90). The comic in *How It Is*, almost indistinguishable from nonsense, torture, and the torturously senseless reading experience it entails, can hardly be said to arouse actual laughter. Rather the text effects a deranged, grimacing expression in its reader. In *Beckett, Literature, and the Ethics of Alterity*, Weller departs from Adorno's analysis of genre in Beckett as a "posthumous appearance," (Adorno, "Trying" 260) and proposes the term *post-humorous* for the later works' gradually receding sense of humor. Weller explains:

And in Beckett's later works, there is a radical reduction of the comic, such that by the time of his last play, *What Where* (1983), there can scarcely be said to be anything humorous at all, and this despite the use of flagrantly clownish names: Bam, Bem, Bim, Bo . . . we are left to reflect once again upon the possibility of a last laugh that is not necessarily pure, a laugh opening not just onto the posthumous but also onto what might be termed the *posthumorous*. (132)

For Weller, Beckett's late works depart from Adorno's reading of critical laughter as a type of weeping. In this posthumorous Beckett, humor is not salvaged. Here, the spectator isn't even laughing about the impossibility of laughter. Thus parody itself is outmoded and incapacitated: "It is not simply that laughter has been left behind, however, but rather that one is no longer in a position to determine whether there is anything to laugh at, and, if not, who, if anyone, might have had the last laugh" (133).

Even laughter that suffocates the ones who laugh may be overstating the case for a work like *How It Is*. The reading experience comes as a kind of aftermath to the possibility of even the painful and awkward laughter of *Endgame*. The silence of the text itself and the reader's emphasized solitude arouse perhaps the nauseating beginnings of such a laugh, but don't necessarily cause one to erupt in cacophony. Adorno essentially says as much immediately after his claim about *Endgame's* suffocating regressive laughter: "This is what has become of humor now that is has become obsolete as an aesthetic medium and repulsive, without a canon for what should be laughed about, without a place of reconciliation from which one could laugh, and without anything harmless on the face of the earth that would allow itself to be laughed at" ("Trying" 257). Perhaps the condition of humor in *How It Is* affirms this statement, an exaggerated aftermath of laughter that chokes the ones who laugh before they even get the chance. The parodic element, while nevertheless present, appears overwhelmed by the repulsive. It isn't simply the case that nothing is harmless. Rather, every element becomes harmful to itself and others, paralyzing laughter before it can be evoked.

Adorno does indeed identify a kind of "pleasure" produced by artworks that embody "the process of their own production," such as *Finnegans Wake*. Adorno writes of this phenomenon in *Aesthetic Theory*:

> Today every work is virtually what Joyce declared *Finnegans Wake* to be before he published the whole: *work in progress*. But a work that in its own terms, in its own texture and complexion, is only possible as emergent and developing, cannot without lying at the same time lay claim to being complete and 'finished.' Art is unable to extricate itself from this aporia by an act of will. (26)

In the sense that Adorno ascribes to *Finnegans Wake*, *How It Is* can be read as a work that rewrites itself each time it is read. A voice dictates words to a narrator who attempts to reconstruct them in the text, to reenact the process of its own creation. The narrator says it as he hears it, not only by attempting to copy or mime what is heard, but also by refashioning the event of articulation. This happens in the case of words that are constantly figured in the present, said at the moment of being heard and thus always posited as an unfinished process of articulation. But as Adorno has noted, Beckett's work produces meaninglessness by repeating otherwise familiar language, opposite to the *Wake's* production of meaning out of nonsensical sound. In this sense, *How It Is* can be read rather rejecting the pleasure of the process of production. Rather than a work in progress, *How It Is* is a work in *regress*, a regressive articulation of a creative process that is no longer possible. A work in regress, it approaches an impossible beginning that comes in the wake of its own end, a ghostly afterlife.

The closing pages of *How It Is* mockingly reiterate the positive potentiality for meaning in Joyce's work, echoing Joyce's "yes" in all of its hollowed out impossibility: "there was something yes but nothing of all that no all balls from start to finish yes this voice quaqua yes all balls yes only one voice here yes mine yes when the panting stops yes" (127). Humor in this passage is relatively apparent; the childishly vulgar assertion that "something" or "nothing" is "all balls" mocks the regurgitated yeses that spastically erupt into the text. The yeses, situated at the closing of the book—just as in *Ulysses*—become emptier as the narrator acknowledges that he is alone and that the voice is "all balls." This brutal parody of the voice emphasizes the impassable distance between the narrator of *How It Is* and the subject of the first-person novel, a point Adrienne Janus develops in "Listening to Laughter in Joyce and Beckett." For Janus, after *Malone Dies* "the traditional first-person novel ceases to operate and a new mode of writing responds in its place," a writing made up of "indistinct murmurs" reiterated by the "listening scribes" that populate the later works (152). Laughter in these texts is characterized by uncertainty and anxiety:

> In the texts following the *Trilogy*, [laughter] is most frequently second-hand, mediated by the body of the listening narrator. But when brought to those limit conditions of not knowing the origin, purpose, or meaning of the voices, the listening narrator transcribes for us, our body responds with an eruption of that agitated, nervous laughter typically produced by Beckett's texts. (Janus 154)

Such laughter momentarily relieves the reader of the attentive and emotional endurance required by a text like *How It Is*. With a "conspicuous absence of bodies capable of producing laughter," the reader can only make up for the absence by laughing at it nervously. The narrator confronts this very task in the self-parodying finale of the text, in which its own minimally assertive title is stripped of any remaining force: "that wasn't how it was no not at all no how then no answer HOW WAS IT screams good" (*HII* 126). The aggressive capitals expose the enormous question mark looming over the reader of *How It Is*, and answer their own question with a snidely derisive "good." Arousing laughter through its own brutal self-parodying, the voice torments itself and exposes its own incapacity to say anything at all.

How It Is transcribes a voice quoting events after they have taken place. All that can be gathered and reconstructed to produce the work is always "ill-said ill-heard ill-recaptured ill-murmured." In his "Notes on *The Unnamable*," Adorno situates *The Unnamable* in a time after death. *How It Is* occurs in the aftermath of this already residual moment: an afterlife of the spectral subject in *The Unnamable*. In the fifth fragment in the notes, Adorno mentions *How It Is* (*Comment c'est*) as a title better suited to capture Beckett's "no man's land," the time after death that is also a beginning:

> Simplest answer to why [*L'Innommable*] is] so enormously significant:
> because it comes closest to the conception of what
> it will really be like after death (the *innomable* dreams it).
> Neither spirit nor time nor symbol. This is precisely
> the Beckettian no man's land. With that the *obvious*
> (the Kafkan moment): the title of the next
> book, *Comment c'est*, perhaps suits this one
> better. (176–7)

Arriving after the dream of the aftermath of death, *How It Is* marks the resurrection of the subject as a lack thereof, a beginning that sets out at the time of its own end, and in which the subject can only regress in repeat. Adorno mentions *How It Is* again in the last fragment of the notes, pointing out that the novel figures within the "disenchanted world" of modernism:

> Modern art is the radical heir not only of
> avant-garde movements but also
> of Naturalism: a disenchanted world, the illu-
> sionless, '*comment c'est*' (177)

How It Is operates within the moment Adorno refers to in the *Endgame* notes as "the obsolescence of the modern," the impotent afterlife of modernism that demolishes itself with its own "regressive language" (171). *How It Is* arrives at its own birth too late, already in the waning of modernism. The "disenchanted world" is a precondition for this work, not its result. The subject of *How It Is* is born too late for laughter, a muted parody of hope that commences over and again, repeating itself into a world abandoned, "the illusionless."

The torture scenarios of *How It Is*—though briefly affirming the existence of others—often appear sadomasochistic, since one Pim is indistinguishable from the other. Among a number of violent gestures, the carving of the narrator's name onto the other conflates the infantile scenario of learning to write one's name—and wanting to scribble it everywhere—with the obviously sadistic branding of and cutting into another. The narrator describes it thus: "with the nail then of the right index I carve and when it breaks or falls until it grows again with another on Pim's back intact at the outset from left to right and top to bottom as in our civilisation I carve my Roman capitals" (*HII* 60). Set in the second part of the narrative, *with Pim*, this scene exemplifies the conflation of self and other that becomes the major conflict in the work. Pim's existence becomes questionable at best, suggesting that the work regressively self-destructs before its own mirror image.

Weller writes of this conflict in the work as providing insight into the condition of solitude, owing to "the fact that each and every other proves on closer inspection to be a disintegrative projection of the self" (*TN* 165). Solitude, like the infantile element, is both an imposition and impossible. The lessening of distinctions between self and other, between torture and play, mirrors the ambivalent reading experience. The production of meaning exerts the voice's dictatorial violence, while also providing the reader with the pleasure of sense-making. Weller writes of this interpretative impasse: "If we decide for *How It Is* by identifying its truth (as being or as voice), we ourselves have cut into the text with a violence which doubles that of the narrator when he cuts into a body that resembles his own; and not only that, for we have dictated the text, spoken from beyond it, imitated the very dictatorial manner with which the text opens but which it ends by rejecting" (168–9). The more work is done onto the text, the more the text undoes itself. The reader experiences something like a cry of pain from the ill-understood text, which is also laughter at one's inability to move forward. The narrator speaks to this experience in a moment of self-conscious regression: "I know less and less that's true of myself since the womb the panting stops I murmur it" (*HII* 81).

This is the subject alienated and othered before itself, who knows less and less true of its own being, the subject that Adorno finds so crucial in Beckett. The enduring horror of the reading experience that *How It Is* requires is perhaps where its meaningfulness is (dis)located. In "Commitment," Adorno writes of Beckett's work producing a potentially useful brand of horror: "everyone shrinks from them [Beckett's works] in horror, and yet none can deny that these eccentric novels and plays are about things everyone knows and no one wants to talk about" (90). The voice that doesn't stop talking, murmuring a painfully dislocated past, is ever-present in *How It Is*: "in a word once more once and for all Pim's voice then nothing nothing then Pim's voice I make it stop suffer it to stop then set it off again that I at last may be no more then at last be again something there that escapes me since how can I opener capitals and not be it's impossible it stands to reason there's reason in me yet" (81). The narrator wants the other to stop talking as well. In the impossibility of this feat, he finds his own first-person pronoun lodged inside a can opener, the very torture device he uses on the other: "how can I opener." This moment resounds with Adorno's observation in "Commitment" about Beckett's characters, who peer out from within their own words. Adorno writes:

> They look mutely out from his sentences as though with eyes whose tears have dried up. The spell they cast and under which they stand is broken by being reflected in them. The minimal promise of happiness which they contain, which refuses to be traded for any consolation, was to be had only at the price of a thoroughgoing articulation, to the point of wordlessness. (90)

According to Adorno, hope lies in the torturous impossibility of wordlessness, the desecration of silence imposed by the artwork. Although positive articulation pays the price here, "wordlessness" remains one of those unreachable asymptotes in Beckett, like worseness, lessness, and silence. In *Very Little . . .*

Almost Nothing, Simon Critchley claims that this impossibility is crucial for the reconstruction of meaning: "the inability to mean something in Beckett does not mean that we stop speaking, but rather that we are *unable* to stop—*pour finir encore*" (178). The impossibility of wordlessness and the ceaseless repetition of the familiar into oblivion is a potentially meaningful experience. Although Critchley reads Adorno as arguing that humor evaporates in Beckett's work, Critchley's own proposal comes quite close to Adorno's. Critchley writes: "Humour does not evaporate in Beckett; rather laughter is the sound of language trying to commit suicide but being unable to do so, which is what is so tragically comic" (185). The inability of language to cease ironically causes it to regress, thus affirming the enduring presence of the work: the persistent face of the other staring back, at once the cause of suffering and pleasure.

"BECKETT'S WORST UNDERSTOOD PROSE" OR, THE POSSIBILITY OF TWO

Taking alterity as the starting point for an analysis of Beckett's hermetic late works, Badiou's readings of *How It Is* are helpful for thinking past the impasse of the incapacitated subject Adorno identifies. In "Tireless Desire," Badiou emphasizes how critics of Beckett have been distracted from enabling a profound understanding of the late works. Badiou claims this is due to a "confusion between [the works'] methodical ascesis—staged with a tender and voluble humour—and some sort of tragic pathos of the destitution and the misery of man" (46). Instead of identifying this tragi-comic opposition or short-circuit as the conclusive element of Beckett's work, Badiou proposes a reading of Beckett's subjects as those of "generic humanity," who affirm meaning through the achievement of fully apprehending the other. For Badiou, this humanity is not stuck or paralyzed in the endtimes or no-man's-land, but is instead reduced to basic capacities that become even more significant in their minimalist presentation. The subject here is engaged in the relational functions of "going, being, and saying."

Setting out from Adorno's claim in "Commitment" about the horror that readers of Beckett experience, which speaks of what everyone knows but "no one wants to talk about," Badiou argues for an understanding of *How It Is* that doesn't merely stare blankly in horror at its repulsive depictions. Badiou proposes that these elements are precisely what we "know," as Adorno claims. They are also what we reluctantly must apprehend and identify with:

> We cannot understand the text [*How It Is*] if we immediately see it as a concentration camp allegory of the dirty and diseased human animal. On the contrary—admitting that we are indeed animals lodged upon an earth which is insignificant and brimming over with excrement—it is a matter of establishing that which subsists the register of the question, of thought, of the creative capacity (in this case, the will to movement, as opposed to flight). Thus reduced to a few functions, humanity is only more admirable, more energetic, more immortal. (46)

Here, Badiou posits the possibility of hope alongside the subtractive and regressive elements in Beckett. What he finds enduring in the work is not the disgust or sadistic fulfillment it arouses, but the potential for identification with the subject. This activity works as a repetition of the creative impulse, an experience which for Badiou necessarily implicates an encounter with the other.

In an essay that attempts to reconcile Adorno's and Badiou's accounts of Beckett, Jean-Michel Rabaté acknowledges the unrelenting and possibly vicious nature of Adorno's Beckett, who "derides philosophical abstraction and all the remainders of late modernism by creating an impasse, a dead end from which one can only be saved by a regressive laughter that spares nothing" (101). Yet while this account centers on the unsparing, suffocating laughter Adorno writes of, Rabaté sees the possibility of hope within a damaged world and the identification with a regressed subject, which marks a significant meeting point with Badiou. Adorno's account surprisingly resounds with Badiou's conception of the late works, which Rabaté describes as "a systematic and serious investigation of 'thinking humanity,' and if [Beckett] proceeds by way of destruction, it is in order to discover what resists, what remains indestructible at the bottom" (109).

Badiou marks *How It Is* as a point of departure in Beckett's oeuvre, the beginning of a new approach toward the subject and the generic conditions of humanity. Rabaté identifies this shift in *How It Is* as "a new minimalism" that pervades the late works, eventually leading Beckett to "daring experiments with the theater and new media like film and television" (108). In Badiou's *Conditions*, the chapter on Beckett titled "The Writing of the Generic" explores the possibility of reconciliation through alterity in the late works. Following from a section earlier in the book on "Philosophy and Love," Badiou identifies the search for the number Two—in which one and one come together without totalizing each other within the subsuming sameness of the One couple—at the crux of Beckett's post-1960 works, of which *How It Is* designates the beginning. Badiou writes:

> *How It Is*, ultimately a little-known work, marks a major mutation in the way that Beckett fictioned his thought. This text breaks with the confrontation between the torturing cogito and the neutrality of the black-grey of being. Beckett attempted to set out from entirely different categories, namely, that of the 'what happens' (which was present in his work from the beginning but is reworked here), and that, above all, of alterity, of the encounter, of the figure of the Other, which fissures and displaces solipsistic imprisonment. (264)

The subject here is found in the midst of an encounter, rather than in the self-reflective ironizing mode of earlier texts. The possibility of the Other is figured fully through the elements of surprise, mirroring, naming, torture, and love. The tortured, lonely creatures that crawl around the mud of *How It Is* constantly search for the possibility of an encounter, simultaneously longing for and repulsed by the other.

For Badiou, this moment marks Beckett's shift "from a programme of the One—the relentlessness of a trajectory or an interminable soliloquy—to the fecund theme of the Two, by which it opens up to the infinite" (*Conditions* 266).

Beckett's "larva of essential humanity" manages to crawl toward the possibility of reconciliation through the recognition of the other and the event of the encounter—the event of love (255). As Rabaté notes, Badiou's reading finds in *How It Is* "less a meditation of post-apocalyptic survival than a deployment of everyday-life paradoxes centering on love—defined by Badiou as making two with 'ones'" (110). In this account, torture itself becomes an opening up to the existence of others, a problematic central to *How It Is*. Crucially, such a reading holds on to the possibility of hope to be found somewhere within the black mud in which beings crawl, murmur, and sometimes even find one another.

"Beckett's worst understood prose," *How It Is* shifts between a gradual subtraction of the subject and of language—and the movement *towards* 'what happens,' towards an encounter with the other (Badiou, "What Happens" 117). Although this search for an encounter is reduced to its minimal capacity, it nevertheless resists being subsumed into nothingness, impossibility, and the suffocation of laughter. Adorno writes of *The Unnamable* (the conceptual precondition for *How It Is*) as positing a subject that is alienated and othered before itself, and thus relentlessly asserting the impossibility of solipsism. He summarizes: "On the situation: absolute alienation is / the absolute subject. But precisely that subject is alienated / from itself, it is the other, it is nothing. / B[eckett]'s novels are the critique of solipsism" ("Notes on *The Unnamable*" 172). Adorno finds embodied in Beckett's novel the "formula of the solipsist without *ipse*," which "comes to its own" in the unnamable subject that Beckett fashions (175). This subject is reduced to the brink of nothing, but never quite becomes nothing, feebly clinging onto the most minimal proof of difference. Adorno's Beckettian subject is reduced to *solus* lacking *ipse*, alone without itself. The subject is alone with the other, with itself as other, with an image of the other that threatens to engulf the self. This threat is carried out with the recognition of the other, with its relentless language, and with its name carved over and over again—a name that always points to the self as other and renders impossible their being subsumed into One. The infantile and humorous are intimately attached to the decrepit and sadistic, producing this very subject: born at the moment of an impossible end, forever bound to its capacity for incremental movements whose minimal mark powerfully asserts an inexhaustible endurance for going on. The possibility of hope is congealed within this formula of the self, alone without itself, constantly asserting its presence as a form of untotalizable lack that, as such, becomes a marker of alterity. The subject, reduced to an irreducible other crawling in the mud, goes on as pure difference. This very difference is marked by its ceaseless worseness, lessness, and torturous wordlessness.

Works Cited

Adorno, Theodor W. *Aesthetic Theory*. Edited by Gretel Adorno and Rolf Tiedemann. Translated by Robert Hullot-Kentor. U of Minnesota P, 1997.

———. "Commitment." *Notes to Literature: Volume Two*. Edited by Rolf Tiedemann. Translated by Shierry Weber Nicholsen. Columbia UP, 1992, pp. 76–94.

———. "Dossier: Adorno's Notes on Beckett." Translated by Dirk Van Hulle and Shane Weller. *Journal of Beckett Studies*, vol. 19, no. 2, 2010, pp. 158–178.

———. *Minima Moralia: Reflections on a Damaged Life*. Verso, 2007.

———. "Trying to Understand *Endgame*." *Notes to Literature: Volume One*. Edited by Rolf Tiedemann. Translated by Shierry Weber Nicholsen. Columbia UP, 1991, pp. 241–275.

Adorno, Theodor W. and Max Horkheimer. *Dialectic of Enlightenment*. Translated by Edmund Jephcott. Stanford UP, 2002.

Badiou, Alain. *On Beckett*. Edited by Alberto Toscano and Nina Power. Translated by Nina Power. Clinamen Press, 2003.

———. "Tireless Desire." *On Beckett*, pp. 37–78.

———. "What Happens." *On Beckett*, pp. 113–118.

———. "The Writing of the Generic." *Conditions*. Translated by Steven Corcoran. Continuum, 2008, pp. 249–284.

Beckett, Samuel. *Endgame: A Play in One Act*. Grove Press, 1958.

———. *How It Is*. Faber and Faber, 2009. Cited as *HII*.

Coulson, Shea. "Funnier Than Unhappiness: Adorno and the Art of Laughter." *New German Critique*, vol. 34, no. 1, 2007, pp. 141–163.

Critchley, Simon. *Very Little . . . Almost Nothing: Death, Philosophy, Literature*. 2nd ed. Routledge, 2004.

Freud, Sigmund. "Humour." *International Journal of Psycho-Analysis*, vol. 9, 1928, pp. 1–6.

———. *Jokes and Their Relation to the Unconscious*. Translated by James Strachey. Norton, 1960.

Janus, Adrienne. "From 'Ha he hi ho hu. Mummum' to 'Haw! Hell! Haw!': Listening to Laughter in Joyce and Beckett." *Journal of Modern Literature*, vol. 32, no. 2, Spring 2009, pp. 144–166.

Rabaté, Jean-Michel. "Philosophizing With Beckett: Adorno and Badiou." *A Companion to Samuel Beckett*, edited by S. E. Gontarski. Blackwell, 2010, pp. 97–117.

Salisbury, Laura. *Samuel Beckett: Laughing Matters, Comic Timing*. Edinburgh UP, 2012.

Weitzman, Erica. "No *Fun*: Aporias of Pleasure in Adorno's *Aesthetic Theory*." *The German Quarterly*, vol. 81, no. 2, 2008, pp. 185–202.

Weller, Shane. *Beckett, Literature, and the Ethics of Alterity*. Palgrave Macmillan, 2006.

———. *A Taste for the Negative: Beckett and Nihilism*. Legenda, 2005.

MICHELLE RADA is the Franke Postdoctoral Fellow at the Whitney Humanities Center at Yale University. Her writing on psychoanalysis, aesthetics, modernism, and critical theory has appeared in *differences: A Journal of Feminist Cultural Studies*, *The Comparatist*, *James Joyce Quarterly*, *The Journal of Beckett Studies*, and *Room One Thousand*. She is senior editor of *Parapraxis*, and associate editor of *differences* and of *Critical Times: Interventions in Global Critical Theory*.

Editors

Jean-Michel Rabaté, professor of English and comparative literature at the University of Pennsylvania, co-editor of the *Journal of Modern Literature*, co-founder of The Slought–Public Trust Foundation, is a fellow of the American Academy of Arts and Sciences. Rabaté is author or editor of fifty books on modernism, psychoanalysis, philosophy, and literary theory.

Laurel Garver is the managing editor of the *Journal of Modern Literature*. She has a master of journalism degree from Temple University, runs a freelance editing and writing coaching business, and has published several fiction writing resources as well as the novels *Never Gone, Ever Near*, and *Almost There*.

Index

Actes sans paroles I, see *Act without Words*.
Acts without Words, 137, 222.
Adorno, Theodor, 3–4, 9, 26, 36, 40, 74, 85–86, 120, 122–123, 129, 133, 140, 254–270.
Agamben, Giorgio, 37, 40–41, 92, 122–123, 125, 128–129, 141.
Algeria, 132, 135–138.
Alleg, Henri, See *La Question*.
alterity, 8–9, 154, 163–167, 169–171, 173, 176–177, 189, 255, 261–262, 267–270.
animal, 7, 46, 48, 53–54, 94, 103, 105, 163–171, 173–181, 229, 267.
Arendt, Hannah, 129, 140–141.
Aristotle, 5, 48, 163, 197, 201.
art, 4, 6–7, 15, 23, 36, 40, 50, 58, 69, 71, 78, 80, 89, 92, 94, 97–99, 101–103, 106–116, 118, 121–125, 127, 133, 140, 154, 186, 200, 213, 216, 223, 227, 229, 231–232, 234, 252, 256, 260–261, 263, 265, 270.
arte povera, 6, 109, 112.
Awaiting Oblivion, 6, 73, 75–76, 84–85.

Bachelard, Gaston, 37, 40.
Badiou, Alain, 3–4, 54, 140–141, 154, 159–160, 267–270.
Bakhtin, Mikhail, 218, 227–229, 231–233.
Beauvoir, Simone de, 110, 185–186, 196, 200.
Benjamin, Walter, 129, 141.
Bion, Wilfred, 6, 58, 62–63, 67–69.
Blanchot, Maurice, 6, 71–87, 92, 95, 117, 122–123, 214, 218.
body, 2, 5–6, 14, 20, 22, 32, 38–39, 42–43, 48–52, 55, 57–60, 62, 64–67, 69, 74, 83–84, 87, 101, 109, 116, 119, 131, 135–136, 147–148, 153–154, 159, 166, 177, 183, 188, 190, 203–205, 207, 210, 213, 215, 217–218, 220–221, 227, 231, 236–239, 244, 249, 251, 264, 266.
Braque, Georges, 14, 93, 97–99, 102–103, 108, 118.
Burri, Alberto, 6, 109–110, 112–115, 118–125.
Butler, Judith, 96, 107.

Cartesian, 2–3, 8, 15, 43, 58, 110, 154, 163, 165–167, 169, 189–190, 209, 213–214.
Cézanne, Paul, 93, 98–99, 101.

Cixous, Hélène, 74–75, 86.
Cohn, Ruby, 53, 63, 68, 85, 107, 116, 123–124, 158, 160, 233.
Comment c'est, See *How It Is*.
Company, 17, 59, 84, 165, 172, 179, 189, 199, 201, 245.
confine, 91, 113, 172, 175, 177, 215.
containment, 58–60, 63–67.
Coetzee, J.M., 49, 53, 86, 207, 218.

Dante [Alighieri], 3–4, 52–53, 149–152, 158–159, 161, 165, 192, 201–202, 206, 222, 229, 233.
"Dante and the Lobster", 150–152, 165.
"Dante ... Bruno . Vico .. Joyce", 53.
Davis, Lennard J., 203–204, 218.
deixis, 5, 27, 30–33, 35–36, 38.
Deleuze, Gilles, 5, 24, 27–29, 36–41, 62, 69, 77, 86, 92, 107, 161, 167, 179, 205, 216, 218–219.
Derrida, Jacques, 7, 26, 30–31, 36, 39–40, 86, 92, 105, 107, 144, 156, 160–161, 163–165, 171, 175–179, 205, 218.
Descartes, René, 3–4, 15, 59, 67, 69, 163, 165, 179–180.
desire, 5, 16, 29–30, 35, 38–39, 46, 64, 66, 71, 96, 106–107, 150–151, 153, 155, 157, 171, 173, 192, 210, 221, 229, 236–237, 267, 270.
Deucalion, 131.
disability, 8, 25, 203–206, 211, 213, 215–219, 253.
dog, 5, 7–8, 163–174, 176, 178–181, 212, 226, 228, 231.
Dream of Fair to Middling Women, 7, 150, 159, 178–179.

Eleutheria, 6, 92, 104, 107, 134, 141, 158–159.
En attendant Godot, See *Waiting for Godot*.
Endgame, 9, 18, 64–65, 130, 134, 136–137, 141, 198, 236, 240, 242, 245–246, 249, 252, 254–259, 261, 263, 265, 270.
ethics, 1, 3–4, 7–8, 54, 69, 72, 87, 111, 122, 125, 149, 154–162, 164–165, 169–170, 176, 180–181, 183, 189, 191–193, 197, 201–202, 219, 262, 270.

Index

exception, 7, 86, 127–129, 132–133, 135, 139–141, 170, 203, 216, 231.
excrement, 8, 154, 220–232, 267.
exhaustion, 5, 8, 26–28, 30, 32, 36–38, 51, 120, 205, 216.

face, 16, 22–23, 34, 39, 44, 49–50, 52, 81, 91, 100, 103, 111–112, 152, 156–158, 169–171, 177–178, 180, 185, 190, 194, 208, 229–231, 260, 262–263, 267.
fatigue, 29, 65, 120.
Film, 2, 41, 127, 161, 222, 268.
Fin de partie, See *Endgame*.
Fontaine, 92, 99, 104, 106–107, 131.
Foucault, Michel, 107, 214, 218.
Freud, Sigmund, 160, 226, 228, 230, 232–233, 238, 246, 252, 254, 258–259, 270.

Gell, Alfred, 58–59, 69.
Geulincx, Arnold, 8, 154, 159–160, 191–193, 196, 201–202.
Gontarski, S.E., 15, 23–24, 54, 68–69, 123–125, 138, 141, 178–179, 181, 187–188, 201, 270.
Gothic, 8–9, 235–236, 239–252.
Guattari, Felix, 62, 69, 167, 179, 216, 218.

habit, 5, 19, 25–41, 82, 194–196.
Happy Days, 65, 121, 136–138, 141.
Haraway, Donna, 164, 176, 180.
Hayles, N. Katherine, 145, 147–149, 156, 160.
Hegel, Georg Wilhelm Friedrich, 3, 29–30, 32, 39–40, 96, 100, 144, 160.
Heidegger, Martin, 6, 76, 91, 95, 103–107, 124, 160, 163, 169, 174.
homunculi, 58–60, 62, 64, 67.
horror, 134, 152, 165, 180, 208, 242, 261–262, 266–267.
How It Is, 5–6, 9, 33, 68–69, 74, 79, 80–82, 84–86, 106–107, 136, 139, 141, 178–179, 186, 201, 221, 254–255, 257–270.
humanism, 91–92, 94–100, 102–105, 107–108, 110–111, 115, 118, 145, 162–164, 169, 177–178, 180–181.
humiliation, 8, 185, 191, 193, 195–196, 198, 200, 202, 227.
humility, 8, 154, 191–193, 195–197, 201–202.
humor / humour, 8–9, 44, 48–50, 161, 170, 201, 221, 229–230, 233, 238, 241, 244–246, 252, 254–256, 257–264, 267, 270.
Hugo, Victor, 57, 69.

impairment, 204–207, 211–212, 214–215.
Inferno, 120, 192, 202.
Ireland, 41, 57, 66, 83, 127, 132, 141.

Joyce, James, 1, 4, 9, 19, 52–53, 65–66, 69, 87, 126–127, 132, 142, 150, 158–159, 161, 213, 222–223, 230, 232–234, 263–264, 270.

Kenner, Hugh, 19, 24, 43, 54, 187.
Kierkegaard, Søren, 202.
Knowlson, James, 16, 23–24, 52, 54, 65–67, 69, 83, 86, 92, 107, 132, 142, 178–180, 185–186, 202.
Krapp's Last Tape, 178, 186.

language, 1, 3–5, 8, 21, 24, 27, 35, 38, 42–54, 58, 71–72, 75, 78–79, 82–84, 86–87, 105, 110, 117–118, 124, 162–163, 173, 181, 194, 200, 204, 206, 212, 217, 220–223, 227–229, 232, 244–245, 258–261, 264–265, 267, 269.
La Question, 138.
laughter, 4, 8–9, 48–53, 80, 86, 183, 195, 199–200, 231, 235–270.
Les Temps Modernes, 92, 96–97, 100, 106–108, 111, 124, 131, 185, 202.
Levinas, Emmanuel, 7–8, 124, 160, 162–165, 168–171, 174–176, 178–180.
L'Innommable, See *The Unnamable*.

Malabou, Catherine, 37, 39–40, 160.
Malone Dies, 6–7, 17, 33, 36, 40, 59, 68, 110, 130, 141, 153, 159, 162, 166, 179, 186–187, 191, 201–202, 218, 241, 252, 264.
Malone meurt, See *Malone Dies*.
Marx, Karl, 4, 9, 95–97, 100, 103, 107, 160.
Marxism, 100, 103–104, 108.
Mauthner, Fritz, 5, 44–46, 48, 52–54.
memento mori, 93.
memory, 7, 18, 20–22, 24, 29, 38, 46, 64, 75, 80, 86–87, 114, 117, 119, 127–128, 135, 138–140, 148, 174, 189, 214, 226, 243.
Mercier and Camier, 17, 130, 135, 141, 178–179, 187.
Mercier et Camier, See *Mercier and Camier*.
Merleau-Ponty, Maurice, 6, 91, 95–96, 98–101, 106, 108.
Molloy, 5–8, 17, 19, 27–28, 31, 33–36, 38–41, 45, 50, 53, 56, 60–61, 68, 72, 92, 104–105, 107, 112, 130–131, 141, 153, 159, 162–164, 166–167, 170–175, 177–181, 185–193, 196–206, 211–218, 220–231, 233, 236, 241–242, 249–250, 252.
monstrous, 64, 85, 240–241, 244, 249–251, 261–262.
More Pricks Than Kicks, 7, 129, 141, 149, 153, 159, 178–179.
mourn, 48.
Murphy, 5, 17, 28, 43, 53–54, 58, 62–68, 167, 173, 178–179, 185, 187, 191, 197, 201, 217–218.

Nancy, Jean-Luc, 5, 13–14, 16, 18, 21–25.
Nazi, 105, 129, 132–134, 138, 164, 168, 175, 179.
neuter, 6, 11, 72–73, 76–77, 117.
nihilism, 25, 72, 75, 86–87, 105, 202, 224, 248, 253, 270.
nonhuman, 6, 55–56, 58, 163, 173, 176.
nothing, 4–6, 9, 13–23, 25, 27, 32–36, 39, 45, 60, 64, 66, 71–72, 74–79, 81–86, 96, 109, 112–113, 117, 129–130, 139, 146, 155–156, 160, 165–167, 176, 186–187, 192–193, 197–198, 200, 202, 215, 217, 221, 229–230, 236, 248–249, 252, 254–256, 258, 263–264, 266–270.
Not I, 5, 13–14, 16–18, 20, 22–24, 53, 62, 114.

O'Brien, Flann, 8, 126, 161, 203–204, 208–211, 218–219.
Oh les beaux jours, See *Happy Days*.
Orpheus, 71, 78, 85.

painting, 6, 23, 91–94, 98–99, 101–103, 106, 109–115, 118–123, 125, 173, 223, 232.
Pascal, Blaise, 191, 202.
Peirce, Charles Sanders, 27, 31–32, 35, 41.
Phenomenology, 5, 54, 99–101, 108, 114, 124.
Pochade radiophonique, 136.
Ponge, Francis, 6, 95–98, 102–103, 106–108, 118, 125.
posthuman, 6–8, 86, 144–149, 156–158, 160–162.
prosthesis, 203–205, 207–211, 214–216, 219.
Proust, Marcel, 5, 14, 27.
Proust, 4–5, 9, 14–15, 23–24, 27, 29–30, 37–38, 40, 61, 63, 68, 71, 85, 191, 194–195, 200–201.

Rabaté, Jean-Michel, 1, 9, 47, 54, 72, 86, 106, 108, 117, 121, 125, 159, 268–270.
Rancière, Jacques, 91, 108.
religion, 8, 69, 221, 226–227, 229, 233.
Rough for Theatre, 57, 136, 198.

Sartre, Jean-Paul, 6, 54, 95–97, 102, 105–108, 230–231, 233.
satire, 8, 135, 166, 218, 221, 225, 227–229.
scatology, 8, 185, 220–221, 224–227, 229.
slaughter, 165–166, 174–176, 179–180.
sound, 3, 5, 23, 33–34, 43, 46–52, 83, 118, 150, 176, 232, 239, 258, 260–262, 264, 267.
subjectivity, 6–7, 34, 37, 39–40, 57, 60, 62, 72, 82, 92, 97, 99–100, 144, 148, 155–157, 163–164, 169, 189–190, 203–206, 209, 214, 216–217, 255, 257–258.

suffering, 7–8, 21, 38, 62, 122, 128–129, 163, 165–167, 170, 174, 177, 194–197, 199–200, 237, 239–242, 244, 246, 248, 254, 261, 267.
"Suite", 110, 185–186, 201.

Texts for Nothing, 6, 79, 82–85, 109, 112, 117, 187, 236, 248–249, 252, 254–255.
theology, 38, 96, 227, 239.
"Three Dialogues", 71, 92, 101–103, 110–111, 121.
The Third Policeman, 8, 203–207, 211–213, 215–216, 217, 219.

Uhlmann, Anthony, 14–15, 25, 54, 68, 112, 121, 125, 154, 159, 161, 202, 216–217, 219.
The Unnamable, 1, 5, 7, 9, 33, 36–37, 39–41, 54, 56, 58, 61–62, 68, 77–79, 116–117, 123, 130, 137, 141, 153, 157, 159, 162, 175, 179, 186–187, 191, 193–194, 201–202, 205, 218, 241–242, 244, 248–250, 252, 254–255, 257, 264–265, 269.

van Velde, Bram, 91–93, 97–99, 101–103, 105–106, 109–112, 119, 121, 202.
vessel, 56–57, 59, 61–63, 65, 127, 142, 192.
Vichy, 134–135, 140.
voice, 6, 34, 37, 44, 69, 72–74, 79–82, 84, 106, 117, 122, 131, 149–150, 159, 225, 257, 263–264, 266.
void, 5, 16, 20, 69, 73–75, 78, 83, 93, 122, 134.
Voyage au bout de la nuit, 139.

Waiting for Godot, 6, 18, 23, 25, 47, 53-54, 62, 75–76, 84–86, 92, 130, 141, 187, 198, 236, 241, 245, 249, 252, 254.
war, 4, 6–7, 42, 44, 57, 80, 86, 91–92, 94–96, 98–99, 102–105, 107, 111–112, 115, 122–124, 127–129, 131–132, 134–140, 155, 162, 164, 169, 198, 253.
Watt, 4–5, 7, 23, 42–54, 56, 68, 72, 75, 86, 112, 120, 123, 162–164, 166, 168, 170, 178–179, 193, 201, 236, 240–241, 252.
Weller, Shane, 23, 25, 72–73, 75, 83–84, 86–87, 107, 123, 163, 165–166, 181, 194, 202, 248–249, 253, 255, 262–263, 266, 270.
What Where, 69, 261, 263.
"Whoroscope Notebook", 52, 62, 68.
World War II, 162, 164, 169. See also: war.